THE LAW OF HABEAS CORPUS IN IRELAND

FOUR COURTS PRESS • DUBLIN

Published 10 January 2006

The Law of Habeas Corpus in Ireland

Kevin Costello

288pp, hardback £55

The publisher will be obliged if the Editor sends a copy of the review, when it appears, to the address below.

The author
Kevin Costello is a lecturer in the School of Law, University College Dublin.

For additional details about the book and publisher, or to arrange an interview with the author, contact:
Anthony Tierney
Four Courts Press, 7 Malpas Street, Dublin 8.
Tel.: (00 353 1) 453 4668; Fax.: 453 4672
E-mail: anthony.tierney@four-courts-press.ie.

The Law of Habeas Corpus in Ireland

History, Scope of Review, and Practice under
Article 40.4.2 of the Irish Constitution

KEVIN COSTELLO

FOUR COURTS PRESS

Set in 11.5 on 14 point Ehrhardt
by Mark Heslington, Scarborough, North Yorkshire for
FOUR COURTS PRESS
7 Malpas Street, Dublin 8, Ireland
e-mail: info@four-courts-press.ie
and in North America
FOUR COURTS PRESS
c/o ISBS, 920 58th Avenue, Suite 300, Portland, OR 97213

© Kevin Costello 2006

A catalogue record for this title
is available from the British Library.

ISBN 1-85182-836-2

All rights reserved. No part of this publication may be
reproduced, stored in or introduced into a retrieval
system, or transmitted, in any form or by any means
(electronic, mechanical, photocopying, recording or
otherwise), without the prior written permission of
both the copyright owner and the publisher of this book.

Printed in England by
MPG Books, Bodmin, Cornwall

Contents

Acknowledgments	vii
Text of Articles 40.4.1-5 of the Constitution of Ireland	ix
1 The development of habeas corpus in Irish law, 1600-1941	1
2 The grounds of review on an Article 40.4.2 enquiry	39
3 Procedure on an Article 40.4.2 application	105
4 Article 40.4.2 and the criminal process	183
5 Habeas corpus review of administrative detention, and detention ancillary to civil litigation	227
Table of cases	247
Table of statutes	259
Index	263

Acknowledgments

This book was completed while on a period of leave under an Irish Research Council for the Humanities and Social Sciences senior research scholarship. I would like to record my gratitude to the IRCHSS. Financial support for the publication of this book was provided by the University College Dublin Publications Scheme and by a grant in aid from the National University of Ireland. Again, I wish to acknowledge the assistance of these two institutions.

A number of practitioners provided me with information otherwise unrecorded: Garrett Sheehan, Robert Eagar, Hugh O'Flaherty SC and Patrick MacEntee SC. I wish, in particular, to thank Dr Gerard Hogan who perceptively identified the law of habeas corpus in Ireland as a fruitful topic of research. Betty McGuigan of the Four Courts enabled me to consult files in the Central Office of the Four Courts. Professor Conor Gearty (University College London), Professor Joseph McMahon (University College Dublin) and Desmond Greer (Queen's University Belfast) helpfully read sections of the book. The information on the drafting of Article 6 of the Constitution of the Irish Free State derived from the Stephens' manuscripts is produced by permission of the Board of Trinity College Dublin. Finally, I owe a considerable debt of gratitude to Vandra Carolyn Dyke to whom, in recognition, this book is dedicated.

Text of Articles 40.4.1-5 of the Constitution of Ireland – Bunreacht na hÉireann

ARTICLE 40

4. 1° No citizen shall be deprived of his personal liberty save in accordance with law.

4. 2° Upon complaint being made by or on behalf of any person to the High Court or any judge thereof alleging that such person is being unlawfully detained, the High Court and any and every judge thereof to whom such complaint is made shall forthwith enquire into the said complaint and may order the person in whose custody such person is detained to produce the body of such person before the High Court on a named day and to certify in writing the grounds of his detention, and the High Court shall, upon the body of such person being produced before that Court and after giving the person in whose custody he is detained an opportunity of justifying the detention, order the release of such person from such detention unless satisfied that he is being detained in accordance with the law.

4. 3° Where the body of a person alleged to be unlawfully detained is produced before the High Court in pursuance of an order in that behalf made under this section and that Court is satisfied that such person is being detained in accordance with a law but that such law is invalid having regard to the provisions of this Constitution, the High Court shall refer the question of the validity of such law to the Supreme Court by way of case stated and may, at the time of such reference or at any time thereafter, allow the said person to be at liberty on such bail and subject to such conditions as the High Court shall fix until the Supreme Court has determined the question so referred to it.

4. 4° The High Court before which the body of a person alleged to be unlawfully detained is to be produced in pursuance of an order in that behalf made under this section shall, if the President of the High Court or,

if he is not available, the senior judge of that Court who is available so directs in respect of any particular case, consist of three judges and shall, in every other case, consist of one judge only.

4. 5° Nothing in this section, however, shall be invoked to prohibit, control, or interfere with any act of the Defence Forces during the existence of a state of war or armed rebellion.

CHAPTER ONE

The development of habeas corpus in Irish law, 1600–1941

HABEAS CORPUS IN IRELAND, 1590–1690

By the early seventeenth century habeas corpus had become an established means of relief against imprisonment ordered by inferior tribunals. In 1638 the Court of Common Pleas[1] granted a writ of corpus cum causa at the request of the waterbailiff of Dublin, in order to test the legality of an order of committal for contempt which had been issued by the Court of Admiralty of Leinster.[2] In 1700 an application for habeas corpus was submitted to the Court of King's Bench to secure the discharge of the under-sheriff of Dublin (who had been committed for contempt to Kilmainham Gaol by the Court of Claims for executing a warrant of arrest in a civil action against a witness appearing before the Court). The King's Bench held that the return to the habeas corpus, which did not set out the grounds of contempt, was insufficient, and ordered the prisoner's release.[3] The Chancery remedy of corpus cum causa, was, in the later Elizabethan period, being routinely used to challenge orders of committal by courts of local civil jurisdiction: in 1588, one Gregory French, a Galway merchant sought corpus cum causa from the Lord Chancellor, alleging that the lord mayor of Galway, Andrew Maries, had imprisoned him without proper cause in order to give him better poundage, and had sworn to keep him imprisoned during the period of his mayoralty.[4] In the same period

---

[1] The seventeenth-century English Court of Common Pleas did not exercise a general habeas corpus jurisdiction, but only issued the writ at the instance of a person privileged to sue or be sued in that Court: *Wynne v. Boughey* (1666) O Bridge 570, 124 ER 750; *Wood's Case* (1770) 2 Wm Bl 745, 96 ER 436. It is unclear whether this condition was being insisted upon by the Irish Court of Common Pleas.
[2] Cooke to Northumberland, 23 Aug. 1638 (Alnwick Castle, Duke of Northumberland MSS, vol. 14, f. 184).
[3] Methuen to Vernon, 23 Nov. 1700, *Cal. S.P. Dom. 1700–2*, pp 150–1.
[4] NAI, Chancery pleadings, CP/E/189.

Edward Bee of Dublin, who described himself as 'an appotigary', submitted a bill for corpus cum causa on the ground that he had been imprisoned by the Mayor for refusing to join the Trinity Guild.[5]

Habeas corpus was also being deployed against some of the most superior institutions in the constitutional order, the House of Commons and the Privy Council. In 1666, the House of Lords challenged, by means of a writ of habeas corpus issued from the Court of Chancery, the imprisonment of Robert and William Barnewall by the Serjeant-at-Arms of the House of Commons. The House of Commons expressed itself 'amazed, nay astonished' at the issue of the writ against it by the Court of Chancery[6] on an application by the House of Lords. In its address to the Lords the Commons argued:[7]

> The House of Commons acknowledge a writ of habeas corpus is a prerogative writ, and of much advantage to the subject, but yet that they always issue from a higher to an inferior court, the end being to judge whether a person is legally committed, or justifiably detained, and in this case the House of Commons humbly hope their Lordships will not assume to themselves such a superiority.

By the middle of the seventeenth century there is the first evidence that the writ was being employed in Ireland as a mechanism for the bail or release of prisoners who had been committed for criminal offences, and were still awaiting trial in breach of the common law entitlement to an expeditious trial.[8] State prisoners detained by the Privy Council were also

---

[5] NAI, Chancery pleadings, CP/G/362.

[6] In 1647, the House of Commons asserted a general claim of privilege against the arrest of its members, and directed the Lord Chancellor to release by habeas corpus persons arrested in violation of parliamentary immunity: 'it is hereby ordered by the several Lords and commons, that if any member of the said houses, or their waged men, or all necessary attending servants by them employed, shall, at any time during the Prorogation be molested or imprisoned, that the Lord Chancellor, or Keeper of the Great Seal for the time being, shall grant to all person or persons, so molested, a supersedeas or writ of habeas corpus, under the foot of the Great Seal of the Kingdom, for enlarging and setting at liberty the said persons, so molested and imprisoned, and upon such supersedeas or habeas corpus, to set him or them at liberty; the said writs to be issued to the said person or persons without fees to be thereafter taken by any officer or Minister whatsoever,' *Commons' jn. Ire.*, i, p. 584 (18 June 1647).

[7] *Commons' jn. Ire.*, ii, p. 550 (27 July 1666).

[8] The account of the Irish criminal prosecution, *A particular deduction of the case*

availing of the remedy. In 1642 a number of suspected Confederates threatened habeas corpus proceedings against the Lord Lieutenant when he rescinded an earlier order not to prosecute, and instead had ordered them to be detained.[9] Two years later, in June 1664, a group of Dominican friars had been discovered in Connaught assembling for the purpose of holding a provincial chapter meeting, and had been committed by the Crown. The Lord Lieutenant's secretary, apparently troubled about the prospect that the men would challenge the legality of the detention in the Court of King's Bench, informed Ormond that 'the Lord Chief Justice had just assured him that if they sue for a habeas corpus he will find way to avoid it'.[10]

In 1641 the Irish House of Commons sought to positively assist the development of habeas corpus as a remedy against executive detention. A series of cases decided by the English courts in the Elizabethan era had established a distinction between detention ordered by a single member of the Privy Council, and imprisonment ordered by the entire Privy Council or by the Queen.[11] In the case of the former the Court of Queen's Bench was allowed to scrutinise the warrant, and if insufficient cause for the detention was demonstrated, the court could direct unconditional or, more usually, conditional discharge. However, in the case of detention ordered by the Queen personally, or by the entire Privy Council, there was no obligation to record the ground of detention on the warrant; since no defect or abuse would be apparent on the record the court had no jurisdiction to intervene. The English Parliament, in an attempt to subject detention by the Council to effective judicial control, enacted the Habeas Corpus Act, 1640 which provided that every person committed, restrained of his liberty or suffering imprisonment should be entitled to a habeas corpus; that 'the person detaining should certify the cause of such his detainer', and that the court 'shall proceed to examine and determine whether the cause of such commitment appearing upon the said return be just and legal

---

of William Eyre Esq. (London, 1675), includes a reference to the writ being used for this purpose: 'the said Eyre to vindicate his innocence to the world brought himself to a trial [in the King's Bench] some time since in Ireland by habeas corpus.'

[9] Aylmer to Ormond, Mar. 1642 (Bodl., Carte MSS vol. 4, f. 237).

[10] Ossory to Ormond, 6 & 28 June 1664 (Bodl., Carte MSS vol. 219, ff. 142–3; Carte MSS vol. 215, ff. 4–6.).

[11] *Searche's Case* (1587) 1 Leon 70, 74 ER 65; *Howel's Case* (1587) 1 Leon 70, 74 ER 66; *Darnel's Case* (1627) 3 St Tr 1.

or not, and shall thereupon do what to Justice shall appertain, either by delivering, taking or remanding the prisoner'.

The objective underlying the Act of 1640 was to override the old prerogative immunity enjoyed by the Privy Council from filing a full return. An attempt to introduce a similar reform was promoted in Ireland. Early in 1640 the Irish House of Commons drew up 'The Queries',[12] a catalogue of written questions scrutinising the content of a range of prerogative powers about which it was unhappy. Those Parliamentary queries were then submitted to a conference of the judges sitting in the Irish House of Lords. Dissatisfied by the judicial response the Commons, in turn, reacted by passing its own 'Declaration to the Queries'.[13] Although none of the original queries touched on habeas corpus, there was slipped into the Declaration a provision on habeas corpus drafted in exactly the same terms as the English Act of 1640, and intended to obtain for Ireland the same constitutional advance as that secured in England the previous year:[14]

> If in any case, any person or persons shall be committed, by the command or warrant of the Chief Governor, or Privy Council of the realm, or any of them, that in every such case every Person or Persons so committed, restrained of his or their liberties, or suffering imprisonment, upon demand or motion made by his or their counsel, or other employed by him or them for that purpose, unto the judges of the Court of King's Bench, or Common Pleas, in open court, shall without delay upon any pretence whatsoever, for the ordinary fees usually paid for the same, have forthwith granted unto him or them a writ or writs of habeas corpus to be directed generally unto all and every sheriff, gaoler, minister, officer, or other person in whose custody the party or parties so committed or restrained shall be, shall at the return of the said writ or writs, and according to the command thereof, upon due and convenient notice thereof given unto him, at the charge of the party or parties who requireth or procureth such writs, and upon security given upon his or their own bond or bonds, to pay the charge of carrying back the prisoner or prisoners, if he or they be remanded by the court to which he or they shall be brought, as in like cases hath been used, such charges of bringing up and carrying back the prisoner or prisoners to

---

[12] *Commons' jn. Ire.*, i, pp 247–8 (16 Feb. 1640).
[13] *Commons' jn. Ire.*, i, p. 270 (26 July 1641).
[14] Ibid.

be always ordered by the court, if any difference shall arise thereabout, bring or cause to be brought the body or bodies of the said party or parties, so committed or restrained unto and before the judges or justices of the said court from whence the said writ or writs shall issue, in open court, and shall then likewise certify the true cause of such his or their detainer or imprisonment; and thereupon the court, upon such return made and delivered in open court, shall proceed to examine and determine whether the cause of such commitment, appearing upon the said return, be just and legal, or not, and shall thereupon do to what justice shall appertain, either by delivering, bailing or remanding the prisoner.

Though the Declaration never became law it at least indicated the constitutional ambition of the Irish Parliament to have a habeas corpus law as extensive as that in England. A struggle to accomplish such constitutional equivalence was carried on for the following one hundred and forty years.

THE CAMPAIGN FOR THE ENACTMENT OF A HABEAS CORPUS ACT, 1692-1782

In England, Parliament, following the Restoration, renewed its efforts to provide effective habeas corpus control over long-term executive detention without trial, and after several frustrated attempts achieved success in the form of the Habeas Corpus Act 1679.[15] The most important provision of that Act, section 7, created a mechanism for the relief of state prisoners. Prisoners committed for high treason or felony were given the right to submit a prayer or petition in the first week of the following term to the Court of King's Bench, or at the first day of the next sessions of oyer and terminer, requesting that they be tried at that session. If not indicted at that session they were automatically entitled to be bailed. If not indicted at the following session they were entitled to be discharged, unconditionally. The prerogative power of indefinite internment without trial was overridden where, as became common in the late seventeenth century, a prisoner took the precaution of submitting a section 7 prayer.

[15] A. Nutting, 'The most wholesome law – the Habeas Corpus Act of 1679' (1959–60) 65 *American Historical Journal* 527.

The campaign to have a habeas corpus act enacted in Ireland went on to the Irish political agenda at the first parliament following the Glorious Revolution – the Parliament which opened in 1692. By the time that the Act eventually passed in 1782, no less than seventeen such liberty of the subject bills had been passed by the Irish House of Commons, only to be set aside (under the mechanism laid down in Poynings' Law) by the Privy Council in Dublin or London.

The first effort at enactment was made at the Parliament of 1692. A select committee appointed to 'enquire and examine what laws have been made since 10th of Henry 7th and may be beneficial to this kingdom' recommended the enactment of legislation equivalent to the English Act of 1679. The proposal was endorsed by Parliament, but with the proviso that it be restricted to those taking the oath of supremacy, thereby excluding members of the Roman Catholic faith:[16]

> Resolved that this House doth agree with the said committee in this resolution, that an Act made in England, Anno. 31 Chas. II, entitled an Act for the better securing of the Liberty of the Subject, and for prevention of imprisonment beyond the seas, is fit to be made of force in this Kingdom, with such alterations, as may make it practicable in this Kingdom; and that one alteration be, that there be a proviso annexed to the above Act, that no person or persons, shall have the benefit of the same, unless they take the oath, and subscribe the declaration mentioned in a late Act of Parliament made in England, for this Kingdom, entitled an Act for Abrogating the Oath of Supremacy of Ireland.

But the proviso was not enough to ensure approval. The Bill, like the other constitutional demands of the Parliament of 1692,[17] was regarded with horror by the Irish administration. The Lord Lieutenant, Viscount Sydney, described the Commons as behaving 'like a company of mad men, for they don't know themselves what they will have ... at present they talk of freeing themselves from the yoke of England, of taking away Poynings' law, of making an address to have a habeas corpus bill, and twenty other

---

[16] *Commons' jn. Ire.*, ii, p. 10 (18 Oct. 1692).
[17] W.N. Osborough, 'The failure to enact a Bill of Rights: a gap in Irish constitutional history' (1998) 33 *Ir. Jurist* 392.

extravagant discourses'.[18] The demand for a habeas corpus act was renewed in 1695. On this occasion the proviso restricting the application of the measure to Protestants was dropped.[19] Under considerable pressure from the Commons (including a threat to disrupt supply measures), the Irish Privy Council was unable to set aside the measure, and it was conveyed to London. It arrived there accompanied by an apology from the Lord Deputy, who protested that he was sending the Bill, although he did not agree with the measure, and did not expect it to be passed. The Lord Keeper, at the meeting of the cabinet assembled to discuss Irish legislation, irritably enquired why, if he did not agree with the measure, and did not expect that it would be passed, he had bothered to send it.[20] The Bill was set aside.

Between 1698 and 1710, a further six liberty of the subject bills were passed: the Irish Parliament approved measures in 1698,[21] 1703,[22] 1705,[23] 1707,[24] 1709[25] and 1710.[26] The Irish House of Commons demanded that

[18] *Cal. S.P. Dom.1695 and Addenda*, p. 213; Sydney to Nottingham, 17 Oct. 1692 (TNA: PRO, SP 63/354, f. 178).
[19] *Commons' jn. Ire.*, ii, pp 518–19 (13 Sept. 1695).
[20] 13 Nov. 1695 (BL, Trumbull MSS, Add MS 72566). I owe this reference to John Bergin (Queen's University, Belfast).
[21] *Commons' jn. Ire.*, ii, pp 804–5, 809 (27 Oct., 1 Nov. 1698).
[22] *Commons' jn. Ire.*, iii, pp 53, 89 (14 & 30 Oct. 1703). Privy Council Register, 26 Dec. 1703 (TNA: PRO, PC/2/79, ff. 484–85).
[23] *Commons' jn. Ire.*, iii, p. 250 (1 Mar. 1705); The Lord Lieutenant, Ormond, noted: 'Tomorrow the bills be sent to England. There are three which I believe will be sent back, which are the habeas corpus, the qualification of Parliament and the registry of justices, but they are so popular here that they are not to be set aside by the Council' (TNA: PRO, SP 63/365, ff. 168–169, 29 Mar. 1705). A report on the bill, which does not survive, was apparently made by the English law officers. In 1758 the English Lord Chancellor was informed by the Privy Council Office that none of the Irish Liberty of the Subject Bills of the late seventeenth and early eighteenth centuries had been retained by the English Privy Council: Sharpe to Hardwicke, 1 Apr. 1758 (BL, Hardwicke papers, Add MS 35595, f. 163).
[24] *Commons' jn. Ire.*, iii, p. 382 (18 July 1707); The proceedings before the English Privy Council took place on 8 and 11 Sept. 1707 (TNA: PRO, PC 2/81, ff. 438, 453).
[25] *Commons' jn. Ire.*, iii, pp 578, 585, 597 (12, 16 & 23 May 1709). The bill was set aside by the English Privy Council following meetings on 11 & 15 July 1709 (TNA: PRO, PC/2/82, ff. 347 & 350).
[26] *Commons' jn. Ire.*, iii, pp 718, 725, 726, 729, 774 (22 & 27 May 1710, 1, 5 & 22 June 1710). The English Privy Council rejected the bill following the report of a committee on 29 July 1710 (TNA:PRO, PC 2/83, f. 361).

they be approved by the Irish Privy Council and transmitted to the English Privy Council. All but one of these measures, the Bill of 1698, was systematically transmitted by the Irish Privy Council to London. Such was their popularity in Parliament that the Irish Privy Council dared not exercise its prerogative to set them aside. As with the first Bill of 1693, it was the English Privy Council which laid aside all of these measures, with the decision to set aside usually following consultation with the English law officers.[27] Writing much later in the century, Christopher Robinson noted[28] that orders were sent from the Privy Council in London to Dublin directing the Lord Lieutenant that no further liberty of the subject bills were to be sent over. No record of this instruction survives. But of the six liberty of the subject bills passed by the Irish House Commons between the years 1711 and 1755, none reached the table of the Privy Council in Whitehall;[29] it is likely, accordingly, that the embargo dates from about 1710.

The absence of a statutory right of state prisoners in Ireland to immediate prosecution, such as that contained in section 7 of the English Habeas Corpus Act, 1679, left intact the prerogative of indefinite detention. On the other hand, the right to bail or the immediate initiation of prosecution was enforceable in Ireland through habeas corpus as a common law right. In 1766 Christopher Robinson, whose assertions on matters of crown practice in mid-eighteenth-century Ireland must be regarded as highly authoritative, declared:[30] 'The habeas corpus act is unnecessary for Ireland, because for the cases that fall within the reason of it – the Court of King's Bench has always looked upon the English Act as a good guide for their direction, tho' not a declaratory or binding law.' The proposition that the English Act had the force of custom in Ireland was regularly asserted. In 1782, on introducing in the House of Commons what was to become the Habeas Corpus Act of 1782, the Chief Secretary, William Eden, is reported as having said 'that from the usage of Ireland,

---

[27] The English law officers were consulted on the bills of 1698, 1703, 1705, 1707 (TNA: PRO, PC 2/77,f. 9; PC 2/79, ff. 484,489; PC 2/80, f. 312; PC 2/81, ff. 438).

[28] TNA: PRO, SP 63/442, ff. 120–1 (7 Mar. 1774).

[29] Liberty of the subject bills were enacted by the Irish Parliament in 1711; 1715; 1743; 1749; 1751 & 1755.

[30] TNA: PRO, SP 63/442, ff. 120–1; Christopher Robinson was justice of the King's Bench, 1758–87. F. E. Ball, *The Judges in Ireland* (2 vols, London, 1926), ii, pp 169–71, 210.

which was the common law of the realm, and from the conduct of the judges, the habeas corpus was in operation here, though not under the authority of statute'.[31] The fullest published account of the application in Ireland of the principle that a subject detained on a criminal charge was entitled either to be tried or released, can be found in the proceedings in 1707 in *Weynell v. Camocke*.[32] Mosley Weynell, the purser of a naval ship, the *Speedwell*, docked at Poolbeg in Dublin, was being held on a charge of mutiny. An application to the Court of Queen's Bench for habeas corpus was made on behalf of Weynell, and was granted returnable the following day. Camocke, the captain of the ship, refused to obey, saying 'he was resolved to have him tried as soon as he could meet with five captains in any harbour'.[33] Camocke persisted in his refusal to accept service of the writ. An unsuccessful attempt to serve the writ was attempted at Lucas's Coffee House on Cork Hill: 'the said James Moore went into Lucas's Coffee House and offered it again to him, but the said Captain refused it; then the said Moore laid it on a chair just beside him, and told him what it was.' Camocke continued to ignore the writ. In response to Captain Camocke's contempt a Grand Committee of the House of Lords was constituted 'to consider the misbehaviour of Captain George Camocke in the undue refusing of a habeas corpus issued out of the Court of Queen's Bench, and the affront given him to that Court.' The Grand Committee censured Captain Camocke in a declaration intended to confirm the operation of the remedy of habeas corpus as part of the Irish constitution: 'It is the undoubted right of every free-born subject of Her Majesty who is in restraint in any part of the Kingdom, to have a writ of habeas corpus, in order to his trial or enlargement. That the Court of Queen's Bench, in granting a habeas corpus to Mosley Weynell discharged their duty according to law and justice.'[34]

The practical recognition of the entitlement to trial or enlargement did not, however, quell the demand for the enactment of a habeas corpus act.

---

[31] *Parliamentary Register* (2nd ed., Dublin, 1784), p. 31 (2 Nov. 1781). Records of the Irish Court of King's Bench for the eighteenth century have now been lost. However, an original writ of habeas corpus issued by Marlay CJ of the Irish King's Bench on 18 Nov. 1749 in respect of John Brown, a prisoner detained by the sheriff of Mayo, is preserved in Dublin City Library & Archive, Robinson MSS, vol. 34, f. 119.

[32] *Lords' jn. Ire.*, ii, pp 157, 158, 163, 166 (10, 11,16 & 18 July 1707).

[33] *Lords' jn. Ire.*, ii, p. 166 (18 July 1707).

[34] Ibid.

There appear to be two reasons. First, legislation along the lines of section 7 of the English Act was still necessary to override the Crown's prerogative right of detention without trial.[35] In addition, the absence of a habeas corpus act seems to have supported a popular perception that the abuse of pre-trial detention was not as well protected by the judiciary as it was in England. By the middle of the century the earlier injunction against transmitting habeas corpus bills was dropped. The Habeas Corpus Bill passed by the House of Commons in 1764 was, late the following year, sealed at a meeting of the Irish Privy Council, and transmitted to London.[36] The Bill proposed that the remedy would not extend to treasonable offences until 25 December 1766, and included a suspension provision under which the operation of the statutory right to be brought to trial could be suspended by proclamation issued by the Chief Governor or Chief Governor and Privy Council during invasion or rebellion or while Great Britain was engaged in war.[37] In November 1766 the English law officers were requested to provide an opinion on the proposed Irish legislation; an additional opinion was commissioned from Christopher Robinson, judge of the Court of King's Bench of Ireland.

Four grounds of objection emerge from these opinions. The first was that the prerogative power of detention without trial was essential to the maintenance of civil order in Ireland. The English law officers argued that while a habeas corpus act may have been feasible in the conditions of relative stability which prevailed in England, it was completely unrealistic in Irish conditions:[38]

> Bills of this nature have been rejected at least five times as appears upon searching the books of the Privy Council of England since the revolution, by your Lordships, and still more frequently we are informed in the House of Commons in Ireland, from an anxious

---

[35] J.A. Froude, *The English in Ireland in the eighteenth century* (3 vols, London, 1887), ii, 178–9.

[36] *Commons' jn. Ire.*, viii, pp 242–3 (27 Jan. 1764); Hertford to Conway, 14 Dec. 1765 (TNA: PRO, SP 63 /424, f. 121).

[37] Irish Privy Council to English Privy Council, 29 Mar. 1766 (TNA: PRO, PC 1/ 8/ 21).

[38] Opinion of Yorke and de Grey, 6 May 1766 (TNA: PRO, PC 1/8/21). Charles Yorke, who had earlier been Solicitor General, served as Attorney General of England 1762–1763 and 1765–1766. William de Grey was Solicitor General, 1765–1766.

concern for the safety of Government, and for the better support of the laws made in that country against the Papists. This Bill makes no distinction between Protestant and Papist. And the truth is that to enact such distinction in favour of the Protestants with an express exclusion of the Papists would be productive of perpetual jealousy amongst his majesty's subjects. Therefore, it is thought wiser in policy to rest this matter in the common law and the well regulated course of the courts in Ireland, than to try a new experiment by legislative provisions.

A second ground, teased out particularly in the Robinson opinion,[39] was the practical difficulty in framing an appropriate suspension provision. Robinson argued that none of the suggested mechanisms was workable: suspension by Parliament was impracticable in emergencies given the long intervals between sittings of the Irish Parliament, while executive suspension might intensify anti-government feeling:[40]

The papists of Ireland are ... five to one of the inhabitants. These must either be admitted to the benefit of this law, or excluded from it, and then the dilemma stands thus. If they are admitted any commotion may be of the utmost danger. If they are excluded, it will be invidious to deprive four fifths of the people from the constitutional right of subjects as the habeas corpus act will be esteemed, and it will be called an unprovoked throwing them out of the public protection. The only expedient will be a power of suspension somewhere. In England this is commonly done by Parliament which meets every year. Here we meet but once in two years, and therefore the suspending power must be vested in Government, and what distress that may be to a Government, either by provoking the papists against them on the one hand by suspending, or of the Protestants by not suspending it, is a matter for consideration, but it seem a most embarrassing dilemma.

The peculiarities of the Irish law of riot and affray provided a subsidiary objection. In Ireland the crimes of riot and affray were misdemeanours; in

[39] TNA: PRO, SP 63/442, ff. 120–1.
[40] Ibid.

England they were, by statute, felonies. But one of the effects of the enactment in Ireland of legislation equivalent to the English legislation of 1679 would have been to grant automatic bail to a person detained during the vacation for a misdemeanour, including, in Ireland, where these offences were classified as misdemeanours, the offences of riot or affray. The English law officers noted this difference in the criminal codes of the two jurisdictions:

> The third and last observation is that the late frequent and dangerous disorders in Ireland, both in time of war and peace, which is thought with reason, received encouragement from foreign enemies, make the Bill liable to weighty objections, especially as it comes unaccompanied with a Riot Act, framed in the same manner and with the same or like remedies as are in the English statute 1 Geo 1 c. 4 whereby some offences which were misdemeanors are constituted felonies, in order to prevent the crimes and mischiefs too often committed in the progress of tumults. The consequence of this is that such offences are not bailable in England which still remain misdemeanors bailable in Ireland. And as many provisions in the habeas corpus act are adapted to accelerate the bailing in misdemeanors, it seems unwise and inexpedient by a new law in Ireland to make the discharge or bailing of rioters or insurgents, as they are called there, more easy than it is in England.

A final objection identified by Robinson was that the prohibition laid down in the Irish Bill against sending persons out of the jurisdiction into England was inconsistent with an English criminal jurisdiction act of 1543[41] which gave to the English King's Bench jurisdiction over 'treason, misprision of treason, or concealments of treason, perpetuated or committed out of the King's Realm in England'.[42] The proposed Irish

[41] 35 Hen. VIII, c. 2 (1543).
[42] 'For so much as some doubts and questions have been moved that certain kinds of treason and concealments of treason done, perpetrated or committed out of the King's Majesty's realm of England and other his Grace's Dominions cannot be by the common law of the realm enquired of, heard and determined within his said realm of England, for a plain remedy order and declaration therein to be had and made, be it enacted by authority of this present Parliament, that all manner of offences, being already made or declared, or hereafter to be made and declared, by any the laws and statutes of the realm, to be treasons, misprision of

liberty of the subject legislation, with its prohibition on the transmission of persons outside the jurisdiction, would, Robinson argued, be in direct conflict with that measure: 'for making it a binding statute might interfere with the English Act of 35th Hen 8th for Tryal of Foreign Treasons, a power which is essential in the very idea of relations between a mother country and her dependants and it is a most absurd solecism in politics to think of making the Constitution of Colonies the same with that of the mother country.'[43]

In 1767 the Lord Lieutenant was instructed by the cabinet to make it known that the Crown had no objection in principle to a habeas corpus measure. However, approval would depend upon the country being politically settled, a condition which, as Townshend noted, 'in the present state of the country will be very difficult.'[44] The 1767 Bill was again a transcription of the English Act of 1679, though with two modifications: there was provision for suspension, and the provision in the 1679 Act forbidding transmission out of the jurisdiction contained a qualification exempting from the prohibition the extradition of offenders accused of capital offences. The Irish Privy Council reported to London that[45]

> the Bill took its rise in the House of Commons and is a literal transcript of a Bill passed in Great Britain in the Thirty First year of the reign of King Charles the Second for the like purposes so far as is suitable to the circumstances of this Kingdom. A clause is inserted in

treasons, or concealments of treasons, and done, perpetrated or committed, or hereafter to be done, perpetrated or committed, by any person or persons out of the realm of England, shall be from henceforth enquired of, heard and determined before the King's Justices of his Bench, for Pleas to be holden before himself, by good and lawful men of the same shire where the said Bench shall sit and be kept, or else before such Commissioners, and in such shire of the realm, as shall be assigned by the King's Majesty's Commission, and by good and lawful men of the same shire, in like manner and form, to all intents and purposes, as if such treasons, misprision of treason or concealment of treason had been done, perpetrated and committed within the same shire where they shall be so enquired of, heard and determined as aforesaid.'

[43] Robinson also noted (TNA: PRO, SP 63/442, f. 120) that the provision in the Statutes of Kilkenny against the trying in England for offences in Ireland 'is passed with an express exception for the offence of treason so that the English statute of 35th Henry 8th so far as Ireland is affected, is founded on the original constitution of this country.'

[44] Townshend to Shelbourne, 5 Nov. 1767 (TNA: PRO, SP 63/425, f. 70).

[45] 26 Dec. 1767 (TNA: PRO, PC 1/9/11).

this Act by which a power is given to the Chief Governor for the time being and Privy Council of this Kingdom to suspend this Act by proclamation during such time only as there shall be an actual invasion or rebellion in this Kingdom, or in Great Britain. We therefore desire your Lordships will be pleased to have the said Bill returned to us in the usual form.

The Bill was sent to the English law officers who, again, recommended that the legislation was unnecessary, and also possibly dangerous in the unsettled conditions of contemporary Ireland:[46]

> Upon this Bill we think it incumbent upon us to observe to your lordships that Bills of the same or of a similar import have been sent over six times since the revolution, and they have been as often rejected. The last was sent over in one thousand seven hundred and sixty six, and your lordships postponed it, as we presume, from an opinion that however wise and just such provisions have been found by experience in this country, they are not yet safe and expedient in Ireland where the Roman Catholic religion is still prevalent, tumultuous disorders and insurrections so frequent, and dangerous riots still continue, as they were at common law misdemeanors only and not made (as they are in England by the Statute of 1st Geo 1st c. 5th under certain aggravating circumstances, capital offences). This Bill goes further than the last in one thousand seven hundred and sixty six by transcribing from the Act of 35th Car 2 what that had omitted, certain clauses, by which it is declared that if any inhabitant or resident of Ireland should be sent a prisoner into Great Britain, or elsewhere out of that kingdom, it should be deemed a false imprisonment and should subject all concerned to damages not exceeding five hundred pounds, tho' with a proviso amongst others, that where such resident should have committed a capital offence in another country he might be sent to take his trial there, in such manner as he might have been before. But we do not find that any thing has happened in Ireland to call for the measure. The recital of the Bill does not import it, and we

---

[46] Opinion of de Grey and Dunning, 10 Apr. 1768 (TNA: PRO, PC 1/9/11). William de Grey, was Attorney General, 1766–71, and John Dunning was Solicitor General, 1768–70.

understand that the established practice of the courts with regard to the writ of habeas corpus is in practice, very easy and salutary to the subject.

Again the Irish measure was respited.[47] A similarly framed proposal forwarded in 1774 was also set aside.[48] The English Attorney General suggested that the Irish Parliament of the 1770s was guilty of affectation in pressing for the extension to Ireland of the Liberty of the Subject Act of 1679:[49] 'The Liberty of the Subject Bill, 1774 recites for its foundation, the imagination of a possible grievance, whereas the English Act went upon grievances which frequently occurred, and cried loudly for redress.' Objection was taken that the legislation purported to impose sanctions and expenses more onerous than those laid down in the English legislation:[50]

> This tenor of a Bill is nearly a transcript from the statute of the third of Charles chapter the second in England; except that it would compel the gaoler to bring up the prisoner at a lesser rate per mile, than it is profitable to convey him at ... When under the colourable pretence of better securing liberty, new encumbrances are proposed to be laid upon the magistracy, and the execution of public justice, it is sufficient answer that liberty has suffered no wrong from the Laws as they stand and it would be extremely unjust to subject judges and magistrates to captious prosecutions, and the danger of heavy penalties, who have afforded no cause of complaint. The administration of justice in Ireland has been so clear in that respect, that the authors of the tenor of a popular bill have not ventured further in their recitals than that delays *may be caused*.

The push for a habeas corpus act was relaxed during the height of the wars with the Americans in the late 1770s. No proposal was introduced during the three parliamentary sessions occurring between 1775 and 1779. However, in 1780 Sir Samuel Broadstreet moved another Liberty of the

---

[47] TNA: PRO, PC 2/113, f. 131.
[48] The Bill was respited by the English Privy Council in April 1774: TNA: PRO, SP 63/442, f. 139.
[49] Opinion of Thurlow and Wedderburn (TNA: PRO, PC/1/10, f.7). Edward Thurlow, later Lord Chancellor, was Attorney General 1771–8; Alexander Wedderburn was Solicitor General 1771–7.
[50] Ibid.

Subject Bill. The Lord Lieutenant advised that he 'did not feel Bill would be opposed here with any success'[51] and the Bill was sealed and transmitted at the Irish Privy Council.[52] The Bill never passed: consideration of the proposal by the Privy Council in Whitehall was postponed, and the measure lapsed.[53]

Finally, in 1782, Parliament got its way. Government support was secured by the insertion of a proposal providing for suspension by means of executive proclamation. The Chief Secretary joined the committee appointed to draft heads for the Bill, saying that 'as the Recorder had added a clause to empower the Lord Lieutenant and Council to suspend it in time of war and rebellion he was very willing'.[54] In transmitting the measure to London in December 1781 the Lord Lieutenant again drew attention to the presence of the suspension clause, and warned London of the risk of a constitutional crisis if the measure was interfered with.[55] On 17 January 1782,[56] the Irish Committee of the English Privy Council met, and, having held out for ninety years against such a measure, approved the Bill and returned it to Ireland, without amendment, Sir Samuel Broadstreet's Liberty of the Subject Bill, 1781,[57] which became law as 21 & 22 Geo. II, c. 11.

But, as some contemporary English commentators pointed out, the Irish Parliament, in seeking no more than a replica of the English legislation of 1679, had failed to appreciate how marginal that legislation had become, and failed to address the principal weaknesses with the remedy.[58] A series

---

[51] Buckingham to Hillsborough, 10 Feb. 1780 (TNA: PRO, SP 63/468, ff. 220–2).
[52] 10 Apr. 1780 (TNA: PRO, SP 63/469, f. 31).
[53] 27 June 1780 (TNA: PRO, PC 2/125, f. 196).
[54] Sir Henry Cavendish's parliamentary diary, vol. 21, f. 57, 2 Nov. 1781 (NLI, microfilm P. 7002). The proposal for a power of executive suspension was justified by reference to the long intervals between parliamentary sittings in Ireland.
[55] Carlisle to Hillsborough, 29 Dec. 1781 (NAI, Calendar of Departmental Letters and Official Correspondence, 1760–89, f. 254).
[56] 17 Jan. 1782 (TNA: PRO, PC 2/127, f. 117).
[57] Relieved, the Lord Lieutenant wrote to Hillsborough that 'upon the return to Parliament of the Habeas Corpus Bill the Recorder expatiated upon the advantage which the country is likely to receive by the return of the Habeas Corpus Act and I think His Majesty's Grace in this instance will have good effect in the course of future debates in this session'; Carlisle to Hillsborough, 29 Jan. 1782 (NAI, M 2446).
[58] Anon., *Account of some proceedings on the writ of habeas corpus* (London, 1781). This pamphlet was written in the form of a letter to an Irish Member of

of decisions in the mid-eighteenth century by the King's Bench under Mansfield CJ had held that the application of the 1679 Act was restricted to persons detained for criminal offences, and did not extend to administrative or private detention. In these cases the only remedy was the writ of habeas corpus at common law. But the common law remedy was deficient in a number of respects. During the long intervals between court terms there was no jurisdiction to issue attachment for disobedience of the writ: although it had become common to issue the writ in vacation, the jurisdiction to enforce compliance with the writ by attachment was restricted to term time. Nor did the legislation deal with the principal complaint about the operation of the common law remedy, the inability of the applicant to contradict untrue assertions of fact contained on the return to the writ. The details of a modern habeas corpus statute had been drawn up by the English judges in 1758.[59] However, no attempt was made by the Irish Parliament to accomplish the enactment of a modernized habeas corpus statute for Ireland. These reforms came only in 1816 with the passing by the United Kingdom Parliament of the Habeas Corpus Act, 1816 (56 Geo. III, c. 100).

HABEAS CORPUS AND THE POLITICAL DISTURBANCES OF THE 1790S

The Government's long-standing fears about interference by habeas corpus during periods of political disturbance in Ireland were soon realized when the remedy begun to be used by prisoners detained during the rebellion of the late 1790s.

Although there was a power of detention without trial by order of the Privy Council under the procedure laid down by the Habeas Corpus Suspension Act, 1797,[60] the military appear to have practised long-term preventive detention without attempting to operate the inconvenient mechanism laid down in that legislation. The writ was employed on a number of occasions by prisoners who were being detained by the military without charge, but against whom the precaution of a warrant issued

---

Parliament apprising the Irish legislature of defects in the contemporary English law of habeas corpus, and advising that these be addressed in the Irish measure.

[59] W. Cobbett, *Parliamentary history of England* (London, 1813), xv, pp 871–926.
[60] 37 Geo III, c. 1. This Act is dealt with below, pp 20–1.

under the Habeas Corpus Suspension Act, 1797, had not been taken.[61] In January 1799, for instance, three prisoners, O'Neale, Murray and Graham, who had been detained in Wicklow gaol without either the initiation of criminal proceedings or the issue of a warrant under the 1797 Act, were discharged by the Court of King's Bench.[62] Secondly, the remedy was used, often with certiorari, as a means of challenging the legality of imprisonment of persons convicted under the Insurrection Act, 1796.[63] Most famously, habeas corpus was used to challenge the detention of those detained under the process of the martial law regime proclaimed by the Lord Lieutenant in the spring of 1798.[64] In *Wolfe Tone's* case[65] a writ directing the production of the prisoner was granted following the submission of Tone's counsel, John Philpot Curran, that the Crown had no jurisdiction to exercise martial law while the ordinary criminal courts still functioned. Although *Tone's* case did not come on for trial, and while it did not authoritatively determine that prosecutions before military tribunals were illegal, an instruction was issued 'in consequence of the proceedings in the case of Tone as other considerations' to cease trials under military law.[66] In late 1798 a series of habeas corpus applications were made on behalf of prisoners detained either prior to military trial or following conviction under military law.[67] These writs were resisted by senior military commanders who asserted their entitlement to act according to the 1798 proclamation of martial law, and the King's Bench, in turn, responded with orders of attachment for contempt. Attachment orders were issued against senior military officers, including the Chief

---

[61] Writs of habeas corpus were issued in the case of a prisoner against whom no charge had been laid and was detained in Mullingar gaol, and another in the case of an uncharged prisoner, James Byrne, being detained without charge, on board a prison ship: *Dublin Evening Post*, 29 Nov. 1798.

[62] *The Times*, 10 Jan. 1799.

[63] See the case of *Barry* reported in *Dublin Evening Post*, 15 Feb. 1798.

[64] R. Keane, '"The will of the general"; martial law in Ireland, 1535–1924' (1990–2) 25–27 *Ir. Jurist* 150, 159–60.

[65] (1798) 27 St Tr 613.

[66] 16 Nov. 1798 (TNA: PRO, HO 100/ 86, f. 43).

[67] An order of attachment was made when, in the course of an application taken by a prisoner called Lyons, General Johnston had refused to observe the writ claiming that he was justified by the martial law proclamation (TNA: PRO, HO 100/86, f. 45, 26 Nov. 1798); Daniel Kennedy's case (TNA: PRO, HO 100/86, f. 96, 5 Feb. 1799); Moore's case (TNA: PRO, HO 100/79, f. 243, 10 Dec. 1798); *Anon.* (n.d.) Rowe's Reports 415.

Commander of Crown forces in Ireland, General Johnson.[68] Constitutional crisis was averted by the firm advice of the law officers, that the military must yield to the rule of law. Cornwallis recorded that[69]

> The Attorney General and Solicitor General have stated to me that they have thought it their duty under all the difficulties of clashing jurisdiction not to involve the executive power and the courts of law in any embarrassment in any question that may effect the principles of the common law, which induced their advising an obedience to the writ of habeas corpus issued in Wolfe Tone's case.

The problem of the legal basis of martial law was solved with the enactment in 1799 of the Rebellion Act[70] which authorized the Lord Lieutenant to empower the military to administer martial law. The issue of interference by writs of habeas corpus was addressed by a specific clause, section 6, which provided that 'if any party who shall be detained in custody under the powers created by this act shall sue forth a writ of habeas corpus it shall be good and sufficient return that the party suing forth the same is detained by virtue of a warrant under the hand and seal of some officers or other persons, duly authorised by the chief governor.'

EIGHTEENTH- AND NINETEENTH-CENTURY HABEAS CORPUS SUSPENSION ACTS

The power of suspension by proclamation under section 16 of the Habeas Corpus Act, 1782 (21 & 22 Geo III, c. 11) was never used.[71] Instead,

---

[68] TNA: PRO, HO 100/86, f. 45, 26 Nov. 1798; *R. v. Carrick* (n.d.) Rowe's Reports 67. The Chief Secretary introducing the Rebellion Bill told the House of Commons that 'General Johnson, the man who saved Ireland, was at this moment under attachment of that court for not instantly bringing up from New Geneva a mob of convicts of the kind who only waited there for transportation,' *The Times*, 27 Feb. 1799.

[69] Cornwallis to Duke of Portland, 10 Dec. 1798 (TNA: PRO, HO 100/79, f. 244); *Correspondence of Charles, first marquis of Cornwallis*, ed. C. Ross (3 vols, London, 1859), iii, pp 10–12.

[70] 39 Geo. III, c. 11.

[71] A petition was introduced in the House of Commons in 1832 praying that the power under s. 16, which it was rumoured was to be put into operation, not be activated: *Hansard 3*, vol. 14, cols 1303–11 (10 Aug. 1832).

beginning in 1797, and continuing throughout the nineteenth century, Parliament enacted a series of statutes, popularly but misleadingly known as habeas corpus suspension acts. Fifteen such acts were enacted.[72] These statues did not completely suspend the operation of habeas corpus at common law. Neither did they directly suspend the operation of all of the rights constituted by the 1782 Act (21 & 22 Geo III, c. 11). What they did instead was to indirectly supersede the right given to a state prisoner under section 6 of 21 & 22 Geo III, c. 11 to submit a petition for trial or enlargement, by enabling the Lord Lieutenant or Privy Council to detain persons suspected of treason or treasonable practices without any requirement to initiate a criminal prosecution. The Act of 1782 had contained a power of suspension in cases of actual invasion or rebellion.[73] The suspension acts did not require actual invasion or rebellion, applying instead in cases of treasonable practices, regardless of whether a rebellion or invasion had occurred. Section 1 of the Habeas Corpus Suspension Act, 1797 (37 Geo III, c. 1) was to provide the standard formula for all subsequent habeas corpus suspension acts:

> That every person or persons that is, are, or shall be in prison within the Kingdom of Ireland, at or upon the day upon which this Act shall receive his Majesty's Royal Assent, or after by warrant of his Majesty's most honourable Privy Council of this Kingdom, signed by six of the said Privy Council, for high treason, suspicion of high treason, or treasonable practices, or by warrant signed by the Lord Lieutenant or Chief Secretary, for such causes, as aforesaid may be detained in safe custody without bail or mainprize, until the first day of August, one thousand seven hundred and ninety-seven, and until the end of the then next session of Parliament; and that no judge or justice of the peace shall bail or try any such person or persons so committed, without order from his said Majesty's Privy Council signed by six of said Privy Council, until the said first day of August, one thousand seven hundred and ninety-seven, and the end of the

---

[72] 37 Geo. III, c. 1 (1797); 38 Geo. III, c. 14 (1798); 40 Geo. III, c. 18 (1800); 41 Geo. III, c. 15 (1800); 41 Geo. III, c. 26 (1801); 43 Geo. III, c. 116 (1803); 44 Geo. III, c. 8 (1803); 45 Geo. III, c. 4 (1805); 3 Geo. IV, c. 2 (1822); 11 & 12 Vict., c. 35 (1848); 12 & 13 Vict., c. 2 (1849); 29 & 30 Vict., c. 1 (1866); 30 & 31 Vict., c. 1 (1867); 30 & 31 Vict., c. 25 (1868); Protection of Life and Property (Ireland) Act, 1871.
[73] S. 16.

next session of Parliament, any law or statute to the contrary notwithstanding.

The suspension acts did not forbid judicial review of whether the findings or procedural conditions to a valid commitment order under the acts had been properly pursued.[74] In *R. v. Despard*,[75] the Court of King's Bench in England rejected an argument that a writ of habeas corpus obtained to review a warrant of detention under the English Suspension Act of 1797 had been issued *qua improvide emanavit*. 'It did not follow' the Court stated 'that because the Court might not bail or discharge that the writ was irregularly issued.' In *Houston and Byrne v. Lake*[76] thirteen members of the United Irishmen had been detained under section 1 of the Irish Act of 1797 by warrant of the Chief Secretary in a military barracks. In a habeas corpus application their counsel, Robert Emmett, successfully argued that the Act of 1797 only authorized detention in a prison, and that a military barracks was not a prison. The Government responded to the ruling by including, in its next suspension act,[77] a provision authorizing the detention of prisoners committed for treason or treasonable practices 'in any place whatever within the Kingdom':

> And be it further enacted, by the authority aforesaid, that in cases where any person or persons have been before the passing of this Act, or shall be during the time this Act shall continue in force, arrested, committed, or detained in custody by force of a warrant or warrants of his Majesty's most honourable Privy Council of this Kingdom, signed by six of the said Privy Council for high treason, suspicion of high treason, or treasonable practices, or by warrant or warrants signed by the Lord Lieutenant or Chief Secretary for such causes as aforesaid, it shall and may be lawful for any person or persons to whom such warrant or warrants have been, or shall be directed, to

---

[74] However, the view that such legislation did forbid habeas corpus review was initially taken in Ireland: in *R. v. Anon.* (n.d.) Rowe's Reports 640 the Irish Court of King's Bench, in dismissing an application for habeas corpus, is quoted as saying that the production of a warrant from the Lord Lieutenant 'puts an end to our authority.'

[75] (1798) 9 TR 736; 101 ER 1226.

[76] *Dublin Evening Post*, 25 Nov. 1797; R.B. McDowell, *Ireland in the age of imperialism and revolution* (Oxford, 1979), p. 574.

[77] 40 Geo. III, c.18 (1800).

detain such person or persons so arrested or committed in his or their custody in any place whatsoever within this Kingdom;[...] And that such place or places where such persons so arrested, committed or detained, are, or shall be, detained in custody, shall be deemed and taken, to all intents and purposes, to be lawful prisons and gaols for the detention in safe custody of such person and persons.

The risk of a successful challenge to executive committal orders was further reduced by clauses, such as that in the Protection of Life and Property Act, 1871, which deemed the Privy Council or Chief Secretary's warrant evidence of full compliance with all of the required procedural steps. In *Re Patrick Casey's* case[78] an application made by the father of a prisoner detained under the Protection of Life and Property Act, 1871, was abruptly terminated when Barry J in the Court of Queen's Bench, simply ruled that 'the warrant of the Lord Lieutenant suspends the action of the Court'.[79]

HABEAS CORPUS IN IRELAND, 1888–1922

Two habeas corpus cases decided in Irish courts in the period 1888–1921, *Re Sullivan*[80] in 1888 and *Egan v. Macready*[81] in 1921, both regarded as calamitous by the executive, and as triumphs by its nationalist opponents, secured the recognition in early twentieth century Irish legal culture of habeas corpus as a high-priority civil right. Both of these cases, but particularly *Egan v. Macready*, lie at the background of the incorporation of habeas corpus in the Irish Constitution. But these decisions were also of considerable doctrinal significance in their own right.

---

[78] 29 Apr. 1874. See 'Affidavits on a Motion in the Queen's Bench in Ireland on a Writ of Habeas Corpus' (HC, 1874 (210) liv, 523).

[79] In 1893 a Private Members' Bill, 'To Amend the Law relating to the writ of habeas corpus in Ireland', was laid before the Commons (HC, 1893–1894 (452) iii, 367). The bill proposed to repeal s. 16 of the Liberty of the Subject Act, 1782. However, it is difficult to establish the purpose of the measure: habeas corpus suspension had never been based on the suspending power in s. 16 but was always based on positive legislative provisions authorising indefinite internment without trial along the lines of the Act of 1797.

[80] (1888) 22 LR Ir 98.

[81] [1921] 1 IR 265.

Habeas corpus and the Plan of Campaign

Re Sullivan[82] concerned the right to remedy, on grounds of misconstruction of law, convictions under the Criminal Law and Procedure Act, 1887, the legislation introduced to suppress the boycotting practised during the agrarian rent campaign (the Plan of Campaign) of the late 1880s. In *Re Sullivan* the applicant's conviction under section 2(1) of the 1887 Act had been based on a clear error of law committed by a Resident Magistrate.[83] Even the Crown accepted that the conviction proceeded from a misunderstanding of section 2(1). The question was whether a remedy lay for misconstruction of law, or whether, following the doctrine laid down in the English case, *R. v. Bolton*,[84] which had held that an error of law within jurisdiction was irremediable on certiorari or habeas corpus, the miscarriage was inaccessible to review on the prerogative writs. The doctrinal issue split the Irish courts. The Queen's Bench Division, presided over by Lord Morris CJ, endorsed the rule in *R. v. Bolton* and held that 'where a charge has been well laid before the magistrate, and it is an offence within his jurisdiction, this Court will not inquire into the grounds of the decision.'[85] Following defeat at the hands of the Queen's Bench, Sullivan's lawyers made an application for habeas corpus in the Exchequer Division of the High Court.[86] The Exchequer, intellectually dominated by Palles CB, in an exceptional act of defiance of prevailing common law doctrine, refused to be bound by the principle in *R. v. Bolton*. Palles CB boldly developed a novel theory of review on habeas corpus quite at odds with what was regarded as orthodoxy in England. The premise underlying the Palles theory was that the subject had a 'constitutional right' to the intervention of the courts where the evidence was insufficient to sustain a

---

[82] (1888) 22 LR Ir 98.
[83] S. 2(1) of the Criminal Law and Procedure Act, 1887 had incriminated every person 'who shall take part in any criminal conspiracy now punishable by law to compel or induce any person or persons either not to fulfill his or their legal obligations, or not to let, hire, use or occupy any land, or not to deal with, work for or hire any person or persons.' The Act had been deliberately designed to avoid the prosecution of those who had simply participated in a boycott. Instead it targeted those who organized and pressurized others into participating in a campaign of excommunication. The only evidence against Sullivan, a blacksmith, was that he had refused to work for a boycotted family.
[84] (1841) 1 QB 65; 113 ER 1054.
[85] (1888) 22 LR Ir 504, 505–6.
[86] (1888) 22 L R Ir 98.

conviction.[87] The Exchequer Division, having found that Sullivan's conviction was based on a misreading of the Criminal Law and Procedure Act, 1887, directed Sullivan's release. The decision in the *Sullivan* case was a cause of significant irritation to the Crown (and of jubilation in political nationalist circles). The Attorney General reported to the Irish Secretary that the expanded scope of review now available on habeas corpus in the Exchequer 'may lead to the bringing up of a good many cases, but you need not trouble yourself about it if there is what, in effect, is an appeal ... We must bow to the majesty of the law which always was, is and always will be, an ass.'[88] Within a few weeks the Queen's Bench Division in England took the opportunity to make clear that it disapproved of the theory of habeas corpus review propounded by the Irish Exchequer.[89]

The internal dispute between the Queen's Bench and Exchequer Divisions in Ireland, as to the extent to which error of law was reviewable on habeas corpus or certiorari, remained in suspension until 1910 when the certiorari application, *R. (Martin) v. Mahony*,[90] came before the High Court. A court of eight judges of the High Court[91] was assembled to settle the point. Every member of the Court, bar one (Palles CB), supported the *Bolton* rule, holding that mere insufficiency of evidence, or misconstruction of law would not impair jurisdiction; these were merely errors within jurisdiction. The decision of the Queen's Bench in *Re Sullivan* (with its conservative view of the scope of review) was restored. It was soon confirmed that the principle in *Mahony* also established the scope of review for habeas corpus.[92]

---

[87] Ibid., p. 119.
[88] Peter O'Brien to Arthur Balfour, 22 Feb. 1888 (BL, Balfour papers, Add. MS 49808).
[89] In the course of *R. v. Northumberland JJ*, *The Times*, 13 Mar. 1888, a certiorari case heard just three weeks after the Exchequer in Ireland had handed down its decision in *Sullivan's* case, counsel for the respondents is reported as saying that the proposition that a magistrate's decision might be re-opened simply on grounds of legal error was incorrect. Huddlestone B confirmed this, saying 'that certainly has always been taken to be the law in this country, and though there is a recent decision in Ireland the other way, I do not think I could have concurred in it'.
[90] [1910] 2 IR 695.
[91] Lord O'Brien LCJ, Palles CB, and Gibson, Madden, Boyd, Kenny, Wright, and Dodd JJ.
[92] *R. (Ryan) v. Starkie* (1920) 54 ILTR 15; *R. v. Murphy* [1921] 2 IR 190.

Habeas corpus review of martial law in 1921

Egan v. Macready[93] decided in 1921 had a thrilling effect on a generation of Irish lawyers, and the decision, taken a year later, to incorporate habeas corpus in the Constitution of the Irish Free State can almost certainly be attributed to the prominence given to the remedy by that decision. John Egan was been being detained in a Limerick awaiting execution, under a martial law regime which had been instituted by the Crown acting under the royal prerogative. Egan's argument was that statutory system of martial law established by the Restoration of Order in Ireland Act, 1920 superseded the prerogative entitlement to proclaim martial law. A similar argument had been made and rejected four months earlier by the King's Bench Division in February 1921 in *R. v. Allen*.[94] The King's Bench held that 'it seems competent, if war exists, for the military authorities to use special military courts, and to impose any sentence, even death, without being disabled in another case from applying procedure of a more moderate and limited character.'[95] *Allen's* case was followed in a number of habeas corpus applications, *R. (Garde) v. Strickland*[96] and *R. (Ronayne) v. Strickland*,[97] submitted in the following months.

However, a different conclusion was reached by the Master of the Rolls, Sir Charles O'Connor, in *Egan v. Macready*. Following (according to some accounts) an unsuccessful attempt before the King's Bench Division,[98] Egan's counsel proceeded to the Chancery Division. O'Connor MR disagreed with the King's Bench, and decided that Parliament in enacting the 1920 Act had eclipsed the common law prerogative power.[99] The 1920 Act was, he held, exhaustive of the power to exercise military law against

---

[93] [1921] 1 IR 265.
[94] [1921] 2 IR 241.
[95] Ibid., at p. 272.
[96] [1921] 2 IR 317.
[97] [1921] 2 IR 333.
[98] The fact that such an application was made and rejected is referred to in the Dáil Debates during the proceedings on the Second Amendment of the Constitution Act, 1941: *Dáil Debates*, vol. 82, col. 1244 (2 Apr. 1941). There is, however, no reference to such an earlier application in either the law report, the Commons debates, or in the newspaper accounts of the proceedings.
[99] The premise of O'Connor MR's argument, that martial law resulted from an exercise of the prerogative, and, as such, could by superseded by legislation, is assessed critically in R. Keane, '"The will of the general"; martial law in Ireland, 1535–1924' (1990–1992) 25–27 *Ir. Jurist* 150, 172.

civilians, and since it had not been established that the tribunal had acted by reference to the Act, Egan's detention was unlawful.

Sensationally, General Macready, the General Officer Commanding of the military in Ireland, refused to comply with the order of the Chancery Division that he produce John Egan and make a return describing the cause of his detention. Macready believed that the decision was aberrational, and referring to the earlier judgments in *Allen*, *Garde* and *Ronayne*, argued that the decision was 'direct opposition to the rulings of every other judge on the Irish bench by whom similar cases had been heard.'[100] Macready took the view that the Crown, before complying with the ruling of the Irish Chancery Division, should await the judgment of the House of Lords in *Re Clifford and O'Sullivan*[101] where the point was in the course of being argued. In response, O'Connor MR made a rule directing General Macready to show cause why he should not be attached for contempt. Macready, in turn, defied that order and made it clear that he 'would not have hesitated to arrest anyone, including the Master of the Rolls himself, who attempted to carry out the service of the writs.'[102] Macready's mistrust of the Master of the Rolls appears to have been shared by Lloyd George's cabinet;[103] however, crisis was avoided when the Government,[104] advised by the Irish Lord Chancellor, Sir John Ross,[105] that 'the movement for peace in Ireland would be gravely prejudiced if the order of the High Court were flouted,'[106] undertook to discharge Egan. The Government, which does not appear to have been entirely comfortable with the appease-

---

[100] N. Macready, *Annals of an active life* (2 vols, London, 1924), ii, 592.

[101] [1921] 2 AC 570.

[102] N. Macready, *Annals of an active life* (2 vols, London, 1924), ii, 589; C. Campbell, *Emergency law in Ireland, 1918–1925* (Oxford, 1994), pp 37–8.

[103] The cabinet was relieved to learn on 2 Aug. 1921 that O'Connor MR was unlikely to sit again that term (TNA: PRO, CAB 23/26, p. 195).

[104] A cabinet sub-committee (consisting of the Lord Chancellor, Viscount Birkenhead, Austen Chamberlain (Lord Privy Seal), Sir Hamar Greenwood (Secretary for Ireland), Denis Henry KC (the Irish Attorney General), Sir L. Gordon Hewart (the Attorney General of England), and T.W. Brown (the Irish Solicitor General)) was established 'to examine, with special reference to recent events in Ireland, the steps to be taken to establish firmly the position of the Military Governor under martial law so that his proceedings shall be recognised as final and unaffected by proceedings in a court of law' (1 Aug. 1921, TNA: PRO, CAB 27/155).

[105] Ross was exercising vice-regal authority in place of the Lord Lieutenant, Lord FitzAlan, who was absent from Ireland.

[106] Cabinet minutes, 2 Aug. 1921 (TNA: PRO, CAB 23/26, p. 195).

ment urged by the Lord Chancellor,[107] continued, however, to insist that the decision of O'Connor MR was incorrect in law,[108] and resolved to initiate an appeal.[109]

THE DRAFTING OF ARTICLE 6 OF THE CONSTITUTION OF THE IRISH FREE STATE

In January 1922, Darrell Figgis, the chairman of the Irish Provisional Government Constitutional Drafting Committee, acting under great pressure of time, assembled a document, 'Document Number 2', which was intended to serve as a rough draft of a constitution for the new state which it would be the function of the Committee to refine. Article 9 of that draft included a provision dealing with habeas corpus. The Committee had before it the Constitution of the Realm of Germany, 1919, and Article 9[110] of this draft drew heavily on the constitution of the Weimar Republic:[111]

> The liberty of the person is inviolable. No restriction on, or deprivation of, that liberty shall be imposed by any authority except in respect of a law, and persons who have been deprived of their liberty must be informed within twenty four hours of the ground and the authority

---

[107] The cabinet minutes for 5 Aug. 1921 record the Prime Minister as indicating that if pressed in the Commons to explain the reason for compliance with the habeas corpus order 'he would be bound to say that the men had been released on the advice of the Lord Chancellor of Ireland' (TNA: PRO, CAB 23/26, p. 201, 5 Aug. 1921).

[108] In the House of Commons Austen Chamberlain explained that the release of Egan 'was based solely upon the existing situation in Ireland and the importance at the present time of avoiding a conflict between the civil and military authorities. The releases were not due to any decision given by a civil court in Ireland.' When asked 'have not the civil courts declared that the military courts are illegal?' Chamberlain, in a bizarre denial of the decision of the Master of the Rolls in *Egan*, replied 'No'; *Hansard 5*, vol. 146, cols 437–8 (10 Aug. 1921).

[109] Cabinet minutes, 2 Aug. 1921 (TNA: PRO, CAB 23/26, p. 195). That appeal was not pursued.

[110] TCD, Stephens papers, MS 4236.

[111] Article 114 of the German Constitution 1919 provided: 'Liberty of the person is inviolable. Restrictions on, or deprivation of, personal liberty may not be imposed by the public authorities except by virtue of a law. Persons who have been deprived of their liberty must be informed on the following day at latest by what authority and on what grounds their arrest has been ordered.'

for that deprivation. If such person not be brought for trial within six months of arrest he or she shall be set at liberty and such arrest must be held a wrongful arrest.

Hugh Kennedy KC, law advisor to the Provisional Government (and counsel in *Egan v. Macready*), pencilled in his copy of Figgis's Document 3: '*Idea* right not words'.[112] Instead, Kennedy emphasized that the priority should be to put in place a habeas corpus-type procedural mechanism.[113] The minutes of the drafting committee record the decision: 'an article to embody the principles of habeas corpus, to be drafted by a sub-committee comprising C.J. French and Hugh Kennedy.'

The first draft of this habeas corpus article emerged in February 1922 in Document 28, the first serious preliminary draft of the new constitution. What emerged from this sub-committee was part-Weimar Republic, part-eighteenth-century common law. The proposed article opens in the language of the constitution of the Weimar Republic: 'The liberty of the person is inviolable, and no person shall be deprived of his liberty save in accordance with law.' The second part incorporated the common law procedure by way of habeas corpus:

> Upon complaint made by or on behalf of any person that he is being unlawfully detained, the High Court and every judge thereof shall forthwith enquire into same and may make an order requiring the person in whose custody such person shall be detained to produce the body of the person so detained before such court or Judge without delay and to certify in writing as to the cause of the detention and such Court or Judge shall thereupon order the release of such person unless satisfied that he is being detained in accordance with the law.

This draft underwent just three alterations between February 1922, and December 1922. The object of the first amendment was to establish a right to renew an application for habeas corpus after refusal on an earlier occasion. When the various rival drafts of the new constitution were submitted, the Provisional Government sought the advice of the lawyer and academic, Dr George O'Brien. O'Brien in his detailed analysis[114] suggested that the phrase 'the High Court and every judge thereof' should be replaced by 'the

---

[112] UCD, Kennedy papers, MS P4/320.
[113] TCD, Stephens papers, MS 4236.
[114] Document no. 56 (UCD, Kennedy papers, MS P4/339).

High court or any judge thereof'; O'Brien's concern was that the committee's draft appeared literally to direct every judge of the High Court to enquire into every habeas corpus application submitted to the High Court. However, there were objections to the O'Brien formula: it appeared to imply that the individual be restricted to a single application, and that the common law right of successive application, which had just been confirmed in *Egan v. Macready*,[115] would be abolished. Writing to Michael Collins on behalf of the committee, Figgis argued in defence of the original wording:[116] 'the wording in the Article is the correct wording. The phrase "every judge thereof" enables an applicant to go to all the judges in turn to seek release. The phrase "or any judge thereof" limits him to one judge.' The Provisional Government accepted the advice of the drafting committee. Following consideration of the draft by the Government, and before submission to the legislature, Kennedy made one further refinement: in place of the phrase 'the High Court and every judge thereof' there was substituted 'the High Court and any and every judge thereof' so as to make it even clearer that the jurisdiction might be exercised by any single judge, and that it was irrelevant that an earlier judge had rejected the application.

Two further amendments, both more restrictive in effect, were proposed during the legislative process. It was, firstly, proposed to delete the word 'person' and to replace it with 'citizen'.[117] The word 'person' implied, it was pointed out, that an enemy alien would be entitled to the remedy. Although the proposal was apparently accepted by O'Higgins at committee stage,[118] the amendment was never formally incorporated into the text of Article 6, which, in its final drafts, continued to use the word 'person.' The second amendment was prompted by the same concern which had preoccupied Government lawyers since the eighteenth century: the problem of reconciling the right of habeas corpus with the existence of circumstances

---

[115] [1921] 1 IR 265.

[116] Figgis to Collins, 13 Apr. 1922 (UCD, Kennedy papers, MS P4/339).

[117] The change originated in an observation during the committee stages by Professor W.M. Magennis that the word person suggested that an alien enemy would be guaranteed the security of Article 6: *Dáil Debates*, vol. 1, col. 687 (25 Sept. 1922).

[118] *Dáil Debates*, vol. 1, col. 694 (25 Sept. 1922): An Ceann Comhairle: 'In Article 6 is an alteration of a word suggested by Deputy Magennis, that is, that the word "person" should be changed to "citizen" in the first line.' Mr Kevin O'Higgins: 'I accept that.'

of exceptional public emergency. At the time that the Constitution of the Irish Free State Bill 1922 came to be discussed at committee stage in September 1922 the Provisional Government was defending its very existence in a civil war. At committee stage Eamon Duggan TD, on behalf of the Government, proposed[119] that the phrase 'in time of peace' be inserted in the first sentence of Article 6, so that the declaration was qualified to read 'the liberty of the person is inviolable, and no person shall be deprived of his liberty in time of peace except in accordance with law.' The corollary of this was that the right of personal liberty did not operate in non-pacific times. The final draft resulted from Kevin O'Higgins's concern to tighten this wording. First, it was considered that the existence of a right to suspend the protection of personal liberty merely on the occurrence of conditions which were not peaceful was too loose.[120] The phrase in 'time of war or armed rebellion', a phrase lifted directly from the wording of the Act of 1782, was proposed instead. Second, it was pointed out that it was necessary to define who was to exercise the right to act in derogation of the right of personal liberty; merely to provide that ordinary personal liberty protections were suspended in times of war or armed rebellion implied that any person might deprive another of his personal liberty in circumstances of war or armed rebellion. On the fourth stage debate on the Bill, the Minister for Home Affairs, Kevin O'Higgins, proposed that these various points were best accommodated in a dedicated martial law provision:[121] 'Provided, however, that nothing in this Article contained shall be invoked to prohibit, control or interfere with any act of

[119] 'The Government proposes to insert the words "in time of peace" after the words "deprived of liberty"' (UCD, Kennedy papers, MS P4/340). At committee stage the proposal was made by Eamon Duggan TD, Minister without portfolio.
[120] 'I wonder if the mover of the Amendment "in times of peace" has not a sufficient safeguard, as there may be a danger that simple local commotion or industrial disturbances would not be regarded as times of peace in that particular area. I would suggest perhaps better words "except in time of peace or armed rebellion." They are certainly somewhat better than "in time of peace,"' *Dáil Debates*, vol. 1, col. 692 (25 Sept. 1922).
[121] *Dáil Debates*, vol. 1, col. 1689 (18 Oct. 1922). Kevin O'Higgins TD: 'Deputy Johnson pointed out quite rightly to me that the Article as it presently stands might mean this extraordinary thing, that once a state of war or armed rebellion was in existence anyone could arrest anyone else, so that there would be no such thing as liberty of the person at all. The effect of the amendment now proposed is to limit it strictly to the armed forces of Saorstát Éireann, and to confine it to them strictly to the period during which a state of war or armed rebellion exists.'

the military forces of Saorstát Eireann during the existence of a state of war or armed rebellion.' O'Higgins's report stage solution endures today in the form of Article 40.4.5 of the Constitution of 1937.

THE TEXTUAL EVOLUTION OF THE MODERN ARTICLE 40.4.2 PROVISION AND THE SECOND AMENDMENT OF THE CONSTITUTION ACT, 1941

Article 6 of the Constitution of the Irish Free State was re-incorporated, but considerably re-modelled, by the Constitution of 1937. The preponderance of those revisions and additions derived not from the original text of the Constitution of 1937, but from amendments introduced by the Second Amendment to the Constitution Act, 1941.

The Second Amendment of the Constitution Act, 1941

In the transitional period between the coming into operation of the Constitution and the expiry of the period allowed for amendment by legislation, Government Circular 3/40 of 29 January 1940[122] requested each Government department to submit amendments to the Constitution to be considered by the Committee on the Amendment of the Constitution under Article 46. In response, the Secretary of the Department of the Taoiseach minuted two suggestions for the amendment of Article 40.4.2.[123] Two rulings in *The State (Burke) v. Lennon*[124] evidently underlie both these proposals. Firstly, Gavan Duffy J had held[125] that it was a neces-

---

[122] NAI, Taoiseach files, S. 10299.
[123] NAI, Taoiseach files, S. 11663.
[124] [1940] IR 136.
[125] The final straw for the Government may have been the ruling by Gavan Duffy J in December 1939 that under Article 6 a detainee was entitled to the determination of 'such judge' as had granted the initial order. In November 1939 counsel for the applicant in *The State (Burke) v. Lennon* [1940] IR 136, who had been granted an initial order by Gavan Duffy J, took objection when it emerged that the return was not to be argued before the same judge (who may have been perceived to be politically sympathetic), but was to be heard before a divisional court consisting of three judges. It was argued that it was a corollary of the applicant's right to proceed from judge to judge that the enquiry be heard by the judge who had granted the initial enquiry. Gavan Duffy J agreed that this was, in principle, correct. However, the exercise of the right to have a habeas corpus

sary corollary of the right to go from judge to judge that an application could be submitted to, and should be heard by, the judge approached by the complainant. Secondly, the Supreme Court had ruled that the common law principle prohibiting habeas corpus appeal against release applied also to Article 40.4.2, preventing an appeal where the ground of release was that legislation was constitutionally invalid. It is obvious that *Burke's* case had prompted both of the changes suggested by Michael Moynihan:

> (a) Amend the provision under which an applicant in a habeas corpus case can have the matter dealt with by 'any and every judge of the High Court'.
> (b) Provide that where a habeas corpus application is granted on the ground that a particular statute is unconstitutional there shall be an appeal to the Supreme Court.
>
> Reasons for the amendment.
>
> (a) It may be necessary or desirable to take steps to ensure that persons are not released from custody on purely technical grounds or because of some trifling flaw in procedure. There is also the issue that habeas corpus proceedings are of such importance as to justify their being heard by more than one judge.
> (b) It is undesirable that constitutional issues should in a habeas corpus case be decided by the judgment of a single member of the High Court without appeal to the Supreme Court.

In the Autumn of 1940, the Committee reported.[126] It proposed that Article 40.4.2. be amended so as to provide for an appeal where legislation was found to be unconstitutional:

> The Committee are of opinion that no change should be made in the present position in regard to habeas corpus save in the direction of an

application determined by the judge to whom the application was originally submitted was, he held, conditional on its being expressly requested. This had not occurred here. Therefore, on aborting the divisional court proceedings costs were awarded against the applicant. Later that day an *ex parte* application, with a request that the proceedings be heard by Gavan Duffy J, was made to Gavan Duffy J at his residence: *Irish Times*, 29 Nov. 1939; 'Habeas corpus procedure under the Constitution of Éire' (1940) 74 *Irish Law Times & Solicitors' Journal* 1.

[126] NAI, Taoiseach files, S 11663.

appeal to the Supreme Court in cases where the applicant obtains his release on the ground that the law under which he is detained is unconstitutional. In this respect, they agree with the proposal and recommend that provision should be made by way of an amendment of Article 40.4 for enabling a Court or judge who is of opinion on an application under the section, that the applicant is detained in accordance with the law, but the law is unconstitutional, to refer the question of constitutionality to the Supreme Court, and not to release the applicant until the question is determined.

Secondly, the Committee recommended that the wording be corrected so as to withdraw the basis for the interpretation that the Article permitted a right to proceed from judge to judge in habeas corpus cases.[127] Thirdly, the Committee advised that there be an amendment to the effect that the full hearing be before a divisional court of not less than three judges (and no longer before a single judge of the High Court). Finally, the Taoiseach, Mr de Valera, insisted that an amendment be introduced providing for the suspension of the administration of the death penalty, pending determination of the legality of the applicant's detention.[128]

The Committee concluded its deliberation by submitting three drafts for a revised text of Article 40.4.2.[129] The Committee's proposals were, in turn, translated into the Second Amendment of the Constitution Bill,

---

[127] 'It is suggested that this subsection should be amended by removing the jurisdiction thereby conferred from a single judge of the High Court' (NAI, Taoiseach files, S 11663).

[128] The Department of the Taoiseach file on the proposed amendment (NAI, Taoiseach files, S. 11663) includes a handwritten interlineation: '24/10/40, Taoiseach desires suspension of death provision.'

[129] One of these, draft 'C' provided:

> Upon complaint being made by or on behalf of any person to the High Court or such judge thereof alleging that such person is being unlawfully detained, the High Court or any judge thereof shall forthwith enquire into the said complaint and may order the person in whose custody such person is detained to produce the body of such person before the High Court on a named day and to certify the grounds of his detention, and the High Court, consisting of not less than three judges shall upon the body of such person being produced before that Court, and after giving the person in whose custody he is detained an opportunity of justifying the detention, order the release of such person from such custody unless satisfied that he is being detained in accordance with the law.

1941, which provided: (i) that the right to renew an application before 'any and every judge of the High Court' be abolished; (ii) that there be a mandatory case stated to the Supreme Court where the High Court found the legislation under which the complainant was detained constitutionally invalid.[130] (iii) However, the Committee's proposal that the application be determined before a divisional court was diluted in favour of a presumption that the application be determined before a single judge unless the President of the High Court directed that the application be heard before a divisional court.[131] De Valera's concern that sentence of death be suspended pending the determination of a habeas corpus challenge was incorporated in a special provision.[132]

Of these proposals the most contentious was that which proposed the abolition of what was regarded as the historical right to go from judge to judge. The extent of this historical entitlement was controversial, but was probably not as expansive as it came to be believed in the 1920s. Prior to the Judicature Act, 1877 there certainly was a right to go from court to court. However, there was no example of detainee being entitled to go from judge to judge. The earliest reported example of the practice in Irish law is probably the *Case of the Honourable Mr Justice Johnson*,[133] where the applicant had submitted habeas corpus applications before the King's Bench, then before the Court of Exchequer, and finally before the Court of Common Pleas.[134] When, following the enactment of the Judicature Act, 1877, the four courts of common law and equity were dissolved into a single High Court of Justice, the right to proceed from court to court was

---

> It is here that a number of notable textual changes make their first appearance. Each of these are concerned with adjusting the procedural balance in favour of the authorities: thus, the enquiry is to be heard on a 'named day' (rather than 'without delay'); the obligation to give the person in whose custody the applicant is detained an opportunity of justifying the detention was inserted. Most controversially of all the draft abolished the right, which had been recognised under Article 6, to proceed, following an earlier refusal, from judge to judge.

[130] The provision became incorporated in the Constitution as Article 40.4.3
[131] The provision became incorporated in the Constitution as Article 40.4 4.
[132] The provision became incorporated in the Constitution as Article 40.4.5. It was deleted by the twenty-first amendment of the Constitution, 2001.
[133] (1805) 29 St Tr 81.
[134] See also *In re Simon Flood, Saunders Newsletter*, 20 May 1818 (applicant moving from the Common Pleas to King's Bench); *Page v. Williams* (1851) 1 ICLR 527 (where the applicant having been unsuccessful before the Court of Queen's Bench then moved before the Court of Exchequer).

converted into a right to proceed from division to division.[135] However, in *Egan v. Macready*[136] O'Connor MR, probably incorrectly, derived from these authorities a much more radical proposition: that there was a common law right to go from judge to judge: 'it is the right of the subject under arrest to apply to any judge of the High Court for a writ of habeas corpus, and, if the writ is refused, to proceed from judge to judge, and it is the duty of each judge to form his own opinion and act upon it.' O'Connor MR did not cite authority for this supposed right to proceed from judge to judge. But, however unfounded the proposition, it came, particularly because of the celebrity of the decision, to be accepted as representing a common law right of the subject. The soundness of the proposition would be a source of controversy for the next twenty years.

Little more than six months separated the decision in *Egan v. Macready* in July 1921 and the first meeting of the Irish Free State Constitution drafting committee in January 1922, and it is not surprising that Article 6 of the Constitution of 1922 referred to a right to renew applications for habeas corpus from judge to judge. Article 6 provided that an enquiry could be presented before 'the High Court and any and every judge thereof'. The return was then to come before 'such Court or judge'. In *The State (Dowling) v. Kingston (No. 2)*[137] the Supreme Court divided on the question. Murnaghan and Fitzgibbon JJ held that there was no right to reapply after refusal.[138] Sullivan CJ, on the other hand, interpreted Article 6 as establishing the right to proceed, despite an earlier refusal, from judge to judge. The unqualified duty of 'every' judge to hold an enquiry implied that the duty existed even where an earlier judge had refused to make an order. This interpretation was supported by the requirement that the enquiry be heard before such judge as had disposed of the earlier

---

[135] *Re Sullivan* (1888) 22 LR Ir 98 (prisoner moving from the Queen's Bench Division on certiorari to the Exchequer Division on habeas corpus).
[136] [1921] 1 IR 265.
[137] [1937] IR 699.
[138] Murnaghan and Fitzgibbon JJ interpreted the right given to 'the High Court and any and every judge thereof' to dispose of an application as meaning that any single judge of the High Court had jurisdiction in addition to the jurisdiction of the High Court itself. It meant that in an emergency the prisoner could, when the High Court was not sitting, make an application before a single judge of the High Court. The proposition that every judge must hear an application despite an earlier refusal by the High Court, involved, they argued, imputing to the framers a tolerance of consequences disruptive of ordered legal administration.

application. The phrase 'such court or judge' imposed a mandatory continuity between the court or judge to which the application was originally submitted and the court or judge deciding the merits of the application. An obligation that the application be heard by the same judge who granted the initial enquiry maximised, in case the application failed, the number of judges unaffected by prejudgment.

The 1941 Bill proposed to reverse Sullivan CJ's interpretation in *State (Dowling) v. Kingston (No. 2)* by restricting the judges to whom the initial complaint could be made. The new wording 'upon complaint being made to the High Court *or any judge* thereof ... the High Court or any judge thereof shall forthwith enquire into the same ...' reduced the right of election available to an applicant. The effect of the change was that the right to have the matter renewed before every judge of the High Court was displaced in favour of the much more reduced entitlement to have the matter reviewed in a single determination either before the High Court or before any judge thereof. The proposal to abolish, what was being termed the ancient common law right to go from judge to judge, generated criticism both from the legal press[139] and the opposition benches.[140] However, the historically suspect premise underlying the opposition argument, that the common law recognized an entitlement to go from to judge to judge in habeas corpus matters, prompted FitzGibbon J, now retired from the bench, and writing from his bed in a nursing home, to communicate with de Valera advising him that the view that there existed a historic common law entitlement to renew a habeas corpus application from judge to judge was misconceived. He pointed out that the view that a majority had held against the existence of a right to go from judge to judge in *Kingston's* case, and that the proposition was unsound as a matter of common law:[141]

> the right of the citizen was not to go from one judge to another, but from one Court to another, at a time when there were four independent and co-ordinate courts-our own old Four Courts- Chancery, King's Bench, Common Pleas and Exchequer, and seek the opinion of each of these independent Courts, through one its judges, as to his right to a habeas corpus. But it was never conceded, or even, so far as

---

[139] 'Proposed amendments in habeas corpus procedure in Éire' (1941) 75 *Irish Law Times & Solicitors' Journal* 65.
[140] *Dáil Debates*, vol. 82, cols 1245–51 (2 Apr. 1941).
[141] FitzGibbon to de Valera, 4 Apr. 1941 (NAI, Taoiseach files, S. 11663).

I know, contended in those days that a man could go from one judge to another of the same court. The courts were all fused into one court in 1875, and so the right to go from court to court disappeared. I have not seen your Bill, but if I do not presume may I say that I think it is a most wise provision that when a conditional order for a writ of habeas corpus has been made it should be returnable before a court of two or three judges if possible.

Although the Government was satisfied that FitzGibbon's view represented the approach of the majority of the Supreme Court in *Dowling's* case, it decided, in light of the interpretation being applied in the High Court by judges such as Gavan Duffy J, combined with the unavailability in habeas corpus of an appeal to the Supreme Court to correct such error, to press ahead with the amendment:[142]

> the absence of a remedy from the High Court when an applicant was erroneously discharged meant that there was no way in which a review or correction can be had judicially of a decision by a High Court judge who disregards the observations of the majority of the Supreme Court in *Dowling's* case and who releases an applicant who has already made an unsuccessful application to the High Court.

However, the Taoiseach proposed a moderation of the original amendment[143] based on a distinction between the right to initiate an application before a second judge after refusal of a prior judge, and the entitlement to renew an application after it had been fully considered by the Court following a return. In the first case, a detainee would be entitled to renew the right to submit an application. In the second case there would be no right to renew the application. This was accomplished by providing that the initial application could be renewed before 'any and every judge' of the High Court (in place of 'the High Court or such judge thereof'); however, if an initial application was granted jurisdiction to determine the legality of the detention was entrusted to the High Court. Being a decision with the full authority of the High Court it was binding on all judges of that

---

[142] Philip O'Donohue to de Valera, 8 Apr. 1941 (ibid).
[143] The amendment may have been inspired by a suggestion made earlier in the article 'Proposed amendments in habeas corpus procedure in Eire' (1941) 75 *Irish Law Times & Solicitors' Journal* 65.

Court and could be reviewed only by means of an appeal to the Supreme Court. It was to give effect to this provision that the current version of Article 40.4.2 requires that a complaint be considered by 'the High Court and any and every judge thereof' but that if a full enquiry is ordered it must be before the 'High Court' only.

CHAPTER TWO

The grounds of review on an Article 40.4.2 enquiry

INSUFFICIENCY OF EVIDENCE AS A GROUND
OF REVIEW UNDER ARTICLE 40.4.2

The principle of restricted review of evidential sufficiency

Perhaps the most serious defect affecting the supervisory capacity of habeas corpus has been the ineffectiveness of the remedy in reviewing the sufficiency of the evidence underlying an order of imprisonment. The traditional principle of review of evidential sufficiency holds that review on certiorari or habeas corpus is exhausted once the finding is sustained by a minimal foundation of supportable evidence. This rule has two corollaries: (i) since the jurisdiction is restricted to determining whether there is merely some evidence justifying detention, it follows that review is not available where it is alleged that the finding is against the weight of evidence;[1] (ii) since review is exhausted by the existence of some evidence it follows that a decision sustained by a minimal evidential base cannot be challenged by the production of fresh evidence.[2] *Gutrani v. Minister for Justice*[3] is an example of the application of the second corollary. The complainant, an asylum seeker, attempted to introduce fresh evidence demonstrating that if returned to Libya, he would face political persecution. The Supreme Court refused to admit such fresh evidence holding that the fact that the Minister's original decision was sustained by supportable evidence, exhausted the Court's power of review on Article 40.4.2. McCarthy J said: 'to admit evidence in this Court after the Minister has considered the matter and after he has carried out the proper consultations is, in effect, challenging the finding of fact made by the Minister and, in

---

[1] *R. (Martin) v. Mahony* [1910] 2 IR 695; *R. (Ryan) v. Starkie* (1920) 54 ILTR 15.
[2] *Gutrani v. Minister for Justice* [1993] 2 IR 427; *Farrell v. AG* [1998] 1 IR 203, 226.
[3] [1993] 2 IR 427, 436. The proposition may now, in the light of *Croke v. Smith* [1998] 1 IR 101, possibly no longer be good law.

my opinion, it seems not to be warranted. It is clear in my mind therefore that this would be an incorrect application of the law governing deportation if I were to receive such evidence.'

Under the most extreme application of the traditional doctrine habeas corpus was not available even where there was absolutely no evidence to support a finding. The sufficiency or quality of that evidence was a matter solely for the official or body authorizing detention. In the classical Irish authority, *R. (Martin) v. Mahony*,[4] Lord O'Brien LCJ stated that 'to grant certiorari merely on the ground of want of jurisdiction, because there was no evidence to warrant a conviction, confounds want of jurisdiction with error in the exercise of it,' while in the habeas corpus case *R. (Ryan) v. Starkie*,[5] a subsequent Chief Justice (Molony LCJ) stated that 'when a justice is sitting as a court of summary jurisdiction, and the accused can call evidence, and the order of the Justice shows on its face facts necessary to give jurisdiction to make the order, it cannot be quashed on the ground of the insufficiency of the evidence.'

A later, and marginally more relaxed, view holds that habeas corpus may be used to impeach a finding of fact, but only where there is absolutely no evidence to support the conclusion. In *The State (Hanley) v. Governor of Mountjoy Prison*[6] Finlay P in declining to review the merits of the conclusion that a young person was of 'unruly character' so as to justify his being detained in an adult prison under the Children Act, 1908, stated: 'With regard to the first argument submitted it is clear that I am not, in these applications, concerned with the weight of evidence upon which the District Court decided that the applicant was of an unruly character, nor with the correctness of that decision. I can only be concerned with one question, was there *any* evidence before him upon which he could reach such a decision?' A third formula, less restrictive than the two preceding tests, holds that a finding of fact may be accessible to review where the finding is grossly unreasonable. In *Creedon v. Criminal Injuries Compensation Tribunal*[7] the Supreme Court held that the finding of fact of an administrative tribunal may be impeached where the finding is 'fundamentally at variance with reason and common sense'. But the conditions under which this is likely to be the case are 'limited and rare'[8] and not

---

[4] [1910] 2 IR 695, 707.   [5] (1920) 54 ILTR 15, 16.   [6] (1973) 108 ILTR 102.
[7] [1988] IR 51, 54.
[8] Per Finlay CJ in *O'Keeffe v. An Bord Pleanála* [1993] I IR 39, 71.

surprisingly there are very few cases of applicants succeeding in reaching this very high threshold.[9]

The condition precedent doctrine

The condition precedent doctrine is probably the most significant qualification recognized at common law to the general principle that sufficiency of evidence is not accessible to judicial review. The doctrine works as follows: every statute authorizing the detention of an individual can be broken down into a series of statutory findings. Those findings of fact may be divided into: (i) findings within the unimpeachable competence of the decision-making authority; and (ii) findings which are conditional or collateral to the jurisdiction of the decision making officer, or authority.[10] The correctness of findings in the second category may be reviewed *de novo* on habeas corpus or certiorari.[11] Classification of a statutory finding

---

[9] *McDonagh v. Governor of Mountjoy Prison*, Irish Times, 29 May 1973, appears to provide a rare instance. Here the ground of complaint was that the applicant had been convicted by the District Court despite the fact that there was no material difference in the evidence submitted against the applicant's co-accused, and despite the fact that these co-accused had been acquitted. The complainant's release on habeas corpus was ordered.

[10] *Eleko v. Officer Administering the Government of Nigeria* [1931] AC 662 is a classic illustration of the operation of the doctrine. The case concerned the administration of a Nigerian decree, The Deposed Chief's Removal Ordinance, 1917, which provided: 'When a native chief has been deposed or removed from office the Governor may by order, direct that such chief or native shall leave the area over which he had exercised jurisdiction (a) if the native law and custom shall require that such deposed chief or native shall leave the area over which he exercised jurisdiction or influence by virtue of his chieftaincy or office.' Applying the condition precedent doctrine the Privy Council held that it had jurisdiction to review the applicant's complaints: (i) that he was not a native chief; (ii) that he had not been deposed; (iii) that there was no native law or custom which required that he leave the area. The Privy Council held, in effect, that these were conditions precedent to the jurisdiction to detain; accordingly the Governor's findings were reviewable: 'Their Lordships are satisfied that the opinion which has prevailed that the Courts cannot investigate the whole of the necessary conditions is erroneous. The Governor acting under the Ordinance acts solely under executive powers, and in no sense is a court. As the executive he can only act in pursuance of powers given to him by law. In accordance with British jurisprudence no member of the executive can interfere with the liberty or property of the subject except on condition that he can support the legality of the action before a court of justice' (p. 670).

[11] The collateral fact doctrine was rehearsed by Wills J in the habeas corpus case *Re*

as a condition precedent has two consequences: the reviewing court may reconsider whether the weight of the evidence supports the finding;[12] and the reviewing court may admit fresh evidence not before the original decision-maker.[13] While the factual condition precedent doctrine facilitates the most exacting scope of review recognized at common law, the principal problem with the doctrine is the lack of a certain test for discriminating findings which are conditional, or collateral, from those which are within jurisdiction. In a lecture on the topic of habeas corpus, Simon Brown LJ, then of the English Court of Appeal, openly admitted the extent to which the court, in operating the collateral fact doctrine, was influenced by the impulse to maximize review in cases involving serious deprivation of personal liberty:[14] 'A power is more likely to be held subject to proof of precedent fact if its exercise will result in the deprivation of liberty. Such a holding is in reality a mechanism whereby the court assumes a more intensive review jurisdiction.' Two factors, in particular, have regularly been identified as tending to support recognition as a condition precedent:

> *Guerin* (1888) 60 LT 538, 541: 'With respect to the power of this court to review the finding of the magistrate upon the question of nationality ... it is a well established principle that where a matter of fact which is cardinal to the existence of a magistrate's jurisdiction is collateral to the subject of inquiry the decision of the magistrate is not final, and the court has a right to inquire into the sufficiency of the evidence upon which the magistrate acted, as being a matter on which the jurisdiction to hear the case at all is based.' The *Guerin* case, in which the applicant attempted to establish that he was an Irish national and therefore exempt from extradition, is the subject of a study by R. Sharpe, 'Habeas corpus, extradition and the burden of proof: the case of the man who escaped from Devil's Island' (1990) 49 *Cambridge Law Journal* 422.

[12] *R. (de Vesci) v. Queen's County JJ* [1908] 2 IR 285, 300: 'The decision of the magistrates on the question of fact of whether the place was an orchard or not, being a question on which jurisdiction to make the order depended, can be challenged here not merely on the basis that there was no evidence to support it, but with reference to the weight of the evidence'; *R. (D'Arcy) v. Carlow JJ* [1916] 2 IR 313, 319; *Khawaja v. Secretary for State for the Home Department* [1984] AC 74, 97, 109–10. However, by contrast with this approach is a line of cases holding that classification of a finding as a condition precedent does not permit *de novo* review, the reviewing court's jurisdiction being restricted to merely determining whether there is any evidence: *Re Bailey* (1854) 3 El & Bl 607, 115 ER 1269; *In re Baker* (1857) 2 H & N 219, 157 ER 92; *R. v. Board of Control, ex p. Rutty* [1956] 2 QB 109, 124.

[13] *Re Guerin* (1888) 60 LT 538; *R. v. Governor of Brixton Prison, ex p. Schtraks* [1964] AC 556, 595–7.

[14] 'Habeas corpus – a new chapter' (2000) *Public Law* 31, 37.

(i) that the decision has been taken by an executive official rather than by a judge,[15] and (ii) the absence of a right of judicial appeal.[16]

Equally, a series of factors have been recognized as weighted against classification as a condition precedent. (i) The condition precedent doctrine permits the re-litigation of a finding of the existence of some objective phenomenon. It follows that where the disputed statutory component has a subjective discretionary character the application of the condition precedent doctrine is inappropriate. In *Liversidge v. Anderson*[17] the nature of the findings under the (English) Defence (General) Regulations, 1939, enabling detention where 'the Secretary of State has reasonable cause to believe any person to be of hostile origin or associations or to have been recently concerned in acts prejudicial to the public safety' were held not to be classifiable as conditions precedent. The power was not predicated upon a set of 'specific facts, capable of proof or disproof in a court of law' but upon a value judgment, with discretionary elements. (ii) The fact that the statutory finding has followed an extended fact-finding process, which it may not be practical to undertake again on a subsequent judicial review, may prejudice classification of the finding as a condition precedent. In *R. v. Secretary for State for the Home Department, ex parte Zamir*[18] Lord Wilberforce held that a finding by an immigration officer that an immigrant was an illegal entrant, a finding based on extensive interviews in the immigrant's home country, was not, by reason of its sheer complexity, and the elements of value judgment involved, appropriate for *de novo* re-appraisal as a condition precedent. Lord Wilberforce said that 'the nature and process of decision conferred upon immigration officers by existing legislation is incompatible with any requirement for the establishment of precedent objective facts.' (iii) It has been held in English case law that where one of the components upon which a power of detention is predicated is the anterior determination of an administrative agency such a component is not capable of being classified as a condition precedent. The concern is to prevent complex decisions of administrative tribunals being re-opened on habeas corpus or judicial review. In *R. v. Secretary for State for the Home Department, ex parte Bugdaycay*[19] the power of removal under the immigration code was contingent upon the immigrant being 'an

---

[15] *R. v. Governor of Brixton Prison, ex p. Ahsan* [1969] 2 QB 222, 232, 248.
[16] *R. (de Vesci) v. Queen's Co. JJ* [1908] 2 IR 284, 305.
[17] [1942] AC 206, 273.   [18] [1980] AC 930, 948.   [19] [1987] AC 514.

illegal immigrant not given leave to enter or remain in the United Kingdom'. The second component (the fact that a decision had been made refusing leave to enter) differed from the first (being an illegal immigrant) in that it referred to an underlying administrative determination; accordingly, it was not subject to *de novo* review. (iv) The High Court in *The State (AG) v. Durcan*[20] held that a finding would only be regarded as a condition precedent where the statutory phrasing clearly provided that the particular finding was conditional to the exercise of the statutory power. Where, the Court held, a statutory power is divided into a conditional subordinate clause, and a main clause, the finding in the subordinate clause may be regarded as a collateral fact since it is clearly designated as conditional to the main set of findings. But where, on the other hand, a statutory power merely follows a sequence of statutory findings, and none of these findings are explicitly phrased as conditional to the others, the doctrine will, according to this test, not operate. However, the *Durcan* criterion has not always been applied subsequently, and later Irish and English authorities have not adopted such a restrictive version of the doctrine.[21]

Misappreciation, or failure to take account of, material primary facts

The range of the common law has recently been extended by two doctrinal developments. Firstly, there has been the recognition by the High Court that a failure, in assessing an evidential issue, to properly take into account an evidential submission made by one of the parties may constitute a breach of fair procedures, and, on this basis, a ground of judicial review.[22] A second doctrine is concerned with the case where a decision-maker has misunderstood, or is misinformed as to some primary data.[23] The doctrine is targeted not against errors in the decision-maker's evaluation of the evidence, but to cases where the decision maker has not been properly apprised of the accepted primary facts. The classical example is *Daganayasi v. Minister for Immigration*.[24] Here the New Zealand Minister for Immigration had rejected a plea against the enforcement of a deporta-

---

[20] [1964] IR 279.
[21] *R. v. Secretary of State for the Home Department, ex p. Khawaja* [1984] AC 74.
[22] *Trarore v. Refugee Appeals Tribunal*, High Court, 14 May 2004.
[23] T. Jones, 'Mistake of fact in administrative law' (1990) *Public Law* 70; D. Blundell, 'Material error of fact' (2004) *Judicial Review* 36.
[24] [1980] 2 NZLR 130.

tion order based on a claim that the child of one of the deportees suffered from a dangerous medical condition which would be aggravated if returned to its country of origin because of poor medical facilities in that country. The Minister had sanctioned the deportation order on the basis of information which misleadingly gave the impression that the doctor in charge of the clinic treating the child had agreed that the deportation would not prejudice the child's condition. The New Zealand Court of Appeal held that it would be unfair that the individual should bear the cost of this administrative error and that a decision based on misinformation as to some critical item of primary evidence was subject to judicial review. This proposition was endorsed by the House of Lords in *R. v. Criminal Injuries Board, ex parte A*.[25] In the *A* case the applicant, in an application for compensation to the Criminal Injuries Board, had claimed that she had been seriously sexually assaulted. Corroborative evidence from a police doctor that she had probably been raped was, through error, not made available to the Board, and acting upon the assumption that there was no evidence supporting the allegation, it dismissed her claim. The House of Lords accepted that there was jurisdiction to quash on grounds of misinformation as to a decisive primary fact. The House of Lords approved of the formulation of the rule propounded in Wade's *Administrative Law*:[26]

> Mere factual mistake has become a ground of judicial review, described as 'misunderstanding or ignorance of an established and relevant fact', or 'acting upon an incorrect basis of fact'[27] ... This

---

[25] [1999] 2 AC 330.
[26] Ibid., pp 344–5. The Wade formula was also accepted by Lord Slynn in *R. (Alconbury Ltd) v. Environment Secretary* [2001] 2 WLR 1389, 1407.
[27] H.W.R. Wade and C. Forsyth, *Administrative law* (9th ed., Oxford, 2004), pp 316–18. This ambivalent phrase 'acting on an incorrect basis of fact' may be loose enough to suggest that misevaluation of primary facts can constitute a ground of review. This would go further than indicated in the case law. The *A* and *Daganayasi* cases, and the earlier authority, *Secretary of State for Education v. Tameside BC* [1977] AC 1014 (from which the phrase is derived) were instances where the source of the factual error was misinformation by a third party as to the primary facts. Interpreted literally the 'incorrect basis of fact' formula would considerably expand the scope of review exercisable on judicial review (and, therefore, habeas corpus) so as to include instances of misappreciation of the primary facts. Most disputed factual conclusions derive from an allegedly wrongful evaluation of one of the primary facts, and the error can be classified as 'acting upon an incorrect basis of fact.' Recognition of review on grounds of

ground of review has long been familiar in French law and it has been adopted by statute in Australia. It is no less needed in this country, since decisions based upon wrong facts are a cause of injustice which the courts should be able to remedy.

Intensified review and fundamental rights

Under a doctrine first developed by Lord Wilberforce in his speech in *R. v. Secretary of State for the Home Department, ex parte Khawaja*,[28] and later adopted by the House of Lords in *R. v. Secretary of State for the Home Department, ex parte Bugdaycay*,[29] the scope of review on judicial review or habeas corpus may intensify according to the interest at stake and according to the degree to which the basic human rights of the individual are engaged:[30]

> [The court] should appraise the quality of the evidence and decide whether that justifies the conclusion reached, e.g. whether it justifies a conclusion that the applicant obtained permission to enter by fraud or deceit. An allegation that he has done so being of a serious character and involving issues of personal liberty requires a corresponding degree of satisfaction as to the evidence.

Therefore, while it is not usually the function of a reviewing court to assess *de novo* the weight of evidence, a duty may arise, particularly in cases involving personal liberty or bodily integrity, to appraise the quality of the fact-finding process in order to determine whether it has been discharged in a satisfactory manner. By contrast with the collateral fact doctrine the

'acting upon an incorrect basis of fact' does not seem easily reconcilable with the general principle that in the common law system factual error is corrected by dedicated appellate jurisdictions, and not, save in exceptional cases, by judicial review or habeas corpus. In *Aer Rianta v. Commissioner for Aviation Regulation*, High Court, 16 Jan. 2003, the High Court declined to recognize the existence of a general 'incorrect basis of fact' ground of review, saying that to follow such authority would 'entail a significant departure from clear and established principle in our own jurisprudence.' Earlier in *Ryanair v. Flynn* [2000] 3 IR 240 the High Court had been sceptical about the existence of such a wide ground of review.

[28] [1984] AC 74.
[29] [1987] AC 514.
[30] *R. v. Secretary for State, ex p. Khawaja* [1984] AC 74, 105, per Lord Wilberforce.

court does not always itself review the sufficiency of the evidence *de novo*; rather, if there is an apprehension that the issue has not been satisfactorily determined, the matter may be remitted to the decision-making body or officer to re-appraise the issue.

The Wilberforce doctrine was applied in *R. v. Secretary of State for the Home Department, ex parte Bugdaycay*,[31] an asylum case in which the applicant, who claimed that he had suffered persecution in Uganda, sought to challenge a proposal to deport him to Kenya on the basis that, if removed to Kenya, he would be likely to be re-deported to Uganda. The House of Lords identified a 'suspicion' that the Secretary for State had not properly resolved the dangers involved in sending the applicant to Kenya. The Lords justified this development by reference to the leading judgment on the capacity of judicial review at common law, *Associated Picture Houses v. Wednesbury*.[32] In *Associated Picture Houses* the scope of review was famously limited to determinations 'so unreasonable that no reasonable authority could have come to it'. However, the judgment recognized a series of exceptions to this strict abstentionist policy. One of those exceptions was the case where a decision-maker failed to take into account a relevant consideration. The House of Lords in *Bugdaycay* exploited that qualification to provide a justification for the doctrinal innovation initiated in *Khawaja*. The authorities' action in failing to have proper regard to Kenya's policy of returning refugees to Uganda was classified as a 'failure to take account of a relevant consideration.' Lord Templeman expressly justified the exercise of this more intense standard of review by reference to the relevant considerations doctrine:[33]

> The action of an authority entrusted by Parliament with decision-making can be investigated by the court:
>
> > 'with a view to seeing whether they have taken into account matters which they ought not to take into account, or, conversely, have refused to take into account or neglected to take into account matters which they ought to take into account.' Lord Greene MR in *Associated Provincial Picture Houses Ltd. v. Wednesbury Corporation* [1948] 1 KB 223, 233-4.

---

[31] [1987] AC 514; *R. v. Secretary for State, ex p. Turgut* [2001] 1 All ER 719.
[32] [1948] 1 KB 223, 233-4.
[33] [1987] AC 514, 537-8.

In my opinion where the result of a flawed decision may imperil life, or liberty a special responsibility lies on the court in the examination of the decision-making process ... I am not satisfied that the Secretary for State *took into account* or adequately resolved the ambiguities and uncertainties which surround the conduct and policy of the authorities in Kenya.

In *Mohsen v. Minister for Justice*[34] the High Court was pressed to recognize as part of Irish law, the English 'anxious scrutiny' standard. However, the High Court was not convinced that such an intrusive scope of review was capable of being reconciled with the non-interventionist doctrine in *Wednesbury*, and dismissed the application. A similar scepticism that the 'anxious scrutiny' test could be reconciled with the canonical *Wednesbury* principle was expressed by the Supreme Court in *Z v. Minister for Justice*[35] where McGuinness J enquired: 'can it mean that in a case where the decision maker is subject to anxious scrutiny the standard of unreasonableness or irrationality is to be lowered? Surely not.'

There are, as the Supreme Court has pointed out, great difficulties in reconciling the 'anxious scrutiny' standard with the *Wednesbury* principle. Lord Templeman's argument in *Bugdaycay*, that the more rigorous standard is permitted by the 'failure to take account of relevant considerations' exception to the *Wednesbury* test, is particularly problematic. All errors of adjudication of issues of fact can be classified as failures to take account of relevant considerations. This, in turn, causes problems in containing the doctrine: it is not logical to classify only factual errors in which human rights are engaged as involving the improper taking into account of irrelevant considerations. To admit the operation of an exception based on this premise risks corroding the basic rule that the court does not review the evidential findings of administrative agencies or inferior courts. This does not mean that the anxious scrutiny doctrine might not be capable of being justified by reference to an alternative basis in Irish law. In *O v. Minister for Justice*[36] Fennelly and McGuiness JJ appeared to suggest that the 'anxious scrutiny' test should be adopted, not necessarily as an application of the

---

[34] High Court, 12 Mar. 2002. *Mohsen* was an asylum case in which it was alleged that the adjudicator had incorrectly assessed the allegation of a Shia Muslim who had fled Bahrain that he had suffered torture in his country of origin.
[35] [2002] 2 ILRM 215, 236.
[36] [2003] 1 IR 1.

failure to take account relevant considerations doctrine, but rather as an application of the courts' duty to protect fundamental constitutional interests.[37]

Review of the weight of evidence and Article 5(4) of the European Convention on Human Rights

Article 5(4) of the European Convention on Human Rights provides:

> Everyone who is deprived of his liberty by arrest or detention shall be entitled to take proceedings by which the lawfulness of his detention shall be decided speedily by a court and his release ordered if the detention is not lawful.

What is the standard by reference to which a person is entitled under Article 5(4) to have the legality of their detention tested?; and is that Article 5(4) standard enforceable against the High Court in conducting an enquiry under Article 40.4.2?

In *X v. United Kingdom*[38] the European Court of Human Rights held that the traditional limited scope of review of factual issues under habeas corpus did not provide the effective system of proceedings for the review of the legality of detention required by Article 5(4). In *X* the English High Court had, on a habeas corpus challenge to the legality of executive detention under the Mental Health Act, 1959, followed conventional doctrine and declined to determine whether the evidence supported the conclusion that the applicant's mental disorder was of a type which warranted detention. The European Court of Human Rights held that the traditional common law scope of review was a denial of the right guaranteed by Article 5(4). The scope of review should, it said, be:[39]

> wide enough to bear on those conditions which, according to the Convention, are essential for the 'lawful' detention of a person on the ground of unsoundness of mind ... This means that in the instant case Article 5(4) required an appropriate procedure allowing a court

---

[37] A similar justification was suggested by Laffoy J in *G (OE) v. Minister for Justice*, High Court, 27 May 2004.
[38] (1982) 4 EHRR 188. The principle was confirmed in *L v. United Kingdom* (2005) 40 EHRR 761.
[39] Ibid., p. 209.

to examine whether the patient's disorder still persisted and whether the Home Secretary was entitled to think that a continuation of the compulsory confinement was necessary in the interests of public safety.

It was held that a scope of judicial review as confined as that on habeas corpus at common law did not comply with the standard required by Article 5(4). On the other hand, Article 5(4) did not guarantee 'a right to judicial control of such scope as to empower the court, on all aspects of the case, to substitute its own discretion for that of the decision-making authority'.[40] The distinction between items which, according to the Convention, are essential for lawful detention, and those aspects in which the decision-making authority enjoys a margin of appreciation, was clarified in *E v. Norway*.[41] The European Court of Human Rights defined the distinction as being between, on the one hand, findings upon which the ultimate decision is predicated, and, on the other hand, the exercise of discretion which then arises, once the findings have been made, whether to operate that power of detention. The Norwegian Penal Code had provided that where a punishable act was committed by someone with an underdeveloped or impaired mental capacity, and where there was a danger that the person would repeat the act, the state could impose any one of a series of measures, including assigning him to a place of residence, placing him under supervision, forbidding him to consume alcoholic beverages or detaining him in a mental hospital. The Court held that Article 5(4) required that there be full review of the conditions required before a decision to order detention could be made; on the other hand, the discretionary decision to order detention in a mental home, as opposed to any of the other available options, was a matter of 'expediency' not necessarily requiring such an intense scope of review.

The European Court of Human Rights has long held that the right of access to proceedings for testing the legality of detention under Article 5(4) does not guarantee a right of review by a court of superior jurisdiction (equivalent to the High Court conducting an enquiry on Article 40.4.2). Review of detention may be discharged by lower level mechanisms. Firstly, the review guaranteed by Article 5(4) may be discharged internally within

[40] Ibid.
[41] (1990) 17 EHRR 30.

the original decision-making process where that process is judicial. This is because where the original process is judicial 'the supervision required by Article 5(4) is incorporated in the decision.'[42] Secondly, even where the original process is administrative, Article 5(4) does not require that the proceedings by which the legality of the detention is to be tested be before a superior court analogous to the High Court. Review may be entrusted to any tribunal so long as it satisfies the characteristics of 'a court' required by Article 5(4).[43] It follows that in the majority of cases the State already complies with its obligation under Article 5(4) to have in place proceedings for testing the evidential basis of detention. This is either because the initial determination is judicial, or because there is an appeal on the evidence to an institution possessing the characteristics of 'a court.' It is only where the initial process of imprisonment is administrative, and where there is no facility for evidential appeal, that the High Court under Article 40.4.2 or judicial review will be required to perform the role of 'proceedings' capable of testing evidential sufficiency, as required by Article 5(4).[44] Powers of investigative Garda detention, and detention pending removal or deportation appear to be the only examples of cases where by reason of detention being both administrative and otherwise unappealable, the higher standard of scrutiny required by Article 5(4) applies.

But there remains the problem as to whether the enquiry under Article 40.4.2 is, as a matter of constitutional doctrine, capable of being affected by the European Convention on Human Rights. It is doubtful whether the incorporation of the Convention by the European Convention on Human Rights Act, 2003 has altered the capacity of the High Court under Article

[42] *De Wilde, Ooms, Versyp v. Belgium* (1971) 1 EHRR 373, 407; *Winterwerp v. Netherlands* (1979) 2 EHRR 387, 407–8.
[43] *De Wilde, Ooms, Versyp v. Belgium* (1971) 1 EHRR 373, 407.
[44] In *Toth v. Austria* (1991) 14 EHRR 551 the European Court stated that where contracting states set up a second level of jurisdiction for the examination of the legality of detention, that second level must also comply with guarantees constituted by Article 5(4). Applying this analysis, in the case of many forms of detention in Irish law, the initial judicial determination, or an administrative appeal, may provide the primary means of review. However, further techniques of appeal or review, including review under Article 40.4.2, may be regarded as 'second levels of jurisdiction.' It is arguable that since under Convention law such second levels of review must comply with the guarantees of Article 5(4) such systems of review must still comply with the requirement that the substantive findings are subject to review. The point has not yet been raised.

404.2. Section 3(1) of the Act obliges every organ of State to perform its functions in a manner compatible with the State's obligations under the Convention. However, this cannot apply to the High Court exercising its jurisdiction under Article 40.4.2 since (under section 1(1)) 'a court' is expressly excluded from the definition of 'organ of state.' Section 2(1) might provide an alternative means of incorporation. This provides that 'in interpreting and applying any statutory provision or rule of law, a court shall, in so far as is possible, subject to the rules of law relating to such interpretation and application, do so in a manner compatible with the State's obligations under the Convention.' But it is questionable whether the interpretation and application of the process under Article 40.4.2 corresponds to the interpretation and application of a 'rule of law'. The exercise of Article 40.4.2 review appears closer to the 'interpretation and application' of a jurisdiction or a procedure.

A second difficulty originates in the doctrine propounded by Walsh J in *The State (Aherne) v. Cotter*[45] that Article 40.4.2 is a constitutional right 'in respect of which the whole procedure is set out in the Constitution itself.' A corollary of the perception of Article 40.4.2 as a self-executing procedure is that it is incapable of being regulated by legislation. In *Cotter* it was held that it was constitutionally improper to regulate by secondary legislation (the Rules of the Superior Courts, 1986) the procedure under Article 40.4.2. It follows that primary legislation which attempts to regulate the scope of review under Article 40.4.2 would be equally inappropriate. That, of course, would be the case if section 2(1) of the European Convention on Human Rights Act, 2003 was interpreted to require that Article 40.4.2 be processed in accordance with the standard established under Article 5(4).

Constitutionally-derived review of evidential quality

An alternative source of this more rigorous standard is the guarantee in Article 40.3.1 that the state 'by its laws' will defend and vindicate the personal rights of the citizen. 'Laws' for the purpose of Article 40.3.1 must include the common law principles regulating judicial review of administrative action. If, as has been argued by some members of the Supreme Court, the current standard of judicial review 'fall well short' of what is

---

[45] [1982] IR 188, 200. See pp 109–10 where the doctrine in *Cotter* is considered.

required for the protection of fundamental rights[46] Article 40.4.3 would seem to require that those 'laws' be modified in order to ensure effective defence and vindication of personal rights. This theory may underlie some existing case law. In *Clarke v. McMahon*[47] the applicant who was being returned to Northern Ireland in order to serve the balance of a sentence imposed following conviction, sought, on Article 40.4.2 proceedings, to challenge the soundness of the original conviction. He alleged that the confession on which the conviction was based had been irregularly obtained, and raised a new alibi. Although not prepared to exercise post-conviction review, both the High Court and Supreme Court indicated that they possessed a reserve jurisdiction to re-open, in exceptional cases, a judicial finding, including the finding of a foreign court, if the protection of the constitutional rights of the individual required it. In the Supreme Court Finlay CJ endorsed this proviso:[48]

> In the course of his judgment [the High Court judge] acknowledges that the court has in addition to its powers under section 50 of the Act of 1965, inherent powers for the protection of constitutional rights. The statement that the Court cannot in an extradition case properly undertake an investigation into the validity of a conviction recorded in a requesting country must be understood as being subject to this inherent power.

Clarke v. McMahon suggests that there is an exceptional power to conduct a full evidential re-appraisal where there is a sufficiently strong indication of the occurrence of a miscarriage of justice such as to engage the courts' inherent power for the protection of constitutional rights. In *Croke v. Smith*[49] the Supreme Court, in a radical break from conventional doctrine, held that on a complaint under Article 40.4.2 taken in respect of detention under the Mental Treatment Act, 1945, the High Court was

---

[46] Per Fennelly J in *O v. Minister for Justice* [2003] 1 IR 1, 203; McGuinness J concurred, ibid., p. 126. Denham and Hardiman JJ declined, in the absence of argument, to consider whether a more rigorous standard should operate: ibid., pp 61, 164–5.
[47] [1990] 1 IR 228.
[48] Ibid., p. 236.
[49] [1998] 1 IR 101, 124.

obliged to determine matters of administrative judgment. The Court, in epitomizing the scope of Article 40.4.2 review of mental health detention under the Mental Treatment Act, 1945 said:

> Upon the hearing of an application under Article 40.4.2 the High Court must be satisfied that (i) the person detained is a person of unsound mind, and in need of care and attention; (ii) that the procedures outlined in the Act have been complied with; (iii) that the person concerned has not recovered; (iv) that the person detained is not being unnecessarily detained.

Propositions (i), (iii), and (iv) greatly increase the scope of review of the merits of the committal decision, suggesting an unrestricted power of judicial review of the detainee's condition, and of the administrative decision that detention is necessary. But a power of review of such depth is difficult to reconcile with the established principle that a court in discharging judicial review is supposed to abstain from reviewing the merits of an administrative order. If the *Croke* formula is reconcilable with general constitutional principle it can only be on the ground that the circumstances fell within an acknowledged exception to the general principle such as the exceptional inherent jurisdiction recognized in *Clarke*. The context in which the *Croke* doctrine was propounded was that of administrative detention, of a long-term and non-appealable character; the decision suggests that an unusually interventionist standard of review may be required in the case of non-appealable, administrative detention where the consequences of an erroneous finding of fact upon the individual's rights are so significant as to engage the exceptional protective jurisdiction.

The various strands, common law, European and constitutional, may be combined into the following propositions:

(i) Evidential error is subject to review by reference to traditional common law standards: where there is no evidence to sustain the decision; where the decision is unreasonable; where the contested finding can be classified as a collateral fact.
(ii) The common law has been supplemented by the recognition of two modern doctrines: that decisions affecting high order

personal rights are accessible to appraisal on a strict scrutiny standard; and that judicial review is available where the decision maker misunderstands, or is misinformed as to, some basic, uncontested fact.

(iii) Supplementing these common law principles is an exceptional reserve power to investigate the weight of evidence where the courts' 'inherent powers for the protection of Constitutional rights' requires it.

(iv) European human rights standards require full evidential review on Article 40.4.2 in that category of detention which results from an administrative process from which there is no adequate internal appeal. It is unclear, however, whether this standard can affect the scope of review on Article 40.4.2.

ERROR OF LAW AS A GROUND OF REVIEW ON ARTICLE 40.4.2

Article 40.4.2 and the power to review errors of law

It is now clear, notwithstanding the earlier prohibition on this ground of intervention, that review on habeas corpus extends to cases where detention has resulted from a misconstruction of law. But the recognition of error of law as a ground of review is relatively new. The mid-twentieth century view of the scope of review on habeas corpus was the product of two propositions: (i) that the principle in *R. (Martin) v. Mahony*[50] (that an error of law or an erroneous finding of fact committed by a court acting within jurisdiction was unreviewable on certiorari) continued to describe the true scope of review on certiorari; and (ii) that the scope of review on Article 40.4.2 was equivalent to that on certiorari. Both of these premises are now unsound. The first proposition, that the scope of review on Article 40.4.2 is equivalent to that on certiorari, disregarded the description of the scope of review prescribed in Article 40.4.2 itself. Under Article 40.4.2 the High Court is under a duty to determine whether detention is 'in accordance with the law'. In *The State (Furlong) v. Kelly*[51] the High Court, applying traditional common law doctrine, held that the question of

---

[50] [1910] 2 IR 695. See above, at pp 23-4.
[51] [1971] IR 132.

whether a District Court judge had properly determined whether an offence referred to in the warrant transmitted to Ireland corresponded to an offence in Irish law was a matter within the jurisdiction of the District Court, and not reviewable by the High Court. On appeal, in a strong expression of censure of the High Court, Ó Dálaigh CJ described the High Court's application of the common law rule on certiorari to the Article 40.4.2 enquiry as 'a wholly unacceptable view of the duty of the High Court in this matter.' The Chief Justice based the duty to review allegations of error of law, or statutory misconstruction, on the explicit wording of Article 40.4.2:[52]

> The duty on the court in such a case is no less than in any other habeas corpus application: it is forthwith to enquire into the complaint and to order the release of the person detained unless satisfied that he is being detained in accordance with the law. Whether there is under the law of the State any offence corresponding to the offence specified in the warrant is not a matter upon which the District Justice could make a determination binding on the High Court ... That question is a question of law, and the correctness or otherwise of the District Court's determination thereon is clearly open to review in the High Court.

The same justification was applied by the High Court in *Russell v. Fanning*.[53] The complainant, who had been remanded pending extradition to Northern Ireland alleged, on an application for certiorari and for release under Article 40.4.2, that the District Court had misconstrued the phrase 'judicial authority in a place in relation to which this Part applies'. The High Court separated its jurisdiction on certiorari (under which it would not ordinarily be competent to review for error of law) and its jurisdiction under Article 40.4.2 (under which the High Court is constitutionally obliged to review whether the complainant's detention is in accordance with the law):[54]

> Even if he were wrong in [interpreting the judicial authority requirement] I am satisfied that his error was within jurisdiction and, therefore, not reviewable by way of certiorari proceedings. However, it is reviewable by this court on foot of a habeas corpus application

---

[52] Ibid., pp 136–7.   [53] [1988] IR 505.   [54] Ibid., p. 525.

under Article 40 of the Constitution where it is appropriate to look again at the whole proceedings by way of judicial review and determine in the light of all the evidence now available whether it is proper that the extradition orders in question should have been made.

But even if it had not been recognized that the scope of review under Article 40.4.2 has a legal basis independent of that on certiorari, and even were the two remedies still considered of equivalent range, the law of certiorari has now evolved to a point where all errors of law are accessible to review. In England, the common law prohibition against review for error of law was conclusively jettisoned in *R. v. Hull University Visitor, ex parte Page*.[55] In Ireland there has been no formal repudiation of the earlier doctrine. Indeed, there have been some suggestions that there may be a distinction between two categories of error of law, routine misconstructions of law within jurisdiction (which remain unreviewable) and error of law committed by an agency which has misconceived the basic character of the enquiry entrusted to it[56] (which alone is reviewable on certiorari). However, the balance of recent Irish authority[57] supports the proposition that error of law is now a general ground of judicial review.

The principle of the strict construction of legislation affecting personal liberty

Statute affecting personal liberty is interpreted subject to the principle of the strict construction of legislation affecting personal liberty. But the extent to which the strict construction principle actually affects the outcome of the interpretative process is probably quite limited. At its most extreme, the principle requires that legislation be construed in a strained way so as to avoid to the greatest extent possible any interference with the liberties of the individual. There are some Irish nineteenth century cases, particularly in the area of revenue legislation, where statements that legislative interference with the property rights of the subject must be clear beyond reasonable doubt appear.[58] However, even at the height of the nine-

---

[55] [1993] AC 682.
[56] *Harte v. The Labour Court* [1996] 2 IR 171; *Killeen v. DPP* [1997] 3 IR 218.
[57] *Radio Limerick One Limited v. IRTC* [1997] 2 IR 291, 312–13; *Ryan v. Compensation Tribunal* [1997] 1 ILRM 194; *Farrell v. AG* [1998] 1 IR 203, 224–5.
[58] In *R. (Wilson) v. Guardians of the Poor of Mallow Union* (1860) 12 ICLR 35, 41

teenth century, few examples of the application of the beyond all reasonable doubt doctrine can be found, and it is clear now that the presumption against interference may, in fact, be displaced 'by something short of clear express language'.[59]

A second version of the strict construction principle, somewhat misleadingly expressed, suggests that wherever there is some ambiguity in the statutory language, that ambiguity must be construed in favour of the liberty of the individual. The principle was so expressed by McCarthy J in *The People v. Ferris*:[60]

> The rule of strict liability arises if and when there is doubt or ambiguity as to the meaning of the provision being construed; for example, if there is an interpretation open which would avoid the imposition of a penalty then that is the interpretation that should be applied. The first rule is to look at the provision in its ordinary meaning. If examination reveals a doubt, then the doubt must be resolved in favour of the person accused.

However, again, the suggestion that mere ambiguity is sufficient to activate the presumption does not reflect the principle as it is actually operated (and as it was actually operated in *Ferris*). The practice is to resolve a legislative ambiguity by processing the issue through the conventional techniques of statutory construction. The strict construction doctrine usually only has a role where the application of these tests produces internally contradictory results, some pointing towards, others against operation, causing a genuine uncertainty as to whether the legislation applies. Where there is such a genuine doubt the courts may hesitate before sanctioning a power which might gravely intrude upon personal liberty:[61] *in dubio pars mitior est sequenda*. The presumption against interference with liberty is, accordingly, dispositive, not at the beginning of the process of statutory construction, but at the conclusion, when the ordinary principles of statutory construction have been exhausted.

---

it was stated that 'if a statute is intended to impose a tax upon the subject its construction must be clear beyond all reasonable doubt.'

[59] *Wills v. Bowley* [1982] 2 All ER 654, 661.
[60] *Judgments of the Court of Criminal Appeal, 1984–1989*, 114.
[61] *Bowers v. Gloucester Corporation* [1963] 1 QB 881; *Mullins v. Harnett* [1998] 4 IR 426.

The principle is, in the second place, employed for the proposition that language should not be strained, or have words added to it, in order to force a construction which might encroach upon personal liberty. Article 2A of the Constitution of the Irish Free State (which had been inserted by the Constitution (Amendment No. 17) Act 1931) instituted a power of 36-hour Garda detention. However, that power was qualified by the procedural requirement that 'whenever a person is removed to a station of the Garda Síochána the member of the Garda Síochána then in charge shall communicate the fact of such removal to a member of the Garda Síochána not below the rank of Superintendent.' In *Re O'Duffy*[62] the respondent argued that the provision only applied where the member himself was below the rank of superintendent, and that, in effect, the words 'provided he is himself under the rank of superintendent' be inserted into the statute. The High Court repudiated this attempt to add words to the provision: 'In construing an enactment of this kind which confers very wide powers on the police in regard to the liberty of the subject, I am of opinion that I should construe it in the manner most favourable to the liberty of the subject, and that for the purpose of holding that a detention is lawful I should not insert words which are not there and which could easily have been inserted by the legislature if it were so desired.' Again, in *The State (O'Duffy) v. Bennett*[63] the High Court in analyzing the Constitution (Amendment No. 17) Act, 1931, found that the Act had omitted to provide an express power enabling the Constitution (Special Powers) Tribunal to issue a bench warrant. It went on to reject the contention that such a power of arrest could be implied: ' A penal statute must', it was said, 'be construed strictly according to its expressed intent' and no power of arrest could be implied.

However, even in the limited senses in which it does operate, the presumption in favour of liberty may be overridden by the public interest in liberalizing the scope of operation of certain types of legislation. It has been recognized that there may be certain powers of detention where the social risks which might result from a narrow application of the legislation render a doctrinaire application of the strict construction principle inap-

---

[62] [1934] IR 550, 563–4.
[63] [1935] IR 70, 103. The principle was applied in *DPP v. Corcoran* [1995] 2 IR 261 in order to reject the argument that there existed as part of the Road Traffic Act, 1978 an implied power to require a urine sample where a blood sample could not be recovered.

propriate. The potential risk to a patient, or to others, arising from a narrow construction of mental health legislation was referred to by the English Court of Appeal in *R. v. Canons Park Mental Health Review Tribunal, ex parte A*[64] as a reason for not applying the principle that ambivalent wording should be read in favour of liberty. Kennedy LJ questioned 'whether the principles which operate in favour of personal liberty have any real part to play in the construction of legislation which in terms seeks to have regard to the potentially conflicting interests of the health or safety of the patient on the one hand and the protection of other persons on the other.' A similar displacement of the rule that ambivalence be construed in favour of personal liberty has been recognized in the context of extradition legislation. In *R. v. Governor of Ashford Prison, ex parte Postlethwaite*[65] it was said that it was inappropriate 'unless constrained by the language used, to interpret any extradition treaty in a manner which would hinder the working and narrow the operation of most salutary arrangements.' The normal principle against the addition of words to statutes has also been dis-applied. The Supreme Court, in construing the Mental Treatment Act, 1945, preferred to add words into the legislation rather than apply a literal interpretation which would have compromised the effectiveness of the involuntary commitment procedure in the case of persons who were dangerously mentally ill.[66]

Finally, the strict construction principle may be applied in the sense of a presumption that the legislature does not intend disproportionate interference with the right to personal liberty. The presumption will, in this context, be used so as to prefer a moderate, or limited, interpretation in place of an interpretation which would disproportionately intrude upon personal liberty. In *The State (Quinlan) v. Kavanagh*[67] the respondents argued for an interpretation of the Constitution (Amendment) Act, 1931 which would have authorized automatic, long-term imprisonment until trial of a person sent forward for trial. The High Court invoked the presumption against disproportionate interference, in order to justify a more restrictive interpretation of the power of pre-trial remand: 'There is no obligation on the tribunal to have a hearing within any fixed time and, accordingly, a construction favourable to the liberty of the citizen is to be

[64] [1995] QB 60, 86.
[65] [1988] AC 924, 974.
[66] *Gooden v. Waterford Regional Hospital*, Supreme Court, 21 Feb. 2001.
[67] [1935] IR 249, 270–1.

preferred to one which must encroach upon such liberty. I do not see why it is so necessary to arrive at a construction which involves the detention of the accused in custody in every case until the actual hearing.'[68]

HABEAS CORPUS REVIEW ON GROUNDS OF DOCUMENTARY ERROR

In *Re Peerless*,[69] a habeas corpus case which came before the English Court of Queen's Bench in 1841, the applicant had been convicted of possession of smuggled goods contrary to the Prevention of Smuggling Act, 1834. Under the Act[70] jurisdiction was limited, in a case where an offence had been committed on the high seas, to the magistrates' court sitting in the place to which the accused had first been taken following apprehension, and the warrant, although reciting that the offence had been committed on the high seas, did not recite the fact that the applicant had first been apprehended, and tried, at Kent. That failure to set out this essential preliminary to jurisdiction was held to be a sufficient basis for discharging the prisoner. Coleridge J said: 'of the conviction we know nothing, except through the warrant. By a warrant I mean a warrant which upon the face of it shows a right to detain; and that right cannot exist unless there be jurisdiction in the magistrates. To deny that this must appear upon the face of the proceedings is to call into question one of the must important rules of the common law.' In *R. v. Oldham JJ, ex parte Cawley*[71] decided almost 150 years later in 1997, two youths, both aged under 21, had been convicted and sentenced to detention in an adult prison. The order did not, as required by the Magistrates' Court Act, 1980, set out the grounds for the

---

[68] The principle of statutory construction against disproportionate detention was applied in *R. v. Hallstrom, ex p. W* [1986] QB 1090 where the English High Court, in rejecting a construction of the Mental Health Act, 1983, which would have involved the long-term detention of psychiatric out-patients who had refused to undergo medical treatment, said of such an unreasonable result: 'Even a night's detention is an infringement of personal liberty. Had Parliament intended to grant the power to overbear the refusal to consent of patients such as W who could be maintained in the community provided they were given appropriate treatment, it would have so provided by a clear provision which would have involved no unnecessary detention.'
[69] (1841) 1 QB 143; 113 ER 1084.
[70] 3 & 4 Will. IV, c. 53.
[71] [1997] 1 QB 1, 13.

magistrates' findings that there was no suitable place of imprisonment. However, on a habeas corpus application taken by the detainees, the failure to set out jurisdiction was dismissed as a legally insignificant technicality. Illustrating the evolution in this area of the law by reference to *Re Peerless* Simon Browne LJ said: 'it is clear that cases like *Peerless* have receded into history and ... the courts have become concerned rather with the legality of the underlying court order than with the face of the warrant.'

But if documentary irregularity as a ground of review has, as Simon Browne LJ put it, 'receded into history' in English law, the doctrine occasionally still flickers in Irish law.[72] In *Greene v. Governor of Mountjoy Prison*[73] two girls under the age of seventeen had been ordered to be detained in an adult place of imprisonment under the exceptional power in section 108 of the Children Act, 1908, which permitted the imprisonment of a young person if the person was 'of so unruly a character that he is not a fit person' to be detained in a place of detention for young offenders. The order in this case, in a very slight deviation from the statutory formula, recited that the young person was of so unruly a character that she 'could not' be detained in a place of detention for young offenders (not that young person was 'not fit' to be so detained). The Supreme Court, on this ground alone, discharged the two girls.[74]

The doctrine makes the documentary order itself an independent condition of the validity of the detention. It is not sufficient that the order actually be within jurisdiction. It must show jurisdiction: 'Every order of a justice must not only be within jurisdiction, but must show on its face the facts which brought the matter within his jurisdiction.'[75] Two principles regulate the appearance of an order of imprisonment: (i) the principle that an order display jurisdiction on its face, and (ii) the misdescription principle. The jurisdiction on the face of the order principle requires that the procedural conditions to the validity of an order be set out on the face of

---

[72] K. Costello, 'Documentary error as a ground of judicial review in Irish law', (1993–95) 28–30 *Ir. Jurist* 148.
[73] [1995] 3 IR 541.
[74] The complainant in *The State (Costello) v. Governor of Mountjoy Prison, Irish Times*, 8 Aug. 1987, had been convicted of an offence under the Dublin Police Act, 1842, and then jailed by the District Court for failing to sign a bond to keep the peace. The certificate returned by the governor on an Article 40.4.2 enquiry recited the conviction under the Dublin Police Act, 1842, but through oversight, omitted the refusal to sign the bond to keep the peace, and on that ground the complainant was, on an Article 40.4.2 enquiry, discharged.
[75] Per Palles CB in *R. (Boylan) v. Londonderry JJ* [1912] 2 IR 347, 379.

the order or warrant. The misdescription principle requires that information which is contained on the order be completely accurate: a misdescription, or an inaccuracy, in the data set out in the order or warrant may be a ground of habeas corpus.

The requirement that jurisdiction be set out on the face of the order

The doctrine requiring that jurisdiction be displayed *ex facie* may be organized in three parts. Firstly (and, in practice, most commonly) the fact of compliance with the preliminary procedural conditions to jurisdiction may be required to be set out on the face of the order. The exercise of statutory authority encroaching upon the liberty of the individual will, in all cases, be contingent upon compliance with a set of procedural preliminaries. The rule that jurisdiction be shown on the record requires that compliance with these procedural conditions be set out on the face of the order. Burke, the complainant in *The State (Burke) v. Lennon*,[76] had been the subject of an internment order made under Part IV of the Offences Against the State Act, 1939. It was a condition precedent to the activation of that power that the Government had published a proclamation declaring that the power of executive internment without trial was necessary to secure the preservation of the public peace. Burke was released by Gavan Duffy J on the ground that the warrant did not set out the publication of the warrant: 'if the document was an ordinary act of a civil department administering its functions it would have to be liberally construed without reference to technicalities derived from the necessity of surrounding personal liberty with safeguards against courts administering laws of a penal character. But it is nothing of the kind.'[77] Secondly, the concluding part of the order must detail precisely, and without ambiguity,[78] the manner in which the order is

[76] [1940] IR 136, 156.
[77] See, also, *The State (Browne) v. Feran* [1967] IR 147.
[78] The doctrine requiring that the action to be taken under the order must be described without ambiguity or duplicity was applied in *The State (Caddle) v. McCarthy* [1957] IR 359. Here the Circuit Court on appeal had confirmed a District Court conviction under which imprisonment was ordered and following which the District Justice had issued a temporary warrant for the apprehension of the convict. Seven days later the Circuit Court drew up a formal warrant reciting the sentence of imprisonment, but not making it clear that the period of imprisonment spent under the temporary warrant was to be discounted. Although it was understood that the period was to be taken into account, the Supreme Court decided an application under Article 40.4.2 in the complainant's

to be executed. In *The State (Holmes) v. Furlong*[79] the Supreme Court held that it was insufficient for an extradition warrant simply to recite the statutory language of Part III of the Extradition Act, 1965 and direct delivery 'from some convenient point of departure from the State.' Instead it was held that in order to show jurisdiction it was necessary that the order identify the exact point of departure from the State. Similarly, in *Kajli and Nisli v. Minister for Justice*[80] it was held insufficient for a deportation order (following the terms of the Aliens Order, 1946) simply to direct the applicant to 'leave and to remain thereafter out of the State.' The deportation order, it was held, must detail the country to which the deportee was to be deported. Thirdly, the rule may exceptionally require that the findings on which the decision is based be set out. The circumstances in which this requirement now applies are rare: common law doctrines on documentary appearance may be displaced by statute, and most orders of detention are regulated by model forms which do not require a narrative of the findings. However, there are some residual cases where a recital of the findings may still be required. An order binding a person to keep the peace may have to set out the underlying findings from which an inference of a future breach of the peace may be inferred.[81] An order of committal for civil contempt

> favour, holding that the ambivalence was serious enough to warrant the applicant's discharge: 'It seems to me that an authority to keep a man in prison must state with precision and without possibility of ambiguity the duration of imprisonment, and that such duration and any other incident of imprisonment stated in the warrant must correspond with the sentence legally imposed. Though I do not think that there was any risk that the prisoner would have been kept from his liberty for an hour more than was justified by the sentence, yet where habeas corpus is concerned I prefer to err on the side of strictness' (p. 379). The principle in *Caddle* was applied in *Carroll v. Governor of Mountjoy Prison*, High Court, 12 Jan. 2005 where an order of imprisonment made by the Circuit Court was held to be ambivalent as to the precise date of commencement of that sentence. The complainant was, on an Article 40.4.2 application, discharged on that ground alone.

[79] [1967] IR 210.
[80] High Court, 21 Aug. 1992.
[81] In *R. (Boylan) v. Londonderry JJ* [1912] 2 IR 374 it was held that an order requiring a person to find sureties to keep the peace must show on its face facts necessary to give jurisdiction. The principle was applied in *Kelly v. O'Sullivan*, High Court, 11 July 1990: the applicant, who had been involved in a dispute over fishing rights in Lough Ree, had been bound over to keep the peace, and in default of entering into the bond, or keeping the peace, to be committed to prison for a period of 12 days. The High Court held that the order was defective for failing to set out facts from which the apprehension of a future breach of the

of the Circuit Court may also attract the requirement that the findings be set out on the order.[82]

Exceptions to the operation of the doctrine; circumstances in which non-compliance may be excused

The documentary doctrine is subject to two principal exceptions: it does not apply in the case of orders made by courts of superior jurisdiction, which are presumed to act within jurisdiction and are not required to affirmatively demonstrate compliance with jurisdiction.[83] Secondly, the doctrine may be modified by statute.[84] Accordingly the legislature has long provided for statutory models in order to reduce the operation of the doctrine. It is only where there is no statutory model the common law rule continues in its original form.

As with all procedural rules, non-compliance with the rules of documentary form may, on habeas corpus or judicial review, be excused or cured. It is, in practice, common to excuse omissions, or clear up ambiguities, by reference to other documentation in the same set of proceedings.[85]

---

peace might be inferred. The rule does not apply where an inference of a future apprehended breach of the peace may be derived from the terms of the summons: *R. (Mulholland) v. Monaghan JJ* [1914] 2 IR 156; *Clarke v. Hogan* [1995] 1 IR 310. In the light of *Mulholland* it is questionable whether *Kelly v. O'Sullivan* was correctly decided since the summons did appear to set out grounds upon which such an apprehension might have been derived. By contrast, in *Clarke v. Hogan* [1995] 1 IR 310, where the applicant was a witness who had not been summoned to answer in respect of any behaviour of her own, and where there were no grounds either in the complaint or in the binding over order, from which an inference of a future breach of the peace could be sustained, the order was sustained. Applying the *Londonderry* case it is questionable whether *Clarke* was correctly decided.

[82] *Levy v. Moylan* (1850) 10 CB 189, 138 ER 78; *Re McAleece* (1873) IR 7 CL 146; *The State (Conneely) v. Governor of Limerick Prison*, Irish Times, 3 Feb. 1937; *McIlraith v. Grady* [1968] 1 QB 468. The Circuit Court Rules, 2001 do not describe a model form of order so that the matter would seem to continue to be regulated by the common law. A model form order for committal, making no provision for setting out evidence, is prescribed by Schedule C, No. 46B.2 District Court Rules, 1997.

[83] *Ex p. Fernandez* (1861) 10 CB NS 3, 142 ER 349; *In re Keller* (1888) 22 LR Ir 158.

[84] *AG (O'Gara) v. Callanan* (1958) 92 ILTR 74; *The People (AG) v. O'Brien* [1965] IR 142, 161; *The People v. Kelly (No. 2)* [1983] IR 1, 16–17.

[85] *The State (Brien) v. Kelly* [1970] IR 69; *Carroll v. Governor of Mountjoy Prison*, High Court, 15 Jan. 2005.

In *Re Tynan*[86] Henchy J held that an alleged informality in the manner in which the prisoner's sentence had been recorded might be cured by reference to the transcript. Ambivalence may also be cured by affidavits showing compliance in fact with the omitted conditions.[87] A documentary slip may be excused on the ground that the applicant has not been prejudiced by the documentary imperfection.[88] At common law a defective warrant appendixed to the gaoler's return could, at the discretion of the court,[89] be replaced by an order or warrant which was technically compliant;[90] this remedial technique continues to be recognized under Article 40.4.2.[91]

NON-COMPLIANCE WITH PROCEDURAL CONDITIONS AS A GROUND OF REVIEW

Where individual liberty is engaged the traditional rule has been to insist upon an exceptional degree of compliance with the procedural conditions to the exercise of the power.[92] However, breach of procedural conditions may, firstly, be forgiven where the statutory condition is directory rather than mandatory. Secondly, even where the condition may be classified as mandatory, the consequence of the breach may be so insignificant, or non-prejudicial, that it may be disregarded. Thirdly, even if the manner of the breach is regarded as significant, the procedural breach may, in certain

---

[86] [1969] IR 273 n.
[87] *R. v. Governor of Brixton Prison, ex p. Pitt-Rivers* [1942] 1 All ER 207; *The State (Brien) v. Kelly* [1970] IR 69; *Jahromi v. Secretary of State for the Home Department* [1996] Imm AR 20.
[88] *People (AG) v. O'Brien* [1965] IR 142; *In re Tynan* [1969] I.R. 273; *The State (Brien) v. Kelly* [1970] I.R. 64; *The State (Shannon) v. Clifford*, Irish Times, 25 Oct. 1983; *The People v. Kelly (No. 2)* [1983] IR 1; *AG v. Borek*, High Court, 11 Sept. 2003.
[89] *R. v. Mountnorris* (1795) Ir Term Rep 460 where the Court of King's Bench declined to exercise its discretion to allow amendment of the return.
[90] *R. v. Feeny* (1842) 5 ILR 437; *R. v. Dillon* (1888) *Judgments of the Superior Courts in Ireland* 181, 185.
[91] *In re Francis* (1963) 97 ILTR 151, 169.
[92] *In re Keller* (1888) 22 L.R Ir 158, 201: 'the exercise of any special statutory jurisdiction, especially one affecting personal liberty, must be strictly in accordance with the statute creating it' per Fitzgibbon LJ; see also *In re O'Neill* [1932] IR 548; *McMahon v. Leahy* [1984] IR 525, 547; *In re Mahmod* [1995] Imm AR 311, 314.

circumstances, be regarded as capable of being cured, or retroactively validated, or the proceedings remitted.

The mandatory/directory distinction in powers affecting personal liberty

The argument is sometimes made that where personal liberty, or other important rights are at stake, all procedural conditions which precede the making of the order are necessarily mandatory.[93] However, the more common tendency in modern case law has been to require some nexus between the procedural condition and the protection of the individual. A procedural condition is, according to this view, more likely to be regarded as mandatory according to the importance of the right or interest which it is designed to protect, and according to the proximity between non-compliance and prejudice to the individual. Particular weighting will be attributed to factors such as the extent to which compliance may affect the outcome of proceedings, or non-compliance may reduce the safeguards put in place for the protection of a person in jeopardy of his liberty.[94] In reviewing the procedural importance of a provision the court is not confined to reviewing the impact of the procedural breach on the particular applicant before it. Instead, the court may hypothesize on the prejudicial affects which a directory construction may produce in future cases;[95] thus, a mandatory construction may be justified by the consideration that what may appear technical in the case before it may be highly prejudicial in different circumstances.

However, where the procedural condition is shown to serve some purpose other than the protection of the individual, there is a greater chance that it may be regarded as directory and not mandatory. In *Re Philip Clarke*[96] the Supreme Court held, on two grounds, that compliance with

---

[93] *The State (Doyle) v. Carr* [1970] IR 87, 91: 'Where powers, rights or immunities are granted with a direction that certain regulations, formalities or conditions are complied with, it seems neither unjust nor inconvenient to exact a rigorous observance of them as essential to the acquisition of the right or authority conferred, and it is, therefore, probable that such was the intention of the legislature.'

[94] E.g. *In re J* (1954) 88 ILTR 120; *R. (McCann) v. Belfast JJ* [1978] NI 153; *The State (Kenny) v. Ó hUadhaigh* [1979] IR 1; *The State (Williams) v. Kelleher* [1983] IR 112.

[95] E.g., *Walsh v. R.* (1888) 22 LR Ir 314, 320.

[96] [1950] IR 235.

the requirements of the form which a member of the Garda Síochána applying for committal under the Mental Treatment Act, 1945 was obliged to submit to a medical practitioner was directory. Firstly, it was stated that to read the provision as mandatory would, because of the practical difficulty of exact compliance, frequently lead to the breakdown of the procedure. Secondly, the Court was influenced by the fact that the information required to be filled up could not serve any purpose which would enhance the protection of the patient (but was purely for the use of the medical practitioner). Even less sympathy to a claim for mandatory construction will be shown where the procedural condition is one which, if it was rigidly insisted upon, would positively prejudice the individual. In *The State (Coveney) v. The Special Criminal Court*[97] the applicant, who was being prosecuted following the withdrawal by *nolle prosequi* of an earlier charge on the same facts, argued that the original *nolle prosequi* was irregular (with the consequence that the first prosecution was still active and the second prosecution could not proceed). The argument was based on section 12 of the Criminal Justice (Administration) Act, 1924 which provides that a *nolle prosequi* may be entered 'at any time after the indictment is referred to the jury and before a verdict is found thereon.' Here the *nolle prosequi* had been entered before the indictment had been submitted to the jury. The High Court dismissed the argument that the *nolle prosequi* must be entered after the empanelling of the jury, observing that it was difficult to see what interest of the accused would be served by this construction since the 'expense incurred by an accused in his own defence and the anxiety associated with a pending criminal charge would be intensified if strict adherence were in all cases paid by the DPP to the provisions of the section appearing to provide that it was only when the accused had been put in charge of the jury that he could and should enter a *nolle prosequi*.'

A close assessment may show the procedural consequences of non-compliance to be otherwise compensatable, and therefore less serious than originally claimed. In *R. v. Canterbury Prison, ex parte Craig*[98] a condition in the (English) Prosecution of Offences Act, 1985, requiring that the prisoner be given advance notice of the prosecutor's intention to apply for an extension of the custody period, had been disregarded. The Court of

[97] [1982] ILRM 284, 288.
[98] [1991] 2 QB 195.

Appeal, having conceded that non-compliance might prejudice the prisoner, pointed out that any such prejudice might be minimized by granting only the shortest extension of the custody period, and by obliging the authorities to renew on notice their application for a longer extension period. Since the defect was compensatable, it was held that a purely directory construction was justified. Alternatively, a cost/benefit analysis, balancing the cost to the public interest against the gain to the individual, may be undertaken in order to assess whether a directory or mandatory construction is appropriate. The legislature, it is inferred, could hardly be credited with intending that procedural conditions be given a mandatory construction where the effect would be that a mechanism which is important in the public interest, might have to be nullified on relatively technical grounds. In assessing whether the conditions to a custodial extension order were directory or mandatory, the Court of Appeal in *R. v. Canterbury Prison, ex parte Craig* weighed[99]

> the importance of the requirement in question, such prejudice as may be occasioned to the defendant by non-compliance, and any competing claims of the public interest; in short, by balancing the inconvenience of holding non-compliance immaterial against the inconvenience of insisting rigidly upon it.

In *The State (D) v. Groarke*[100] the Supreme Court adopted a similar approach, rejecting an argument that section 23 of the Children Act, 1908 (which required that an order placing a child in care should specify the religious persuasion of the child who was being placed) was a mandatory condition to a place of safety order. Weighing the benefits of compliance against the costs of nullification the Court stated: 'Having regard to the intention and purpose of the statutory provisions with which we are concerned in this appeal, namely, the urgent protection of the welfare of the child, I do not consider that this particular omission from the terms of the order would, if it were the only frailty in that order, entitle the prosecutors to a declaration that the child was in unlawful custody and a consequent order for its return to their custody.'[101]

---

[99] Ibid., p. 204.
[100] [1990] 1 IR 305, 315.
[101] The Supreme Court indicated that such an argument should be disposed of by declining release and remitting the matter to the District Court in order to have the form perfected in compliance with s. 23.

Of course, the issue of whether a mandatory or directory construction is appropriate may often be resolved by the application of conventional linguistic techniques of statutory construction. In the English habeas corpus case *Re Philpot*[102] the applicant argued that section 21(4) of the Criminal Justice Act, 1948, which made it a condition to a sentence of preventive detention that 'before sentencing any offender to corrective training or preventive detention, the court shall consider any report or representations which may be made to the court by or on behalf of the Prison Commissioners on the offender's physical and mental condition and his suitability for such a sentence' was mandatory. The Queen's Bench Division contrasted the language in section 21(4) with what it considered the more imperative language in section 23(1) which provided that 'no account shall be taken of any previous conviction or sentence unless notice has been given to the proper officer of the court at least three days before the trial that it is intended to prove the conviction or sentence.' The language in section 23, it was argued, made it abundantly clear that the condition was mandatory; by contrast, the absence from section 21(4) of language as imperative as that in the later section justified a directory construction.

Excusing purely technical defects

The classification of a requirement as mandatory does not exhaust a court's capacity to deny relief. Judicial review or habeas corpus is regularly refused on the ground that the alleged irregularity is non-prejudicial or of no significant importance.[103] Marginal non-compliance may be excused where there has been substantial compliance.[104] A common excusatory technique is to identify the overall statutory purpose underlying the procedural condition, and to excuse non-compliance where that underlying purpose has been accomplished by some other means. In the extradition case *Smithers v. Governor of Mountjoy Prison*[105] there had been a slight

---

[102] [1960] 1 All ER 165.
[103] *In re Rice* (1873) IR 7 CL 74, 78; *R. (O' Neill) v. Tyrone JJ* [1917] 2 IR 96, 102; *The State (Bond) v. Governor of Mountjoy Prison* (1964) 102 ILTR 93, 101; *Application of McLoughlin* [1970] IR 197, 202; *The State (McGinley) v. Durcan*, High Court, 5 May 1975; *The State (O'Dare) v. Sheehy* [1984] ILRM 99, 102; *DPP v. Somers* [1999] 1 IR 115, 119; *R. v. Home Secretary, ex p. Jeyeanthan* [2000] 1 WLR 354, 358.
[104] *R. v. Home Secretary, ex p. Jeyeanthan* [2000] 1 WLR 354.
[105] [1998] 2 IR 392.

deviation from the condition that a request for a provisional arrest should recite the intention to seek the extradition of the individual. The High Court identified the purpose underlying the procedural requirement as being the prevention of the abuse of the provisional arrest procedure in a case where there was no clear intention to continue proceedings. However, there was no risk of such abuse since it was clearly the intention of the United States Government to proceed with extradition, and since there were other items in the documentation which clearly established this intention. The defect was, accordingly, classified as non-invalidating.

Where the source of the defect is an omission to make a mandatory finding, or lies in the fact that the finding has been defectively arrived at, the defect may be cured where the respondent can demonstrate that there in fact existed the circumstances which would have justified the making of the finding. In *R. v. Brixton Prison, ex parte Servini*[106] no proof had been given before the magistrates' court, which had ordered the applicant's extradition to Italy, of the Order in Council extending the Extradition Act, 1870 to Italy. The Court held that the fact (proven on the habeas corpus application) that the Order in Council had, in fact, been properly made at the time of the original hearing concluded the matter against the applicant:[107]

> We have seen the *London Gazette* and know there is an Order in Council, and it is admitted that there is nothing in it which, if it had been given in evidence, would have benefited the prisoner. In these circumstances should the Court grant the writ of habeas corpus- a writ which has been of the greatest value in the history of England and one of the greatest securities for the liberty of the subject? I agree that we must approach the question from the point of view of the liberty of the subject, but while the courts have always used the writ of habeas corpus as a very strong defence of the subject they have always used it to effect justice.

It was this technique also which underlay the principle propounded in *The State (Furlong) v. Kelly*[108] which operated when, in Anglo-Irish

---

[106] [1914] 1 KB 77.
[107] Ibid., pp 83-4.
[108] [1971] IR 132, 142: 'If it should appear, on application to the High Court for an order of habeas corpus, that the offence under the law of the State found by the

extradition proceedings under Part III of the Extradition Act, 1965, a District Judge inaccurately identified the offence in Irish law to which the offence named in the English warrant was supposed to correspond. Under the *Furlong* principle that irregularity might be disregarded if, in the light of all of the materials before the High Court on a subsequent Article 40.4.2 enquiry, it could be shown that the English offence did in fact correspond to some other offence in Irish law.

The combination of a technical defect with delay or acquiescence in prosecuting the point may have the effect of neutralizing any potentially invalidating effect. In *Re MacCurtain*[109] a prisoner who had been tried, and was on remand awaiting execution, was not, at this late stage, permitted to argue that, on technical grounds, the order sending him forward for trial was defective. It would, the Supreme Court held, 'be reducing the law to an absurdity to allow an objection of this kind to prevail now after a trial which had been allowed proceed to the end.' In *The State (Bond) v. Governor of Mountjoy Gaol*[110] post-conviction release was sought on the ground that the depositions, on the basis of which the accused had been sent forward for trial, were defective. The High Court was, in the light of the applicants' failure to raise the issue when the order sending the case forward was made, sceptical of the seriousness of the alleged defect.

Rectifying procedural omissions at the habeas corpus hearing

A well-established remedial technique on habeas corpus is to permit the retroactive validation of the defectively performed procedural step at the habeas corpus hearing itself. The earliest application of this principle is the ancient common law rule under which a defective warrant may, in the course of habeas corpus proceedings, be replaced by a corrected warrant.[111] This general principle has been extended to permit the correc-

> District Justice is not, in fact, a corresponding offence under the law of this State, I do not think such a position would be fatal to the validity of his order provided it could be shown in the High Court, or on appeal to this Court, that the offence in the warrant did correspond with some offence under the law of the State.'

[109] [1941] IR 83, 87.
[110] (1964) 102 ILTR 93.
[111] *Anon.* (1673) 1 Mod 103, 86 ER 765; *Leonard Watson's Case* (1839) 9 A & E 731, 112 ER 1389; R.J. Sharpe, *The law of habeas corpus* (Oxford, 1989), hereafter *The law of habeas corpus*, p. 182.

tion of procedural conditions other than the warrant. In *Re Allen*[112] it was a condition to the transfer of military prisoner that an order establishing the alternative place of detention have been made by the commanding officer; this had not been done at the time of the transfer. The court was, however, prepared to grant the authorities a second chance at compliance: 'If the Solicitor General can obtain further information, sufficient to satisfy us that Lord Clyde had ordered the place of the prisoner's imprisonment to be changed from Agra to England, the Court will pause before ordering the liberation of the prisoner.'

The retrospective compliance principle has been applied in the operation of Article 40.4.2. In *McMahon v. Leahy*[113] one of the proofs essential to an extradition order under Part III of the Extradition Act, 1965 (an affidavit establishing that a warrant of arrest had been issued by a magistrate or justice of the peace) had been irregularly presented. Nonetheless, Keane J was prepared to grant an adjournment in order to permit a fresh affidavit to be prepared and the omission rectified. However, the jurisdiction to permit retroactive compliance is discretionary. Whether late correction is permitted may depend on factors such as the relative seriousness of the illegality, or the extent to which the authorities have been guilty of maladministration. In *McMahon v. Leahy* McCarthy J hearing the Supreme Court appeal felt that, in light of the seriousness of the process of extradition and the careless approach of the authorities, it was inappropriate to allow an amendment of proofs. A similar reluctance is apparent in *The State (Dowling) v. Kingston*,[114] where, in response to the prisoner's argument that the Assistant Commissioner of the Garda Commissioner had not been formally constituted a successor to the Inspector General of the Royal Irish Constabulary, the respondent sought an adjournment so that a proper adaption order could be made and proven. Gavan Duffy J, however, refused to permit the submission of supplementary proof. Ordinarily, he said, he would be prepared to grant such an order[115]

> were this not an application for habeas corpus; but, in my opinion, it is now too late to seek any such way of solving the doubt, in view of the very solemn and stringent language of Article 6 of the

---

[112] (1860) 30 LJ QB 38.
[113] [1984] IR 525.
[114] [1937] IR 483.
[115] Ibid., pp 505–6.

Constitution. That Article, in my judgment, requires that clear authority for the arrest shall be forthcoming upon the arrest being challenged in the High Court.

However, Gavan Duffy J's understanding that the 'solemn and stringent language' of Article 6 forbade amendment is not necessarily transferable to its successor, Article 40.4.2. Article 6 required that the detainer 'certify in writing as to the cause of the detention, and such Court or judge shall thereupon order the release of such person unless satisfied that he is being detained in accordance with the law.' The requirement in the text of Article 6 that the High Court determine 'thereupon' the legality of the imprisonment could plausibly be read as implicitly excluding any amendment of this original justification. Article 40.4.2, on the other hand, is not so urgently expressed. Adjudication is postponed until, firstly, the return has been made, and, secondly, the detainer has been afforded the opportunity of justifying the detention. Since the opportunity to justify the detention (and not just the original return) may, in some cases, be most effectively exercised by revising the original process, Article 40.4.2 may accommodate technical amendments in a way in which Article 6 did not.

Remittal

Irregularities may be corrected by the exercise by the High Court of its jurisdiction to remit. There are two species of remittal. In both cases the exercise of the power is discretionary.[116]

The stronger version of the remittal order operates ancillary either to an adjournment of the habeas corpus proceedings, or on refusal of release on habeas corpus proceedings, and directs the lower court or agency to correct the element of the process which has been defectively executed.[117] Here, of course, the objective is to cure the defective process and to avoid release.

The second (but weaker) variety operates where the order has already been found to be invalid. Here the order of remittal directs that the process defectively taken on the first occasion be re-commenced from the beginning again. The objective of this form of remittal is to secure the

---

[116] *R. v. Governor of Brixton Prison, ex p. Percival* [1907] 1 QB 696.
[117] *Ex p. Carpenter* (1824) Sm & Bat 81; *R. v. Governor of Brixton Prison, ex p. Percival* [1907] 1 QB 696; *R. v. Governor of Brixton Prison, ex p. Shuter* [1960] 2 QB 89; *The State (D) v. Groarke* [1990] 1 IR 305.

re-initiation of the original process and consequently the re-arrest of the complainant.

Doubts, however, have been expressed about whether there exists any power to order remittal on Article 40.4.2 proceedings: there certainly exists express authority under O. 84, r. 26 (4) of the Rules of the Superior Courts, 1986 to direct remittal following quashing on judicial review. However, the jurisdiction in O. 84, r. 26(4) is restricted to applications for judicial review, and there is no express jurisdiction to order remittal ancillary to Article 40.4.2. In *McSorley v. Governor of Mountjoy Prison*[118] the Supreme Court assumed that there was no power of remittal following release on Article 40.4.2. However, the procedure under Article 40.4.2 is not entirely self-contained,[119] and the High Court possesses a series of incidental jurisdictions not expressly referred to in the Article. There is authority dating back to the middle of the nineteenth century to the effect that the High Court possessed an inherent power to order remittal ancillary to quashing on certiorari.[120] It is difficult to think of any reason why that inherent power should not also operate ancillary to the court's jurisdiction on habeas corpus. Indeed, in a number of decisions prior to *McSorley* the Supreme Court assumed that the High Court did possess an inherent jurisdiction to remit to the trial court following release under Article 40.4.2.[121]

EVIDENCE ON THE ARTICLE 40.4.2 ENQUIRY

Article 40.4.2, it has been said, envisages 'the widest possible powers to be conferred on the judge or Court conducting the enquiry'.[122] Accordingly, the full range of evidence-generating procedures are available on the

---

[118] [1997] 2 IR 258. See below, pp 86–88.
[119] *Gallagher v. Director of Central Mental Hospital* [1996] 3 IR 1.
[120] K. Costello, 'Certiorari followed by remittal' (1993) 3 *Irish Criminal Law Journal* 145, 147–8.
[121] In *The State (O) v. O'Brien* [1973] IR 50, 61 the Supreme Court assumed that it had a power to remit for re-sentencing. However it refused to exercise that jurisdiction on the basis that the complainant had already undergone sixteen years' imprisonment. *The State (Aherne) v. Cotter* [1982] IR 188, 201, and *McConnell v. Governor of Castlerea Prison*, Supreme Court, 26 Oct. 2001, both assume the existence of an ancillary power of remittal following release.
[122] *Gallagher v. Director of Central Mental Hospital* [1996] 3 IR 1.

enquiry.[123] Further, the capacity on Article 40.4.2 may be greater than that under the common law remedy,[124] or in ordinary civil litigation: common law principles, or rules of court, which might impede the elicitation of evidence necessary for the determination of an enquiry under Article 40.4.2 may, in light of the overriding constitutional duty, have to be disapplied.[125]

Burden and standard of proof

The topic of the burden of proof is clarified by separating, firstly, the issue of the initial burden and, secondly, the issue of the standard of proof.[126] As to the first issue, the initial burden, the general, though not unanimous, understanding is that the onus of raising a preliminary case rests with the complainant. This follows as a corollary of the principle *omnia praesumuntur rite esse*. In *The State (Dowling) v. Kingston*[127] Maguire P rejected

---

[123] In *Gallagher v. Director of Central Mental Hospital* [1996] 3 IR 1, it was stated that 'although Order 84, Rule 1(2) of the Rules of the Superior Courts expressly excludes from the definition of "Order of Habeas Corpus" an order made pursuant to Article 40, Section 4, the Constitution itself, in my view envisages the widest possible powers to be conferred on the Judge or Court conducting the inquiry, which power could not be delineated or cut down by the rule-making Committee.'

[124] At common law the affidavit is, in practice, usually the only evidential source on habeas corpus. There has been in English practice a reluctance to permit to accede to applications for cross-examination. By contrast, the use of cross-examination on Article 40.4.2 has been relatively routine: *The State (C) v. Minister for Justice* [1967] IR 106; *The State (Magee) v. O'Rourke* [1971] IR 205; *The State (Trimbole) v. Governor of Mountjoy Prison* [1985] IR 550; *Finucane v. McMahon* [1990] 1 IR 165; *Hegarty v. Governor of Limerick Prison* [1998] 1 IR 412. In *The State (Harrington) v. Garda Commissioner*, High Court, 14 Dec. 1976, the parties gave their evidence orally, but did not cross-examine; Finlay P himself recalled both the complainant and the respondents and examined them.

[125] In *Duncan v. Governor of Portlaoise Prison* [1997] 1 IR 558, the High Court, in refusing to follow the common law rule prohibiting cross-examination on an affidavit of discovery, attributed weighting to the fact that it was engaged upon an enquiry under Article 40.4.2 and to its obligation 'to be astute to ensure that the remedy provided for in Article 40 may be obtained efficaciously'. In *Re Quigley* [1983] NI 245 the Northern Ireland High Court declined to enforce the conventional prohibition against a judge calling a witness not called by the parties 'having regard to the duty of the court to make a searching inquiry' on an application for habeas corpus.

[126] *The law of habeas corpus*, pp 85–91.

[127] [1937] IR 483, 494.

an argument to the effect that the *omnia* principle did not apply to habeas corpus proceedings: 'It is said that the onus is on the respondent here to show that Assistant Commissioner Brennan is endowed with authority... in my opinion, the onus is the other way, the presumption is that everything has been done regularly, and no evidence has been given by the prosecutor to rebut this presumption.' In *Re Ó Laighléis*[128] the applicant who had been interned under the machinery established by section 4 of the Offences Against the State (Amendment) Act, 1940, on grounds that 'he was engaged in activities which were prejudicial to the safety of the State' submitted, on a habeas corpus challenge, that it was for the Minister to establish that he was engaged in such activities. Davitt P, implicitly applying the principle that the onus of proof rested with the applicant, said that 'the mere denial by the applicant of such activities does not suffice to put the respondent upon proof of the Minister's opinion, already stated in a warrant in the statutory form and good on its face.' There is, however, one authority, the decision of the Supreme Court in *The State (Griffin) v. Bell*,[129] which points in the opposite direction. Here the applicant was being held under the Petty Sessions Act, 1851, which authorized the execution in Ireland of a warrant issued by a justice of the peace in England for 'any crime or offence under English law.' The Supreme Court held that the burden of positively demonstrating that the offence was an offence under English law, and the burden of proving compliance with each of the conditions prescribed by statute, lay on the respondent. It was stated that when detention was predicated upon compliance with a series of conditions precedent it was, on an application under Article 40.4.2, for the respondent to show compliance with each of these conditions, even if no challenge to their fulfillment had been raised by the complainant:[130]

> Article 40 section 4.2 of the Constitution makes it mandatory upon the Court to order the release of a person who has complained that he is unlawfully detained unless the party detaining the complainant satisfies the Court that the detention is in accordance with the law. I respectfully agree with the view expressed by Mr Justice Kingsmill Moore in *The State (Hully) v. Hynes* that the effect of this portion of

---

[128] [1960] IR 93, 105.
[129] [1962] IR 355.
[130] Ibid., p. 362.

the wording of the Constitution is to throw upon the party showing cause the onus of justifying detention in all aspects to the satisfaction of the court. In this case there is no evidence that the matters complained of against the applicant in the warrants are crimes under English law, and, in my view, it is no answer for the respondents to say that the applicant has not adduced evidence to prove that these matters do not constitute crimes or offences.

However, this understanding of the burden of proof is not necessarily justified by the language of Article 40.4.2. That Article is predicated upon a complaint being made by a person alleging that he is 'being unlawfully detained.' Had, instead, the Article been framed so that an enquiry was activated simply 'upon complaint that a person is being detained' it could be contended that the full burden of establishing the propriety of the detention would fall upon the respondent. But the fact that the applicant is implicitly required to specify the basis of the complaint that he is being illegally detained is difficult to reconcile with the proposition that the detainer is, even in the absence of a controversy being raised by the prisoner, required to give positive evidence that it has fulfilled every legal condition required by law. Secondly, the fact that Article 40.4.2 obliges the High Court to release the applicant 'unless satisfied that he is being detained in accordance with the law' (a point relied upon in *Griffin*, and elsewhere)[131] does not necessarily prove that the burden of proof rests upon the respondent. Article 40.4.2 is more neutral on the question of the burden of proof than is suggested in these cases. While Article 40.4.2 may oblige the High Court to release unless satisfied as to the legality of the detention, it does not restrict the sources of that satisfaction: it does not actually state that the only source is an affirmative case made by the gaoler. There is some support in the academic literature for the view that at common law the detaining party carries the burden of affirmatively demonstrating the legality of the detention. In Wade's *Administrative Law*[132] the editors state that the respondent 'must be able to give positive evidence that it has fulfilled every condition expressly required by statute, *even in the absence of contrary evidence from the prisoner*'. In support of the proposition the editors cite *R. v. Governor of Brixton Prison, ex parte*

---

[131] *The State (Trimbole) v. Governor of Mountjoy Prison* [1985] IR 550.
[132] H.W.R. Wade and C. Forsyth (9th ed., Oxford, 2004), 300–1.

Ahsan[133] and *R. v. Secretary of State for Home Affairs, ex parte Khawaja*.[134] But in *Ahsan's* case the High Court deliberately distinguished the initial burden of identifying a defect, which it held was on the applicant,[135] and the situation 'after a challenge to the validity of the order [in which] it will be for the executive at the end of the day to negative that challenge',[136] while in *Khawaja*[137] Lord Scarman said that 'whatever the process the party seeking relief carries the initial burden of showing he has a case fit to be considered by the court' (a statement hardly supportive of the editors' contention).

The ultimate burden and standard of proof; issues of evidential sufficiency on de novo *review*

Assuming that the applicant ordinarily carries the initial burden of proof, the second question, the issue of the standard of proof, then arises. The authorities fall into two groups: in the first group are cases where it is said that the complainant is required to establish the existence of the alleged illegality on the balance of probabilities. In the second category are cases in which it has been held that the gaoler is required to contradict the complainant's case on the balance of probabilities, or to a high probability, or even beyond reasonable doubt. It is the ground of complaint, and the nature of the investigation which the court is allowed conduct, which usually determines into which category a case is placed. In cases where the enquiry is concerned with the evidential basis of the detention, and where the High Court is competent to conduct a full evidential appraisal of the findings upon which detention is predicated, the detainer will generally be required to establish the case on at least the balance of probabilities. But where the ground of challenge is extrinsic to the evidential sufficiency of the finding (for instance, breach of procedural or constitutional requirements), or where the ground of challenge is to evidential sufficiency, and

---

[133] [1969] 2 QB 222.
[134] [1984] 1 AC 74.
[135] [1969] 2 QB 222, 234; the Court expressly approved the dictum of Gordon LJ in *R. v. Secretary of State, ex p. Greene* [1942] 1 KB 87, 113: 'In my opinion, when once it is shown that he is detained under a warrant or order which the executive has power to make, it is for the applicant for the writ to show that the necessary conditions for its making do not exist.'
[136] Ibid., p. 235.
[137] [1984] AC 74, 111.

where the habeas corpus court does not have jurisdiction to conduct *de novo* review, the position is much less settled.

Where the applicant disputes the evidential basis of the detention, and where (because, for instance, the condition precedent standard operates) the court also has jurisdiction to undertake a full evidential review,[138] the detaining party will usually carry the burden of contradicting the detainee's case to a high balance of probabilities, or beyond reasonable doubt. This standard of proof is a corollary of the statutory framework: if the legislation establishing the power of detention requires proof on a high standard of probability, or proof beyond reasonable doubt, and if, on habeas corpus, the court has power to conduct a full re-appraisal of the evidential foundation of detention, then it necessarily follows that the standard of proof on habeas corpus will equate to the statutory standard.[139] The proposition underlies the approach taken to the burden of proof in *R. v. Governor of Brixton Prison, ex parte Ahsan*.[140] Under the Commonwealth Immigrants Act, 1962 the power of removal could only be activated where an immigrant had been detained within twenty-four hours of landing in the United Kingdom. The applicants argued that they had arrived clandestinely at Dover three days before their presence had been detected, with the result that they had not been apprehended within the statutory period of twenty-four hours. Parker CJ held that the fact of the applicants having arrived within twenty four hours was a condition precedent to the exercise of the power of detention; that, being a factual condition precedent, the court had full power to review compliance with this condition; and that in conducting this review the Governor carried the burden of establishing the reliability of the finding on a beyond reasonable doubt standard.[141]

In *R. v. Secretary for State, ex parte Khawaja*[142] the House of Lords

---

[138] See pp 41–4.
[139] *R. (H) v. N & E London Mental Health Tribunal* [2002] QB 1.
[140] [1969] 2 QB 222, 230.
[141] Ibid., p. 230. Parker CJ concluded: 'Has the respondent, through the immigration officers and the police, satisfied me that the applicants could not have been here more than 24 hours? I, for my part, could not find beyond doubt, because this would, I think, be the standard of proof, that they had been here for less than 24 hours. True, they had told somewhat differing stories, and two are said to have confessed but with the language difficulties involved, and the known propensities of men such as these to say whatever they think will suit their case, I could not be sure that they had been here for less than 24 hours.'
[142] [1984] AC 74.

refined somewhat the assertion in *Ahsan* that the standard, where the court is competent to conduct review of evidential findings, is always proof beyond reasonable doubt. The standard of proof required, it said, to exercise a power of detention was proof to a high standard of probability, with the degree of probability required proportionate to the nature and gravity of the issue. It followed that where a court on habeas corpus was competent to review the quality of the evidence that the authorities would carry a similar burden:[143]

> I would adopt as appropriate to cases of restraint put by the executive upon the liberty of the individual the civil standard flexibly applied in the way set forth in the cases cited ... The reviewing court will therefore require to be satisfied that the facts which are required for the justification of the restraint have been put upon liberty do exist. The flexibility of the civil standard suffices to ensure that the court will require the high degree of probability which is appropriate to what is at stake. '... the nature and gravity of an issue necessarily determines the manner of attaining reasonable satisfaction of the truth of the issue'; Dixon J in *Wright v. Wright* (1948) 77 CLR 191, 210. I would therefore adopt the civil standard flexibly applied in the way described.

Lord Scarman's speech appears to treat the 'balance of probabilities flexibly applied' as a general principle of law, establishing a standard to be applied in all cases in which the court on habeas corpus conducts a full factual reappraisal of the findings. But this may be over-rigid. The function of a court conducting a *de novo* review is to reassess for itself whether the statutory findings have been determined; this process necessarily involves re-determination in accordance with the conditions prescribed by the legislation. A court conducting habeas corpus review cannot ask for proof to a degree higher, or lower, than that required by the legislation being applied. It does not, therefore, follow that the standard in every case is proof to a high degree of probability. What counts is the standard of proof required by the legislative code under scrutiny. Where the legislation

---

[143] Ibid., pp 113–14, per Lord Scarman. Lord Scarman's approach was adopted by the Supreme Court in *Georgopoulus v. Beaumont Hospital Board* [1998] 3 IR 132, 149–50.

requires that the detaining institution be satisfied beyond all reasonable doubt, or to a high standard of probabilities, then the standard of proof on habeas corpus *de novo* review is proof beyond all reasonable doubt, or proof to a high degree of probability; where, on the other hand, legislation authorizes detention on a mere balance of probabilities then a court exercising *de novo* review is only required to re-examine the correctness of the findings on the balance of probabilities. The standard of proof on a habeas corpus re-examination is not a general, fixed standard, but an incident of the statutory framework.

The ultimate burden and standard of proof; extrinsic defects

Where, on the other hand, the ground of complaint is independent of the evidential sufficiency of the determination, or where it relates to the issue of evidential sufficiency, but the court has no jurisdiction to conduct a full factual reappraisal, the case law divides. One line of authority holds that the detainee must establish the alleged defect on the balance of probabilities. Another line holds that the predominant burden of proof lies upon the gaoler. *The State (Harrington) v. Garda Commissioner*[144] is representative of the first category. Here the applicant sought release on the ground that he had been assaulted while in police custody. He presented evidence that the interrogating Gardaí had punched him and pulled out a portion of his hair. The Gardaí produced evidence in rebuttal. Finlay P found the evidence to be evenly suspended. But since, he held, the burden rested upon the detainee to prove his case on the balance of probabilities, he dismissed the complaint:[145]

> My function is to decide as to whether on all this evidence I am satisfied as a matter of probability that the prosecutor was assaulted while in detention in Fitzgibbon Street Garda Station. If he was assaulted that would in law constitute an illegal act making his entire detention unlawful and entitling him to be released from that detention. Viewing all the evidence however given on this issue as it was presented before me I am not satisfied that the prosecutor was assaulted in Fitzgibbon Street Garda Station. In so far as his applica-

[144] High Court, 14 Dec. 1976.   [145] Ibid., p. 10.

tion therefore is based on this allegation I must find his detention to be lawful.

Harrington's case was followed by the High Court of Northern Ireland in *Re Gillen's Application*[146] a case also involving allegations of assault committed in police custody. Hutton J distinguished cases where the court was competent to fully assess the statutory findings (where the court would have to be satisfied to the extent required by the legislation) from cases (such as the case at hand) where the ground of challenge was extrinsic to the statutory findings:[147]

> Where the issue before the court on an application for habeas corpus is whether an order has been validly made and the applicant claims that a condition precedent to the making of an order has not been satisfied, the onus rests on the respondent to negative the challenge and to prove that the condition precedent has not been performed, and if the respondent fails to discharge that onus, the applicant will be released (see *R. v. Governor of Brixton Prison, ex parte Ahsan* [1969] 2 QB 222). But where it is not in dispute that the detention was initially lawful and the applicant claims that the detention has become unlawful because he has been assaulted, then we consider, as held by Finlay P in *Harrington's* case, that the onus rests on the applicant to prove on the balance of probabilities that the assaults took place.

The judgment of the Supreme Court in *Russell v. Fanning*[148] also falls within the collection of cases in which the burden of proof of an extrinsic defect was imposed on the complainant. Here the complainant claimed, in attempting to resist extradition, that he would, if returned, be subjected to ill-treatment and assault at the hands of prison officers. Again the location of the burden of proof was decisive. The application failed because the complainant failed to reach the minimal standard of proof, proof on the balance of probability.

On the other hand, there is a line of cases stretching back to the 1920s holding that the ultimate burden, or the burden of adducing the preponderance of proof, rests upon the respondent. In *R. (O'Brien) v. Military Governor of North Dublin Union Internment Camp*[149] Molony CJ held that it was for the authorities to establish that there existed a 'state of war or

---

[146] [1988] NI 40. [147] Ibid., p. 54. [148] [1988] IR 505. [149] [1924] 1 IR 32, 38.

armed rebellion' within the terms of the derogation in Article 6 of the Constitution of the Irish Free State:[150] 'In the circumstances it is clear that Mrs O'Brien is entitled to a writ of habeas corpus unless a state of war or armed rebellion exists in Dublin, and the onus of establishing this clearly rests with the person who seeks to justify the detention.' In *Finucane v. McMahon*[151] the applicant claimed that if extradited to Northern Ireland he would suffer retaliatory beatings by members of the prison service. The Supreme Court, in direct contrast to the 'reasonable likelihood' standard applied in *Russell v. Fanning*, held that it was sufficient that the applicant merely establish a 'real danger' or a 'real possibility' that he would be subject to inhuman or degrading treatment. A corollary of the proposition that the complainant was merely required to establish a real possibility was, of course, that the authorities carried the burden of disproving this real possibility, i.e. of proving to a very high degree of probability that the order did not threaten the constitutional rights of the applicant.

Again, in *The State (Trimbole) v. Governor of Mountjoy Prison*[152] where the complainant alleged that his initial arrest under section 30 of the Offences Against the State Act, 1939 had been motivated by an improper purpose (the intention to have the complainant *in situ* while an extradition treaty was being negotiated with Australia) it was held that the burden fell upon the respondent to displace the case made by the applicant. That ultimate burden not having been discharged, the applicant's release was ordered. The Supreme Court in *Trimbole*, in support of its view that the ultimate burden lay on the custodian, referred to the proviso in Article 40.4.2, requiring release 'unless satisfied that the detention is in accordance with the law.' But it is difficult to see how this advances the argument that the burden is imposed on the custodian. The ordinary meaning of the proviso appears to be that the only ground upon which release may be refused is that the detention is lawful; the effect is that release may not be refused on any ground extraneous to the issue of legality (such as the behaviour of the complainant). The proviso is not concerned with the allocation of the burden of proof.

---

[150] The proviso to Article 6 had provided: 'Provided, however, that nothing in this Article contained shall be invoked to prohibit control or interfere with any act of the military force of the Irish Free State (Saorstát Eireann) during the existence of a state of war or armed rebellion.'

[151] [1990] 1 IR 165.   [152] [1985] IR 550, 577.

Hearsay

Hearsay evidence is, as a general principle, inadmissible on an Article 40.4.2 enquiry (although the prohibition may not be so strict on the initial application for an enquiry).[153] In *The State (Magee) v. O'Rourke*[154] the Supreme Court refused to admit (in rebuttal of the applicant's allegation that he would, if extradited, be liable to be prosecuted for a political offence) copies of correspondence between senior officers in Ireland and Northern Ireland, who were not witnesses in the Article 40.4.2 enquiry. The evidence was hearsay and the High Court, it was held, was quite correct to refuse to admit it. On the other hand, there is an inherent discretion to disapply the strict rule in circumstances in which an inflexible application might produce an injustice. The two principal determinants regulating the admissibility of such evidence appear to be the reliability of the evidence, and the risk of an injustice being produced by its exclusion. In *R.(O'Brien) v. Military Governor of North Dublin Union Internment Camp*[155] the prisoner's internment was predicated upon the existence of a 'state of war or armed rebellion,' circumstances which, under Article 6 of the Constitution of the Irish Free State, permitted the executive to exercise detention without reference to ordinary criminal procedure. The Court of Appeal permitted both sides to furnish hearsay evidence, mostly newspaper accounts of statements made by protagonists on both sides of the civil war, and accounts of statements printed in the *Dáil Debates*. Molony CJ, in admitting the evidence, referred to the court's entitlement to flexibly apply the hearsay rule in habeas corpus: 'We regard with great doubt the admissibility of some of the exhibits and statements referred to; but as this is a case affecting the liberty of the subject we thought it better to give every latitude to both sides regarding the evidence, whether by affidavit or exhibit that they desired to lay before the court.' The detainer as well as the detainee may be entitled to the benefit of this flexibility. In *R. v. Secretary for State, ex parte Rahman*[156] the Home Office sought to prove that the applicant had fraudulently entered the United Kingdom by introducing statements collected by entry clearance officers from villagers in

---

[153] In *DPP v. Early* [1998] 3 IR 158, 161, McGuinness J said: 'whereas hearsay is permissible to an extent in an affidavit for the purpose of an *ex parte* application for leave to issue judicial review proceedings, it is contrary to the provisions of the Superior Court Rules in the case of affidavits to be used in a plenary hearing.'

[154] [1971] IR 205.   [155] [1924] 1 IR 32.   [156] [1996] 4 All ER 945.

Bangladesh. Since it would have been impractical to produce the villagers as witnesses in London, the Queen's Bench Division and the Court of Appeal held that the necessity principle applied, and, subject to the power to regulate the weight to be attached to the evidence, the material (though hearsay) was admissible. The costs to the public interest in not having such evidence available exceeded any prejudice to the interest of the applicant, which could be accommodated by the court monitoring the reliability of that evidence.[157]

THE RELATIONSHIP BETWEEN CERTIORARI AND HABEAS CORPUS

Currently there appear to be three categories of case in which a challenge to the legality of detention must be prosecuted by means of an application for certiorari instead of by an application under Article 40.4.2: (i) where the complaint involves factual allegations directed against a party other than the immediate detainer – the principle in *McSorley v. Governor of Mountjoy Prison*;[158] (ii) where statute requires that a challenge to the order on which the detention is predicated be processed through judicial review; and (iii) (according to a line developed by the English Court of Appeal) where the ground of challenge is directed to the prior underlying administrative decision on which detention is based.

Where the complaint implicates parties other than the detainer: the principle in McSorley v. Governor of Mountjoy Prison

In *McSorley v. Governor of Mountjoy Prison* the Supreme Court held that Article 40.4.2, was inappropriate, and that instead judicial review was the proper remedy, where the complaint implicated the conduct of some party other than the actual detainer. Thus, the High Court was held to have been in error in processing under Article 40.4.2 (as opposed to judicial review) a complaint of breach of fair procedures allegedly committed by the trial

---

[157] In the analogous context of pre-trial bail, the Supreme Court in *The People (DPP) v. McGinley* [1998] 2 IR 408 held that statements by persons who were too intimidated to present evidence *viva voce* might, subject to the court's power to assess the weight to be attached to such evidence, be admissible.

[158] [1997] 2 IR 258.

judge in the course of a District Court prosecution. Two considerations underlay the Supreme Court's preference for judicial review over Article 40.4.2: (i) the principal reason appears to have been a concern that fair procedures could only be accomplished by judicial review, since Article 40.4.2 did not facilitate representation by parties other than the immediate detainer; (ii) the second, subsidiary, ground was that in the event of the application succeeding, the ancillary order of remittal could only be ordered on judicial review, and that there was no jurisdiction to order remittal on Article 40.4.2. O'Flaherty J said:[159]

> the District Judge should have been given an opportunity of offering his observations, especially in a case in which some of the suggestions of what took place contained in Mr McSorley's affidavit were dubious to say the least, and were so found by the learned High Court judge. It might have been that the District Judge would have concurred in what was alleged and might have nothing to offer. On the other hand, he might have had pertinent observations to make. So, I conclude that in the circumstances of a case such as this where the District Judge's conduct is called into question the correct course for the learned High Court judge to have followed would have been to give leave to apply for judicial review in such manner that the District Judge and the Director of Public Prosecutions could have been given an opportunity to make their observations. He could, of course, have stipulated that the matter should proceed with the same degree of expedition, or nearly so, as an enquiry under Article 40 but, that way, both the requirements of making sure that no one was in unlawful detention, on the one hand, and preserving the rights of other parties would be preserved. It should be said, too, that if the matter had proceeded by way of judicial review, the judge of trial would bring his discretion to bear on whether the provisions of r. 26 (4) of O. 84 of the Rules of the Superior Courts, 1986, should be invoked.

The ultimate effect of the *McSorley* principle, if pushed to its logical conclusion, would be to virtually displace entirely the use of Article 40.4.2. The overwhelming preponderance of challenges on Article 40.4.2 concern allegations of legal error by some party other than the immediate custo-

---

[159] Ibid., pp 262–3.

dian, so that if applied rigorously, the *McSorley* rule would entirely marginalize Article 40.4.2. The effect of this, if it were to occur, would be to frustrate what may be assumed to have been the framers' primary intention: that Article 40.4.2 provide an effective, accessible remedy in all cases of unlawful detention. Article 40.4.2 would hardly ever be accessible if the *McSorley* principle was enforced thoroughly. The premise of the *McSorley* argument, that Article 40.4.2 denies proper representation to parties other than the detainer, derives from the requirement in Article 40.4.2 that only 'the person in whose custody the complainant is detained be given an opportunity of justifying the detention.' But 'opportunity of justifying detention' requires, presumably, an effective opportunity; and an effective opportunity must include the right of participation by the party who is actually responsible and best able to defend the legality of the detention.[160] It is not disputed that Article 40.4.2 is modeled on the common law remedy of habeas corpus. But the rule at common law was that notice of the application had to be served on the relevant responsible parties, as well as on the detainer.[161] The constitutional right to fair procedures and the procedure under Article 40.4.2 are not mutually irreconcilable.

Where legislation requires that detainees challenge underlying administrative decision by way of judicial review: Re Article 26 and the Illegal Immigrants (Trafficking) Bill, 1999[162]

Section 5(1) of the Illegal Immigrants (Trafficking) Act, 2000 prohibits a person from challenging by any means other than by way of an application for judicial review the legality of *inter alia* an order of refusal of leave to land, or of deportation.[163] The result is that a person detained in conse-

---

[160] *Re Maguire* [1996] 3 IR 1, 6.
[161] So the Irish Queen's Bench in the first half of the nineteenth century insisted that, where habeas corpus was issued on behalf of a prisoner convicted in summary criminal proceedings, notice of the day on which the prisoner was due to be produced should be given to the Attorney General: *R. v. Feeny* (1843) 5 ILR 437.
[162] [2000] 2 IR 360.
[163] S. 5(1) of the Illegal Immigrants (Trafficking) Act, 2000 (as amended by s. 10 of the Immigration Act, 2003 and s. 16 of the Immigration Act, 2004) provides:

> A person shall not question the validity of
>
> (a) a notification under section 3(3) (a) of the Immigration Act, 1999,
> (b) a notification under section 3(3)(b)(ii) of the Immigration Act, 1999,

quence of an order of refusal of leave to land, or of a deportation order, cannot, as he or she previously could, challenge the legality of the order underlying that detention by means of an application under Article 40.4.2; any such challenge must, instead, be taken by means of an application for judicial review. In *Re Article 26 and the Illegal Immigrants (Trafficking) Bill, 1999* the Supreme Court rejected the argument that section 5(1) amounted to an unconstitutional abridgement of the right to challenge the legality of detention by means of an application under Article 40.4.2. The Court held that section 5(1) did not abridge the individual's rights under Article 40.4.2 since a complainant could still proceed by means of the binary procedure of judicial review with habeas corpus in aid. The Court

- (c) a deportation order under section 3(1) of the Immigration Act, 1999,
- (d) a refusal under Article 5 of the Aliens 1946 (S.R. and O. No. 395 of 1946),
- (dd) a refusal under section 4 of the Immigration Act, 2004,
- (e) an exclusion order under section 4 of the Immigration Act, 1999,
- (f) a decision by or on behalf of the Minister to refuse an application for refugee status or a recommendation of an Appeal Authority referred to in paragraph 13 of the document entitled "Procedures for Processing Asylum Claims in Ireland" which, as amended, was laid by the Minister for Justice, Equality and Law Reform before the Houses of the Oireachtas in March 1998,
- (g) a recommendation under section 12 (as amended by section 11(1)(h) of the Immigration Act, 1999) of the Refugee Act, 1996,
- (h) a recommendation of the Refugee Applications Commissioner under section 13 (as amended by section 11(1)(i) of the Immigration Act, 1999) of the Refugee Act, 1996,
- (i) a decision of the Refugee Appeals Tribunal under section 16 (as amended by section 11(1)(k) of the Immigration Act, 1999) of the Refugee Act, 1996,
- (j) a determination of the Commissioner or a decision of the Refugee Appeals Tribunal under section 22 (as amended by section 11(1)(p) of the Immigration Act, 1999) of the Refugee Act, 1996,
- (k) a refusal under section 17 (as amended by section 11(1)(l) of the Immigration Act, 1999) of the Refugee Act, 1996,
- (l) a determination of an officer appointed under section 22(4)(a) of the Refugee Act, 1996,
- (m) a decision of an officer appointed under section 22(4)(b) of the Refugee Act, 1996, or
- (n) a decision under section 21 (as amended by section 11(1)(o) of the Immigration Act, 1999) of the Refugee Act, 1996,

otherwise than by way of an application for judicial review under Order 84 of the Rules of the Superior Courts (S.I. No. 15 of 1986).

held that the substance of the Article 40.4.2 right, to have the legality of the detention examined, and to release if that detention was not in accordance with the law, was not compromised by a requirement to challenge the underlying administrative order by means of an application for judicial review. It could equally be discharged through an enquiry into the detention conducted on judicial review, with Article 40.4.2 functioning as a purely consequential remedy, activated if the detention was found to be unlawful on the judicial review application:[164]

> Nothing in the section can be interpreted as restricting the right of any person to bring proceedings pursuant to Article 40.4.2 of the Constitution. The only question is whether the validity of the deportation order can be determined by the courts in a manner consistent with that Article. The validity of the deportation order may be challenged in judicial review proceedings and the issue determined before any question arising of the person being detained. As already stated, the legitimate object of the provision is to ensure that challenges to the validity of the relevant decisions and other matters are brought promptly. In proceedings brought pursuant to Article 40.4.2 challenging the legality of a person's detention, that detention may be justified by reason of the existence of a deportation order. The fact that the deportation order has previously been unsuccessfully challenged in judicial review, or had not been challenged at all within the time permitted by s. 5, may be sufficient to constitute the deportation order as a lawful basis for that person's detention.

Arguably, however, Article 40.4.2 rights are compromised. Article 40.4.2 can be viewed as composed of a collection of procedural rights. A number of these rights can be identified as being infringed by the statutory requirement to proceed by way of judicial review. (i) Under Article 40.4.2 the High Court is obliged to conduct an enquiry where the applicant establishes an arguable case (or according to a rival formula, raises sufficient doubt as to the legality of the order).[165] However in immigration cases an application for judicial review is, under the Rules of the Superior Courts, 1986 as modified by section 5(2) of the Illegal Immigrants (Trafficking)

---

[164] [2000] 2 IR 360, 398.
[165] See below, pp 134–5.

Act, 2000, only admissible where the High Court is satisfied that the application reaches a higher standard and raises 'substantial grounds.'[166] (ii) Under Article 40.4.2 the High Court is obliged to determine the initial application for an enquiry upon the material submitted by the complainant (or a person acting on his behalf) alone. Under the Illegal Immigrants (Trafficking) Act 2000 the individual loses the entitlement to an *ex parte* application; instead, the application must be on notice 'to the Minister [for Justice, Equality and Law Reform] and any other person specified for that purpose by order of the High Court.' (iii) There is no maximum time limit after which the right to submit an application under Article 40.4.2 expires. Section 5(2)(a) of the Illegal Immigrants Act 2000, on the other hand, interferes with the right of challenge at any time during the currency of detention, requiring that an application shall be made within the period of '14 days commencing on the date on which the person was notified of the decision ... unless the Court considers that there is good and sufficient reason for extending the period within which the application shall be made.' The Supreme Court did indicate that the High Court could, where detention was involved, exercise the jurisdiction to extend the time for applying for judicial review where an application was initiated after the expiry of the fourteen days' period. An applicant for habeas corpus, it said, 'would be entitled, concurrently with the habeas corpus proceedings, to apply for an extension of time within which to seek leave to apply for judicial review *on showing that there are good reasons for doing so*.' But the entitlement to an extension on the fourteen-day period is still subject to showing 'good and sufficient reason'; no equivalent burden is carried by an applicant on Article 40.4.2. (iv) There is an unqualified right to appeal a refusal of release on Article 40.4.2 to the Supreme Court. A detainee under the immigration code loses that unqualified right. Under section 5(3) of the 2000 Act the determination of the High Court of an application for judicial review is final, and no appeal lies to the Supreme Court unless the High Court certifies that its decision involves a point of law of exceptional public importance.

There are at least two constitutional problems with such section 5-type clauses. Firstly, by obliging the applicant to proceed by means of judicial

---

[166] S. 5(2)(b) provides that 'leave shall not be granted unless the High Court is satisfied that there are substantial grounds for contending that the decision, recommendation, refusal or order is invalid or ought to be quashed.'

review, the applicant is subjected to the procedures which regulate the application of judicial review. The effect of this is that the rule in *The State (Aherne) v. Cotter*[167] that Article 40.4.2 may not be regulated by statutory rules of procedure is indirectly avoided.[168] Secondly, the effect of clauses such as that in section 5 is to depreciate Article 40.4.2; the remedy plays no independent role, except the purely technical, consequential one of releasing a person whose detention has been found illegal on judicial review (and the same result would follow if no Article 40.4.2 application was initiated). There is no logical limit to the cases in which devices equivalent to those endorsed by the Supreme Court in *The Illegal Immigrants (Trafficking) Bill, 1999 Reference* might be used. In theory it might become a standard clause regulating every power of detention, with the ultimate effect that judicial review could gradually supersede Article 40.4.2 altogether. It is inconceivable that, when the decision was taken to institutionalize habeas corpus in the Constitution, it could have intended that the legislature would have the power to entirely displace Article 40.4.2 in this indirect way.

The Muboyayi *principle*

The general historical understanding has been that the scope of review on habeas corpus and certiorari evolved in a similar fashion from the early eighteenth century. In the case of certiorari the original rule determining the scope of review, a principle under which review was confined to review of the order alone, was supplemented by a later rule allowing the use of affidavits to prove extraneous jurisdictional defects not apparent on the record. A similar development occurred on habeas corpus. Originally on habeas corpus the court would only look at the return. Since the information contained on the return reproduced the data contained on the original court orders the scope of review on the two remedies was equivalent.[169] By

---

[167] [1982] IR 188.
[168] See pp 108–10.
[169] In *R. v. Riall* (1860) 11 ICLR 279, 290–1 Lefroy CJ denied that a writ of habeas corpus was essential to bring up an order of committal made by justices on the ground that the same documentation would necessarily be included on the return to habeas corpus as would be before the court on certiorari. Describing a writ of certiorari additional to a writ of habeas corpus as superfluous Lefroy CJ said: 'No such necessity [for certiorari] exists; indeed, it is not the proper course, according to the opinion of Lord Kenyon in the case of *R. v. Bowen* 5 TR 156

the early nineteenth century it came to be accepted in the English Court of King's Bench that a prisoner could bring to the attention of the court jurisdictional defects affecting the underlying order of detention but which were not apparent on the warrant. The facility to demonstrate extra-documentary jurisdictional defects was recognized as existing both on certiorari and habeas corpus.[170]

In 1992, in *R. v. Secretary for State for the Home Department, ex parte Muboyayi*[171] the previously uncontested understanding that habeas corpus and certiorari had followed the same evolutionary course was challenged. In *Muboyayi* the Court of Appeal propounded a description of the scope of review on habeas corpus which effectively denied that the remedy was capable of reviewing most categories of extra-documentary jurisdictional defects. The Court of Appeal held that on habeas corpus the court was restricted to two grounds: to reviewing errors patent on the face of the committal order, or allegations of the non-existence of a condition precedent to the original exercise of jurisdiction. The Court of Appeal sought to re-instate the original understanding of the remedy as concerned only with defects appearing *ex facie*:[172]

> While it is true that in dim and distant times a writ of habeas corpus used to be coupled with a writ of certiorari, but as time went on the issues arising in the context of certiorari were considered and decided upon the return of the writ of habeas corpus (see Sharpe, *The law of habeas corpus*, 2nd ed. (1989), at pp 5 and 44–5), this submission is not I think well founded. Habeas corpus was originally confined to errors of jurisdiction which were patent on the face of the committal order, certiorari being required to bring up the record on which it was based
>
> > ... in which he says that that, where an order of Sessions involves the liberty of the party, the proper mode of obtaining relief is, not to apply for a writ of certiorari to remove the order of sessions, for the purpose of quashing it, but for a writ "on a return to which the cause of commitment would be specified; and upon those the Court would be enabled to form an opinion whether or not those causes were sufficient to justify his detention." In that case [Lord Kenyon's] opinion clearly was that the proper course of proceeding was by writ of habeas corpus upon the return to which the several documents in the case would necessarily be before the court.'

[170] See the cases cited at fnn 176–9 below.
[171] [1992] 1 QB 244. The decision was followed in *R. v. Oldham JJ, ex p. Cawley* [1997] QB 1.
[172] Ibid., p. 257.

94   THE LAW OF HABEAS CORPUS IN IRELAND

with a view to quashing the committal if latent jurisdictional errors emerged.

It followed that there was no power to review by habeas corpus defects (other than the two exceptional categories) affecting the legality of the prior underlying administrative decision. The result was that the applicant, who was being detained in consequence of an order refusing leave to land, could not, on an application for habeas corpus, argue that the decision had been vitiated by a failure to take account of relevant considerations; such a complaint would engage the legality of the 'prior underlying administrative decision,' and this was not one of the accepted grounds of habeas corpus review.

The *Muboyayi* doctrine is an extraordinary attempt to reverse several hundred years of doctrinal evolution. The basic accuracy of the understanding of the law propounded in the *Muboyayi* decision has been strongly contested by academic commentators.[173] The Parliament of New Zealand has even enacted legislation to override the doctrine.[174] The assertion that there could on habeas corpus be no demonstration of jurisdictional defects occurring off the record appears to disregard the character of the remedy as it operated from the early nineteenth century onwards. Although stray statements could still be found as late as the 1880s that only matters appearing on the face of the warrant could be raised on habeas corpus[175] it had, by the end of the nineteenth century become

[173] The decision has been criticized in: H.W.R. Wade and C. Forsyth, *Administrative law* (9th ed., Oxford, 2004), 597–8; S. De Smith, H. Woolf and J. Jowell, *Judicial review of administrative action* (5th ed., London, 1995), 678–9; Law Commission, *Consultation paper no. 126: Judicial review and statutory appeals* (London, 1983), pp 48–50; H.W.R. Wade 'Habeas corpus and judicial review' (1997) 113 *Law Quarterly Review* 55.
[174] S. 14 (2) of New Zealand's Habeas Corpus Act, 2001 reverses the *Muboyayi* doctrine by providing that 'a judge dealing with an application must enquire into the matters of fact and law claimed to justify the detention and is not confined in that enquiry to the correction of jurisdictional errors'. This provision incorporates the recommendation of the Law Commission of New Zealand in its report *Habeas corpus procedure* (Report No 44, Wellington, 1997) that the *Muboyayi* doctrine be extinguished in that jurisdiction.
[175] The old view appears to underlie the following passage in *In re Keller* (1888) 22 LR Ir 158, 163 Morris CJ stated: 'The cause suggested in this case is that the warrant of committal is illegal. That subject alone can be heard before us, and we have only to see whether the committal was legal, and cannot enter into any question as to the propriety or legality of any proceedings other than so far as

accepted that affidavits could be used to show breach of jurisdiction occurring outside the record and affecting 'the prior underlying order.' In *Re Eggington*[176] the applicant was permitted to demonstrate by affidavit that he had been arrested on a Sunday contrary to the provisions of the Sunday Observance Act, 1677. Habeas corpus operated although the defect was one which did not appear on the warrant. In *Re Bailey*[177] the prisoner who had been convicted of unlawfully absenting himself from a contract of service was held entitled to show that the nature of the relationship was not one of service; again this review of an extraneous defect was allowed despite the fact that no certiorari had been taken out, and despite the fact that the error was not apparent on the record. Similar developments had occurred (though at a slightly later period) in Ireland. In *R. (Gallagher) v. Martin*[178] it was held that an applicant for habeas corpus (without certiorari) could show by affidavit that his conviction had occurred on a day which was not a valid petty sessions day. In *Re Sullivan*[179] Palles CB held that the capacity of habeas corpus to correct jurisdictional defects affecting the prior underlying order was exactly equivalent to that on certiorari:[180]

> they are embodied in the warrant of committal.' In *R. v. O'Brennan* (1854) 3 ICLR 589, 595 Lefroy CJ had stated: 'a party imprisoned is entitled to a certiorari to have the proceedings removed and that for obvious reasons. The return upon the habeas corpus would only set out the warrant of committal; and if on the face of that, his detention appeared to be legal he would have no remedy unless he was entitled to have the proceedings removed, for then only the court would have everything before them to decide whether they would properly exercise their jurisdiction in discharging him.' A similar understanding was expressed in *Re Ramsey* (1867) 1 *Irish Law Times & Solicitors' Journal* 622.

[176] (1853) 2 El & Bl 717; 118 ER 936.
[177] (1854) 3 El & Bl 607; 118 ER 1269. Further examples include *Re Blues* (1855) 5 El & Bl 291, 119 ER 490 and *In re Baker* (1857) 2 H & N 219, 157 ER 92.
[178] (1874) IR 8 CL 556. *In re Rea (No. 2)* (1879) 4 LR Ir 345 a majority (May CJ dissenting) appear to have considered that on habeas corpus (without a complementary certiorari) affidavits could be used to show that an order of imprisonment for contempt had been made in circumstances amounting to a beach of natural justice. In *Ex p. Clarke* (1890) 26 LR Ir 1 a prisoner on habeas corpus (without certiorari) was permitted to prove on affidavit that one of the Petty Sessions Justices who had convicted him had subsequently presided at the applicant's unsuccessful appeal to Dungannon Quarter Sessions.
[179] (1888) 22 LR Ir 98.
[180] Ibid., pp 110–11. In *The State (Burke) v. Lennon* [1940] IR 136, 157 Gavan Duffy J returned to Palles CB's judgment in *Re Sullivan* as authority for the proposition that 'it is well settled in this country that the absence of an application for certiorari does not affect the duty of the Court, with regard to habeas corpus when satisfied that the detention is not in accordance with the law'.

But the jurisdiction of this Court upon habeas corpus is clearly the same as that of the Queen's Bench in a case in which the latter court instead of issuing both habeas corpus and certiorari issued the former writ only ... A conviction under which a warrant of commitment is issued is examinable on habeas corpus to the same identical extent as on certiorari, viz. to ascertain whether in making the conviction, the justice acted outside his jurisdiction. The same result can also be arrived at from consideration that habeas corpus and certiorari are but separate remedies for what is substantially the one wrong – one of such remedies being directed to the void judgment, and the other to the execution under it.

But even if the *Muboyayi* principle, that habeas corpus is concerned only with the formal sufficiency of the return, is correct as a matter of common law, it can have no effect on Article 40.4.2. Article 40.4.2 operates whenever detention 'is not in accordance with the law,' and not just where there is a defect on the warrant, or a misevaluation of a jurisdictional fact.[181] The consultative case stated procedure in Article 40.4.3 is also difficult to reconcile with the *Muboyayi* theory of limited review. The case stated to the Supreme Court under Article 40.4.3 is activated when the High Court finds that the legislation upon which detention is predicated is 'invalid having regard to the provisions of the Constitution'. Article 40.4.3 necessarily assumes that Article 40.4.2 review applies to one species of ulterior defect (the constitutional invalidity of the underlying legislation). But it is highly improbable that the Constitution should admit review of one type of extraneous defect (the constitutional invalidity of the underlying legislation) while prohibiting review of other categories of jurisdictional defect.

---

[181] In *The State (Hully) v. Hynes* (1966) 100 ILTR 145, 163 Kingsmill Moore J noted: 'a very wide field of enquiry is open to the court on an application for habeas corpus and when the detention is by an act of the executive, the court can enquire into all of the circumstances. It is concerned not only to see that the documents are correct in form: it can investigate whether the necessary conditions exist to justify the execution of such documents, and can enquire whether they have been executed by mistake or whether their execution has been procured by fraud.'

Conversion of an application under Article 40.4.2 into an application for judicial review or alternative remedy

The Rules of the Superior Courts 1986 permit, on an application for judicial review, the High Court to grant any other of the public law remedies 'notwithstanding that it has not been specifically claimed.'[182] But there is no equivalent provision where the matter originally comes before the Court by way of an application under Article 40.4.2. The High Court has, on a number of occasions, terminated proceedings where the applicants were not entitled to redress under Article 40.4.2, but did have good grounds for the alternative remedy of judicial review.[183] In one case the High Court refused to accept an Article 40.4.2 complaint into the validity of a District Court conviction until an application for certiorari had been made, and remanded the prisoner until such an order had been obtained.[184] In *Cahill v. Governor of Military Detention Barracks, Curragh Camp*[185] the High Court held that where a prisoner complained of conditions of detention by means of an Article 40.4.2 application, and where (as is usually the case) the character of the allegation fell below the standard required to justify an Article 40.4.2 investigation, the applicant must re-institute proceedings for the alternative relief. The Court could not, it said, convert the Article 40.4.2 application into an application for the proper, alternative remedy. The severity of the rule by which alternative relief is withheld from a prisoner who wrongly proceeds by way of habeas corpus is well illustrated by *The State (Comerford) v. Governor of Mountjoy Prison*.[186] Here the complaint concerned what appears to have been a relatively serious breach of the Prison Rules: the applicant, who was a pre-trial remand prisoner, was being detained in a section of Mountjoy Prison known as 'the Base', a section of the prison set aside for convicted prisoners undergoing punitive or preventive detention. This was in clear breach of Rule 192 of the Rules for the Government of Prisons, 1947[187] which provided that prisoners awaiting trial should be kept apart from convicted prisoners.' The High Court held (i) that the complaint under Article 40.4.2 was inappropriate, and (ii) following *Cahill* the High Court

---

[182] O. 84, r. 19, RSC, 1986.
[183] *Cahill v. Governor of Curragh Military Detention Barracks* [1980] ILRM 191; *The State (Comerford) v. Governor of Mountjoy Prison* [1981] ILRM 86; *The State (Wilson) v. Windle, Irish Times*, 19 Aug. 1987.
[184] *The State (Wilson) v. Windle, Irish Times*, 19 Aug. 1987.
[185] [1980] ILRM 191.   [186] [1981] ILRM 86.   [187] S.R. & O. No. 320 of 1947.

did not have power on an Article 40.4.2 application to issue a mandamus requiring transfer to the remand wing. The application of the *Cahill* principle in this case was certainly rigorous. The prisoner was required to re-institute proceedings (it is unclear whether he ever did) and while waiting for those proceedings to be determined, to undergo a prison regime which, it was accepted, was unlawful.

However, subsequently both the High and Supreme Courts have exercised an inherent jurisdiction to convert a misdirected application for Article 40.4.2 into judicial review proceedings, and *vice versa*.[188] The English Court of Appeal has also exercised such an inherent jurisdiction.[189] More recently the High Court appears to have disregarded its earlier rule in *Cahill*. In *Nicholls v. Governor of Mountjoy Prison*[190] the complainant on an Article 40.4.2 application, a paraplegic, complained that the conditions of detention did not provide appropriate treatment for his condition, and, thereby infringed his right to bodily integrity. While the High Court dismissed the Article 40.4.2 application, it also (without requiring the complainant to institute judicial review proceedings) directed that the Governor give an undertaking that Nichols be provided with special facilities. Such a mandamus-type order would not, under *Cahill* have been appropriate without an independent, and subsequent, application for judicial review.

THE OPERATION OF DISCRETIONARY CONSIDERATIONS ON ARTICLE 40.4.2

The basis of the common law principle

In an opinion delivered to the House of Lords in the mid-eighteenth century Sir John Wilmot, then a judge of the Court of King's Bench, famously propounded the formula that habeas corpus was a writ of right, but not a writ of course.[191] The statement that habeas corpus was a 'writ of

---

[188] *The State (Aherne) v. Cotter* [1982] IR 188, 205; *Sheehan v. Reilly* [1993] 2 IR 81, 89; *Bolger v. Garda Commissioner*, High Court, 15 Dec. 1998.
[189] *R. v. Home Secretary, ex p. Muboyayi* [1992] 1 QB 244.
[190] *Irish Times*, 24 July 1998.
[191] *Notes of opinions and judgments delivered in different courts by the Right Honourable Sir John Eardley Wilmot, Knt.* (London, 1802), pp 77, 82. Wilmot was a justice

right' has, over the last two centuries, become the principal support for the proposition, now constantly rehearsed,[192] that habeas corpus is a non-discretionary remedy and that release cannot be withheld on grounds extraneous to the legality of the detention. In *Re Heaphy*[193] Palles CB distinguished the writ of certiorari which he accepted was 'in the discretion of the court' from habeas corpus which, he said, was not, 'for the writ of habeas corpus differs from certiorari, and is as of right.' The doctrine was repeated in *R. v. Governor of Pentonville, ex parte Azam*[194] where Denning MR said that 'if a man can make out a prima facie case ... he is entitled to a writ of habeas corpus of right ... the court has no discretion to refuse it.'

However, the conclusion that because habeas corpus is of right it is also non-discretionary does not necessarily follow. Wilmot's statement, which seems to be the principal authority for the proposition that habeas corpus is of right, has its immediate origin in a constitutional controversy arising out of a series of impressment cases in which the Court of King's Bench had refused to issue a writ of habeas corpus to impressed soldiers and sailors whose affidavits did not show that their detention was probably unlawful.[195] The practice on habeas corpus of requiring a prima facie case of illegality as a condition to intervention in impressment cases generated parliamentary protest, and led to a demand, subsequently taken up by William Pitt, for a further Liberty of the Subject Act which would require the issue of the writ merely on proof of detention and without a showing a prima facie case of illegality.[196] In 1758 the judges of the superior courts were summoned by the House of Lords to give their opinion as to whether 'writs of habeas corpus ad subjiciendum, by the law as it now stands, ought to issue of course, or upon probable cause verified by affidavit'[197] Justice Wilmot's response was that although never a writ of course habeas corpus

---

of the King's Bench 1756–1765, and Chief Justice of the Common Pleas, 1766–1771.

[192] *The law of habeas corpus*, 58–9; S. De Smith, H. Woolf and J. Jowell, *Judicial review of administrative action* (5th ed., London, 1995), p. 676.
[193] (1888) 22 LR Ir 500, 516. An earlier rehearsal of the principle may be found in *R. v. Riall* (1860) 11 ICLR 279, 291–2.
[194] [1973] 2 WLR 949, 961.
[195] W. Cobbett, *Parliamentary history of England* (London, 1813), xv, pp 871–926.
[196] M. Peters, *Pitt and popularity; the patriot minister and London opinion during the Seven Years' War* (Oxford, 1980), pp 108–13.
[197] W. Cobbett, *Parliamentary History of England* (London, 1813), xv, pp 898–9.

was a writ of right, by which he meant that it was not a remedy which issued without judicial scrutiny, but that it was a remedy which issued as a matter of entitlement upon probable cause that the detention was unlawful.[198] In the mid-eighteenth century the issue of a writ of habeas corpus merely initiated the enquiry by calling on the detainer to have the body; it was not an order of liberation. What Wilmot meant when he asserted that a writ of habeas corpus was 'of right' was that an enquiry would commence of right once probable cause was established. The statement was concerned with the initial application, and not with the ultimate decision to order release. The statement that habeas corpus was a writ of right does not, when read in the light of the historical context in which it was expressed, sustain the conclusion that habeas corpus is never discretionary.

Withholding release on extrinsic grounds under common law and under Article 40.4.2

Whether historically sound or not, the classification of habeas corpus as non-discretionary is now generally accepted. The rule, however, is not, even at common law, absolute. The unqualified assertion that the remedy is non-discretionary is difficult to reconcile with cases where the remedy has been withheld on the ground that the applicant has been guilty of abuse of process,[199] or where release has been denied on the ground that the public welfare, or the welfare of the prisoner, might be compromised by discharge.[200]

Literally, the text of Article 40.4.2 appears to suggest that circumstances extraneous to the issue of legality may never be used as grounds for denying release. The proviso to Article 40.4.2 ('unless satisfied that he is being detained in accordance with the law') limits the jurisdiction to refuse release to one ground only: cases where the High Court is satisfied that the detention is in accordance with the law. By implication, the release may not

---

[198] 'I am of opinion that in cases not within the Act of the 31 Car II. writs of habeas corpus ad subjiciendum, by the law as it now stands ought not to issue of course, but upon probable cause, verified by affidavit. A writ which issues upon a probable cause verified by affidavit is as much a writ of right, as a writ which issues of course.'

[199] *R. v. Governor of Pentonville Prison, ex p. Tarling* [1979] 1 WLR 1417; *R. v. Governor of Brixton Prison, ex p. Osman* [1992] 1 WLR 36.

[200] *Re Shuttleworth* (1846) 9 QB 651, 662; 115 ER 1423, 1428.

be refused on any extraneous ground. On a literal interpretation the Court is forbidden from taking into account matters other than the issue of the legality of the detention.

This raises the general problem as to whether the Article may only be read in a literal sense, or whether the literal provisions in Article 40.4.2 may be conditioned by competing constitutional interests. There certainly have been cases where the provisions of Article 40.4.2 have been given a rigidly literal interpretation.[201] But in as many, if not more, instances there has been adopted a more flexible approach, under which the strict text has been regarded as accessible to qualification in the interests of competing constitutional concerns. Thus, the literal right of any third party to make an application in behalf of another is now interpreted as a right restricted to a third party 'acting bona fide'.[202] The unrestricted right of a person who is detained to make a complaint may be withdrawn where the ground sought to be raised by the complainant is one which could have been submitted on an earlier occasion.[203] The requirement that the custodian produce the body, although literally mandatory, has been read as a purely enabling power[204] exercisable only where it is necessary for a proper judicial enquiry to be conducted.[205] Arguably, the same flexible approach should also be available so as to permit a more qualified interpretation of the apparently categorical direction in Article 40.4.2 to order release once a person is found to be undergoing illegal detention.

There is also a significant body of case law which can only be explained on the basis that the release on Article 40.4.2 is not determined solely by reference to the legality of the detention, and that release may be denied on extrinsic grounds. The overriding constitutional interest which is most usually invoked is the integrity of the administration of justice. Thus, the

---

[201] The literal approach underlies the interpretation (in cases such as *The State (Trimbole) v. Governor of Mountjoy Prison* [1985] IR 550, 567–8) of the right of release under Article 40.4.2 as an absolute entitlement, and the consequential refusal to recognize a jurisdiction to subject an order of release to a stay in the event of appeal.

[202] *Cahill v. Governor of Curragh Military Detention Barracks* [1980] ILRM 191, 201.

[203] *Re Thomas McDonagh*, High Court, 24 Nov. 1969; *Re Gallagher, Irish Times*, 26 July 1983; but contrast *Application of Michael Woods* [1970] IR 154.

[204] *The State (Woods) v. Kelly* [1969] IR 269; *The State (Rogers) v. Galvin* [1983] IR 249; *RT v. Director of Central Mental Hospital* [1995] 2 IR 65.

[205] *The State (Rogers) v. Galvin* [1983] IR 249.

Supreme Court has held that where a prisoner has not presented all available grounds of challenge in the one complaint, but has been guilty of unjustifiably staggering complaints over a succession of applications, an Article 40.4.2 enquiry may be dismissed.[206] The High Court has refused relief on Article 40.4.2 where the application is of a technical nature, particularly where the circumstances, such as a long delay in raising the complaint, suggest that there is something disingenuous about the character of the complaint.[207] The abuse of process rule was applied in *The State (Byrne) v. Frawley*[208] a case which involved a jurisdictional complaint of a higher order of seriousness to that line of cases in which jurisdiction has conventionally been applied, and misconduct of a lower level than is usually classified as abuse of process. Two days after the complainant had been arraigned before a jury empanelled in accordance with the Juries Act, 1927 the Supreme Court declared the 1927 Act unconstitutional.[209] Nonetheless the trial proceeded and the accused was convicted before such an unconstitutionally empanelled jury. The Supreme Court declined to proceed with a post-conviction Article 40.4.2 enquiry on the ground that since neither at the trial nor in his grounds of appeal to the Court of Criminal Appeal, nor on a subsequent appeal to the Supreme Court, had (presumably on the advice of his legal advisors)[210] the question of the constitutionality of the jury been raised. The prisoner's apparent acquiescence, it was held, had compromised his complaint. The Court, notwithstanding the relatively serious jurisdictional defect involved,[211] refused redress.

---

[206] *Re Gallagher*, Irish Times, 26 July 1983; *Re Thomas McDonagh*, High Court, 24 Nov. 1969. See pp 131–4.
[207] *In re MacCurtain* [1941] IR 83, 87; *The State (Bond) v. Governor of Mountjoy Gaol* (1964) 102 ILTR 93, 99, where the High Court held that it would be 'utterly absurd' that an accused person who had pleaded guilty to an offence could be released on habeas corpus on the ground of a pure irregularity in the proceedings taken against him.
[208] [1978] IR 326; See, also, *The State (Bond) v. Governor of Mountjoy Gaol* (1964) 102 ILTR 93, 99.
[209] *de Burca v. AG* [1976] IR 38.
[210] In *R. v. Governor of Brixton Prison, ex p. Osman* [1992] 1 WLR 36 the English High Court excused an alleged abuse of process on habeas corpus on the ground that the prisoner had followed an erroneous legal path on the recommendation of his legal advisors.
[211] In *R. v. Governor of Pentonville Prison, ex p. Tarling* [1979] 1 WLR 1417, 1423 it was stated that the abuse of process doctrine on habeas corpus was a flexible one

Finally, the unconditional obligation to discharge persons detained in breach of positive law may be avoided by an alternative device: the principle that circumstances of constitutional necessity may act as a justificatory defence to illegal detention; so justified the detention can be said to be 'in accordance with the law' and it follows that there is no need to rely on the discretionary jurisdiction to deny relief on Article 40.4.2. The defendant in *The People (DPP) v. Shaw*[212] had been one of the principal suspects in a case in which a young woman had recently been abducted, and was feared (although it was not certain) to be dead. Sensing that by continuing the defendant's detention past the point when the defendant ought either to have been released or taken before a District Judge, they might be able to locate, and possibly save the life of the victim, the Gardaí illegally detained her in excess of the period permitted by the Offences Against the State Act, 1939. The Supreme Court engaged in a speculative debate about what the proper response would be had an application under Article 40.4.2 been taken during the course of the defendant's detention. Walsh J, on the one hand, held that the interests of the victim could not qualify the rights of the complainant under Article 40.4.2 and so the High Court would have no alternative but to order the release of the applicant.[213] On the other hand, Griffin J (with whom the majority agreed) held that right to personal liberty was not an absolute one, but could be

and that the complainant's mishandling of the procedure may be overridden by the seriousness of the complaint.

[212] [1982] IR 1.
[213] 'To take the example which was considered by the trial judge, if an application for the release of the appellant at the time in question had been made to the High Court under Article 40 of the Constitution and the only justification which could be offered by the custodians, namely, the Garda Síochána, was their belief, albeit a reasonable one, that holding the appellant under continued arrest might lead to the saving of the life of Mary, the High Court would have no alternative but to order release of the appellant forthwith on the grounds that he was not being detained in accordance with the law. The custodians would not have been able to point to any law which justified the appellant's continued detention. If it were sought simply to justify it by showing a good motive, such as an effort or hope to save a life in so doing, the Court would have had to hold in accordance with Article 40.4, sub-s.2, of the Constitution, that such detention, however well intentioned, was not in accordance with the law-whether it be the law stated in the Constitution or the law in force by virtue of statute or common law. To do otherwise would be to disobey the mandatory express injunction of Article 40' (ibid., p. 41).

subordinated to the right to life of another. The effect of an overwhelmingly superior interest may, it was said, justify a deprivation of liberty, otherwise unlawful, and so render it a detention which is in accordance with the law for the purpose of Article 40.4.2.

CHAPTER THREE

Procedure on an Article 40.4.2 application

SOURCES OF HABEAS CORPUS LAW

The Habeas Corpus Act, 1782 as a source of habeas corpus

It is still sometimes assumed that the old Habeas Corpus Act of 1782 (21 & 22 Geo. III, c. 11) continues to function as a source of modern habeas corpus law: on at least two occasions[1] habeas corpus applications have been processed, not under Article 40.4.2, but under the Act of 1782, while in *The State (Aherne) v. Cotter*[2] Walsh J appeared to assume the continued existence of the 1782 Act when he stated that, while the Rules Committee had no jurisdiction to constrict by rules of court the process under Article 40.4.2, it was competent to regulate 'such provisions as are still operative of the Habeas Corpus Acts and the procedures thereunder,' implying that the old acts were still active. The Superior Courts Rules Committee, apparently in response to the view expressed by Walsh J that the Act of 1782 continued to operate, drew up a set of rules, Rules 2–12 of Order 84 of the Rules of the Superior Courts, 1986, intended to regulate applications under the 1782 Act.[3]

But the notion that the Act of 1782 could still act as a source of habeas corpus law is probably misconceived. The Act of 1782[4] prescribed (i) a general set of duties to be observed by persons served with writs of habeas corpus in criminal-related applications, and (ii) created a number of criminal procedural rights totally independent of habeas corpus. However, none of the general criminal procedural rights or duties created by the Act

---

[1] *Re Zwann* [1981] IR 395; *Bolger v. Garda Commissioner*, High Court, 15 Dec. 1998.
[2] [1982] IR 188, 200.
[3] O. 84, r. 3(a) provides that applications for habeas corpus shall be entitled 'in the matter of the Habeas Corpus Act, 1782.'
[4] See K. Costello, 'A constitutional antiquity? – The Habeas Corpus Act, 1782 revisited' (1988) 23 *Ir. Jurist* 240.

of 1782 are still in force.[5] Furthermore, that part of the Act which regulates habeas corpus procedure, section 1, also appears to have been superseded. Section 1 did not create an independent form of habeas corpus. Section 1 provides:

> That whenever any person or persons shall bring any habeas corpus directed to any sheriff or sheriffs, gaoler, minister, or other person whatsoever, for any person in his or their custody, and the said writ shall be served on the said officer or left at the gaol or prison with any of the under-officers, under-keepers or deputy of the said officers or keepers, that the said officer or officers, his or their under officers, under keepers, or deputies, shall within three days after the service thereof as aforesaid (unless the commitment aforesaid were for treason or felony, plainly and specially expressed in the warrant of commitment) upon payment or tender of the charges of bringing the said prisoner, to be ascertained by the judge or court that awarded the same, and endorsed upon the said writ, not exceeding six pence per mile ... make return of such writ, and bring or cause to be brought the body of the party so committed or restrained unto, or before the Lord Chancellor or Lord Keeper of the great seal of Ireland for the time being, or the judges or the barons of the said court from whence the said writ shall issue, or unto or before such other person and persons before whom the said writ is made returnable, according to the command thereof, and shall then likewise certify the true causes of his detainer or imprisonment, unless the commitment of the said party be in any place beyond the distance of twenty miles from the

---

[5] The two principal procedural rights created by the Act were the right created by s. 2 (which created a virtually automatic right to bail for persons committed for offences other than felony during vacation), and the right under s. 6 (which provided for persons committed for felony or treason a right to bail if not indicted within the first term following committal, and to complete discharge if not indicted and tried in the second term following indictment). However, s. 2 was repealed by the Third Schedule of the Criminal Law Act, 1997, while s. 6 is a casualty of the abolition of the distinction between felonies and misdemeanors: s. 6 of the 1782 Act was restricted to persons charged with a felony; however, s. 3(2) of the Criminal Law Act, 1997, provides that in all matters on which a distinction had previously been made between felonies and misdemeanors the law and practice applicable to a misdemeanor shall apply. Since the statutory right to bail or discharge on the passage of one or two terms, applied only to felonies and not to misdemeanors it follows that the s. 6 right has ceased to exist.

place or places where such court or person is or shall be residing, and if beyond the distance of twenty miles, and not above one hundred miles, then within the space of ten days, and if beyond the distance of one hundred miles then within the space of twenty days after such the delivery aforesaid, and not longer.

There are constitutional difficulties compromising the continued recognition in Irish law of the procedure under 21 & 22 Geo. III, c. 11. During the enactment of the English Habeas Corpus Act of 1679 (the English legislation of which the Irish Act is a virtual transcription) a series of procedures were inserted in the original bill which were designed to protect the authorities from abuse of the process;[6] these rights were retained in the Irish legislation of 1782. Custodians certainly have rights under Article 40.4.2, but they are far less elaborate than those required by 21 & 22 Geo. III, c. 11. Article 40.4.2 does not limit the time within which production may be required; section 1 of the legislation of 1782, on the other hand, concedes time periods of up to twenty days before production is required. It is not a condition of the custodian's obligation to produce the prisoner under Article 40.4.2 that he first have been furnished with his expenses; section 1, on the other hand, requires the payment of such charges or expenses.[7] The legislation of 1782 created a series of procedural rights which interfere with the detainee's rights of complaint under Article 40.4.2, and which must, accordingly, have been superseded by Article 40.4.2. It is difficult also to see how these offensive parts of section 1 could be severed from the rest of section 1, since to do so would alter the fundamental sense of the arrangement. It follows that the constitutionality of the entire of section 1 of 21 & 22 Geo. III, c. 11 would appear suspect.

The High Court has, on a number of occasions, made orders of habeas corpus 'under the Act of 1782.'[8] That description is not technically accurate. The Act of 1782 (21 & 22 Geo. III, c. 11) was not constitutive of an independent form of habeas corpus. Section 1 merely strengthened the manner in which judges could administer habeas corpus at common law. Following the enactment of the legislation a writ of habeas corpus did not issue 'under the Act of 1782.' It issued under common law as modified by

[6] A. Nutting, 'The most wholesome law – the Habeas Corpus Act of 1679', (1959–60) 65 *American Historical Journal* 527.
[7] *Re Scott* (1841) 2 Leg Rep 77.
[8] See fn. 1 above.

the Act of 1782. Further, the common law remedy was only partly regulated by the Act of 1782. Section 1 only operated in the case of persons 'in prison for any such criminal or supposed criminal matters.' Accordingly, even if the Constitution does tolerate the co-existence of the legislation of 1782 alongside the remedy under Article 40.4.2, it is only correct to refer to the Act of 1782 in the case of detainees under criminal process.

The power to regulate Article 40.4.2 by rules of court

The issue of the co-existence with Article 40.4.2 of the Rules of the Superior Courts 1986 has also been problematic. The current understanding is that the Superior Court Rules Committee has no power to elaborate by rules of court the application under Article 40.4.2. Since 1986 all rules relating to the procedure have been removed, and, according to one reading of a line of an argument pursued by the Supreme Court,[9] no future Rules Committee would have jurisdiction to put in place rules dealing with the procedure under Article 40.4.2.

The issue of the relationship between the two procedures was first considered by Lavery J in *Re Singer*:[10]

> The procedure by way of conditional order adopted has been that customary for many years, notwithstanding the provisions of Article 40(4)(2) of the Constitution as amended. It may be necessary to consider in some appropriate case whether the procedure prescribed by the Constitution should not be used in place of the old procedure by conditional order, cause shewn and motion to make absolute or to discharge the conditional order.

The main difficulty identified by Lavery J was the failure to align the procedure prescribed in the Rules with the procedure required under Article 40.4.2: the nineteenth century practice[11] of a conditional order followed by an order absolute upon which the body was to be produced and a formal return made, was not reincorporated in Article 40.4.2. There is, however, no suggestion in Lavery J's comments that he considered the

---

[9] *The State (Cotter) v. Aherne* [1982] IR 188, 200.
[10] (1960) 97 ILTR 130, 138–9.
[11] The practice of a conditional order of habeas corpus came to be applied in Ireland by the mid-nineteenth century: see, e.g., *R. v. Riall* (1860) 11 ICLR 279.

promulgation of rules of court constitutionally offensive *per se*. However, that more radical proposition was sanctioned by Walsh J (and seemingly by a majority of the Supreme Court)[12] in *The State (Aherne) v. Cotter*:[13]

> The application to challenge the legality of the deprivation of someone's personal liberty is enshrined as a constitutional right in respect of which the whole procedure is set out in the Constitution itself. It is outside the competence of any rule-making body to make any rules whatever to regulate this procedure. Indeed it is questionable, as it has previously been questioned, whether the method of a conditional order followed by the procedure of an order absolute is the appropriate procedure - however convenient it may appear to be. The rules of the Superior Courts which refer to habeas corpus do not refer to the Constitutional procedure but would refer to such provisions as are still operative of the Habeas Corpus Acts and the procedures thereunder.

The essential concern underlying the very doctrinaire approach of Walsh J in *Aherne's* case appears to be that if Article 40.4.2 were to be regulated by rules of court the rights given by Article 40.4.2 might be compromised, or distorted by those rules. This concept of the procedurally transcendent character of Article 40.4.2 has had the consequence that the Superior Court Rules Committee has, ever since, been careful not to promulgate any rules touching on Article 40.4.2. While Rules 2–12 of Order 84 of the Rules of the Superior Courts, 1986 prescribe the procedure for an application for an order of habeas corpus ad subjiciendum, it is expressly provided[14] that the expression 'order of habeas corpus does not include an order made pursuant to Article 40 section 4 of the Constitution.'

However, the *Aherne* approach is difficult to reconcile with the subsequent decision of the Supreme Court in *Re Article 26 and the Illegal Immigrants (Trafficking) Bill, 1999*[15] where the Court upheld the constitutionality of a statutory provision requiring that a challenge to immigration-

---

[12] O'Higgins CJ and Hederman J, though they did not address the issue, agreed with the judgment of Walsh J.
[13] [1982] IR 188, 200.
[14] O. 84, r. 1(2).
[15] [2000] 2 IR 360.

related detention be directed through an application for judicial review (with Article 40.4.2 playing the function of a purely consequential remedy activated only if the judicial review succeeds). The legislative object in requiring such an application to be processed through judicial review is precisely so that the application may be subjected to the statutory controls prescribed for judicial review (order 84 of the Rules of the Superior Courts 1986 as restricted further by section 5 of the Illegal Immigrants (Trafficking) Act, 2000). This leads to the somewhat anomalous result that, while there may be no direct regulation of Article 40.4.2, the legislature may specify that detention be challenged by means other than Article 40.4.2, such as judicial review, and can then subject that procedure to strict legislative regulation. What may not be done directly may be accomplished indirectly. The approval by the Supreme Court of the judicial review requirement in *Re Article 26 and the Illegal Immigrants (Trafficking) Bill, 1999* provides the legislature with a simple, if indirect, means of avoiding the rule that Article 40.4.2 may not be circumscribed by procedural rules.

THE CONCEPT OF DETENTION

At common law the notion of detention or custody for the purpose of habeas corpus was made up of three strains: firstly, a state of actual, immediate detention; secondly, circumstances in which, although the detainee was not under immediate physical restraint, the detainer enjoyed the present means of enforcing detention. By the late eighteenth century there emerged a third category: habeas corpus was exercisable in a case where one person (although not actually detaining another) exercised continuous dominion or control over another. In the mid-twentieth century the Supreme Court of the United States extended the last category so as to encompass restraints upon mere autonomy as detention sufficient for the purpose of habeas corpus. While the first three categories are recognized as constituting detention for the purpose of Article 40.4.2, there must be considerable doubt as to whether the fourth species can be reconciled with the text of the Article.

Actual custody or the present means of enforcing it

In *Wales v. Whitney*[16] Miller J defined the extent of restraint necessary to make habeas corpus appropriate as being constituted either by a state of actual restraint or by another having the present means of enforcing such restraint:[17]

> Something more than moral restraint is necessary to make a case for habeas corpus. There must be actual confinement or the present means of enforcing it. The class of cases in which a sheriff or other officer, with a writ in his hands for the arrest of the person whom he is required to take into custody, to whom the person to be arrested submits without force being applied, comes within this definition. The officer has the authority to arrest and the power to enforce it. If the party named in the writ resists or attempts to resist, the officer can summon bystanders to his assistance, and may himself use personal violence. Here the force is imminent and the party is in presence of it.

The first of these categories, actual restraint, includes not just the total deprivation of means of egress, but also cases in which there is no reasonable means of egress: 'it is no answer to a writ of habeas corpus to say that there is a means of egress, if that means of egress is not reasonable.'[18] The question of reasonableness of egress for the purpose of amenability to habeas corpus was a central issue in *Victoria Council for Civil Liberties v. Minister for Immigration*.[19] The *MV Tampa*, a Norwegian vessel which had picked up 433 Afghani asylum seekers from a sinking boat, was refused entry to Australian territorial waters. In response to an application for habeas corpus taken on behalf of the crew and passengers, the respondents argued that habeas corpus was inappropriate: the rescuees could simply have turned away from Australian waters. North CJ found that the rescuees did not have a practical means of egress from the vessel, which was on the open seas; and the vessel did not have practical means of egress from Australian waters by reason of the peril of a voyage across open seas in an overcrowded vessel.[20]

---

[16] 114 US 564 (1885).
[17] Ibid., p. 571.
[18] Per Black CJ in *Victorian Council for Civil Liberties v. Minister for Immigration* [2002] 1 LRC 189, 259.
[19] [2002] 1 LRC 189.
[20] On the other hand, French J for the majority, although agreeing that a total

The alternative condition requires that the other party, although not exercising direct custody, have both the present means, and the definite intention[21] of enforcing detention. It is the application of the second condition of the definition that has caused the greatest difficulty. In *O'Shea v. Garda Commissioner*[22] the applicant, who had been injured following an exchange of fire with the Gardaí, was arrested and taken to Galway Regional Hospital where he was treated and maintained under a 24-hour watch. He was refused redress under Article 40.4.2 (and on a subsequent criminal appeal) on the ground that he had not been detained: 'In the present case there is a finding of fact that the applicant remained of his own volition and not from any restraint imposed by the Gardaí. The fact that he was aware that when he left hospital he would be arrested does not affect the Court's finding that he was not in custody.'[23] But, according to the 'present means of enforcing detention' test, the fact that the applicant knew that he would be arrested on leaving hospital is very much in point. It is not a necessary condition of detention that the individual have actually been frustrated in attempting to exercise egress; it is enough that, without egress actually being blocked, the other party has the intention and 'the present means of enforcing custody' should the detainee attempt to break bounds. By contrast with *O'Shea*, in *The State (Rogers) v. Galvin*,[24] also a case where an injured suspect was under constant Garda supervision while in hospital, evidence that the Gardaí intended to arrest the applicant once he tried to discharge himself was held to establish a state of detention. Hamilton J is reported as saying that the applicant was not free to leave when he wished to, and that he was, therefore, in custody. The prisoner, he said, was undergoing detention, for although egress from the hospital was not barred, the evidence established that the Gardaí intended to arrest him if he attempted to leave.

The question of whether it is necessary that the bar on movement operate within a closely confined space or whether it is possible to chal-

---

restraint of movement is not essential for habeas corpus, held that the respondents were not responsible for the detention of the applicants: the fact that the vessel could not sail was not a restraint attributable to the respondents.

[21] *R. v. Bournewood Mental Health N.H.S. Trust, ex p. L* [1999] 1 AC 458.

[22] The habeas corpus application is reported in the *Irish Times*, 15 July 1980. The proceedings in the Court of Criminal Appeal are reported in 2 Frewen 57.

[23] (1981) 2 Frewen 57, 105.

[24] *Irish Times*, 20 Oct. 1980; the ruling was subsequently overturned by the Supreme Court on other grounds: [1983] IR 249.

lenge by means of habeas corpus a restriction on movement within a large geographical expanse has not yet been settled. In *Ex parte Mwenya*[25] the English Court of Appeal reserved to a further occasion the question of whether an order restraining an applicant within a space of 1,500 square miles constituted detention sufficient for habeas corpus. If, however, there was a rule that a condition of close custody was a necessary foundation of habeas corpus significant restrictions upon freedom of movement would be inaccessible to intervention by the remedy. The Chief Justice of the Federal Court of Australia instanced the problems of degree that might be caused were an application taken by a person held in a football stadium: arguably such a person might not be said to be under close custody, and, if a close custody rule applied, would be disqualified from habeas corpus.[26] However, in reality, the problem is something of a non-issue. The wider the geographical limits the less likely it is that there will be a state of immediate detention, or the means of enforcing such detention. The more diffuse the degree of restraint, the more effective will be the individual's means of egress and the more unlikely that there is a complete restraint of liberty. In *Wales v. Whitney*[27] the Supreme Court of the United States held that an order requiring the applicant not to leave the city of Washington did not constitute a detention sufficient to justify habeas corpus. There was no current actual custody. Nor, since there was no means of enforcing the detention, was there a state of conditional custody: 'If Dr Wales had chosen to disobey the order, he had nothing to do but to take the next or any subsequent train for the city and leave it.' Perhaps (since, as suggested earlier, it may be excessively restrictive to limit the application of the remedy to persons confined within a narrow geographical zone) the most satisfactory solution is to accept that there is no categorical prohibition on habeas corpus ever being available in the case of a person detained in a wide spatial zone. That does not necessarily involve a massive extension in the scope of the remedy. There will still only be a state of detention in the most exceptional case: where the person is so closely monitored, or where the means of apprehension are so effective, that the restriction on liberty is practically enforceable.

[25] [1959] 3 WLR 767.
[26] 'It was not suggested that detention for present purposes need be detention in a confined space ... a person might be unlawfully detained within a football field,' per Black CJ in *Victorian Council for Civil Liberties v. Minister for Immigration* [2002] 1 LRC 189, 257.
[27] 114 US 564, 572 (1885).

A state of actual or conditional detention is not affected either by the fact that on complying with some step the prisoner may obtain release. It has, on occasions, been suggested that an immigrant detained pending removal is not really being detained since he is free to return to his country of origin. In *R. v. Secretary of State for the Home Department, ex parte Phansopkar*[28] the English High Court rejected, on these jurisdictional grounds, an application by an immigrant family pending deportation:[29]

> Next there is an application for habeas corpus, the basis of which is of course that the lady and children are wrongly detained and entitled to be released by issue of that writ. But, as has been said more than once, this type of case is not really a habeas corpus case at all. This is not a case in which the lady's movements are restricted. She can leave the country at a moment's notice if she wants to.

Historically, however, habeas corpus has been operated in cases where the prisoner through compliance with some step, might have secured his liberty. The remedy has been invoked by persons committed for civil contempt, or for non-payment of debt[30] (who might have secured their liberty through compliance with the original judgment) and by persons committed in default of sureties (who, again, might have obtained their discharge through simply offering the required sureties).[31] The proposition in *Phansopkar* confuses the historical cause of the prisoner's detention with the legality of that detention. The historical cause of the prisoner's detention (the attempt to gain entry to another country) is irrelevant. What counts is the fact, and legality, of that detention. Habeas corpus is predicated upon the fact that the prisoner is being detained and a claim that that detention is unlawful; it is not a condition that the initial detention cannot be voluntarily cancelled.[32]

---

[28] [1975] 3 All ER 497.
[29] Ibid., p. 501.
[30] *In re Aikin* (1881) 8 LR Ir 50; *In re Keller* (1888) 22 LR Ir 158.
[31] *R. (Gregg) v. Kelly* (1841) 3 ILR 316.
[32] The proposition that an immigrant seeking entry is not being detained on grounds of the theoretical freedom to return has been rejected by the European Court of Human Rights (*Amuur v. France* (1996) 22 EHRR 533), and the Supreme Court of the United States (*Shaughnessy v. US* 345 US 206 (1953)).

Domiciliary control as a form of detention at common law

In *R. v. Johnson*[33] in 1724 the Court of King's Bench doubted whether it had jurisdiction to intervene by the writ of habeas corpus in a dispute as to who should exercise guardianship of a young child: the child, it noted, did not appear to be subject to actual imprisonment and on habeas corpus the Court could 'go no further than to see she was under no illegal restraint.'[34] However, by the seventeen-sixties the Court had begun to extend the limits of the remedy.[35] In *R. v. Delaval*[36] a habeas corpus application was taken by a father seeking the recovery of his daughter who had allegedly been 'apprenticed' to serve as mistress to a peer. The girl was more in a state of concubinage than actual imprisonment; yet Mansfield CJ, in handing the girl over to her father, decreed: 'let the girl be discharged from all illegal restraint' (a rule which suggests that the Court of King's Bench was applying a more relaxed interpretation of the concept of 'restraint' than that which it was applying three decades earlier). The concept underlying this extended definition appears to have been that of the exercise of continuous domiciliary dominion over another. The same principle was applied in a number of cases in the early nineteenth century where habeas corpus was taken by apprentices complaining that their request to be discharged from the relationship of apprenticeship was being unlawfully refused by their master.[37] In *R. v. Eden*[38] habeas corpus was granted to discharge a London apprentice indentured to a goldsmith, who complained that he was refused liberty to leave by his master, even though he had reached the age of 21 and was, consequently, past the age at which

---

[33] (1724) 1 Stra 579; 93 ER 711.
[34] When in *Ex p. Hopkins* (1732) 3 PWMS 152; 24 ER 1009 King LC mentioned *de homine replegiando* and habeas corpus as legal remedies for the recovery of a ward, the editor of the law reports series *Peere Williams* appendixed a rather sceptical annotation doubting the capacity of the writ, at that stage in its development, to function as a mechanism for guardianship disputes 'as to *homine replegiando* and habeas corpus (which last especially seems calculated only for the liberty of the subject) if the parties brought up thereon will acquaint the court that they are under no force, the court will let them go back to the places from where they came; or, if they appear to be under restraint, will set them at liberty, but not deliver them into the custody of another, nor in proceedings of that nature, determine private rights as the right of guardianship evidently is'.
[35] *R. v. Delaval* (1763) 1 Black 411, 96 ER 234; *R. v. Ward* (1762) 1 Black 386, 96 ER 218; *Elizabeth Warman's Case* (1778) 2 Black 1204, 96 ER 709.
[36] (1763) 1 Black 411, 96 ER 234.
[37] *R. v. Eden* (1813) 2 M & S 226, 105 ER 366. *The law of habeas corpus*, p. 170.
[38] (1813) 2 M & S 226; 105 ER 366.

he could be obliged to continue to serve; there was no evidence that he was in actual detention.

It is by reference to this wider interpretation of detention at common law that Article 40.4.2 has been used in cases involving irregular adoption orders,[39] inter-parental guardianship disputes,[40] or challenges to the legality of children's protective care orders.[41] However, Article 40.4.2 appears, on a number of grounds, unsuited for acting as a mechanism for the adjudication of child custody disputes. Article 40.4.2 is concerned with detention which is not in accordance with the law. Applications for the transfer of guardianship, on the other hand, do not usually challenge the legality of the current guardian's custody, but the suitability of that custody. In *Re Corcoran*[42] Murnaghan J said: 'the constitutional remedy of application by way of habeas corpus is designed to determine whether a person is detained in illegal custody ... The child cannot be said to be detained in illegal custody-the matter is in reality an unhappy difference between the parents as to the religious and other upbringing of the child.' Second, the remedial capacity of Article 40.4.2 is limited to one order only: a direction of unconditional discharge. Its use as a transfer of guardianship remedy is a distortion of the remedial character of Article 40.4.2. Third, the use of Article 40.4.2 denies the High Court procedural powers it would have if the statutory procedures were being used: the fact that Article 40.4.2 requires immediate release means that the High Court cannot impose a stay pending appeal to the Supreme Court; it also means that it may not, as it may upon an application under the Guardianship of Infants Act, 1964, require the person entrusted with guardianship to comply with some condition imposed by the court.[43] Section 23 of the Child Care Act, 1991 provides that a reviewing court may, if it finds a care order illegal, but

---

[39] *DG & MG v. An Bord Uachtála*, High Court, 23 May 1996; *Re Baby A* [2000] 1 IR 430 [2001] 1 IR 430.
[40] *Re Kindersley* [1944] IR 111.
[41] *MF v. Superintendent Ballymun Garda Station* [1991] 1 IR 189. Here a challenge to the legality of a place of safety order was pursued under Article 40.4.2. This was permitted despite the view of O'Flaherty J, delivering the judgment of the Supreme Court, that a place of safety order was not equivalent to detention.
[42] (1950) 86 ILTR 6, 12.
[43] The New Zealand legislature, in an attempt to prevent the by-passing of the guardianship acts by the use of habeas corpus in custody disputes, enacted (in s. 13 (2) of the Habeas Corpus Act, 2001) a provision to the effect that 'if the substantive issue in an application is the welfare of a person under the age of 16

also finds that the welfare of the child would be compromised by returning the child, make a new care order as if it were a court of original jurisdiction. One consequence of permitting the use of Article 40.4.2 is that these remedial powers may not be operated.

But however inappropriate Article 40.4.2 may be as a means of challenging the legality of guardianship issues, it is just arguable, and indeed there is authority to the effect, that the strain of habeas corpus at common law which treats domiciliary control as a form of detention subsists in Irish law concurrently with the Constitutional remedy. If this is so then this common law strain (rather than Article 40.4.2) may be used as a means of relieving a person from irregular constructive custody. A contention that the constitutional remedy had displaced the common law remedy was expressly rejected by Gavan Duffy P in *Re Kindersley*:[44]

> [counsel for the respondent] advanced the courageous argument that one baneful effect of the Constitution is to destroy the equitable jurisdiction in habeas corpus, so that we find ourselves back at the common law position before the reform of the seventies. I cannot so read the Constitution; nor do I regard Article 40.4.2 of the Constitution as governing the distinct jurisdiction of this Court in habeas corpus where the custody of infants is concerned and the Court's main preoccupation is their benefit. The duty imposed upon the Court by that Article is in my view irreconcilable with the duty of the Court exercising a delicate discretion in the best interests of young children.

Gavan Duffy P appears to be suggesting that common law guardianship habeas corpus and Article 40.4.2. co-exist. According to this view Article 40.4.2, with its more restricted conception of liberty, operates within a narrower space than the common law strain of habeas corpus, while the common law remedy continues to function outside those categories of detention subject to Article 40.4.2.

---

years, the High Court may, on its own initiative or at the request of a party to the proceedings, transfer the application to a Family Court'.

[44] [1944] IR 111, 119–20.

Restrictions upon personal autonomy as detention for the purpose of habeas corpus

The common law recognition of domiciliary control as detention for the purpose of habeas corpus cases has been built upon by the United States Supreme Court[45] as the justification for a view of detention for the purpose of habeas corpus, as extending beyond deprivation of liberty to encompass restraints on mere autonomy, such as those consequent on temporary release, or on bail,[46] or binding over, or community service orders. But the common law cases involving infants and apprentices do not necessarily justify such an attenuated notion of detention. Those cases are arguably merely an application of the principle that detention at common law included not just actual detention but also cases involving the present means of enforcing detention. In both cases, guardians over infants and masters over apprentices, the respondents were entitled to exercise physical restraint, and might have been expected to resist removal from their custody by physical means. Although not actually continuously detained, the subjects of these cases could be viewed as subject to immediate contingent detention. These authorities do not, therefore, necessarily support the proposition that the remedy was applicable for the relief of persons, not subject to immediate or contingent custody, from restraints upon personal autonomy in the broad sense.[47]

---

[45] *Jones v. Cunningham* 371 US 236 (1963); *Hensley v. Municipal Court San Jose Milpitas Judicial District* 411 US 345 (1973). There is an account of these United States developments in D. Clark & G. McCoy, *The most fundamental right: habeas corpus in the Commonwealth* (Oxford, 2000), pp 194–6.

[46] It is asserted in Clark & McCoy, *The most fundamental right: habeas corpus in the Commonwealth* that 'the balance of authority and the compulsion of principle now leans towards the view that persons on bail may apply for the writ of habeas corpus' (p. 214). But the authorities cited by Clark & McCoy in support of the proposition that habeas corpus is available to a person discharged on bail do not, in fact, support the conclusion: *R. v. Secretary of State for Home Affairs, ex p. O'Brien* [1923] 2 KB 361 (cited at p. 199) involved an applicant who was clearly in custody at the time of the application; *Re Amand* [1941] 2 KB 239 (cited at p. 202 for the proposition that habeas corpus may be granted to a person on bail) involved a case where bail was granted by Bow Street Police Court following the application for habeas corpus taken when the applicant was under arrest; see, *The Times*, 22 July 1942; in *Franic v. Wilson* [1993] 1 NZLR 318 (cited at p. 202) bail was granted by the court hearing the habeas corpus application; the applicant was in custody when the application was submitted.

[47] The strongest authority in favour of the extended version is *R. v. Board of Control, ex p. Rutty* [1956] 2 QB 109. The applicant had earlier been detained

There are also fairly strong grounds, both in the drafting history, and in the overall scheme of the remedy, against the legitimacy of such a wide notion of custody.[48] The evolution of the constitutional guarantee shows a narrowing in the meaning of 'liberty' for the purpose of Article 40.4.2. Article 6 of the Constitution of 1922 had provided that 'no person shall be deprived of his liberty save in accordance with the law.' The equivalent of Article 6 under the 1937 Constitution, Article 40.4.1, is tighter. Article 40.4.1. provides that 'no citizen shall be deprived of his *personal* liberty'. The imposition of restrictions on social freedom through bail conditions, or the withdrawal of a passport, might be regarded as restrictions upon 'liberty' in that broad sense, and might, possibly, have fallen within Article 6. However, the phrase 'personal liberty' in Article 40.4.2, with its suggestion of liberty of the physical person, appears more associated with physical liberty. Furthermore, if the expanded definition were correct it would follow that Article 40.4.3 (the mandatory case stated procedure which applies where the High Court finds invalid the legislation under which a person is detained) would extend to cases where legislation is found to unconstitutionally interfere with personal autonomy. However, Article 40.4.3 contemplates the grant of bail pending the resolution of the case stated to the Supreme Court. The fact that a positive restriction upon autonomy (such as bail) is itself an intermediary *remedy* under Article 40.4.3 is hardly consistent with a theory that Article 40.4.2 functions as a remedy for discharge from mere restrictions upon autonomy.

---

under an order under the Mental Deficiency Act, 1913. However, the habeas corpus application was taken at a point when Rutty had been granted a temporary release under a residential licence. The objection that the applicant was at liberty was, strangely, overlooked and the court issued the process notwithstanding the fact that the detainee was at liberty. The detainee was, of course, liable to have the licence revoked, and it may be that the court regarded the fact that the applicant's liberty was determinable as bringing the case within the 'present means of enforcing detention' limb of the definition of detention. The principal ground upon which the court appears to have been persuaded to grant habeas corpus was the argument of counsel for Rutty that the detention order, as a purely ministerial act, would not be susceptible to certiorari, and that unless habeas corpus was issued he would have no remedy: *The Times*, 22 Feb. 1956.

[48] In *Bolger v. Garda Commissioner*, High Court, 15 Dec. 1998, the Court refused to accept that the 'restriction on movement by virtue of the surrender of the passport constitute[d] detention for the purpose of an enquiry under Article 40.4.2 of the Constitution'.

HABEAS CORPUS AND INITIAL OR INTERVENING LIBERTY

Applicant at liberty at the time of the application; applicant released following initiation of the application

It has been suggested that the Article 40.4.2 process may exceptionally be available to a complainant who is at liberty during the application.[49] Three situations may be distinguished: cases where the applicant is at liberty when the application is submitted; cases when the applicant has been discharged by his or her custodian following the initiation of the application; and cases where the applicant has been discharged on bail by the High Court during the habeas corpus hearing.

The constitutional right is restricted to a complaint made in respect of an allegation that a person is being unlawfully 'detained', and, patently, excludes from the operation of the procedure cases where the applicant is at liberty when the initial application is submitted. The common law remedy was likewise not available to a person at liberty when the application was submitted. The only exception arose where statute deemed, as the extradition acts commonly did, a person at liberty on bail to be in custody for the purpose of habeas corpus.[50] There are no instances of applications by complainants then at liberty being processed under Article 40.4.2. In *Bolger v. Governor of Mountjoy Prison*[51] it was suggested that there might be 'exceptional circumstances' (which the High Court did not elaborate) where Article 40.4.2 might be available to a complainant who is at liberty

---

[49] *Bolger v. Governor of Mountjoy Prison*, High Court, 15 Dec. 1998.

[50] In *R. v. Spilsbury* [1898] 2 QB 615 the applicant having been committed to custody under the Fugitive Offenders Act, 1881 was released from detention on bail; he then applied for habeas corpus. It was held that the statutory scheme envisaged that the right to judicial review would be discharged only through an application for habeas corpus; and that that right would be frustrated if a person, after being committed, was then granted bail, and therefore unable to seek habeas corpus. Accordingly, a person released on bail was, in order to realize the legislative intention, to be regarded as constructively detained. See, also, *Jennings v. Government of the United States of America* [1983] 1 AC 624 and *Launder v Governor of Brixton Prison* [1998] 3 WLR 221. These cases were considered in *Bolger v. An Garda Commissioner*, High Court, 15 Dec. 1998.

[51] High Court, 15 Dec. 1998. O'Higgins J said 'it seems to me to be reasonable that an inquiry under Article 40 of the Constitution should be normally refused in circumstances where at the time of the application the applicant is on bail – though it is possible to envisage exceptional circumstances where this might not apply'.

at the time that the application is first submitted. The proposition that there might be such an exceptional jurisdiction is, nonetheless, very difficult to reconcile with the explicit requirement of detention in the text of Article 40.4.2.

The usual, though not invariable, response where an applicant following the initiation of Article 40.4.2 proceedings has been discharged, is that the High Court terminates the proceedings. Irish practice suggests that such intermediary discharge usually has this effect. In *R. (O'Sullivan) v. Military Governor of Hare Park Internment Park*[52] the applicant, who had sought habeas corpus on the ground that his imprisonment was in error by reason of mistaken identity, was released a day after notice of motion for the conditional order. The King's Bench Division of the Irish Free State High Court held that the only issue was costs and declined to make any order on the application for habeas corpus. The approach is typical of the traditional common law practice.[53] In a case in 1973[54] the applicant, a minor, had allegedly been illegally remanded in custody in Mountjoy Prison. Between the initiation and the determination of Article 40.4.2 proceedings the applicant was again remanded by the District Court, though, on this occasion, on bail. Counsel for the youth argued that on the grant of an Article 40.4.2 enquiry the applicant was within the constructive custody of the Court, so that there was sufficient custody for the purpose of Article 40.4.2. Again, the President of the High Court, Finlay P, is reported as having rejected this argument, saying that habeas corpus was only concerned with ensuring that no person be detained save in accordance with the law, and that since the complainant was no longer detained, there was no jurisdiction to continue the habeas corpus application. The general practice of the High Court has been to disengage in cases where a suspect has, following the ordering of an Article 40.4.2 enquiry, been released from Garda custody.[55] There have, however, been cases where the High Court, in order to maintain judicial review, has continued

---

[52] (1924) 58 ILTR 62.
[53] *R. v. Gavin* (1850) 15 Jur 329: an applicant, who had been detained as a deserter from the Home Guards was released on receipt of notice that a writ of habeas corpus had been issued. The Court of King's Bench held that a return that the respondent no longer held the prisoner was sufficient to determine the application.
[54] *Irish Times*, 24 July 1973.
[55] *The State (de Paor) v. O'Connor*, *Irish Times*, 5 Nov. 1977; *Morgan v. Garda Commissioner*, *Irish Times*, 3 June 1984.

proceedings despite the earlier release of the complainant. In *The State (Breathnach) v. Hennessy*[56] and *The State (Healy) v. Kenny*[57] (which are treated in chapter 4) proceedings were not terminated despite the prior release of the detainee from Garda custody; the jurisdictional basis of this practice is, however, problematic.[58]

It is obvious that the grant of bail by the High Court[59] as part of its Article 40.4.2 jurisdiction does not affect the Court's entitlement to maintain the process;[60] if it were otherwise the absurd result would follow that the enquiry (and bail) would automatically determine, and the complainant's detention resume without the High Court discharging its constitutional duty to enquire into the legality of the detention. It is less clear what is the proper remedy when the Court finds that the detention of a complainant already free on bail is unlawful; is an order of release really appropriate when the complainant is already free on bail? Both the High Court and Supreme Court have directed the release in Article 40.4.2 proceedings of a complainant already freed by it on bail.[61] This, according to one view,[62] is justified by the theory that a complainant who has been bailed is in the 'custody' of his bailsman. This argument, however, is inconsistent with earlier case law[63] where the proposition that a person enlarged on bail is subject to 'the detention' of his or her sureties has been rejected. An alternative view holds that, where the complainant has already been freed by the High Court on bail, the Court cannot order release on Article 40.4.2; some alternative remedy not conditioned upon the detention of the complainant (such as discharge from the conditions of bail) may only be granted.[64]

---

[56] *Irish Times*, 8 Apr. 1976; *Sunday Tribune*, 16 Aug. 1992.
[57] *Irish Times*, 11 Jan. 1975; See, also, *Re Sherman and Apps* (1980) 72 Cr App R 266.
[58] See below, pp 189–91.
[59] The same principle applies where any other court grants temporary bail during a detention under investigation by habeas corpus: *Re Amand* [1941] 2 KB 239.
[60] *Bolger v. Governor of Mountjoy Prison*, High Court, 15 Dec. 1998.
[61] *The State (Caddle) v. McCarthy* [1957] IR 359; *The State (Hully) v. Hynes* (1966) 100 ILTR 145; *Ojo v. Governor of Mountjoy Prison*, High Court, 8 May 2003.
[62] Per McCarthy J in *McMahon v. Leahy* [1984] IR 525. In directing the release of the complainant, who had been bailed during the application, McCarthy J noted that 'while not in custody in the ordinary sense he remains in the custody of his bailsmen' (p. 547).
[63] *AG v. Blennerhasset* (1932) 67 ILTR 136; *R.(Caherty) v. Belfast JJ* [1978] NI 94.
[64] *The State (Hanley) v. Governor of Mountjoy Prison* (1974) 108 ILTR 102.

The most appropriate approach may depend upon whether the terms of the grant of bail provide that bail shall expire at the determination of the enquiry, or whether the terms require the complainant to surrender to the court at each day of the hearing.[65] In the latter case the complainant may, on surrendering, revert to the custody of the original detainer, and, if so, there can be no objection to the issuing of an order of habeas corpus. However, in a case where the bailed complainant is at liberty at the time of the decision, it is more difficult to reconcile the exercise of the order of release with the text of Article 40.4.2: the complainant can only be said to be released from 'detention' on the assumption, which, as we have seen, is difficult to reconcile with the scheme of Articles 40.4.2 and 40.4.3, that detention includes conditions of reduced autonomy.

THE TWO-STAGE PROCESS UNDER ARTICLE 40.4.2 AND ALTERNATIVE PROCEDURAL MODELS

Two procedural models of habeas corpus existed at common law: under the classical, pre-nineteenth century model the court issued the writ of habeas corpus in the first instance, and the argument took place upon the production of the prisoner and the filing of the return. Under the nineteenth and early twentieth-century model, and the model current when the Constitution of the Irish Free State was being drafted, the argument took place upon an intermediary motion (the motion to show cause why a writ of habeas corpus should not issue). The earlier, pre-nineteenth century version was preferred by the framers of the Article 6 of the Irish Free State Constitution (and by the framers of Article 40.4.2 of the Constitution of Ireland when they adopted the provisions of the earlier text). Article 40.4.2 is a two-part process. There is an initial application to determine whether there is an arguable case. If the High Court finds such an arguable case the second part of the process is operated: the detainer is required to produce the body of the detainee and to file a certificate describing the basis of the detention, and the Court enquires into the legality of the detention.

Under the newest version of the remedy, which has been adopted in some Canadian jurisdictions, the two-stage process is replaced by a one-part hearing.[66] The grounds of the application are transmitted prior to

---

[65] See below, p. 150.

the hearing to all of the parties responsible for the detention. The respondents may either have the application dismissed on the basis that it does not raise an arguable case, or on the basis that the detention is in accordance with the law. The third model reduces the number of court hearings by incorporating the admissibility issue into the main hearing. It demotes the role of the immediate custodian; the inquiry is re-orientated away from the anachronistic preoccupation with the custodian's return and on to the wider justification for the detention. One of the consequences of the institutionalization in the Constitution of the pre-nineteenth-century model is that this modernized version, whatever its advantages, could not, in light of the express Constitutional requirement of a two-stage procedure, be adopted in Irish law.

THE COMPLAINANT: 'BY OR ON BEHALF OF ANY PERSON'

The recognition of the entitlement of any person to make a complaint 'on behalf of' a detained person, reincorporates the common law principle of third party intervention on habeas corpus. In an early rehearsal of the principle Marlay CJ sitting in the Irish King's Bench in 1744 stated that 'a habeas corpus for the liberty of the subject is a writ of right and may be applied for without affidavit of the party.'[67] Applications, both at common law, and under Article 40.4.2 have been submitted by fathers,[68] mothers,[69] brothers,[70] sisters,[71] children,[72] wives,[73] fellow prisoners,[74] political

---

[66] The one-stage process has been adopted in the provinces of British Columbia, Alberta and Nova Scotia.
[67] *R. v. Blakeney* (1744) reported sub nom *R. v. Heath* (1744) 18 St Tr 1, 19.
[68] *Wolfe Tone's Case* (1798) 27 St Tr 613; *R. v. Riall* (1860) 11 ICLR 279.
[69] *R. (O'Reilly) v. AG* [1928] IR 83; *The State (Greene) v. Governor of Portlaoise Prison*, High Court, 20 May 1977.
[70] *The State (Burke) v. Lennon* [1940] IR 136; *The State (Woods) v. Governor of Portlaoise Prison* (1974) 108 ILTR 54.
[71] *R. (O'Sullivan) v. Military Governor of Hare Park Internment Camp* (1924) 58 ILTR 62; *R. (O'Brien) v. Military Governor of North Dublin Union Internment Camp* [1924] 1 IR 32.
[72] *R. v. Blakeney* (1744) reported sub nom *R. v. Heath* (1744) 18 St Tr 1, 19.
[73] *Re James O'Reilly* (1895) 29 ILTR 33.
[74] *Application of Woods* [1970] IR 154; *The State (Kinsella) v. Governor of Portlaoise Prison*, High Court, 23 July 1984.

activists,[75] employers[76] and employees.[77] At common law a complaint may be submitted by a corporation as well as by a natural person,[78] and a similar result would follow under Article 40.4.2 since Article 40.4.2 in admitting an application 'by or on behalf of any person' does not restrict the legal identity of the complainant applying on behalf of that other person to any particular category of legal personality.

Although Article 40.4.2 does not indicate a priority between the two categories of complainant, the detainee, or a person acting on his behalf, it has been consistently held that it is the detainee who has the primary control over whether an application should be submitted in respect of the detention affecting him or her. The rule was referred to by Gavan Duffy J in *The State (Burke) v. Lennon*[79] who said that he would 'not endorse an interpretation of Article 40.4.2 which would permit an application by a third party where the party detained could make the application himself.' The principle was also applied in the *Application of Michael Woods*[80] where Kenny J refused to entertain an application submitted by a third party, Richard Tynan, on the ground that there was no evidence that Woods had ever authorized Tynan to act on his behalf. An assertion made in *The People (DPP) v. Pringle*[81] that an application may be made 'without the consent of the detainee' is irreconcilable with this authority, and may go too far.

On the other hand, the primary rule may be overriden where the detainee is not in a position to submit an application on his or her behalf.[82] At its most obvious, lack of capacity may be inferred from the fact that the prisoner is being physically prevented from submitting an application. In *R. (Childers) v. Adjutant General of the Provisional Forces*[83] O'Connor MR ruled on this ground that it was in order for a solicitor acting without

---

[75] *Re O'Duffy* [1934] IR 550; *Re Dolphin*, High Court, 27 Jan. 1972; *McGlinchey v. Ireland* [1988] IR 671.

[76] *The State (Harrington) v. Garda Commissioner*, High Court, 14 Dec. 1976

[77] *R. v. Cody* (1852) 5 Ir Jur 175.

[78] *Victorian Council for Civil Liberties v. Minister for Immigration* [2002] 1 LRC 189, 257.

[79] [1940] IR 136.   [80] [1970] IR 154.

[81] (1981) 2 Frewen 57, 97.

[82] At common law there was a requirement that the detainee have been physically prevented from submitting an application: *Ex p. Child* (1854) 15 CB 238; 139 ER 413.

[83] [1923] 1 IR 5. See G. Hogan 'Hugh Kennedy, the Childers habeas corpus application and the return to the Four Courts' in C. Costello (ed.) *The Four Courts: 200 years* (Dublin, 1996), 177.

instructions to make an application on behalf of a group of unnamed prisoners, whose identity the authorities had refused to disclose.[84] The possibility that the detainee, who could not be located by his solicitor, was being deliberately restrained from submitting an application was held to justify a third party application in *The State (Quinn) v. Ryan*.[85] The denial to a detainee of access to a solicitor has been classified as giving rise to an inference of practical inability to initiate an application. In *The People (DPP) v. Pringle*[86] a solicitor refused access to a client was held to have *locus standi* to submit an application. Lack of practical ability to make a personal application has been inferred from the detainee's withholding consent on grounds of principle, or by reason of an ideological refusal to recognize the court. In *Re Martin Dolphin*[87] an application for habeas corpus had been taken on behalf of a student Maoist who had been committed to the Central Mental Hospital on grounds of unfitness to plead. Kenny J held the third party application admissible, despite the fact that the detainee, for reasons connected with his political extremism, did not recognize the courts. Lack of practical capacity may also be deduced from the detainee's lack of familiarity with the legal system. In 1810 a habeas corpus, taken by the secretary of the African Institution in respect of the alleged enslavement of an African who was being exhibited as a human curiosity in London, was held admissible without any objection to the fact that the detainee had not authorized the application.[88]

A second condition to third party intervention on Article 40.4.2 is that

---

[84] O'Connor MR is reported as saying 'I do not think it is necessary for any person to have instructions from a prisoner. It is a right of every British subject to apply for habeas corpus for any prisoner, and if he had not that common law right, the Habeas Corpus Act would be defeated because you can easily conceive a man incarcerated without being allowed communicate with the outside public'; *Irish Times*, 22 Nov. 1922.

[85] [1965] IR 70. 'It might be, as the Judge thought, that the prosecutor had vanished of his own volition. This is possible, but the probabilities on the information available to this Court are otherwise: they point to an arrest. As to the authority of the prosecutor's solicitor, the Court is of opinion in the circumstances of this case that there is sufficient shown to entitle the solicitor to maintain this application. The indications are that the prosecutor was prevented from consulting with his legal advisors, and the Court cannot permit an Article of the Constitution to be set aside with impunity' (at pp 73-4).

[86] (1981) 2 Frewen 57, 97.

[87] High Court, 27 Jan. 1972.

[88] *The Venus Hottentot* (1810) 13 East 195; 104 ER 344.

the complainant be acting bona fide. In *Cahill v. Governor of Curragh Military Detention Barracks*[89] Finlay P briefly referred to this requirement, saying that the third party complainant should be 'bona fide interested on [the detainee's] behalf.'

'SUCH PERSON'

The right of personal liberty guaranteed by Article 40.4.1 is restricted to 'citizens.' Its predecessor, Article 6 of the Constitution of the Irish Free State, had extended the right of personal liberty to 'persons.' The change in the wording of Article 40.4.1 appears to have been a deliberate contraction in the range of operation of the Constitutional guarantee of personal liberty. On the other, hand the right to an Article 40.4.2 enquiry applies, without discrimination on grounds of citizenship. The right is activated where a complaint is submitted by 'any person,' and it is accepted that the procedure may be invoked by non-citizens.[90] The two provisions are not, however, necessarily irreconcilable. It may be that the framers envisaged certain categories of non-national, such as enemy aliens, as having merely reduced rights of personal liberty, while still allowing such persons the constitutional facility of an enquiry into the legality of the exercise of the more extended powers of detention exercisable in their case.

THE FORUM

'the High Court or any judge thereof'

The provision enabling an application to be made to the High Court or any judge thereof (strange, perhaps, to the modern eye, where the High Court is a typically single judge thereof) is probably explicable by reference to institutional arrangements envisaged at the time when Article 6 of the Constitution of the Irish Free State was being drafted. Early drafts provided that the High Court would, as it did until 1924, sit in two divisions, an equity and common law division. An application to one of

---

[89] [1980] ILRM 191, 201.
[90] *The State (Kugan) v. O'Rourke* [1985] IR 658; *The State (McFadden) v. The Governor of Mountjoy Prison* [1981] ILRM 113.

these divisional courts would have been the ordinary means of submitting an application.[91] The reference to a single judge of the High Court was, perhaps, included in order to preserve the common law right to approach a single judge in emergency cases where a full divisional court of the type envisaged was not accessible.[92] As it turned out, the proposal for a divisional arrangement was discontinued, and what had originally been intended as an exceptional jurisdiction, became, instead, routine.

The phrase 'any judge thereof' includes a judge of the High Court relieved of his or her duties on appointment to the Law Reform Commission. Section 3(9) of the Law Reform Commission Act, 1975 provides that a person holding judicial office who is appointed a Commissioner shall 'not be required to perform his duties *under statute*.' By implication, a High Court judge appointed to the Law Reform Commission retains his duties under *the Constitution*. Indeed, the legislative history of the provision shows that the legislation was drafted precisely with Article 40.4.2 in mind.[93] It was understood by the Oireachtas that to have withdrawn the duty of a High Court judge to hear an application under Article 40.4.2 would have been an infringement of the duty of amenability imposed on judges of the High Court under Article 40.4.2.

Section 2 of the Courts (Establishment and Constitution) Act, 1961 appears to broaden even further the size of the forum, including, on one interpretation, the President of the Circuit Court and the Chief Justice, as judges to whom an application under Article 40.4.2 may be made. Subsections (3)-(5) of section 2 provide:

> (3) The Chief Justice shall be ex officio an additional judge of the High Court

---

[91] Document No. 29 (TCD, Stephens papers, MS 4236, f. 159).
[92] *The State (Dowling) v. Kingston (No. 2)* [1937] IR 699.
[93] Explaining the use of the phrase 'under statute' at Committee stage the Attorney General said: 'under Article 40.4.2 of the Constitution every judge of the High Court to whom a complaint has been made that a person has been unlawfully detained has a duty forthwith to enquire into the complaint. This Constitutional provision could not be removed by statute. The amendment is proposed for the purpose of showing that section 3(9) does not purport to do so. A person appointed to [the Law Reform Commission] could still be a judge and so a person could apply to him for habeas corpus and he would hear him,' Law Reform Commission Bill, 1975, Special Committee, D 18, No. 2, 22. See J.P. Casey, 'The Constitution and the legal system' (1979) 14 *Ir. Jurist* 14, 25–6.

(4) The President of the Circuit Court shall be ex officio an additional judge of the High Court.

(5)(a) where, owing to the illness of a judge of the High Court or for any other reason, a sufficient number of judges of the High Court is not available for the transaction of business of that Court or, on account of the volume of business to be transacted in the High Court or for any other reason arising from the state of business in that Court, the Chief Justice, at the request of the President of the High Court, may request any ordinary judge of the Supreme Court to sit in the High Court as an additional judge thereof, and every ordinary judge of the Supreme Court so requested shall sit in the High Court.

(b) whenever an ordinary judge of the Supreme Court sits in the High Court in pursuance of this subsection, he shall be an additional judge of the High Court for all purposes of that Court.

It has been argued that it follows from section 2 that 'an application [under Article 40.4.2] may competently be made to the President of the Circuit Court, who has, by virtue of office, the status of a High Court judge.'[94] But, this interpretation reads section 2 as if it says that the President or Chief Justice is always, ex officio, vested with the jurisdiction of a High Court judge. On a narrower interpretation section 2 merely endows the President of the Circuit Court, or the Chief Justice, with an (ex officio) contingent entitlement to serve as judge of the High Court. The distinction between the rival interpretations lies in the question as to whether there is any element of discretion allowed. Under the narrower view the President or Chief Justice must first exercise the statutory discretion to act as a judge of the High Court as a condition to capacity to hear a complaint under Article 40.4.2; under the wider interpretation there is no discretion and the President and Chief Justice, being standing judges of the High Court, must always investigate an Article 40.4.2 complaint. Section 2 creates two categories of 'additional judge': the judge ex officio (where the entitlement is inherent) is distinguished from those ordinary judges of the Supreme Court (who are only constituted additional judges following the appointment procedure described in section 2(5)). On the

---

[94] J.P. Casey, *Constitutional law in Ireland* (Dublin, 2000), p. 479.

narrower view the tag 'ex officio' appears to refer to the process by which a judge is entitled to sit as an additional judge. An ordinary judge of the Supreme Court is entitled to sit as a judge of the High Court where there is an insufficient number of High Court judges, where the President requests an extra judge, and where the Chief Justice consents. Because that appointment mechanism would be impracticable in the case of the Chief Justice or the President of the Circuit Court, the legislative intention appears to have been that such judges be entitled to convert their status ex officio, and without necessity for compliance with the statutory procedure. But section 2 does not say that these judges possess the jurisdiction of the High Court even when *not sitting* as judges of the High Court. The Chief Justice and the President of the Circuit Court are described as 'additional' judges of the High Court, and not 'judges' of the High Court. In *The State (Woods) v. Governor of Portlaoise Prison*[95] the President of the Circuit Court, Ó Briain J, while sitting as a Circuit Court judge of Clare, accepted jurisdiction in habeas corpus proceedings. However, the report does not describe the basis on which O'Briain J accepted jurisdiction; whether because he believed himself always an additional judge of the High Court, or because he decided to exercise his intrinsic discretion to act as an additional judge of the High Court.

SUCCESSIVE AND REPEATED APPLICATIONS UNDER ARTICLE 40.4.2

Successive applications in the case of refusal

The Second Amendment of the Constitution Act, 1941 drew a distinction in respect of the right to renew an Article 40.4.2 application between, on the one hand, the refusal of an initial enquiry and, on the other, the rejection of an allegation following an enquiry. The purpose was (a) that a complainant was to have a right to proceed from judge to judge following a refusal to order an initial enquiry, but (b) that a complainant was to have no right of renewal when an enquiry had been held and it had been determined that the detention was in accordance with the law.[96]

The first of these provisions, the right of a person refused an enquiry to

---

[95] (1974) 108 ILTR 54.
[96] See above, pp 34–8.

renew the application before another judge of the High Court is, perhaps, difficult to justify. In practice the right of successive application is very rarely availed of.[97] There may be a number of reasons for this: the test for ordering an enquiry is so low that a decision to the effect that there are no grounds for ordering an enquiry is likely to be followed by another judge of the High Court; and secondly, complainants, in practice, prefer to renew the application by way of appeal to the Supreme Court. A justification referred to during the enactment of the provision was that it provided a means of having a complaint reconsidered when the Supreme Court was not sitting.[98] But it is anomalous that there be this vacation facility available in the (less common) event that a detainee during vacation wishes to argue that an initial application is improperly refused, but not available (in the more common case) when, following an enquiry during the vacation, release has, allegedly, been irregularly refused, but there is no means of appeal to the Supreme Court.

Repeated applications

The practice of complainants challenging the same order or detention by means of a renewed application has been established since the mid-1960s. There are at least three qualifications to this entitlement.

The first of these restrictions prohibits a complainant from raising on a second application, grounds which were available and which could have been submitted on an earlier application. This suggestion, when it was originally forwarded, was dismissed as unconstitutional by the Supreme Court. In the *Application of Michael Woods*[99] the Supreme Court rejected the contention that a rule analogous to the doctrine in *Henderson v. Henderson*[100] (that it is an abuse of process to stagger grounds of challenge

---

[97] See, however, *The State (Richardson) v. Governor of Mountjoy Prison* [1980] ILRM 82 (where Barrington J granted an initial order for an Article 40.4.2 enquiry notwithstanding the earlier refusal of Keane J to do so) and *Payne v. Governor of Portlaoise Prison*, Supreme Court, 7 Apr. 2003 (where O'Higgins J in the High Court granted an initial order despite the refusal of another High Court judge to order an enquiry into the same point).

[98] Anon., 'Proposed amendments in habeas corpus procedure in Éire' (1941) 75 *Irish Law Times & Solicitors' Journal* 65, 66.

[99] [1970] IR 154. See M. Kenny, 'Informality in modern Irish habeas corpus practice' (1974) 9 *Ir. Jurist* 67, 71–5.

[100] (1843) 3 Hare 100, 67 ER 313; *AA v. Medical Council* [2003] 4 IR 302.

over successive sets of proceedings) could apply to the Article 40.4.2 application:[101]

> Neither the High Court nor the Supreme Court warrants by a decision in an application for habeas corpus, that every possible ground of complaint has been considered and ruled ... The duty which the Court has under the Constitution of ordering the release of a person unless satisfied that he is lawfully detained, requires that the Court should entertain a complaint which bears on the question of the legality of the detention, even though in earlier proceedings the applicant might have raised the matter but did not do so. The duty of the courts to see that no one is deprived of his personal liberty save in accordance with the law overrides considerations which are valid in litigation *inter partes*.

In *Re Thomas McDonagh*[102] the applicant had managed to take three separate applications in the twelve months between his conviction in November 1968 and his fourth application in November 1969. Henchy J, although acknowledging that he was bound by *Woods's* case, suggested that failure to include all available grounds of complaint in the same application might constitute an abuse of process:

> While it is understandable because of the special nature and purpose of habeas corpus that more than one application may be made in respect of a particular detention and that failure to state a particular complaint of unlawful detention in an earlier application should not, ipso facto, be a bar to raising it in a subsequent application, I should have thought that where a person has been convicted and sentenced to imprisonment, it could not be said that he will never, during his imprisonment, be debarred from applying for habeas corpus notwithstanding how many previous applications he has already made. The result would be litigiousness and the processes of the court would be abused.

The Henchy view was, notwithstanding its earlier decision in *Woods*, subsequently adopted by the Supreme Court in *Re Gallagher*[103] where the complainant, in a second challenge, attempted to overturn a conviction by

---

[101] [1970] IR 154, 162.
[102] High Court, 24 Nov. 1969.
[103] *Irish Times*, 26 July 1983.

the Special Criminal Court (this time on the ground that one of the convicting judges was not, as required by the Offences Against the State Act, 1939, a barrister of seven years' standing). The Supreme Court rejected the application on two alternative grounds: that the Special Criminal Court judge was properly qualified,[104] and secondly, that the complainant was guilty of an abuse of process in not submitting this ground in the previous Article 40.4.2 application. The newspaper report records Henchy J as stating:

> This was not the first application Gallagher had made to be released on habeas corpus. It was the view of the Court, annunciated in the past, that a person seeking habeas corpus should put forward all his grounds in his application and not hold them over for the purpose of making subsequent applications. On that point alone the appeal should be dismissed, but the Court was prepared to hold that the appeal was properly before it, and dismissed the appeal.

Gallagher strongly suggested that the duty to submit all currently available grounds in the same application now applies to habeas corpus (though the status of the ruling may have been undermined by a series of subsequent assertions in both the High and Supreme Courts repeating the doctrine that there is no limit on the number of challenges which may be brought on Article 40.4.2).[105] But even assuming, that the *McDonagh/Gallagher* principle is governing, it is not, in practice, likely to prove of great significance. Successive applications are only likely to be submitted in the case of orders of detention which are long-term in nature; and in the case of the principal form of long-term detention, imprisonment following conviction on indictment, habeas corpus is hardly ever available.[106] Second, where the defect which is sought to be raised in the renewed application is very serious, the principle may be dispensed with. In English law, where the

---

[104] The Court held that the Special Criminal Court judge (a retired High Court judge) reverted, on his retirement, to being a barrister, and that since he had before appointment to the High Court practiced as a barrister he was, as required by s. 39 (3) of the Offences Against the State Act, 1939, a barrister of more than seven years standing at the time of his appointment to the Special Criminal Court.

[105] *Hardy v. Ireland*, 25 June 1993; *Junior v. Clifford*, High Court, 17 Dec. 1993; *Breathnach v. Manager of Wheatfield Place of Detention*, Supreme Court, 22 Feb. 2001.

[106] See below, pp 206–15.

principle is also recognized, it has been stated that the rule should be applied flexibly:[107] 'the stringency of the application of the principle may be different in cases concerning the liberty of the subject from that in cases concerning such matters as disputes upon property.'

A complainant's right to submit a renewed application is subject to two further restraints. Firstly, the rule of res judicata applies so that an applicant will not be permitted to challenge on a second application grounds which have previously been rejected in a previous hearing.[108] In *McGlinchey v. Governor of Portlaoise Prison*[109] the Supreme Court propounded a related rule: that it is not possible to initiate a complaint under Article 40.4.2 about an issue which is already being investigated following a complaint earlier submitted to another judge of the High Court.

THE COMPLAINT: THE STANDARD OF ADMISSIBILITY

At common law a writ of habeas corpus would not issue unless the applicant could raise a probable cause,[110] or a reasonable ground,[111] or a sufficient cause,[112] that the detention was unlawful.[113] The formulae used in determining whether a complaint has passed the threshold necessary to obtain an initial order under Article 40.4.2 indicate some divergence. According to one strain, the complainant is required to present only an 'arguable case.'[114] But another tendency, closer to the common law

---

[107] *R. v. Governor of Pentonville Prison, ex p. Tarling* [1979] 1 WLR 1417, 1423; see also *AA v. Medical Council* [2003] 4 IR 302, 317.

[108] *Re Charles Wilson (No. 1)*, Supreme Court, 11 July 1968; *Junior v. Clifford*, High Court, 17 Dec. 1993.

[109] *Irish Times*, 28 July 1987.

[110] *Hobhouse's Case* (1820) 3 B & Ald 420, 422; 106 ER 716, 717. The probable causes standard appears to have been influenced by the Habeas Corpus Act, 1816 (56 Geo. III, c. 100) s. 1 of which required that the applicant establish a 'probable and reasonable ground.'

[111] Ibid., pp 423, 718.

[112] *In re Keller* (1888) 22 LR Ir 158, 162.

[113] The only exception to the requirement to show probable cause arose in the case of the statutory right to vacation bail under (the now repealed) s. 2 of the Habeas Corpus Act, 1782 (21 & 22 Geo. III, c. 11).

[114] *Trimbole v. Governor of Mountjoy Prison*, *Irish Times*, 24 Nov. 1984; *Re McGlinchey*, *Irish Times*, 28 July 1987; *Breathnach v. Manager Wheatfield Place of Detention*, Supreme Court, 20 Oct. 2000.

approach, requires that the court have a 'sufficient doubt' as to the legality of the detention.[115] The two tests are not identical: 'sufficient doubt' suggests an evaluation which is more developed, implying that the court has reached a conclusion, albeit a very intermediary one. The 'arguable case' standard suggests minimal evaluation, and that the court is suspending any conclusion, even an intermediary one. The 'sufficient doubt' standard is perhaps the less satisfactory of the rival tests. It is not clear what the court must be 'sufficiently doubtful' of: whether it must be doubtful that there exists a possibility of illegality, or whether it must doubtful to the point of apprehending a reasonable probability that the detention is unlawful. If the higher standard is correct and the court is required to apprehend an intermediary view that the detention is probably unlawful it imposes a standard which is stricter than the standard on judicial review, where only 'an arguable case' is required. It would be difficult to justify an anomaly under which Article 40.4.2 was a less accessible remedy than the procedure by way of judicial review.

'SHALL FORTHWITH ENQUIRE INTO THE SAID COMPLAINT'

The complaint may either be by means of a single application, usually, though not necessarily on affidavit,[116] or letter, or may be built up over a series of submissions, including information derived by the court from sources independent of the complainant.[117] In *Sheehan v. Reilly*[118] Finlay CJ described the more extended complaint:[119]

---

[115] *In re Keller* (1888) 22 LR Ir 158, 162; *The State (Cannon) v. Kavanagh* [1937] IR 428, 436; *Brennan v. Governor of Mountjoy Prison, Irish Times*, 8 Mar. 1975; *Sheehan v. Reilly* [1993] 2 IR 81.

[116] The practice direction, 'State Side Applications other than Bail (Personal Actions)' (undated, but probably drawn up in the late 1970s) provided at para. (1): 'Applications received by post should be by affidavit-except for habeas corpus applications. Should be accompanied by copy of warrant.' On the other hand it may, as a check against abuse of procedure, be desirable that in the interval between the grant of the initial application and the full enquiry, the detainee's allegations be repeated on affidavit. See *The State (Harrington) v. Garda Commissioner*, High Court, 14 Dec. 1976, and *Re Copeland's Application* [1990] NI 301.

[117] In *The State (Williams) v. Kelly* (1969, No.18 SS), [1970] IR 271, following an initial application by letter, the High Court, through an assistant registrar, wrote to the complainant, identifying certain questions which it wished elaborated.

[118] [1993] 2 IR 81.   [119] Ibid., p. 90.

Upon the making of an application to a judge of the High Court, that judge has got a jurisdiction and a discretion, in my view, even prior to reaching a conclusion that a sufficient doubt as to the legality of the detention of the applicant has been raised to warrant calling upon the jailor or detainer of the applicant to show cause, to make inquiries of a speedy and, if necessary, informal nature to try and ascertain the facts.

The complainant's capacity to present a complaint is assisted by the recognition as an incident of Article 40.4.2 of a constitutional right to basic information about the basis of any detention. In *The State (Ward) v. Governor of Mountjoy Prison*[120] Finlay P is reported as holding that 'a person had a constitutional right to know where and by whose authority he was being detained which though not expressly granted, was a necessary corollary of his right to make a complaint under Article 40.4.2.'

The issue as to whether on Article 40.4.2 the complaint must always be processed *ex parte*, or whether the High Court may in cases of doubt invite submissions from the respondent before making an initial order,[121] has yet to be addressed. There appears to be nothing in the text of Article 40.4.2 which positively prohibits this. In eighteenth and early nineteenth century common law practice (the procedural model on which Article 40.4.2 is evidently based) the English Court of King's Bench, where it was in doubt as to whether the grounds stated in the detainee's affidavits were sufficient to justify the initial issue of the writ, had jurisdiction to make an order directing the respondents to show cause why the writ should not issue.[122]

The prisoner has no right to an audience in order to present the initial complaint.[123] But while the complainant has no right to be present,

---

[120] *Irish Times*, 22 Feb. 1975.

[121] For the equivalent jurisdiction on judicial review see *R. v. Secretary of State for the Home Department, ex p. Begum* [1990] COD 107.

[122] *Ex p. Gallile* (1798) 7 TR 673, 101 ER 1192; *Barrow's Case* (1811) 14 East 346, 104 ER 635; *Herbert's Case* (1811) 16 East 165, 104 ER 1051.

[123] *Breathnach v. Manager Wheatfield Place of Detention*, Supreme Court, 20 Oct. 2000; 'State Side Applications other than Bail (Personal Actions)' para. 5; In *Toohey v. Governor of Central Mental Hospital* (1967 No. 158 SS), High Court, 24 Oct. 1967, the President of the High Court ruled that the prisoner's attendance was not necessary in order to consider the application. In *O'Shea v. Governor of Mountjoy Prison*, High Court, 28 June 1991, it was said: 'these ex parte applications are considered by the Court on the evidence submitted by the applicant and unless the Court thinks that there is some special reason why the Court would like to hear the applicant in person, the production of the person is not required.'

production may occasionally be ordered in order to permit the development of the initial complaint.[124] In 1983 Gannon J publicly admonished the Governor of Mountjoy Prison for refusing to comply with a High Court direction requiring him to produce a prisoner before the High Court in order to present an initial application under Article 40.4.2.[125] In considering whether the power to permit the complainant appear at the initial stage should be exercised, it has been suggested that a court should take into account the reality that 'inmates do not always have ready access to materials necessary to make written submissions, and even where they do, many may be unable to express themselves effectively in writing, or in English'.[126] Whether granted[127] or refused,[128] the grounds on which the initial application has been determined should be recorded, and transmitted to the prisoner.

'MAY ORDER THE PERSON IN WHOSE CUSTODY PERSON SUCH IS DETAINED'

The range of persons against whom an order may be made

At common law the primary addressee of an order of habeas corpus was the immediate gaoler. However, where the location of the gaoler could not

---

[124] In *Re Tynan* (1963, No. 39 SS) the prisoner having earlier submitted an application by letter, the High Court, on 8 May 1963 directed the Governor to produce the prisoner on Friday 10 May 1963 in order to present the application for a conditional order. The complainant was also allowed to submit the initial application in person in *Re Singer* (1963, No. 13 SS), (1963) 97 ILTR.

[125] *Re Rowe, Irish Times,* 12 Oct. 1983.

[126] *R. v. Gustavson* (2005) 193 CCC (3d) 545.

[127] The practice direction, 'State Side Applications other than Bail (Personal Actions)' provided at para. 7: 'Draw orders. (Darcy J wants Art. 40 orders to indicate which ground or grounds are to be considered on return).'

[128] Para. 9 of the practice direction 'State Side Applications other than Bail (Personal Actions)' provided: 'In refusals send copy Order to prisoner with covering note stating briefly the reason for refusal (directed by President) and enclose copy order for Governor. If judge has made a suitable note on file a copy of it may suffice as a note of reasons.' One Article 40.4.2 case in which there had been a twelve-month delay in the transmission of the grounds of refusal to a prisoner complainant was the subject of an adjournment debate in Dáil Éireann: *Dáil Debates,* vol. 503, col. 1121 (22 Apr. 1999). The Minister for Justice assured the Dáil that the Chief Registrar of the High Court had been spoken to about the administrative default.

be identified, or where the immediate gaoler might not have the authority to comply with any order of release, the writ might issue to an officer in a position to discover the detainee,[129] or to the officer in effective administrative control,[130] or to an officer in a position to recover the detainee from a third party.[131] On the other hand, the immediate custodian appears to be the only potential addressee of Article 40.4.2. Article 40.4.2 envisages an order directed to 'the person in whose custody such person is detained to produce the body of such person before the High Court.' The general practice is to direct the order to the immediate custodian, usually the prison governor, or the member in charge of the Garda station in which the detainee is held, but there have been cases where the order has been issued to some party other than the immediate custodian. In *The State (Quinn) v. Ryan*,[132] where the location of the detainee could not be established, the order was directed to the Garda Commissioner and Deputy Commissioner Quinn, while, for a period during the mid-1970s the general practice in cases challenging the legality of Garda detention[133] was to direct the order to the Garda Commissioner as well as the station sergeant (possibly because the inclusion of the Commissioner was perceived as essential to the effectiveness of the order). On a literal reading, Article 40.4.2 does not permit orders directed to non-custodians. On the other hand, it has been recognized,[134] that there exists within Article 40.4.2 a range of implied ancillary powers, which enable the court to make the constitutional process effective. In order to make an Article 40.4.2 enquiry effective it may be necessary that the High Court have the ancillary jurisdiction to issue orders attaching parties other than the custodian: orders against parties who are in a position to locate the custodian; or directions to superiors to the custodian in a position to ensure compliance by the custodian with the process. Since the immediate custodian is, under the Constitution, the primary respondent, proceedings originally directed against a third party should, once the immediate detainer is made amenable, be continued against him.

---

[129] *Re Mathews* (1860) 12 ICLR 233; *Barnardo v. Ford* [1892] AC 326.
[130] *R. (Childers) v. Adjutant General of Provisional Forces* [1923] 1 IR 5.
[131] *R. v. Secretary of State for Home Affairs, ex p. O'Brien* [1923] 2 AC 603.
[132] [1965] IR 70.
[133] *The State (Healy) v. Kenny and Garda Commissioner* (10 SS 1975), *Irish Times*, 11 Jan. 1975; *The State (Walsh) v. Garda Commissioner* (32 SS 1975), *Irish Times*, 29 Jan. 1975; *The State (Harrington) v. Garda Commissioner*, High Court, 14 Dec. 1976; *The State (Hoey) v. Garvey* [1978] IR 1.
[134] *Gallagher v. Director of Central Mental Hospital* [1996] 3 IR 1.

The extra-territorial operation of the remedy

The jurisdiction to issue habeas corpus to a person detained outside the territorial jurisdiction of the court was, by way of exception to the common law presumption against the extra-territorial operation of legal processes,[135] well established at common law.[136] First, notice of the issue of the writ within the jurisdiction could be served on persons outside the jurisdiction.[137] Second, the writ itself could be issued outside the jurisdiction of the court to places under the control of the Crown. The common law test enquired whether the place was subject to the effective, though not necessarily legal, sovereignty of the Crown; thus, the remedy might issue to Berwick on Tweed[138] (a place outside the jurisdiction of the Court of King's Bench of England, but a dominion of the Crown); it issued to the Bechuanaland Protectorate;[139] and it issued to the Protectorate of

---

[135] *Dickson v. Capes* (1860) 11 ICLR 345, 346 ('This court never had jurisdiction to order service out of the jurisdiction before this Act'); *Re Bushfield* (1886) 32 Ch D 123, 131 ('apart from statute a court has no power to exercise jurisdiction over anyone beyond its limits.')

[136] In *Adams v. DPP* [2001] 2 ILRM 401 the High Court held that the Court had no jurisdiction to issue an order of judicial review extra-territorially against an officer situated outside the State (in that case the United Kingdom's Secretary of State for Home Affairs). The Court held that the common law did not recognize the extra-territorial exercise of judicial process; that extra-territorial jurisdiction could be conferred only by legislation; and, that the only legislation in the field, O. 11 of the Rules of the Superior Courts, 1986 did not make provision for the extra-territorial operation of proceedings by way of judicial review. But, as the authorities show, the common law presumption against extra-territorial jurisdiction was not unqualified. It was subject to the special exception which applied in the case of the prerogative writs, including habeas corpus. There are, therefore, two sources of extra-territorial jurisdiction: statute in the form of O. 11 of the Rules of the Superior Courts, 1986 and the extra-territorial capacity of the old prerogative writs. O. 11 is exhaustive only of the area outside the public law remedies. Though it is doubtful whether that common law jurisdiction would have operated in circumstances such as those in that case, the account in *Adams* of extraterritoriality and judicial review overlooks this second source. It was by reference to this source that (notwithstanding the omission of the prerogative writs from rules of court equivalent to O. 11) the English courts have recognized a limited jurisdiction to issue habeas corpus extra-territorially.

[137] This continues to be the case under Article 40.4.2: see *The State (Dowling) v. Kingston* [1937] IR 483; *The State (Hully) v. Hynes* (1966) 100 ILTR 145.

[138] *R. v. Cowle* (1759) 2 Burr 834; 97 ER 587.

[139] *R. v. Crewe, ex p. Sekgome* [1910] 2 KB 576.

Northern Rhodesia[140] (again, constitutionally a foreign country, but subject to the administration of the Crown).

It has been assumed that the writ issued from the Court of King's Bench in England into the Kingdom of Ireland.[141] The only authority for the proposition that this did occur is a report entitled *Anon.*[142] in 1681. The point arose during the hearing of a writ of error from the King's Bench in Ireland to the King's Bench in England, when it emerged that the plaintiff was in execution upon the judgment in Ireland. It is reported that 'the Court seemed to be of opinion that a habeas corpus might be sent thither to remove him as writs mandatory had been to Calais, and now to Jersey, Guernsey.' This precedent does not, however, precisely sustain the proposition that the English King's Bench issued habeas corpus for the relief of persons unlawfully detained in Ireland. The writ issued in *Anon.* appears not to have been a writ of habeas corpus ad subjiciendum for the release of the applicant but more in the nature of a writ of habeas corpus ad testificandum in order to secure the attendance of the plaintiff at the hearing on the writ of error. In 1972, in *Re Keenan*[143] Orr LJ asserted that it was 'very probable that between 1719 and 1782 process could have issued out of England into Ireland.' However, a search of the Crown-side rule books of the Court of King's Bench for the period 1740 to 1782 fails to disclose a single instance in which the writ of habeas corpus issued from the English King's Bench into Ireland.

The writ probably did not issue extra-territorially of right but only when it was 'the properest and most effectual remedy.'[144] The principle

---

[140] *Ex p. Mwenya* [1960] 1 QB 241.
[141] *R. v. Cowle* (1759) 2 Burr 834, 97 ER 587; *Re Keenan* [1972] 1 QB 533.
[142] (1681) 1 Vent 357; 86 ER 230.
[143] [1972] 1 QB 533, 543. In *Re Keenan* it was held that the jurisdiction to issue habeas corpus into Ireland was implicitly overridden by 23 Geo. III, c. 28 (Eng.) which recognized the right 'claimed by the people of Ireland ... to have all actions and suits at law or in equity which may be instituted in Ireland decided in his majesty's courts therein finally and without appeal from thence.' *Re Keenan* is the subject of a note by D.E.C. Yale, 'Habeas corpus- Ireland-jurisdiction' (1972) 30 *Cambridge Law Journal* 4.
[144] In *R. v. Cowle* (1759) 2 Burr 834, 97 ER 587 Mansfield CJ stated: 'But notwithstanding the power which the court have, yet where they cannot judge of the cause or give relief upon it, they would not think proper to impose. Therefore, upon imprisonments in Guernsey and Jersey, in Minorca and the Plantations, I have known complaints to the King in Council, and orders to bail or discharge: but I do not remember an application for a writ of habeas corpus. Yet cases have

underlying the extra-territorial operation of the writ was that of effective connection to the Crown: the writ would only issue to a jurisdiction in which the Crown regulated the governmental apparatus in such a way as made it likely that the process would be observed. In *ex parte Mwenya* Romer LJ said:[145]

> The machinery provided by the writ for obtaining this information would obviously be ineffective in relation to any territory in which the Crown had to no extent displaced the sovereign power; and because of this, and also because of the comity of nations, the writ would not issue into, for example, the United States of America for the purpose of inquiring into the detention of a British subject who is imprisoned there. But in a territory in which the Crown, on the advice of Parliament, has assumed such a degree of power and control that the protected State is to all intents and purposes a British possession and in which the writ, if issued, would certainly be effective in its results, it is difficult to see why the sovereign should be deprived of her right to be informed through the High Court as to the validity of the detention of her subjects in that territory.

These common law authorities were relied upon by the Supreme Court of the United States in its ruling in *Rasul v. Bush*[146] that there was jurisdiction to issue habeas corpus for the persons detained in Guantanamo Bay Naval Base in Cuba, a place under the effective control of the United States. Stevens J, relying, in particular, on *Ex parte Mwenya* concluded that 'the reach of the writ [at common law] depended not on formal notions of territorial sovereignty, but rather on the practical question of the exact extent and nature of the jurisdiction or dominion exercised in fact by the Crown.' In the child custody case *JW v. MW*[147] the High Court went much further than the extent permitted by the common law, and apparently directed a habeas corpus to a mother resident in a women's refuge in London. It is not obvious how such an order would be capable of passing

> formerly happened of persons illegally sent from hence and detained there, where a writ of habeas corpus out of this Court would be the properest and most effectual remedy' (p. 856).

[145] [1960] 1 QB 241, p. 305.
[146] 124 S Ct 2686 (2004)
[147] [1978] ILRM 119. The habeas corpus had been issued at an earlier stage in the proceedings.

the effectiveness principle. There certainly would have been no jurisdiction at common law to issue the remedy where the constitutional connection was as remote as that between Ireland and the United Kingdom. In the child custody case *R. v. Pinckney*[148] Collins MR, applying the principle that the writ could not issue into a foreign country where the Crown had no administrative presence, held that habeas corpus could not issue to France.

As an alternative to issuing the process outside the jurisdiction, extraterritorial effect may be accomplished indirectly by directing the writ to issue against a person within the jurisdiction requiring the retrieval of a detainee from another jurisdiction. The most celebrated instance of this is *R. v. Secretary of State for Home Affairs, ex parte O'Brien*[149] where the Court of Appeal issued a writ of habeas corpus to the Home Secretary directing him to return a detainee against whom he had illegally made an order of internment in Ireland under the Restoration of Order in Ireland Act, 1920, after the establishment of the Irish Free State in 1922. The issue of the writ was justified by the information that there existed an informal arrangement between the two Governments under which the Government of the Irish Free State would comply with a request for the return of the detainee by the Government of the United Kingdom. An attempt to apply the *O'Brien* principle was dismissed by the High Court in *The State (Quinn) v. Ryan:*[150] at the time that the complaint was being submitted to the High Court Quinn had been removed from Ireland to England, had been charged in Ealing Magistrates Court, and had been remanded in custody to Brixton Prison. A majority of the High Court held that officers of the Garda Síochána could not be held to have had the effective capacity to produce Quinn before the Court on Article 40.4.2. Implicitly, the High Court held that the initial order under Article 40.4.2 had been improperly issued. However, in the course of legal argument during the subsequent appeal, two members of the Supreme Court expressed the view that the State might, in fact, have been able to secure the return of the detainee to the jurisdiction, and that the Article 40.4.2 order had been properly made.[151]

---

[148] [1904] 2 KB 84.   [149] [1923] 2 AC 603.   [150] [1965] IR 70.

[151] Ó Dálaigh CJ is reported as suggesting that, having regard to the friendly relations between the states, the case against Quinn might have been postponed in order to have the Article 40.4.2 application in Ireland determined. Walsh J is reported as not being satisfied that production was impossible since the respondents were not shown to have made any positive effort to recover Quinn: *Irish Times*, 25 June 1964.

PRODUCTION OF THE PRISONER AND
CERTIFICATION OF GROUNDS OF DETENTION

'to produce the body of such person before the High Court'[152]

Article 40.4.2 is clearly drafted along the lines of the pre-nineteenth-century two-stage common law model.[153] The later version was invented explicitly in order to avoid the requirement necessitated by the earlier procedure of the physical presence of the prisoner.[154] The framers did not adopt that later version and Article 40.4.2 evidently requires the production of the prisoner. However, notwithstanding the literal wording of the provision, neither the initial production of the prisoner, nor the prisoner's presence during the entire hearing, have in practice been regarded as mandatory. In *The State (Woods) v. Kelly*[155] Ó Dálaigh CJ rejected a literal interpretation and ruled that the provision for production of the prisoner was an enabling power. The Chief Justice pointed out that a strict requirement of production might be counter-productive: 'The corollary of the submission [that the complainant must be produced] is that the court cannot make an order setting the prisoner at liberty unless he is present in court.' This construction enables Article 40.4.2 to be used in cases where it is not been practicable to direct the production of the prisoner (because, for instance, the prisoner is already in court, or because the prisoner has waived production)[156] or to have the prisoner present throughout the proceedings (because the prisoner is receiving treatment for injuries or illness).[157] But it has, in addition, been suggested that the High Court's

---

[152] At common law there exited a power to set aside a writ of habeas corpus (*R. v. Reynolds* (1795) 6 TR 497, 101 ER 667; *Carus Wilson's Case* (1845) 7 QB 984, 115 ER 759). The application was processed by means of a motion made by the respondent requiring the applicant to show cause why the writ should not be quashed. The writ could be rescinded where it was established that there was no jurisdiction to issue it, or that it had been obtained by misrepresentation. Article 40.4.2 contains within it a number of latent powers (such as the power to grant interim bail, or to authorize re-arrest following a successful respondent appeal, or to order costs); the question of whether a jurisdiction equivalent to the common law power to quash is included amongst that collection of latent powers has not yet been considered.

[153] See above pp 123–4.

[154] *Re Lloyd* (1845) 9 JP 115; *Re Eggington* (1853) 2 E & B 717, 118 ER 936.

[155] [1969] IR 269, 272.

[156] *The State (Rogers) v. Galvin* [1983] IR 249; *RT v. Director of Central Mental Hospital* [1995] 2 IR 65.

[157] *The State (Trimbole) v. Governor of Mountjoy Prison* [1985] IR 550.

discretion is much broader, and that production is only required where necessary to a proper enquiry. In *The State (Rogers) v. Galvin*[158] Henchy J stated: 'for a proper judicial enquiry to be carried out in certain cases, it may be necessary to exercise that power. But it cannot be said that in all cases its exercise is a necessary preliminary to an order of release from custody.'

At common law, on the other hand, the presumption was in favour of production. This was only exceptionally dispensed with: in the case of mentally disturbed prisoners, or children in child custody disputes where exposure to legal proceedings might be upsetting, or in the case of prisoners who had consented to not being produced.[159] If, as the Article 40.4.2 case law appears to suggest, the prisoner's entitlement to be produced is now only enforceable where production is in some way necessary 'for a proper judicial enquiry', the prisoner's entitlement to production on Article 40.4.2 has fallen below the right which a detainee enjoyed at common law.

'on a named day'

Article 40.4.2 requires that the prisoner be produced 'on a named day.' It may be that the formula, which has appeared in some Article 40.4.2 orders, that the detainee be produced 'at a later date to be agreed between the parties'[160] does not correspond to production on 'a named day' and so is inconsistent with Article 40.4.2. On the other hand, greater flexibility was introduced with the alteration in Article 40.4.2 of the wording originally found in Article 6 of the Constitution of the Irish Free State. While Article 6 had required that the body of the prisoner be produced 'without delay' the less prescriptive Article 40.4.2 does not insist that the full hearing commence at the most immediate point in time. The 'named day' has varied between orders requiring production on the same day and orders requiring production four weeks later, but more typically within less than

---

[158] [1983] IR 249, 252.
[159] *Re Brown* (1852) 18 LT OS 224; *Re Eggington* (1853) El & Bl 717, 118 ER 936, where it is noted editorially (p. 731) 'the prisoner was not brought into Court, upon the return, but remained in gaol probably by consent. This circumstance is not noted by the court. The gaoler had not, in fact, been required to bring up the body according to the exigency of the writ.'
[160] *The State (Trimbole) v. Governor of Mountjoy Prison* [1985] IR 550.

a week where the detention is of a long-term character, and on the day of complaint, or by the following day, where the detention is short term.[161]

'to certify in writing the grounds of his detention'[162]

The return at common law took two forms: either (i) a certificate which contained a full narrative establishing the legal authority for the detention, or (ii) a certificate justifying the detention by reference to the underlying order of commitment which was then attached to the certificate of return.[163] The second version was based on a concern that the detainer should not be required to furnish an independent account of the basis of the detention; otherwise 'it would be in the power of the gaoler to alter the case of the prisoner, and make it either better or worse than it is upon the warrant.'[164] This second type became, by the nineteenth century, the conventional form of return. The common law practice of returning the original order or warrant of committal has been perpetuated in the practice under Article 40.4.2. However, Article 40.4.2 does not literally require the production and endorsement of the order and warrant of committal, and in *Bolger v. Garda Commissioner*[165] it was suggested that under Article

---

[161] *The State (Trimbole) v. Governor of Mountjoy Prison* [1985] IR 550 (order made 4 Nov. 1984; returnable 11 Dec. 1984). Typically, in the case of detention of a longer-term character the return date will be set a number of days, rarely in excess of a week, from the date of the original order: *Re Ó Laighléis* [1960] IR 93 (4-day interval); *Re Singer* (1960) 97 ILTR 160 (6-day interval); *Croke v. Smith* [1994] 3 IR 525 (4-day interval); *McSorley v. Governor of Mountjoy Prison* [1997] 2 ILRM 315 (3-day interval); *Duncan v. Governor of Portlaoise Prison* [1998] 1 IR 433 (5-day interval).

[162] In *The State (Rogers) v. Galvin* [1983] IR 249 Henchy J held that the right to produce a written certificate was fundamental to the detainer's procedural rights. Accordingly, it was held that where a detainer had been given the opportunity to justify detention, but not to furnish a written certificate, Article 40.4.2 had not been constitutionally operated. But, given what appears to be the very technical nature of the written certificate requirement, it is difficult to see why the procedure should be characterized, as it was by the Supreme Court in *Rogers*, as so critical.

[163] The governor's return would recite the origin and date of the warrant under which the prisoner was detained. That warrant was then attached to the return. See, e.g. the return in 1860 of the governor of Fermanagh gaol in *R. v. Butler* (1860) LT NS 730.

[164] *R. v. Clerk* (1697) 1 Salk 349; 91 ER 305.

[165] Supreme Court, 2 Nov. 1998. O'Flaherty J said: 'there is no formality provided for the certificate in writing ... the governor of the prison may, no doubt, certify

40.4.2 it is sufficient that the custodian merely describe the legal basis of the complainant's detention without returning the original documentation.

How much detail is required to be set out in the certificate in order to adequately 'certify the grounds of detention'? The contents of the return at common law were originally determined by the rule that the custodian furnish a 'sufficient' return, demonstrating on the face of the certificate compliance with all of the procedural conditions precedent to the detention.[166] That return could then be quashed for insufficiency where it was technically irregular or did not show jurisdiction on its face. Until the nineteenth century, when the court acquired the means of investigating errors extraneous to the return, a defective return provided the sole ground of review. The evolution of the constitutional texts appears to suggest a contraction in the requirement. Article 6 of the Constitution of the Irish Free State required that the detainer 'certify in writing *as to* the causes of the detention.' The Article 40.4.2 requirement that the detainer 'certify in writing the grounds of his detention' appears to impose a less discursive standard. This textual refinement may support an argument that under Article 40.4.2 the custodian is not necessarily required to furnish a detailed narrative of the circumstances in which the detention power was exercised.[167]

INTERIM ORDERS AND BAIL

It has been suggested[168] that the combination of the express reference to a jurisdiction to grant bail on the case stated procedure under Article 40.4.3, together with the absence of a reference to such a jurisdiction from Article

> in writing that he holds [a prisoner] pursuant to such an order of such a court. He may well annex a copy of the warrant committing him to prison to his certificate in writing. I am not saying that he necessarily has to do so, but for completeness sake it is probably a wise move.'

[166] 'In favour of the liberty of the subject a sufficient cause for the imprisonment must appear on the return, and the place where the imprisonment takes place ought to be set out with certainty' per Crampton J in *Re Gregg* (1841) 3 Ir LR 316, 322; *The law of habeas corpus*, pp 36–9.

[167] The fact that the Article 40.4.2 enquiry is concerned with establishing whether the detainee is being 'detained in accordance with the law' and not with the sufficiency of the return also suggests that the technical content of the return is not of high significance under the Constitution.

[168] The argument was made by counsel in *Hegarty v. DPP*, High Court, 29 Nov.

40.4.2, generates an inference that the High Court has no jurisdiction to grant bail pending the determination under Article 40.4.2. The argument overlooks the fact that Article 40.4.3 was introduced four years later than Article 40.4.2, and, is therefore, not the guide as to the framers' intentions on Article 40.4.2 which it might be were the two provisions contemporaneous.[169] The practice of the High Court has been to continue to exercise on Article 40.4.2 the common law power to grant bail ancillary to habeas corpus.

The principles according to which the High Court acts in determining whether to grant bail on an application under Article 40.4.2 vary according to the objective of the imprisonment, and, in particular, according to whether the detention is preventive (as in extradition, deportation or mental health-related detention) or whether the objective is punitive or coercive (as in imprisonment following conviction, or committal for civil contempt). Where the imprisonment is preventive in character, the applicant may, where the High Court is satisfied that the release will not compromise the objective of the imprisonment, be entitled to bail on Article 40.4.2. Where, on the other hand, the objective underlying the imprisonment is punitive or coercive it is not sufficient that the prisoner will not abscond; release from custody compromises the punitive or coercive objective. Therefore, habeas corpus-associated bail is granted in these cases only where there are strong overriding grounds for disapplying the penal regime.

It is in cases where the purpose of the detention is preventive, and, in particular, in the context of pre-extradition remand, that the jurisdiction to grant habeas corpus-associated bail has been most commonly exercised. The standard of assurance which the court requires before granting bail has been variously expressed. According to the standard endorsed by the Supreme Court in *The People (AG) v. Gilliland*[170] bail must be granted

---

1996. The High Court assumed, though without deciding the question, that it did have such jurisdiction.

[169] In *The State (Whelan) v. Governor of Mountjoy Prison* [1983] ILRM 52 the High Court depreciated the use of Article 40.4.3 as an interpretative guide to the construction of Article 40.4.2.

[170] [1985] IR 643. In *Hegarty v. DPP*, High Court, 29 Nov. 1996 the High Court, in determining a habeas corpus-related application on behalf of remand prisoners, required the DPP establish a 'reasonable probability' of interference. The Court assumed, though without deciding the question, that no special or extraordinary circumstances must be demonstrated as a condition to the grant of bail. In the light of *Gilliland*, which is not referred to, that assumption was clearly correct.

unless the prosecution establishes a reasonable probability that the applicant will abscond. According to a second view, the principle applied in English law (and the principle that used to apply in Irish law)[171] bail may only be conceded in exceptional cases where the prisoner engenders a high degree of confidence that he will make himself available for extradition. According to a third view, a view expressly rejected by the Supreme Court in *The People (AG) v. Gilliland*,[172] the power to grant bail may only be exercised where the court is satisfied beyond all reasonable doubt of the applicant's trustworthiness. In *Gilliland* the Supreme Court expressly rejected the proposition that the court must be satisfied beyond all reasonable doubt of the likelihood of the applicant not absconding; it implicitly rejected the proposition that the applicant establish to a high degree the likelihood of his honouring his conditions of release. Instead, the Court held, a person awaiting extradition is no different from any other untried person, and enjoys a presumptive right to bail. Accordingly, the heavier burden is carried by the State, which must establish a reasonable probability that the complainant will not attend. Practically applied, the *Gilliland* standard means that bail must be granted even where there is a reasonable doubt as to whether the complainant may abscond, or where the evidence is evenly balanced.

However, the *Gilliland* rationale cannot be translated to the case of immigration, or mental health-related detention, where the proceedings are non-criminal, and where there is no presumptive right to liberty. The High Court has not yet determined the issue of the standard of proof required for the grant of bail pending a habeas corpus challenge to deportation or removal. The English High Court, however, has consistently held that bail in immigration-related habeas corpus should only be granted where the applicant establishes special grounds why intermediary release should be granted.[173] The jurisdiction to grant bail to prisoners seeking post-conviction habeas corpus is also highly restricted.[174] This is, in part,

---

[171] *The State (Dowling) v. Kingston* [1937] IR 483, 496.   [172] [1985] IR 643.
[173] It has been held in immigration-related habeas corpus proceedings that bail should be granted only where it is apparent that an error of principle has been committed or the decision has been affected by gross unreasonbleness: *Mohan v. Secretary of State for the Home Department*, Court of Appeal, 20 Dec. 1988; *Vilvarajah v. Secretary of State for the Home Department* [1990] Imm AR 457; *R. v. Secretary of State for the Home Department, ex p. Rahman*, Queen's Bench Div., 16 Aug. 1993.
[174] *The People (AG) v. Sigal* (1946) 12 Ir Jur 21. It was stated in *The State (Dunne)*

because the jurisdiction to exercise post-conviction habeas corpus review is itself quite limited, and, also, because the grant of bail to a convicted prisoner is objectionable in that it defeats the primary objective of imprisonment. There appear to be two conditions to the exercise of this exceptional jurisdiction: that the applicant has a strong prima facie case,[175] and the existence of special circumstances (such as the fact that the application may take time to dispose of,[176] or the fact that the imprisonment is about to expire).[177] In *The State (Langan) v. Donoghue*[178] the Supreme Court reserved[179] the question as to whether it had power on granting bail to suspend the operation of the sentence while the applicant was free on bail, and to reactivate the sentence should the detention be held to be in accordance with the law. The existence of an inherent common law power to suspend the running of a sentence of imprisonment while a prisoner is

---

v. Martin [1982] IR 229, 233: 'the fact that a judge is willing on an *ex parte* application, to grant a conditional order of certiorari is not in itself a good ground for granting bail when the applicant is serving a term of imprisonment imposed by a court of competent jurisdiction.' In *The People (DPP) v. Sweetman* [1997] 3 IR 448, 450 it was stated that 'the situation of a convicted person is in a different class. He now no longer enjoys the presumption of innocence. It is not a question of admitting a person to bail where he will answer to his bail pending the disposal of the hearing before judge and jury. The criteria that are relevant to pre-trial applications for bail are not the same as those that operate post-conviction.'

[175] In *R. v. Watton* (1979) 68 Cr App Rep 293 the English Court of Criminal Appeal stated that bail pending appeal should only be granted under special circumstances, i.e. where it appears, prima facie, that the appeal is likely to be successful or where there is a risk that the sentence will be served by the time that the appeal is heard. In *The People (DPP) v. Sweetman* [1997] 3 IR 448, 450 the Court of Criminal Appeal stated: 'the strength of the case as it appears on the materials placed before it on this application is the proper matter to be brought into the reckoning.'

[176] *The State (Healy) v. Donohue*, Irish Times, 8 Mar. 1975. In *The State (Whelan) v. Governor of Mountjoy Prison* [1983] ILRM 52, 55 Barrington J stated: 'if the application raises difficult questions of law or fact the court may have to consider whether the applicant should be admitted to bail until those procedures are resolved.'

[177] *The State (McKenna) v. Durcan* (1952) 87 ILTR 62 (likelihood of sentence having expired at time of determination of applications for certiorari and habeas corpus); *AG v. Kirwan* (1950) 89 ILTR 120 (court holding that it would be disposed to granting bail if it was satisfied that the delay would be considerable).

[178] [1974] IR 251, 257.

[179] On the other hand, the power was assumed in *The State (Sheerin) v. Kennedy* [1966] IR 379 and *The State (Dunne) v. Martin* [1982] IR 229.

discharged on certiorari or habeas corpus-related bail can be traced to, at least, the early eighteenth century. *R. v. Reader*[180] provides an instance: the Court of King's Bench, in granting bail to a prisoner challenging his sentence by certiorari, stated 'if the conviction was affirmed, they could commit him in execution for the residue of the term.'[181]

Along with the usual requirements of recognizances and sureties, the grant of habeas corpus-associated bail is usually conditioned on a series of undertakings: to appear and surrender before the High Court at every hearing of the habeas corpus application; not to leave the jurisdiction; to prosecute the application with due diligence. The grant of bail may be made subject to a proviso that the period on bail not be reckoned part of the applicant's sentence.[182] However, procedures for the enforcement of bail ancillary to Article 40.4.2 are weaker than the procedures for the enforcement of pre-trial bail. The mechanisms introduced under the Bail Act, 1997 (the requirement that the recognizance be lodged prior to release, and the power of arrest without warrant under section 9 where a person is suspected of absconding) only apply where bail has been granted by a court exercising 'criminal jurisdiction'; it is doubtful whether the High Court exercising jurisdiction under Article 40.4.2 is exercising criminal jurisdiction.[183] The alternative to the re-arrest procedure under the 1997 Act is more cumbersome: at common law the King's Bench had an

---

[180] (1723) 1 Stra 532; 93 ER 681.

[181] It has been suggested that the theoretical basis for this is that, pending the determination of the application, the prisoner is held not under the original warrant of commitment but under the authority of the writ of habeas corpus: *Barth v. Clise* 12 Wall 400; 79 US 393 (1870).

[182] *The State (Hully) v. Hynes* (1959 No. 13 SS), (1966) 100 ILTR 145: to appear before the court at each day of the hearing and abide by the order of the court and not leave the country without leave, and that the person showing cause retain the complainant's passport; *The State (Griffin) v. Bell* (1960 No. 43 SS), [1962] IR 355: recognizance in the sum of £500 together with two independent sureties in the sum of £500 each, sureties to be approved by the District Court, on condition that the applicant surrender himself at each and every hearing of his application; *The State (Magee) v. O'Rourke* (1968 No. 44 SS), [1971] IR 205: to prosecute the hearing with due diligence, attend the proceedings in person, and in the event of the application failing, surrender himself to the custody of the Gardaí; *The State (Sheerin) v. Kennedy* (1966 No. 9 SS), [1966] IR 379: not to leave the jurisdiction, period spent on bail not to be reckoned part of the sentence.

[183] S. 1(1) provides that a court for the purpose of the legislation means any court exercising criminal jurisdiction.

inherent jurisdiction, where it had granted bail, to direct the arrest of a person breaching the conditions of that bail,[184] and it is probably from this common law source that the High Court derives the power to issue a bench warrant where a complainant abuses a grant of bail ancillary to Article 40.4.2.[185] There appears, however, to be no right, as there is under the Bail Act, 1997 to arrest without warrant.[186]

A range of intermediary orders may be made on an application for habeas corpus: that interrogation be suspended;[187] that the prisoner be removed from a police station to hospital;[188] that a detainee be psychiatrically examined; that the detainee be given access to his legal advisor;[189] varying the conditions on which bail has been granted;[190] that a punishment of loss of privileges be suspended.[191] A structured approach to the exercise of the jurisdiction was elaborated by Hutton J in *Re Gillen's Application*,[192] where an application for a stay of the detainee's interrogation was sought pending the determination of the prisoner's habeas corpus application. The High Court of Northern Ireland analogized the application for a stay to an application for an injunction, where a plaintiff is required to establish a prima facie case, and to establish that the balance of convenience favours the grant of an order. Given the risk that police interrogation might be frustrated by disingenuous applications for stay of

---

[184] *R. v. O'Fagherty* (1841) 1 Leg Rep 72.
[185] Bench warrants were issued for the arrest of complainants not surrendering in accordance with the terms of bail in *The State (Whelan) v. Governor of Arbour Hill Prison* (1978 No. 730 SS), [1983] ILRM 52, and *The State (Aherne) v. Governor of Limerick Prison* (1980 No. 328 SS), [1982] IR 188. See, however, Short and Mellor, *Crown practice* (London, 1890), at pp 135–6 expressing reservations as to the power to recommit a prisoner failing to surrender in accordance with the recognizance.
[186] A power to arrest without warrant persons released on bail ancillary to habeas corpus has been created in New Zealand's Habeas Corpus Act, 2001: s. 12 (1) provides that a member of the police may arrest a person who has been released from detention under an interim order if the member of the police believes on reasonable grounds that the person released has absconded or has failed to comply with a condition attached to the interim order; s. 11(4) creates a power of forcible entry for the purpose of carrying out such an arrest.
[187] *The State (Harrington) v. Garda Commissioner*, High Court, 14 Dec. 1976.
[188] *The State (Breathnach) v. Hennessy* (1976 No. 127 SS), *Irish Times*, 8 Apr. 1976.
[189] *R. v. Mountnorris* (1795) Ir Term Rep 460.
[190] *Mangan v. DPP*, High Court, 30 July 2004.
[191] *State (Fagan) v. Governor of Mountjoy Prison*, *Irish Times*, 14 Sept. 1977.
[192] [1988] NI 40.

interrogation pending determination of habeas corpus, the Court required, firstly, the establishment of a strong prima facie case of illegality in the conduct of the interrogation, and, secondly, that the applicant establish a risk of uncompensatable loss were a stay not ordered.

THE HEARING

In camera *hearings*

Applications under Article 40.4.2 are governed by the publicity principle in Article 34.1 of the Constitution. In *The State (Cremin) v. Cork Circuit Court Judge*[193] the Supreme Court censured the policy of ruling epistolary prisoner applications by correspondence, rather than by ruling in open court:

> The broad requirement of Article 34 is that justice should be administered in public. Section 45 of the Courts (Supplemental Provisions) Act, 1961, however, authorizes the disposal of a habeas corpus application elsewhere than in open court in a case of an urgent nature. In the absence of urgency, an application is proper to be ruled in the open and not in chambers. Where an applicant is not represented by counsel and the application is made by correspondence it is perhaps easy to overlook that the Court should after enquiry, rule the application orally in court and not by correspondence.[194]

The Constitution permits two exceptions to the general rule: (i) Article 34.1 itself recognizes that exceptions to the publicity rule may be prescribed by statute, and (ii) there are cases where, even in the absence of a statutory exclusion, the publicity rule may have to be subordinated to some overriding constitutional interest. An exception within the first category is contained in section 45(1) of the Courts (Supplemental Provisions)

---

[193] Supreme Court, 8 Feb. 1965.
[194] The *Cremin* judgment only requires that where an application is submitted in the form of a written complaint that the ruling as to whether the application be admitted or refused be determined in open court; it is not a requirement of Article 34.1 that the documentation upon which the application is based be read in open court: *O'Dwyer v. Boyd* [2003] 1 ILRM 112.

Act, 1961 which provides that 'justice may be administered otherwise than in public in any of the following cases:- (a) applications of an urgent nature for relief by way of habeas corpus, bail, prohibition, or injunction.' It is by reference to this exception that the practice (already established at common law) of hearing applications at judges' homes is justified. The exception is, however, restricted to cases where an extra-curial application is required on grounds of urgency (and not for some other reason). In *Z v. DPP* Hamilton CJ noted:[195]

> The applications of 'an urgent nature' for relief by way of habeas corpus, bail, prohibition, or injunction, to which section 45(1) of the Courts (Supplementary Provisions) Act, 1961 relates, are those which are because of their nature so urgent that they must be made to a judge in his house or some place to which the public do not directly have access, and not to applications which are made in court.

A second qualification to the publicity requirement in Article 34.1 is recognized where the interest served by the publicity requirement is overridden by a constitutional interest of superior weight.[196] It is by reference to this qualification that applications have been disposed of otherwise in public where a public hearing might imperil the physical safety of the complainant or some other party.[197]

The speed of disposal

In *The State (Whelan) v. Governor of Mountjoy Prison*[198] it was held that, 'provided the urgency and importance of the proceedings are kept in mind, the Court is entitled to conduct the hearing in the manner which it thinks best calculated to resolve the issues of law and fact and to achieve justice.' The Court pointed out that the adverb 'forthwith' qualified the manner in which the decision to order an enquiry was to be conducted, but

---

[195] [1994] 2 IR 476, 486.
[196] *The Irish Times Ltd v. Ireland* [1998] 1 IR 359.
[197] In *Re Quigley* [1983] NI 245, the issue as to whether a Ms Linda Quigley (the wife of a man who had undertaken to provide evidence as a supergrass in a terrorist prosecution, and who was under police protection) was being detained against her will, was determined in chambers.
[198] [1983] ILRM 52, 55.

did not govern the time in which the enquiry itself was to be administered, or within which judgment was to be delivered. On the other hand, Article 5(4) of the European Convention of Human Rights requires that the individual have access to proceedings under which the lawfulness of his detention shall be decided speedily. The discretion allowed by the *Whelan* formulation under which urgency is a factor to be 'kept in mind' appears to be less rigorous than the European standard under which the entitlement to a speedy hearing is a positive right. The Article 5(4) notion of speediness requires such minimal operational delay as the complexity of the issues to be determined permits,[199] and may intensify where the authorities have been at fault in delaying access to review, or their conduct may have increased the risk of an injustice.[200] Where there has been a prima facie infraction of the requirement, the burden shifts to the authorities to demonstrate exceptional grounds to excuse the prima facie denial.[201] However, even if binding as treaty duties in international law, these principles of European human rights law are probably not standards capable of regulating the operation of Article 40.4.2 of the Constitution. The European Convention of Human Rights Act, 2003 incorporates the European Convention into Irish law; however, the Act excludes 'a court' (and thereby the High Court under Article 40.4.2) from the range of institutions required to 'perform its functions in a manner compatible with the State's obligations under the Convention.'[202]

The right to select the judge determining the application

Article 6 of the Constitution of the Irish Free State (and for the first four years of its existence, Article 40.4.2 of the present Constitution) by

---

[199] *Sanchez-Reisse v. Switzerland* (1986) 9 EHRR 71; *Jablonski v. Poland* (2003) 36 EHRR 27; delay caused by vacation periods or excessive time spent in the writing of the court judgment is not a legitimate excuse: *E v. Norway* (1990) 17 EHRR 30.

[200] *Van der Leer v. Netherlands* (1990) 12 EHRR 567.

[201] Such exceptional grounds have included the fact that the prisoner has voluntarily waived the right to speedy determination, or has contributed to the delay by his own dilatory conduct: *Musial v. Poland* (2001) 31 EHRR 29, para. 45; *Pereira v. Portugal* (2003) 36 EHRR 49; *Kolompar v. Belgium* (1993) 16 EHRR 197.

[202] S. 3 (1) of the 2003 Act provides that every 'organ of the State shall perform its functions in a manner compatible with the State's obligations under the Convention provisions.' However, s. 1 provides that an organ of State does not include 'a court.'

requiring that the order be returnable before 'such judge' as had directed the initial enquiry, appeared to establish a right to select the judge to determine both the initial application for a hearing and the full hearing. The contention that the Article did confer such a right of selection was accepted by Gavan Duffy J in *The State (Burke) v. Lennon* in 1939.[203] The Government responded to Gavan Duffy's ruling with a constitutional amendment which expressly addressed the issue. In 1941, with the enactment of the Second Amendment of the Constitution Act, 1941, the right of selection was abolished. In place of the direct continuity, which had existed under the original text, between the judge who granted the application and the judge hearing the application, the revised version made the entire High Court competent to hear the application. The right of selection was further undermined by the right in Article 40.4.4 of the President or the senior judge of the High Court to empanel a three judge divisional court. In light of the background, the assertion sometimes made[204] that the complaint must 'if practicable and possible be discharged by [the judge to whom the initial application was submitted]' is difficult to justify. On the other hand, the historical evidence establishes that it was not the framers' intention that the earlier entitlement be totally overriden. Contemporary sources reveal that it was the Government's intention was that, while a complainant would no longer have the right to have the complaint determined by the judge to whom the application was submitted, the entitlement was something to which the President would at least 'advert' or 'have regard to'.[205] In practice, the determination of the application by a judge other than the judge granting the initial application, or by a divisional court, is not at all uncommon.[206]

---

[203] [1940] IR 136; *Irish Times*, 29 Nov. 1939. See above, pp 31–2.
[204] *Cahill v. Governor of Curragh Military Detention Barracks* [1980] ILRM 191; *Barry v. Waldron*, High Court, 23 May 1996.
[205] *Dáil Debates*, vol. 82, cols 1909–10 (24 Apr. 1941); NAI, Department of the Taoiseach, S. 11603.
[206] *The State (D) v. Groarke* [1990] 1 IR 305; *Ellis v. O' Dea (No. 2)* [1991] 1 IR 251; *JG v. Governor of Mountjoy Prison* [1991] 1 IR 373; *RT v. Director of Central Mental Hospital* [1995] 2 IR 65; *Duncan v. Governor of Portlaoise Prison* [1998] 1 IR 433. Divisional courts were assembled in *McGlinchey v. Governor of Portlaoise Prison* [1988] IR 671; *Finucane v. McMahon* [1990] 1 IR 165; *Hegarty v. Governor of Limerick Prison* [1998] 1 IR 412; *Re Gallagher* [1996] 3 IR 10.

PROCEDURAL RIGHTS OF THE DETAINER

'after giving the person in whose custody he is detained an opportunity of justifying the detention'

The requirement that the detainer be given 'an opportunity of justifying the detention' has the obvious corollary that a complaint may not be processed summarily without the detainer being given the opportunity of making a defence. This principle was confirmed in *Re Zwann*.[207] Here the High Court, without hearing the respondent, had made, what was described as an absolute order of habeas corpus under the Habeas Corpus Act, 1782. The Supreme Court held that 'it is implicit in Article 40, s. 4, sub-s. 2 that before an [order of release] may be made an opportunity must be afforded to the detaining person to justify such detention.' The Court then turned to the absolute order made by the High Court and remarked that the extent to which the common law or the Act of 1782 'permit[ted] the granting of an absolute order of habeas corpus without allowing an opportunity to justify the detention complained of, it would appear difficult to reconcile its provisions with the provisions of Article 40, s. 4, sub-s. 2 of the Constitution.' But an absolute order of habeas corpus did not compromise the representative rights of the custodian. An absolute order of habeas corpus at common law was merely an order requiring production of the prisoner and the filing of a return. An order of release would issue subsequent to the order of habeas corpus and the filing of the return, and took the form of a separate rule for the discharge of the detainee. An absolute order of habeas corpus was equivalent to an interim order of production under the Constitution and to characterize it as an order of release is incorrect.

Three further corollaries of the requirement that the detainer be given an opportunity of justifying the detention were established in *The State (Rogers) v. Galvin*:[208] that the detainer must be given adequate time to prepare a justification; that the detainer must be enabled to consult a legal representative; and that the detainer must be allowed exercise his Constitutional entitlement to file a certificate of the grounds of detention. Henchy J described the custodian's right of response as[209]

---

[207] [1981] IR 395.   [208] [1983] IR 249.   [209] Ibid., p. 253.

a constitutional recognition of the rule of natural justice expressed in the maxim *audi alteram partem*. It guards against the risk that on an *ex parte* application, or on an application in which the detainer has not had a proper opportunity of justifying the detainee's complaint, an unjustified order of release from custody may be made. It gives constitutional form and shape to what had been for centuries an essential prelude to release by means of habeas corpus.

Henchy J did, however, acknowledge one exception to this requirement, cases where the detainer 'with full authority, knowledge and intention' consented to dispensation with his procedural rights.

Usually, of course, the custodian will not have been a party to the decision on which the detention is predicated, and an effective justification will only be possible where those who are primarily responsible for the detention are allowed respond to the complainant's argument. This may be done either by making the parties responsible for the detention notice parties to the application,[210] or by the custodian introducing evidence on behalf of the responsible party; or (perhaps less properly, given that the detaining party is the only respondent acknowledged by Article 40.4.2) making the parties responsible for the detention respondents.[211] Of course, it is essential that any materials filed by any of these parties by way of justification for the detention be served on the complainant sufficiently in advance of the hearing in order to facilitate a full response by the complainant.[212]

---

[210] *The State (Ring) v. Governor of Mountjoy Prison* (1971) 105 ILTR 113 (committing creditor notice party); *Quinlivan v. Governor of Portlaoise Prison* [1998] 1 IR 456, and *Duncan v. Governor of Portlaoise Prison* [1998] 1 IR 433 (Director of Public Prosecutions, Minister for Justice, Ireland, the Attorney General and Garda Commissioner, notice parties); *Re Gallagher* [1996] 3 IR 10 (Minister for Justice, Ireland and Attorney General, notice parties). Where the detention follows judicial proceedings the practice has always been to make the party promoting the detention (the Director of Public Prosecutions, or the Attorney General, or the creditor), though not the judge, a notice party to the proceedings. The rule against making the judge a notice party is motivated by a concern that judges should not be amenable to cross-examination in relation to the judicial process: *O'Connor v. Carroll* [1999] 2 IR 160; *McIlwraith v. Fawsitt* [1990] 1 IR 343. In the Article 40.4.2 case *MF v. Superintendent of Ballymun Garda Station* [1991] 1 IR 189,191 a District Court judge was permitted to file a letter outlining the sequence of events.

[211] *The State (Hoey) v. Garvey* (1976 No. 443 SS), [1978] IR 1; *The State (D) v. Groarke* [1990] 1 IR 305 (Midland Health Board, respondent); *McGlinchey v. Ireland* [1990] 2 IR 215 (Ireland and the Attorney General, respondents).

[212] *R. v. Olson* (1987) 38 CCC (3d) 534.

In *Re Maguire*[213] the High Court refused representation, on an Article 40.4.2 application, to the family of the victim of a criminal offence committed by the prisoner. The High Court held that the challenge by the complainant (who had been convicted of murder and was challenging his detention under the Trial of Lunatics Act, 1883) could be adequately defended by the Minister for Justice, and that victim representation on habeas corpus was unprecedented. In fact, historically the representation by victims in habeas corpus applications was by no means unheard of.[214]

The Supreme Court in *The State (Hully) v. Hynes*[215] appeared to require continuity of identity between the person in whose custody the detainee was at the time of the complaint and the identity of the custodian at the time of the enquiry. The Court, in effect, added words into Article 40.4.2 to the effect that release must be ordered unless satisfied *by the person in whose custody he was at the time of complaint* that the detention is in accordance with the law. In *Hully's* case the initial order had been directed to Superintendent Hynes of Bray Garda Station in April 1959, but it was only in October 1961, when Hynes had retired, that the matter was determined. The Supreme Court held that since the respondent, Superintendent Hynes, had no longer any active role in the detention of the complainant, and could not justify the detention of the complainant, the complainant was entitled to his release.[216] The effect of *Hully's* case is that an order of discharge must follow where there is any discontinuity in the identity of the custodian, since the original respondent will lack standing to justify the detention. It would seem to allow the complainant to profit from technical administrative oversight, or delay. The *Hully* construction is not necessarily supported by Article 40.4.2. Instead, Article 40.4.2 appears to require that, upon a transfer of custody from the original custodian to a subsequent custodian, the new custodian be given the right of justifying the detention: the Constitution refers to the detention being

---

[213] [1996] 3 IR 1.
[214] *Re Rumble* (1868) 3 IRCL 271 (next of kin of deceased heard in habeas corpus challenge by soldiers charged with homicide following incident at which they had opened fire on a crowd); *R. v. Metropolitan Police Commissioner, ex p. Melia* [1957] 1 WLR 1065 (wife of complainant, an alleged maintenance defaulter, heard on habeas corpus taken by complainant opposing his extradition).
[215] (1966) 100 ILTR 145.
[216] 'We are all satisfied that because the respondent has retired from the Garda Síochána he cannot in this Court justify his authority to detain the prosecutor,' per Maguire CJ (1966) 100 ILTR 145, 161.

justified by 'the person in whose custody he is' at the time of the hearing, and not by 'the person in whose custody he *was*' at the time of the initial complaint.

CONTEMPT OF ARTICLE 40.4.2[217]

Contempt of habeas corpus has usually taken the form of disobedience of an order of production, or to make a return, or to release. In *Egan v. Macready*,[218] in July 1921, an order for attachment was issued against Sir Nevil Macready, Commander in Chief of the Forces in Ireland, Major General Strickland, and Brigadier General Cameron, following their decision to ignore the order of release made by O'Connor MR. In *Re Mathews*[219] Margaret Aylward was sentenced to six months' imprisonment for furnishing a return which was regarded as 'untrue or evasive' in its denial of knowledge of the whereabouts of a child the subject of a custody dispute. Failure to make a return has also, even where the body has been prduced, been treated as contempt.[220] There is early Irish authority to the effect that the swearing a false affidavit in order to induce the court into issuing habeas corpus may (as well as being indictable as perjury) also be a contempt of court.[221] Under the Constitution frustration of access to, or interference with the operation of the remedy, may, even without disobedience to an existing order, also constitute contempt; it was doubtful at common law whether such conduct was a contempt.[222] In *The State*

---

[217] O. 84, r. 12 provides a specific procedure for the disobedience of habeas corpus. However, 'habeas corpus' is expressly stated not to include an order made pursuant to Article 40 section 4 of the Constitution: O. 84, r.1 (2).
[218] [1921] 1 IR 265.
[219] (1860) 12 ICLR 233.
[220] *In re Thompson* (1888) 5 TLR 540.
[221] *R. v. Blakeney* (1744) reported sub nom *R. v. Heath* (1744) 18 St Tr 1, 20.
[222] In *Barnardo v. Ford* [1892] AC 326 the respondent had allegedly transferred the custody of a child out of the jurisdiction prior to any habeas corpus being sought, and purely in order to avoid future legal process. The House of Lords was not confident that this was conduct for which the respondent could be punished. Lord Watson said that, while a person who parts with the custody of a detainee after service of a writ committed a plain contempt of court, the position was different where the act took place before receipt of the writ: 'No contempt is committed by a person who, lawfully or unlawfully, absolutely gives up the custody and control of a child from the mere apprehension that by

(Quinn) v. Ryan[223] officers of the Garda Síochána, and of the London Metropolitan Police, were found guilty of contempt of the Constitution for organizing an extradition from Ireland with such rapidity that it frustrated the extraditee's right of access to an enquiry under Article 40.4.2. The Supreme Court did not consider it relevant that the respondent had not disregarded any order already made by the court.

Habeas corpus-related contempt has been classified as a form of criminal contempt.[224] There may also be circumstances in which contempt of habeas corpus may be civil in character: Henchy J thought that the application for contempt taken in *Re Earle*[225] (following the refusal of a guardian to comply with an order of habeas corpus in a child custody case) was civil in character. But cases of civil contempt are likely to be rare. The accepted understanding of civil contempt in Irish law is that of a coercive process initiated by one of the parties for the enforcement of an order made in its favour.[226] Since contempt proceedings in the course of an Article 40.4.2 proceeding will typically be initiated by the court *ex mero motu*, and independent of the complainant, the proceedings are, under this definition, criminal in character. A criminal characterization would also appear to be preferable on policy grounds: to classify habeas corpus as civil contempt (with the corollary that the contempt proceedings may be waived by the applicant) might be seen as weakening the constitutional remedy.

In *The State (DPP) v. Walsh*[227] the Supreme Court held that criminal contempt was subject to the guarantee in Article 38.5 of a trial with a jury. Subsequently the Supreme Court has held that the application of Article 38.5 was restricted to acts of criminal contempt committed outside the court; the requirement did not apply to contempt *in facie curiae*.[228] In

---

retaining it he may become liable to a writ of habeas corpus and without any notice that such a proceeding will be taken' (p. 335).

[223] [1965] IR 70.
[224] *Keegan v. de Burca* [1973] IR 223, 227.
[225] [1938] IR 485. In *The State (DPP) v. Walsh* [1981] IR 412, 430 Henchy J said of *Earle's* case 'that case was concerned with a question of what is, perhaps only a civil contempt now, i.e., a failure to obey an order of habeas corpus in respect of a child whose custody was in issue: see per Murnaghan J at p. 502 of the report.'
[226] *Hawkins v. Fackman* (1795) Ridgeway 537; *Smith v. Molloy* (1905) 39 ILTR 221; *Keegan v. de Burca* [1973] IR 223.
[227] [1981] IR 412.
[228] *Kelly v. Deighan* [1984] ILRM 424, relying on *The State (DPP) v. Walsh* [1981] IR 412. This is questionable. *Walsh*, where jury trial was held necessary, was,

proceedings for contempt of habeas corpus the facts are usually admitted and the proceedings discharged without a factual contest.[229] Whether, in the event that findings of fact are required to be made, contempt of Article 40.4.2 is subject to, or free from, the jury trial requirement, depends, therefore, on the breadth of the definition of contempt *in facie curiae*. O'Higgins CJ in *The State (DPP) v. Walsh* defined contempt *in facie curiae* as including conduct which is 'obstructive or prejudicial to the course of justice' and which is committed during court proceedings. On this view any conduct which is obstructive, and which is committed while legal proceedings are current, constitutes contempt *in facie curiae* (and therefore does not attract the inconvenient trial by jury requirement). According to an alternative, and possibly more natural view, contempt *in facie curiae* only extends to conduct which occurs in the presence of the court. It is only if the wider definition of *in facie curiae* represents the correct test, that the highly awkward jury trial requirement is removed from contempt of Article 40.4.2.

THE ORDER OF RELEASE

The requirement of unconditional release

A number of ancillary rules underlie the remedy of release in Article 40.4.2: (i) that the High Court may not place a stay on the order of release; (ii) that the Supreme Court is also prohibited from placing a stay pending an appeal to that Court from an order of release directed by the High

admittedly, a case of contempt out of court, and in *Walsh* counsel for the defendant, in pressing for the application of Article 38.5 expressly refrained from making any submissions on whether the right to jury trial extended to contempt *in facie curiae*. But it also appears that the majority of the Supreme Court did consider that logically the procedure should apply regardless of the nature of the contempt. Henchy J stated that if 'jury trial were to be a permissible or proper mode of trying the factual issues of some major contempt charges, I think that it should be held to be the correct mode of trying such issues in all major contempt charges. A judicial policy that in only some cases should such issues be tried before a jury would seem so arbitrary and discriminatory as not to be consistent with the equality before the law guaranteed by the Constitution' ([1981] IR 412, 441).

[229] An instance is *Egan v. Macready* [1921] 1 IR 265 where attachment proceedings were discharged when counsel for the Crown apologized to the court, explaining that no contempt of the court's authority was intended.

Court; (iii) that once the defect which was the cause of the original enquiry is not perpetuated the complainant may, following release, be re-arrested; and (iv) that the High Court has no inherent power to manufacture its own order of re-arrest.

An order of release may not be qualified by an order staying the release. This prohibition means that the High Court may not place a stay on one of its own orders.[230] It also means that the Supreme Court may not, pending an appeal, place a stay on an order of the High Court.[231] The text of Article 40.4.2 is unambivalent in requiring that the High Court 'shall' release a person whose custody is unlawful; therefore the Court may not (except in the circumstances envisaged in Article 40.4.3) attach a stay to its order of release. However, there is, arguably, nothing in the text which clearly prohibits *the Supreme Court* from directing the suspension of an order made by the High Court. Nonetheless, a contrary view has been taken by the Supreme Court. In *The State (Trimbole) v. Governor of Mountjoy Prison*[232] the Supreme Court held that it had no power to suspend an order of the High Court pending an appeal:[233]

> While it is persuasive to say that any ordinary appellate jurisdiction includes any powers to make it effective, so to constitute that power to order a stay in this case would be inconsistent with the Constitution. I am satisfied from the report of *The State (Browne) v. Feran* that the power of this Court to make an order for re-arrest clearly must be confined to a time when the Court has held the High Court decision is incorrect. There is no question of the High Court ordering re-arrest in order to allow the Court to decide an issue.

Release 'from such detention'

On the other hand, Article 40.4.2 merely directs the release of the person from 'such' detention as he is currently undergoing. Unlike Article 6 of the

---

[230] There appears to have been a power at common law to place a stay on a writ of habeas corpus. In *Egan v. Macready* [1921] 1 IR 265 the court placed a stay on the writ of habeas corpus requiring the production of the applicants following an undertaking by the Crown to release the detainees (*Irish Times*, 1 Aug. 1921).
[231] *The State (Trimbole) v. Governor of Mountjoy Prison* [1985] IR 550.
[232] [1985] IR 550.
[233] Ibid., pp 567–8.

Constitution of the Irish Free State which, in unconditional terms, directed the release *simpliciter* of the detainee, Article 40.4.2 only requires that the prisoner be discharged from the custody which has been established to be unlawful. The text is not irreconcilable with the co-existence of a power of immediate re-arrest under some alternative power. The fact that Article 40.4.2 only requires release from 'such' detention as is the subject of the Article 40.4.2 enquiry is the source of a number of propositions which work in favour of the executive: (i) that an order of release does not require an extended period of liberty; (ii) that once the original order of arrest has been remedied, a prisoner discharged on Article 40.4.2 may, usually, be immediately re-arrested.

An order of release under Article 40.4.2 is sometimes a purely formal remedy. Because Article 40.4.2 only requires the release of the detainee from 'such' custody as he is currently undergoing it appears to be accepted that release does not require a long-term interval of liberty. In *Re Singer (No. 2)*[234] the applicant had, following an application under Article 40.4.2, been discharged from Mountjoy Prison. As he stepped out of prison, and into the enclosed avenue which leads from the prison, members of the Gardaí, standing three to five yards from the prison gates, were waiting for him armed with a warrant of arrest. Within ten seconds of his release he was under arrest again. Walsh J held that the police manoeuvre did not infringe Article 40.4.2: 'It was not contested that in fact the prosecutor was at the time of this arrest enjoying a period of freedom from restraint, although a brief one. Once he was free of the restraint of the Governor of the Prison the order of the Supreme Court had, in my opinion, been complied with ...'[235] The first of the grounds mentioned by Walsh J, that the complainant was at liberty, does not appear convincing: Singer's freedom of movement along the enclosed prison avenue was entirely restricted when the Gardaí blocked the only egress. On the other hand, Singer had been freed from the custody of the unlawful custodian, the Governor of Mountjoy Prison, and the minimal Article 40.4.2 requirement of discharge from 'such' unlawful detention, the detention by the custodian responsible for the unlawful custody, had been complied with.

---

[234] (1960) 98 ILTR 112.
[235] Ibid., p. 124.

The right of re-arrest following correction of the original error

It has always been recognized at common law that a person who has been discharged on habeas corpus may be re-arrested where the defect which invalidated the original detention has been corrected.[236] There are, however, a series of potential restrictions on the power of re-arrest. First, re-arrest affected by the same error for which the applicant was released may be treated as an act of contempt.[237] Secondly, a statutory prohibition on re-arrest (though operating only in the case of persons detained in the criminal process and only to a person delivered or set at large upon any 'habeas corpus')[238] is prescribed by section 5 of the Habeas Corpus Act, 1782:

> For the prevention of unjust vexation by reiterated commitments for the same offence be it enacted that no person or persons who shall be delivered or set at large upon any habeas corpus, shall at any time hereafter be again imprisoned, or committed for the same offence by any person or persons whatsoever, other than by the legal process of such court wherein he or they shall be bound by recognizance to appear, or other court having jurisdiction of the cause.

It has been assumed that section 5 applies to release under Article 40.4.2.[239] But it is difficult to see how this could be so: the 'habeas corpus' referred to in section 5 is clearly a different procedure to the procedure in Article 40.4.2. The range of operation of section 5, assuming it does apply, is unsettled. The narrower interpretation of section 5 is that it only prevents re-arrest in cases where a detainee has applied for, and been granted, bail by means of habeas corpus. It does not apply where habeas corpus has been deployed for the purpose of the person's unconditional release. The conclusion that section 5 was intended to deal with applications for bail by habeas corpus is based on the proviso entitling re-arrest by 'process of such court wherein he or they shall be bound by recognizance

---

[236] *The law of habeas corpus*, pp 205–9.
[237] See, e.g., *R. v. Merrick* (n.d.) Rowe's Reports 550.
[238] The point that s. 5 cannot apply to release under Article 40.4.2 was not taken in any of the recent Irish cases where its application was raised.
[239] *The State (Dowling) v. Kingston (No. 2)* [1937] IR 699; *In re Singer (No. 2)* (1964) 98 ILTR 112, 132; *The State (McFadden) v. Governor of Mountjoy Prison (No.2)* [1981] ILRM 120.

to appear.' The reference to susceptibility to re-arrest by the court to which the person is 'bound by recognizance to appear' suggests, it is contended, that the provision is intended only to deal with a person discharged on bail. In *R. v. Governor of Brixton Prison, ex parte Stallman*[240] Phillimore J (in a passage endorsed by Ó Dálaigh CJ as the most accurate translation of the section 5)[241] stated:[242]

> Some reference to history is necessary ... The section was directed against reiterated commitments, as it says, for the same offence. Persons were committed; they were enlarged upon bail or their recognizances to appear. In those days it was frequently a very lengthy process to persuade the Court to go so far as that; and in addition there was the danger that a fresh warrant would be issued, and that the person again arrested upon it would be compelled to sue out a second writ of habeas corpus, remaining in custody meanwhile; and it was intended by that section to enact that as long as he had done nothing to forfeit his recognizance, or which justified the Court in calling upon his sureties to shew cause why their bail should not be estreated, he should not be recommitted upon the same charge ...

But it is odd, if the intention was to restrict the bar on re-arrest to persons discharged on bail, that the prohibition on re-arrest is phrased as applying to persons 'delivered or set at large', and not (as in section 6) to persons 'set at large *upon bail*' or 'discharged on his or their recognizances' (as in section 2). One of the principal remedies provided by the legislation was that (under section 6) of the unconditional release of a person committed for trial, who having made his prayer to be brought to trial, had not been indicted for two sessions.[243] If the Phillimore interpretation is correct, and only persons released on bail are protected by section 5, it would attribute to the legislature the absurdity of having allowed the Crown to take away at will, simply by re-arresting the detainee, the great remedy under section 6.[244]

---

[240] [1912] 3 KB 424.
[241] *In re Singer (No. 2)* (1964) 98 ILTR 112, 132.
[242] [1912] 3 KB 424, pp 448–9.
[243] See above, p. 5.
[244] The suggestion that the provision was intended only to permit re-arrest by the court which has granted bail is upset by the reference in the second part of the

A rival construction accepts that section 5 applies to unconditional release (and not just release on bail). According to this view section 5 only forbids re-arrest which is infected by the same defect as that which was the cause of the original order of release. In *Attorney General for Hong Kong v. Kwok a Sing*[245] Mellish LJ interpreted the provision so that 'it can only apply when the second arrest is substantially for the same cause as the first, so that the return to the second writ of habeas corpus raises for the opinion of the Court the same question with reference to validity of the grounds of detention as the first.' The 'substantially the same question' test has been adopted by the Irish courts. It provided a means of extrication from the problem which arose in *Re Singer (No. 2)*[246] when the complainant, having been released on the ground that the authority to detain him on pre-trial remand had expired, was re-arrested on a fresh set of charges as he stepped outside the prison gates. It was held that the re-arrest did not raise the same defect as the cause of the first discharge and therefore was not restricted by section 5. In *The State (Dowling) v. Kingston (No. 2)*[247] a prisoner arrested on a Scottish extradition warrant which charged him with neglecting his wife and children, was re-arrested on a marginally different charge. The re-arrest was held not to infringe section 5 on the ground that complainant had not been re-arrested 'for the same charge.' In *The State (McFadden) v. Governor of Mountjoy Prison (No. 2)*[248] the complainant had been discharged on the ground that there had been procedural defects in the processing of an extradition request, and upon release was immediately re-arrested. The High Court held that the re-arrest was not infected by the circumstances which had led to the original order of discharge, and, accordingly, that there had been no infringement of section 5.

> proviso permitting re-arrest not merely by the court which had granted bail, but also by some 'other Court having jurisdiction of the cause.' In attempting to sustain the interpretation that the provision is restricted to release on bail it has been suggested that the words 'other Court having jurisdiction of the cause' were added to meet the case of the indictment in the case of a person discharged on bail having been moved by certiorari from one court to another'; see Mellish LJ in *AG for Hong Kong v. Kwok a Sing* (1873) LR 5 PC 179, 201–2 and *The State (McFadden) v. Governor of Mountjoy Prison* [1981] ILRM 120, 122. However, if this were so the reference to 'some other court having jurisdiction of the cause' would be superfluous, because on removal of a cause to a superior court that court would become a court to which the person was bound by recognizance to appear.

[245] (1873) LR 5 PC 179, 202.   [246] (1964) 98 ILTR 112.   [247] [1937] IR 699.
[248] [1981] ILRM 120.

Even where section 5 applies, a proviso permits re-arrest 'by the legal process of such court wherein he or they shall be bound by recognizance to appear, or other court having jurisdiction of the cause.' The proviso was applied in *The State (Gilheany) v. Officer in Charge of the Bridewell*.[249] Here Article 40.4.2 proceedings had succeeded on the ground that complainant had been detained under section 30 of the Offences Against the State Act, 1939 for a period in excess of the statutory maximum of 48 hours. On being released, the complainant was, apparently on the recommendation of the High Court judge, immediately re-arrested by the Gardaí, taken before the Special Criminal Court, charged, and remanded in custody. A second Article 40.4.2 complaint was made, this time challenging the legality of the re-arrest on the ground it infringed section 5 of the Habeas Corpus Act, 1782. The High Court held that the arrest fell within the proviso to section 5: having been sanctioned by the High Court, the re-arrest was, it appears to have been held, by a 'court having jurisdiction of the cause.' But it is not clear whether this solution really works: the High Court, which had no involvement in trying the offence, was not a court having 'jurisdiction of the cause.'

The High Court possesses an overriding jurisdiction to regulate the manner of re-arrest. The most dramatic instance of the exercise of this jurisdiction occurred in *The State (Trimbole) v. Governor of Mountjoy Prison*.[250] Trimbole, having been illegally detained under the Offences Against the State Act, 1939, not for any of the purposes envisaged under that power, but simply in order to secure his availability when the formalities necessary to enter an extradition treaty with Australia had been concluded, was held to have been the victim of such a serious abuse of process, that the executive power of post-habeas corpus re-arrest was, on the direction of the court, suspended. The conscious and deliberate violation of Trimbole's rights committed on the 25 October 1984 was held to continue, even fifteen weeks later, on 5 February 1985, to inhibit the power of the authorities to effect re-arrest.

The power of the court to manufacture its own order of re-arrest

Distinct from the power of some executive agent to affect re-arrest following release is the question of whether the High Court itself possesses

---

[249] *Irish Times*, 12 Jan. 1984.   [250] [1985] IR 550.

an inherent jurisdiction to order arrest. Precedent establishing a jurisdiction in a court administering habeas corpus, to issue a warrant for the purpose of re-arrest, can be found in the practice at common law. In *R. v. Rumble*[251] the applicant had been illegally committed by a coroner's court on a charge of murder. Granting habeas corpus the Irish Court of Queen's Bench held that the only court with jurisdiction to direct the applicant's committal was the appropriate magistrates' court. Rather than ordering the applicant's unconditional discharge, the Court directed that he be discharged from his current place of detention, and, exercising its own power of arrest, ordered that he be apprehended for the purpose of being carried before the magistrates' court.

However, the power of the High Court under Article 40.4.2, upon releasing a detainee, to issue an order of re-arrest, is restricted only to cases where a detainee has been unlawfully transferred to some alternative place of confinement. Here the practice is to combine the order of release with an order of re-arrest justified by reference to the earlier lawful warrant of commitment. In *The State (Dillon) v. Kelly*[252] the Supreme Court, upon finding that the order transferring the complainant from Mountjoy Prison to Portlaoise Prison, had been unlawfully made, issued an order for the re-arrest of the complainant: 'Therefore, the Court will issue its warrant directed to the Commissioner of An Garda Síochána for the apprehension of the prisoner Joseph Dillon and for his conveyance to, and lodgment in, Mountjoy.' However, subsequent case law establishes that the competence of the High Court to order re-arrest is limited to cases where there is already a lawful *order* of detention in existence; the existence of a lawful *power* of detention will not suffice. Five months after its order in *Dillon's* case the question of the validity of such a 'secondary' warrant was raised again in *State (Williams) v. Kelly (No. 2)*.[253] The applicants, having been sent forward for sentence by the Circuit Court, were illegally convicted by that Court, and, following an Article 40.4.2 application, were released by the High Court. However, that order of release was qualified by an auxiliary order that the applicants be apprehended and detained until produced before the Circuit Court for re-sentencing. The Supreme Court held that the second order decreed by the High Court was unlawful and distinguished *Dillon's* case:[254]

---

[251] (1868) IR 3 CL 271.   [252] [1970] IR 174, 179.   [253] [1970] IR 271.
[254] Ibid., p. 283.

Counsel for the respondent has sought, as an analogy, to rely upon the power which this Court has repeatedly exercised where, having ordered release from one gaol, the Court has ordered a prisoner to be arrested forthwith and committed to another gaol. This power has been exercised only where there is a valid conviction and a valid order exists for the imprisonment of a prisoner in gaol A but he has been invalidly transferred to gaol B. *In such case there is a valid order for detention in existence which the court ensures is carried out.* The present case is not analogous. There is no valid order in existence for the prosecutor's detention.

The ground identified for distinguishing the circumstances in the two cases was that in the irregular transfer case there is a pre-existing *order* of imprisonment in place, whereas in the *Williams* case there was merely an unexercised *power* of detention (the power of the sentencing court to issue a bench warrant) in existence. The reason why the Supreme Court in *Williams* considered that there was no power to issue a warrant of arrest was that an order of re-arrest would be inconsistent with the requirement of unconditional release. Walsh J stated: 'the provisions of Article 40.4.2 make it mandatory that an order for release must be made and furthermore there is no power to put a stay on any such order.'[255] But exactly the same objection affects the use of the binary order in cases where there is already an order of imprisonment in existence. The right to immediate release is compromised; yet here the court is permitted to order re-arrest.

THE CONSULTATIVE CASE STATED UNDER ARTICLE 40.4.3

Within days of Gavan Duffy J's judgment in *The State (Burke) v. Lennon*,[256] to the effect that Part V of the Offences Against the State Act, 1939 was unconstitutional, the Attorney General had lodged an appeal to the Supreme Court. The Supreme Court (with only Johnston J dissenting) declined jurisdiction. Finding a route around the very unequivocal words of Article 34.4.3 ('the Supreme Court with such exceptions, and subject to such regulations as may be prescribed by law, shall have appellate jurisdiction from all decisions of the High Court') the Supreme Court held that

---

[255] Ibid., p. 289.   [256] [1940] IR 136.

the established common law usage prohibiting appeal against release constituted an implicit 'exception' to the right of appeal in Article 34.4.3. The following year the Second Amendment of the Constitution Act, 1941, was enacted, and this reversed in part at least, the jurisdictional ruling in *Burke's* case. Article 40.4.3 envisaged a procedure by way of mandatory case stated to the Supreme Court:

> Where the body of a person alleged to be unlawfully detained is produced before the High Court in pursuance of an order in that behalf made under this section and that Court is satisfied that such person is being detained in accordance with a law but that such law is invalid having regard to the provisions of this Constitution, the High Court shall refer the question of the validity of such law to the Supreme Court by way of case stated and may, at the time of such reference, or at any time thereafter, allow the said person to be at liberty on such bail and subject to such conditions as the High Court shall fix until the Supreme Court has determined the question so referred to it.

Since 1967, and the decision in *The State (Browne) v. Feran*[257] which reversed *Burke* and gave the Supreme Court general competence to hear appeals against release in habeas corpus matters, two systems of Supreme Court review have existed concurrently: the appeal under Article 40.4.3 (where the ground is the invalidity of a law) and the appeal under Article 34.4.3 (where the ground of release is based on some non-constitutionality of legislation ground). At least two significant practical consequences depend on which procedure must be used: perhaps the most important is that while in the ordinary case a person whose custody has been found not to be in accordance with the law must be released, where Article 40.4.3 is engaged the right of release is suspended, and bail is the most that can be hoped for. Secondly, cases processed through Article 40.4.3 will be subject to the one judgment rule in Article 34.4.5, whereas separate opinions may be expressed in appeals involving matters other than the validity of law.

The line of demarcation is determined according to whether the appeal involves an issue as to 'the validity' of a law. In *The State (Sheerin) v. Kennedy*[258] the Supreme Court held that the word 'validity' was restricted to

---

[257] [1967] IR 147.   [258] [1966] IR 379.

a law enacted under the Constitution of 1937, and did not include a pre-1937 statute (such as, in that case, the Prevention of Crime Act, 1908). Walsh J elaborated a terminological scheme in which the phrase 'invalid having regard to the Constitution' was read as a technical term of art referring to post-Constitutional legislation only. Article 28.3 ('nothing in this Constitution shall be invoked to invalidate any law enacted by the Oireachtas which is expressed to be for the purpose of securing the public safety') expressly associated 'validity' and an act of the Oireachtas. Walsh J contrasted 'validity' with the phrase 'repugnant to the Constitution' in Article 26, which referred to the jurisdiction to determine the constitutionality of bills not yet enacted; he then contrasted 'validity' with the term 'inconsistent with the Constitution' in Article 50 which referred to the admissibility of pre-constitutional law. The different contextual usage of the terms suggested that 'validity' was not used in an indiscriminate sense, but was restricted to 'laws enacted by the Oireachtas established by the Constitution.'[259] The formula propounded by the Supreme Court in *Sheerin's* case for determining the applicability of Article 40.4.3, 'laws enacted by *the Oireachtas* established by the Constitution', would appear to have clearly excluded delegated executive legislation from the procedure under Article 40.4.3. However, in *The State (Gilliland) v. Governor of Mountjoy Prison*[260] the Supreme Court extended the range of Article 40.4.3 to include a statutory instrument. The complainant was awaiting extradition to the United States and was detained on a combination of (a) the provisions of Part II of the Extradition Act, 1965 and (b) the statutory instrument incorporating a treaty of extradition between Ireland and the United States of America. That Treaty was held to be unconstitutional on the ground that it infringed the terms of Article 29.5.2 of the

---

[259] Ibid., p. 386. On the other hand, if *Sheerin* is correct does it not also follow that Article 37.1 ('Nothing in this Constitution shall operate to *invalidate* the exercise of limited functions and powers of a judicial nature') has been so deficiently drafted as not to validate those administrative bodies exercising quasi-judicial authority which had been established under legislation enacted prior to the Constitution of 1937? This interpretation would have the effect of not preserving the Land Commission (established under the Land Law (Ireland) Act, 1881), the body which it is understood to have been the principal object of Article 37 to protect: *Bryan v. Irish Land Commission* [1942] IR 185, 198; *Fisher v. Irish Land Commission* [1948] IR 3, 17–18.
[260] [1987] IR 201.
[261] 'The State shall not be bound by any international agreement involving a charge

Constitution;[261] and consequently, the statutory instrument which gave it force in Irish law, was also unconstitutional. A majority of the Supreme Court held that Article 40.4.3 was activated since 'the law in accordance with which the applicant was detained within the meaning of Article 40, s.4, sub-s. 3 [was] a combination of s. 29 of the Act of 1965 and the Government order applying Part II of the Act to the United States of America.'[262] The *Gilliland* interpretation may be supported by the fact that by contrast with, for instance, the phrase in Article 28.3.3 referring to 'the validity of any law *enacted by the Oireachtas*', Article 40.4.3 is more broadly expressed, being predicated on a question involving the validity of 'a law.' Against that, Article 40.4.3 appears to envisage detention which is justified under a single legal basis, and not (as was the case in *Gilliland*) a combination of primary and secondary laws, since the text refers to a the Court being 'satisfied that such person is being detained in accordance with *a* law.'

There appears to be some doubt as to whether the consultative case procedure operates in the case of a detention which is expected to expire before the determination by the Supreme Court of the case stated. Since Article 40.4.3 is based[263] merely on the applicant 'being detained' at the time of the High Court determination it seems to follow that the reference must be made at the point at which the High Court determination is made – even if the detention is likely to have expired by the time the case stated reaches the Supreme Court. On the other hand, the fact that the facility for liberty on bail continues until the Supreme Court has determined the question referred to it, and the fact that the case stated procedure involves remittal of the case to the High Court, suggests that Article 40.4.3 assumes that the detention will still be active following determination of the Supreme Court referral. It follows, according to one view, that the procedure does not operate where detention will elapse pending determination. Support for this interpretation may be derived from *RT v. Director of the*

---

upon public funds unless the terms of that agreement shall have been approved by Dáil Éireann.'

[262] [1987] IR 201, 229.

[263] Although Article 40.4.3 appears to make it a condition to the exercise of the procedure, that the complainant's body have been produced before the High Court, it is been held that (as in Article 40.4.2) the requirement of production is a purely enabling one, so that it is not a pre-condition to the exercise of the power that the person have been produced: *RT v. Director of the Central Mental Hospital* [1995] 2 IR 65.

[264] [1995] 2 IR 65, 82.

Central Mental Hospital[264] where the complainant was, pending the date fixed for the Supreme Court hearing, discharged from detention; the High Court then withdrew the Article 40.4.3 case stated.[265]

Under Article 40.4.3 the High Court has a discretion (which in practice it usually exercises) to discharge the complainant on bail. Bail lapses at the point at which the Supreme Court determines the case stated: Article 40.4.3 provides that that the High Court may allow the said person to be at liberty on such bail 'until the Supreme Court has determined the question so referred to it.' It follows that, where the validity of the detention is sustained, the High Court, and, it seems, in the Supreme Court[266] is immediately invested with jurisdiction to issue a bench warrant for the arrest of the complainant; alternatively, re-arrest may be effected under the original order of detention. Where, on the other hand, the Supreme Court

---

[265] The procedure under Article 40.4.3 is further elaborated by O. 59, r. 4 of the Rules of the Superior Courts, 1986:

> In the case of a case stated under Article 40 of the Constitution, the case shall be signed on behalf of the High Court by the Registrar, and such Court may direct which party is to have carriage thereof. When the case stated is signed the Registrar shall serve notice by registered post on each party to the proceedings in which such case shall have been stated, and shall forthwith transmit the case stated to the Registrar of the Supreme Court. Every such party shall thereupon be entitled to receive from the Registrar of the Supreme Court on payment of the prescribed fee, one or more copies of the case stated. The party having carriage shall lodge with the Registrar of the Supreme Court as soon as may be, five copies of the case stated, and on lodgment thereof the case shall be set down for hearing at such time as the Supreme Court shall direct.

The High Court may direct who is to have carriage of the case stated: in *The State (Sheerin) v. Kennedy* (1966 No. 9 SS), [1966] IR 379, the applicant was directed to have carriage. The party having carriage of the referral is required to obtain a copy of the case stated from the Registrar of the Supreme Court, and then lodge five copies with the Registrar. It is only on lodgment of these copies that the matter may be set down for hearing. It may be that the lodgment precondition in O. 59 is an unconstitutional interference with the Supreme Court's duty of determination under Article 40.4.3.

[266] The power of the High Court would derive from the common law power of a superior court, which grants bail, to issue a warrant of arrest on non-compliance with conditions of bail: *R. v. O'Fagherty* (1841) 1 Leg Rep 72. The Supreme Court has been held to posses an implied power to order re-arrest when it determines an appeal against release (*The State (Browne) v. Feran* [1967] IR 147). By extension, it should have an inherent power to direct arrest following determination of an Article 40.4.3 reference.

finds the legislative basis of the detention invalid, the Court appears to possess an implied power to direct the release of the complainant from the conditions of bail and to restore to the prisoner the security on which bail was conditioned.[267]

SUPREME COURT APPEALS IN ARTICLE 40.4.2 PROCEEDINGS

Appeal against refusal to direct an enquiry or to order release

In *The State (Williams) v. Kelly*[268] the Supreme Court held that where it accedes to an appeal against refusal by the High Court to order an enquiry the Supreme Court possesses a discretion: either to remit the matter to the High Court, or to determine the matter itself. In *Williams* the Supreme Court elaborated upon the nature of the discretion, noting that 'the Court's practice had alternated between requiring the respondent to justify the grounds of detention in the Supreme Court, and remitting the matter to the High Court ... in cases of urgency, and in cases where issues of fact have arisen for determination, the Court's practice has favoured retention.' It is not easy to identify a jurisdictional basis for this power of retention. Under Articles 34.4.1–3 the Supreme Court is a court of appellate, not original jurisdiction.[269] Such original jurisdiction as it possesses (under Articles 12 and 26) does not include habeas corpus, while Article 40.4.2 clearly restricts original jurisdiction in habeas corpus to the High Court. The Supreme Court may subsequently have revised its original view.[270] In *McGlinchey v. Governor of Portlaoise Prison*[271] Finlay CJ defined the juris-

---

[267] In *The State (Gilliland) v. Governor of Mountjoy Prison* (1985 95 SS), [1987] IR 201 the Supreme Court, following its decision that the law under which the complainant was held, was unconstitutional, directed that the complainant be discharged, and that the sum lodged as bail and the complainant's passport be returned.
[268] [1970] IR 259, 262.
[269] *Blehein v. Murphy* [2000] 2 IR 231.
[270] In *O'Connor v. Governor of Curragh Prison*, Supreme Court, 3 Dec. 1999, Lynch J said of an application to raise a point not submitted in the original complaint before the High Court that 'the attempt to raise this for the first time in this Court is to misconceive the function of the Supreme Court which is a court of appeal and not, save in a very few limited exceptions such as a Reference under Article 26 of the Constitution, a court of first instance.'
[271] [1988] IR 671, 700–1.

diction of the Supreme Court in a manner which notably omitted any reference to the Court's having any original jurisdiction: 'The function of this Court on appeal from the determination of an application under Article 40.4.2 for an enquiry as to the legality of the detention of a detainee is to enquire into the complaints and if any one of them shall appear to be arguable then to remit the matter to High Court to hold an enquiry.'

The scope of review on an Article 40.4.2 appeal approximates to that in Supreme Court appeals generally. A full description of the Supreme Court's appellate jurisdiction over findings of fact and law is provided in *McGlinchey v. Governor of Portlaoise Prison*:[272]

> The nature of an appeal from the High Court to the Supreme Court, in this as in every other case, requires a short explanation, and it is that it is the function of this Court, on such appeal being brought and grounds being put before it to examine them so as to ascertain whether an error of law in the adjudication of the court below has occurred, or as to whether an error in inferences from whatever primary facts may have been found by that court has occurred or whether there was evidence to support any finding of fact.

The Supreme Court has an unrestricted power of review over issues of legal interpretation. It also has an unrestricted power of review over the manner in which the High Court has applied the appropriate legal standard to an accepted set of primary facts.[273] But where the primary facts are disputed the Court's power of review will vary according to the sources from which those findings have been derived. Where the finding is based on testimonial evidence the Supreme Court, not having seen the witness, will generally not be in a position to assess demeanor, and will generally be obliged to accept the findings of fact made by the High Court. Unless the finding is unreasonable or lacks credibility the Supreme Court may not set it aside.[274] Where, on the other hand, the finding derives from a process of

---

[272] Ibid., pp 702–3.
[273] *Hay v. O'Grady* [1992] 1 IR 210, 217; *Fusco v. O'Dea (No. 2)* [1998] 3 IR 470, 492.
[274] *Hay v. O'Grady* [1992] 1 IR 210, 217; *Carron v. McMahon* [1990] 1 IR 239, 268. The Supreme Court does, however, have power under O. 48, r. 8 to receive further evidence upon questions of fact, including evidence by oral examination in court.

evaluation of circumstantial evidence, or from an appraisal of documentary evidence, the Supreme Court may re-examine the factual issue.[275] The jurisdiction to review findings of fact within this last category was adverted to by Finlay CJ in *Russell v. Fanning*:[276] 'the evidence before [the High Court] consisted of evidence on affidavit, and [the High Court] judgment therefore does not involve findings with regard to the creditworthiness of witnesses who have given oral evidence. On appeal, accordingly, I am satisfied that I should look at the evidence before the learned trial judge, and reach a conclusion as to whether the inference which he drew from it is not the correct one.'

An appeal to the Supreme Court from refusal to release on Article 40.4.2 is regulated by the same procedural rules as regulate appeals generally; in practice, however, there has, in ease of the complainant, been a greater flexibility on Article 40.4.2-related appeals. The Supreme Court has been prepared to overlook appeals taken outside the prescribed time limit,[277] to overlook notices of appeal which have misidentified the decision appealed from,[278] and to relax the mootness rule in cases where detention has expired.[279] The admission of moot appeals by unsuccessful complainants is, the Supreme Court has held, a matter for the discretion of the Court, and there is no categorical prohibition against such appeals.[280] The Court

---

[275] See, e.g. *Fusco v. O'Dea (No. 2)* [1998] 3 I.R. 470, 510: 'The finding of fact by the learned trial judge, that there was a decision that there be a prosecution under the Act of 1976, was made from documents. The inference in the case that a final decision not to seek extradition was made in 1981 was based on documents and an analysis of the law. It was not based on oral evidence. Thus it was open to this Court to review the decision fully: *Hay v. O'Grady* [1992] 1 IR 210.'

[276] [1988] IR 505, 532.

[277] Under O. 58, r. 3(1) of the Rules of the Superior Courts a notice of appeal is a ten-day notice and notice of appeal must be served not later than 21 days from the passing and perfecting of the order appealed against. However, in *Sheehan v. Reilly* [1993] 2 IR 81, 85, a notice of appeal was permitted against an order refusing an application under Article 40.4.2. made nine months earlier. See, also, *The State (Woods) v. Kelly* [1969] IR 269, 271 allowing late amendment of notice of appeal.

[278] *McGlinchey v. Governor of Portlaoise Prison* [1988] IR 671, 700. O.58, r.4 of the Rules of the Superior Courts, 1986 requires that notice of appeal must state the grounds of appeal.

[279] *Keating v. Governor of Mountjoy Prison* [1991] 1 IR 61.

[280] In *Payne v. Governor of Portlaoise Prison*, Supreme Court, 7 Apr. 2003, the Court noted that that discretion may be influenced by considerations such as delay by the complainant in prosecuting the appeal, and the detail of the information in the High Court record.

has also been prepared to overlook the rule (itself a consequence of the Supreme Court's having a purely appellate and no original jurisdiction) that grounds not raised in the High Court may not be mentioned in the Supreme Court.[281] In *The State (Quinn) v. Ryan*[282] the issue of the constitutionality of the Petty Sessions Act, 1851 appears to have been raised for the first time in the Supreme Court, while in *The State (Holmes) v. Furlong*,[283] *The State (Browne) v. Feran*[284] and *McMahon v. Leahy*[285] the decisive ground upon which the applicant ultimately succeeded had not been argued in the High Court.

Appeal against release

In 1967 in *The State (Browne) v. Feran*[286] the Supreme Court reversed the decision in *The State (Burke) v. Lennon*[287] that no appeal lay against an order of release on habeas corpus. Differing from the decision in *Burke*, the Supreme Court in *The State (Browne) v. Feran* could find no 'exception or regulation prescribed by law' (as required by Article 34.4.3) which could abridge the comprehensive appellate jurisdiction of the Supreme Court. Since 1967 the appellate jurisdiction has been quite regularly exercised.[288] However, as the Supreme Court has pointed out in an analogous context, the fact that Article 34.4.3 gives the Supreme Court an appellate jurisdiction 'means no more than the Court is given competence to accept such appeals. How, and to what extent, that competence will be exercised is a matter for the decision by that Court.'[289]

---

[281] *O'Connor v. Governor of Curragh Prison*, Supreme Court, 3 Dec. 1999; *AG (SPUC) v. Open Door Counselling Ltd (No 2)* [1994] 2 IR 333; *Blehein v. Murphy* [2000] 2 IR 231. In *SPUC* Finlay CJ stated (at pp 341–2) that the Supreme Court had 'consistently declined, otherwise than in the most exceptional circumstances, dictated by the necessity of justice, to consider an issue of constitutional law which though arising in a case not yet determined by it, has not been fully argued and decided in the High Court.'

[282] [1965] IR 70.

[283] [1967] IR 210, 217.

[284] [1967] IR 147 (justified, at p. 153, on the basis that the ground was implicit in the original complaint).

[285] [1984] IR 525 (justified, at p. 539, on the basis that new evidence had become available only after the High Court hearing).

[286] [1967] IR 147.

[287] [1940] IR 136. See above at p. 32.

[288] *The State (O) v. O'Brien* [1973] IR 50; *The State (Royle) v. Kelly* [1974] IR 259; *The State (Langan) v. Donohue* [1974] IR 251.

[289] *The People v. O'Shea* [1982] IR 384, 404.

One established qualification to the jurisdiction arises where the detention has expired so that the controversy is, in an immediate sense, moot. In two earlier decisions, *Re Zwann*[290] and *Lavery v. Member in Charge, Carrickmacross Garda Station*,[291] the Supreme Court accepted jurisdiction in cases involving short-term powers of detention which had long expired by the time of appeal on the ground that the matter of law involved was of 'real concern to the State'.[292] In *Re Zwann* O'Higgins CJ stated:[293]

> It is true that this Court will not entertain questions which are purely hypothetical or academic, and will not hear complaints made by persons who lack a real interest or locus standi in the question raised. However, this is not such a case. Here the matter raised on appeal is of real concern to the Attorney General and to those charged with the duty of initiating prosecutions under the Fisheries Consolidation Acts. It is of no significance that the success of the appeal can now have no practical effect. If this court on appeal is satisfied for any reason that the orders in question ought not to have been made then these orders must be set aside. If the court declined to do so merely because the orders had been acted upon and practical difficulties thereby created, it would be declining to exercise its proper appellate jurisdiction. This view has, I think been implicit in many previous decisions of this court: see, in particular, *The State (Browne) v. Feran* [1967] IR 147, at p. 169 and *The State (Dillon) v. Kelly* [1970] IR 174.

However, in *Clarke v. The Member in Charge, Terenure Garda Station*[294] the Supreme Court pointed out that the authorities cited in *Zwann* (extracts

---

[290] [1981] IR 395.
[291] [1999] 2 IR 390.
[292] Similarly, in *MF v. Superintendent Ballymun Garda Station* [1991] 1 IR 189 the Supreme Court justified its deciding an appeal in the case of a detention which had expired on the ground that the subject matter, the administration of the place of safety order, was a matter of concern to persons involved in the welfare of children.
[293] [1981] IR 395, 400–1.
[294] [2001] 4 IR 171. In *Maloney v. Member in Charge Terenure Garda Station*, Supreme Court, 18 May 2004, the Supreme Court accepted an appeal taken by a detainee who challenged the legality of a period of custody under s. 30 of the Offences Against the State Act, 1939 from which he had long been discharged, on the ground that the question of whether he was in lawful custody might become 'a live issue' in a subsequent criminal prosecution.

from *Browne* and *Dillon*) did not support the proposition that the Court was entitled to act when the controversy had become moot. *Browne* and *Dillon* involved subsisting orders of detention which were still in existence; they were not concerned with a power of detention which had expired. The Supreme Court in *Clarke* reserved discussion of whether *Re Zwann* was correctly decided, and the issue of whether the Supreme Court may exercise appellate jurisdiction where the detention has expired is now unsettled. But even if the authorities cited in *Zwann* do not strictly support the conclusion, the rule against moot appeals is not absolute.[295] Two exceptions to the rule against moot appeals, both pertinent to habeas corpus, have been recognized in other legal systems. One such exception arises in the case of short-term transactions which would, if the mootness rule is strictly applied, make such transactions inaccessible to appellate review. The exception for cases that are 'capable of repetition, yet evading review'[296] would appear particularly appropriate in the case of short-term Garda detention where, if the rule was strictly applied, Supreme Court review would be virtually excluded. Secondly, an exception (similar in its rationale to the approach of the Supreme Court in *Zwann*) has been recognized, under which the State may be allowed to pursue judicial review of a decision made against it, even where the effect of the particular decision has passed, in order to clarify the legal approach to a continuing public responsibility.[297]

LEGAL AID AND COSTS

The Attorney General's Scheme

A dedicated source of habeas corpus funding, the Attorney General's Scheme, was established in 1967 when in *Application of Woods*[298] the

---

[295] *Condon v. Minister for Labour* [1981] IR 62; *Sinnot v. Minister for Education* [2001] 2 IR 545; *Crilly v. Farrington* [2001] 3 IR 251.
[296] *Roe v. Wade* 410 US 113 (1973).
[297] *R. v. Dartmoor Board of Visitors, ex p. Smith* [1987] 1 QB 106; *R. v. Birmingham City Court, ex p. Birmingham City Council* [1988] 1 WLR 337; *R. v. Leicester Crown Court, ex p. DPP* [1987] 1 WLR 1371. J. Laws, 'Judicial remedies and the constitution' (1994) 57 *Modern Law Review* 213; C. Lewis, *Judicial remedies in public law* (London, 1992), pp 289–90.
[298] [1967] IR 154, 166.

Minister for Justice and the Minister for Finance undertook in respect of that application 'and every application for habeas corpus made henceforth' to defray the cost of solicitors and counsel for applicants who were not in a position to defray legal fees and where the court considered assignment proper. The announcement in 1967 formalized an arrangement which has been in place on an informal basis for several years previously.[299] The conditions to the benefit of the scheme, which was revised in 2000,[300] are that the applicant must satisfy the court that he or she is not in a position to retain a solicitor (or, where appropriate, counsel) unless he receives the benefit of the scheme, and that the court must be satisfied that the case warrants the assignment of counsel and a solicitor.[301] No court fees are payable on Article 40.4.2 proceedings. In 1968 the Supreme Court and High Court Fees Order was amended to provide that no fees should be payable to the Central Office of the High Court, or the Registrar of the Supreme Court in connection with habeas corpus proceedings, bail proceedings, or criminal-related judicial review proceedings.[302]

Costs

In practice the unsuccessful complainant is usually not directed to pay the costs incurred by the executive in defending the detention. However, there is no authority for the proposition that Article 40.4.2 proceedings are an established exception to the ordinary indemnity rule. The Constitutional

---

[299] The practice appears to have been first established in *The State (Summers Jennings) v. Furlong* [1966] IR 183. Here the complainant asked the Supreme Court for legal aid. The Court is reported as informing informed him that it had no power to grant legal aid but suggested that he apply to the Attorney General for any books or documents he might require: *Irish Times*, 8 Dec. 1965. The Attorney General responded by assigning both junior and senior counsel. The Attorney General repeated this gesture in *The State (Sheerin) v. Kennedy* [1966] IR 379, and *The State (C) v. Minster for Justice* [1967] IR 106.

[300] The Attorney General's Scheme, 1 May 2000. The 2000 version replaces the version of the scheme promulgated in March 1989. That version had been drafted so as to apply to proceedings for judicial review generally; the amended scheme applies only to application for judicial review concerned with criminal matters or matters where the liberty of the individual is at issue.

[301] Ibid., paras 3 & 4.

[302] Supreme Court and High Court Fees Order, 2001, S.I. No. 488 of 2001. The exemption was first introduced by the Supreme Court and High Court Fees Order, 1968, S.I. No. 157 of 1968.

position does not appear any different from the pre-Constitutional régime where costs on habeas corpus were (after 1877) in the discretion of the court.[303] Orders that unsuccessful complainants pay the legal costs incurred by the respondents in an unsuccessful Article 40.4.2 application are not unprecedented,[304] and the fact that in many cases there is no order as to costs may be as much a result of the fact that no application is made for costs as it is from any rule against making unsuccessful complainants pay costs. At common law there was, exceptionally, jurisdiction to subject an unsuccessful applicant to a unique sanction: an order to pay the expenses incurred by the custodian in producing the prisoner.[305]

While an unsuccessful applicant in public law is usually liable to pay the respondent's costs, at least four categories of case have been recognized (including in proceedings under Article 40.4.2) as operating so as to justify a dispensation from the ordinary rule. These exceptions include cases: (i) where the applicant has raised a point of law of general public importance;[306] (ii) where the public body, although ultimately successful, has, in the course of the challenged transaction, been guilty of a degree of illegality or maladministration;[307] (iii) where the authorities by lack of transparency, or otherwise, can be regarded as responsible for precipitating

---

[303] Prior to the Judicature Act, 1877 the Crown-side of the Court of King's Bench had no legislative power to grant costs to either a successful applicant or a successful respondent on habeas corpus applications. It acquired that power only upon the enactment of s. 53 of the Judicature Act, 1877: *Re Proctor* [1903] 2 IR 117.

[304] *The State (McCarthy) v. Lennon* [1936] IR 485; *In re Singer* (13 SS 1960), (1963) 97 ILTR 130, (applicant ordered to pay costs of unsuccessful High Court proceedings); *The State (Green) v. Governor of Portlaoise Prison*, (214 SS 1977), High Court, 28 Nov. 1977; *The State (O'Shea) v. Chief Superintendent, Galway District* (307 SS 1980), *Irish Times*, 15 July 1980; *Bolger v. Garda Commissioner*, Supreme Court, 2 Nov. 1998.

[305] *Dodd's Case* (1857) 2 De G & J 510; 44 ER 1087.

[306] See *Reynolds v. AG*, High Court, 14 Feb. 1973; *Central Development Trust v. AG* (1975) ILTR 69; *F v. Ireland*, Supreme Court, 27 Feb. 1995; *O'Sheil v. Minister for Education*, High Court, 10 May 1999; *McEvoy v. Meath CC*, High Court, 23 Jan. 2003; *Dunne v. Minister for the Environment*, High Court, 18 Mar. 2005. An Article 40.4.2 example is *Croke v. Smith (No. 2)* (1995 No. 367 SS), [1998] 1 IR 101.

[307] *Hanafin v. Minister for the Environment* [1996] 2 IR 321; *McEvoy v. Meath CC*, High Court, 23 Jan. 2003. The award of costs to the unsuccessful complainant in *The State (Cahill) v. Commissioner of An Garda Síochána* (10 SS 1975), *Irish Times* 15 Apr. 1975, might be explained on this basis.

the litigation;[308] and (iv) where the application has involved a doubtful point of law which the complainant is considered justified in raising.[309] Alternatives to the ordinary indemnity rule may take one of a number of forms: (i) an order that there be no order as to costs; (ii) or an order that the unsuccessful complainant only pay a fixed portion of the respondent's costs;[310] or (iii) exceptionally a reverse costs order under which the successful respondent is directed to reimburse the unsuccessful complainant.[311]

Where the Article 40.4.2 complaint succeeds the custodian will, of course, be ordered to pay the costs incurred in both the initial application[312] and upon the full enquiry. But where a number of institutions are parties to the imprisonment, the institution which has been primarily responsible for the detention, and which may be identified as the target of the complaint, has occasionally been directed to indemnify the custodian for the costs incurred.[313]

---

[308] *An Taisce v. Dublin Corporation*, High Court, 31 Jan. 1973; *O'Connor v. Nenagh UDC*, Supreme Court, 16 May 2002.
[309] *The State (Carney) v. Governor of Portlaoise Prison* [1957] IR 25 where the High Court ordered the respondent pay to the complainant the cost of the conditional order on the ground that the order was doubtful at the time the application was initiated, provides an instance of this principle.
[310] O. 99, r. 5(2) Rules of the Superior Courts, 1986.
[311] *Ring v. Minister for the Environment*, High Court, 27 Feb. 2004; *Dunne v. Minister for the Environment*, High Court, 18 Mar. 2005.
[312] However, in *The State (Rossi) v. Bell* [1957] IR 281,284 the High Court awarded the costs of the motion on notice only to the successful complainant. The ground on which the complainant was denied costs of the initial application is not specified, but it appears that the complainant had not, when the complaint was submitted, fully worked out the grounds on which he alleged that the warrants of arrest were unlawful.
[313] In *Croke v. Smith (No. 2)* (1995 No. 367 SS), [1998] 1 IR 101, the Eastern Health Board and the Attorney General were ordered to pay the costs of the Director of the Central Mental Hospital.

CHAPTER FOUR

Article 40.4.2 and the criminal process

HABEAS CORPUS AND REVIEW OF INVESTIGATIVE ARREST

Habeas corpus has been used in Ireland as a remedy for persons unlawfully detained in police custody since at least the beginning of the twentieth century.[1] However, it was in the mid-1970s that Article 40.4.2 was deliberately developed into a practical remedy for the supervision of this form of detention. It was at this point that there were developed by the High Court a number of doctrinal innovations in habeas corpus procedure, the purpose of which was to overcome the principal difficulty affecting the use of the remedy in this context, the short-term duration of police custody.

The practice on an enquiry into allegedly irregular Garda detention

A number of practices facilitate ease of access and the speed of disposal on enquiries concerned with police detention. (i) The third party application has been commonly employed: enquiries into the legality of Garda custody have been moved at the request of the detainee's employer, sister, mother, and by a legal adviser acting without instruction;[2] (ii) Complaints have been processed by judges at home, and at anti-social hours,[3] with the complainant's legal representative organizing the attendance of a registrar;[4] (iii) Advantage has been taken of the principle that an application for habeas corpus may be informally initiated, and not necessarily by a sworn

---

[1] In 1919 an application for habeas corpus was taken on behalf of a youth John McLaughlin, who was being detained at Castlebar Barracks by the Royal Irish Constabulary: *McLaughlin v. Scott* [1921] 2 IR 51,92; another early twentieth-century example is *Re O'Duffy* [1934] IR 550.
[2] *The State (Healy) v. Kenny* (10 SS 1975), *Irish Times*, 11 Jan. 1975 (complaint by detainee's sister); *The State (Harrington) v. Garvey*, High Court, 14 Dec. 1976 (complaint submitted by detainee's employer).
[3] *The State (Cahill) v. Garda Commissioner* (165 SS 1975), *Irish Times*, 15 Apr. 1975 (application granted by Hamilton J sitting at his residence early on a Sunday morning); *Barry v. Waldron*, High Court, 8 May 1996.
[4] *Barry v. Waldron*, High Court, 8 May 1996.

statement on affidavit. In *Beckman and Dahlstrom*,[5] an Article 40.4.2 application concerned with Garda detention was reported to have been initiated by means of a telephone call made on a Sunday afternoon by the applicant's solicitor; (iv) Notice of the primary order may be conveyed to the authorities by means of fax or telephone;[6] (v) Where the High Court does decide to make a primary order it may, at the same time, make one of a number of intermediary orders: that interrogation cease; that the complainant be given medical treatment; that the complainant be allowed temporary release;[7] (vi) The time within which the complaint is disposed of is accelerated. In *The State (Walsh) v. Garda Commissioner*[8] the application for a conditional order was made on Friday 24 January and a return fixed for Monday 27 January, by which time the Garda custody had terminated. It is arguable that an interval of this length may infringe the requirement of a speedy determination under Article 5(4) of the European Convention on Human Rights.[9] However, in the subsequent practice of the High Court the tendency has been that such applications have been disposed of within the same day[10] or, at the latest, after an overnight adjournment.[11]

---

[5] *Irish Times*, 25 July 1977.
[6] *Barry v. Waldron*, High Court, 23 May 1996.
[7] *The State (Breathnach) v. Hennessy* (127 SS 1976), *Irish Times*, 6 Apr. 1976; *The State (Harrington) v. Garda Commissioner*, High Court, 14 Dec. 1976.
[8] 32 SS 1975; *Irish Times*, 29 Jan. 1975.
[9] See above, at pp 153-4.
[10] In *The State (Trimbole) v. Governor of Mountjoy Prison* [1985] IR 550 the High Court sat at 7 pm in order to dispose of an application initiated at 3 pm The application in *Clarke v. Member in Charge, Terenure Garda Station* [2001] 4 IR 171 was made to the High Court late in the afternoon of 14 April 2000; the respondent was directed to have the body of the detainee before the High Court at 6 pm.
[11] *The State (Harrington) v. Garda Commissioner*, High Court, 14 Dec. 1976, the initial application was made on the afternoon of 10 December 1976 and the enquiry ordered for 11 am on the following morning; in *O'Shea v. Chief Superintendant, Galway*, (307 SS 1980), *Irish Times* 15 July 1980, the application was submitted on Friday afternoon, and the enquiry was directed to be held on Saturday 18 July at 10.45 am. In *The State (Healy) v. Superintendent Kenny*, (10 SS 1975), *Irish Times* 11 Jan. 1975, the full hearing of complaint was directed to be heard on the following day at 2 pm. The application in *The State (Hoey) v. Garvey* [1978] IR 1 was submitted on 11 Nov. 1977 and the full hearing heard at 11 am the following day. In *Gilheany v. Officer in Charge, Bridewell Garda Station, Irish Times*, 12 Jan. 1984, the High Court expressly refused a Garda application for a 48-hour adjournment in order to complete its investigation. The High

The danger, of course, with such ease of access is that the process may be liable to abuse, and a concern with preventing such abuse underlies a number of procedural principles. In *Barry v. Waldron*,[12] Carney J appeared to prescribe a requirement that a direct approach to a judge of the High Court should be made by counsel, and not immediately by the detainee or any other third party.[13] A second device was endorsed by the High Court of Northern Ireland in *Re Copeland's Application*,[14] where it was held that an application must, in order to deter perjury, be made on affidavit, if not on the *ex parte* application then at least by affidavits sworn prior to the full enquiry. Justifying the principle Hutton CJ noted the risk that 'otherwise a person in lawful custody could abuse the process of the court and impede the carrying out of the lawful functions of the police by giving false instructions to his solicitor.' There is support for this condition in the practice under Article 40.4.2: in *The State (Harrington) v. Garda Commissioner*,[15] the enquiry was adjourned in order that the grounds of complaint might be put on affidavit.

The effect of intervening discharge from custody

By the time that the full enquiry commences the complainant will often not be in Garda custody. If Article 40.4.2 review were restricted only to cases where the applicant is, at the time of the enquiry, still in Garda custody then the supervisory jurisdiction under Article 40.4.2 would be capable of being easily evaded: (i) the jurisdiction could be rendered inoperable if, in the period between the initiation of the enquiry and its disposal, the complainant were produced and charged before the District Court; and (ii)

Court ordered that the enquiry, which had been applied for at 7 pm in the evening, be heard at 11 am the following day.

[12] High Court, 23 May 1996.
[13] 'On the material date I was at home. I was telephoned by Mr O' Driscoll as is the normal course of things. The judge is telephoned in the first instance by counsel and asked if he is amenable to sit. In relation to matters under Article 40 of the Constitution the judge has no discretion but to sit and that is the unique procedure in the entire law where a person is entitled to actually select the judge whom he wishes to hear the proceedings. Having communicated with the judge by telephone, counsel – I should say it is not particularly proper for anybody else to do it – having communicated with the judge by telephone, counsel or his solicitor then arranges for the attendance of a registrar.'
[14] [1990] NI 301, 305.
[15] High Court, 14 Dec. 1976.

it would not operate where the applicant had, in the interval between the application and the return, been released. Since the mid-1970s the High Court has developed a number of techniques which have the objective of adapting habeas corpus to the short-term character of Garda detention. Without these the remedy would certainly never have been as successful as it has become in monitoring this form of detention. On the other hand, at least some of these techniques are doctrinally problematic.

One of the most common responses to the initiation of habeas corpus has been to remove the detainee from Garda custody to the District Court in order to have him or her charged. In Irish law a judicial remand will not, it seems, necessarily cancel the High Court's jurisdiction to review the legality of the earlier detention. This innovative principle, which appears to have the approval of the Supreme Court,[16] was first established in *The State (Walsh) v. Garda Commissioner*.[17] Legal representatives of a detainee who was being held in Garda custody beyond the point at which he ought to have been produced before the District Court initiated an Article 40.4.2 enquiry. In response the detainee was discharged from Garda custody, taken before the District Court and charged. Finlay P, however, refused to accept the contention that the District Court's order of remand had terminated the habeas corpus investigation, but held, instead, that the original illegality had subsisted into the subsequent order of remand. Since the earlier detention was found to be illegal, the order of remand was held to be infected and the complainant was discharged. In *Hand v. Governor of Mountjoy Prison*[18] the production before the District Court took place before the habeas corpus proceedings had been initiated. Following legal objections by his solicitor the detainee's detention under section 4 of the Criminal Justice Act, 1984 had been terminated, and he was taken before

[16] The assumption that the High Court's jurisdiction to investigate the legality of Garda custody remains active, notwithstanding a subsequent remand, underlies the following passage in the judgment of Finlay CJ in the decision of the Supreme Court in *Keating v. Governor of Mountjoy Prison* [1991] 1 IR 61, 65: 'Where, however, an issue is raised as to the validity of detention in Garda custody of a person brought before a District Justice, such issue touching, not upon the admissibility of evidence, but upon the actual validity of detention, the proper course for the District Justice is, as was done here, to remand the person concerned, thus enabling him to make such application to the High Court as he may be advised. If the High Court, or any judge thereof, is satisfied that the detention is unlawful, it or he will direct the release of the person detained.'

[17] (32 SS 1975), *Irish Times*, 29 Jan. 1975.

[18] *Irish Times Law Reports*, 29 May 1989.

the District Court where he was charged. An Article 40.4.2 application was then taken on the following day. Notwithstanding the intervening order of remand, the High Court held that the subsequent order was not sufficient to cure the prior illegality, and the prisoner was discharged.[19]

The doctrine of subsisting illegality prevents the frustration of Article 40.4.2 scrutiny of police detention. It permits the Court retain jurisdiction over a complaint made prior to, or immediately after, a judicial remand. It is, however, difficult to reconcile with one of the leading common law doctrines of criminal procedure: that an earlier police arrest does not impair a subsequent order of remand. Subject to a case where there has been a gross abuse of process, the generally accepted understanding is that an order of remand initiates a distinct episode, and that the earlier detention, even if unlawful, terminates.[20] Application of the conventional principle, that an irregular police arrest does not infect a subsequent order of remand, should, in principle, mean that the former detainee's detention is now regularized, and not susceptible to review under Article 40.4.2. Nor is the practice of post-remand review consistent with what is thought of as the only exception to that general principle: cases of grave abuse of process. The proper remedy, where gross abuse of the constitutional right to liberty is established, is a direction that the victim be given a definite, uninterrupted interval of liberty proportionate to the injustice done to the detainee.[21] Yet in the *Walsh* and *Hand* cases the High Court sanctioned immediate re-arrest, which suggests that the High Court did not consider these cases grave enough to qualify as genuine abuse of process cases. Reconciliation with general principle is not easy. The doctrine of subsisting police illegality is probably best regarded as a discrete exception to the general principle: it is an exception exclusive to an application under Article 40.4.2 which has been initiated either prior to, or immediately after, a judicial remand.

A second response to an Article 40.4.2 application has been simply to release the detainee following the order for production. Common law and pre-Article 40.4.2 authority[22] favours the view that the discharge of the

---

[19] In *Re Kelly & Clare*, Irish Times, 3 Aug. 2002, the High Court continued an investigation into the legality of the Garda detention of the two complainants after their remand in custody by the Special Criminal Court.
[20] *R. v. Hughes* [1879] 4 QBD 614; *Keating v. Governor Mountjoy Prison* [1990] IR 61; *DPP (Ivers) v. Murphy* [1999] 1 IR 98.
[21] *The State (Trimbole) v. Governor of Mountjoy Prison* [1985] IR 550.
[22] *R. v. Gavin* (1850) 15 Jur 329; *R. (O'Sullivan) v. Military Governor of Hare Park*

prisoner brings the matter to an end.[23] A similar view has been adopted under Article 40.4.2. In *The State (de Paor) v. O'Connor*,[24] for example, an Article 40.4.2 application had been ordered on the ground that the applicant had been arrested without reasonable cause. Shortly afterwards the Gardaí released the applicant; Finlay P is reported as holding that this put an end to the matter. In June 1984[25] an Article 40.4.2 application, grounded on an allegation that the Gardaí were using section 30 of the Offences Against the State Act, 1939 as a form of preventive custody, was taken on behalf of a number of women peace protesters who had encamped near the American ambassador's residence in Phoenix Park during President Regan's visit to Ireland. The women were released soon after the initial order. In response the enquiry was simply discharged without further investigation by the High Court.

The practice of directing release following the initiation of an enquiry raises a number of questions: (a) does the release of a detainee which is designed to avoid an enquiry ever amount to a contempt?; (b) does the fact that the detainee has been released relieve the respondent from the obligation to make any return?; and, (c) does the release of a prisoner disable the court from further enquiry into the legality of the earlier detention?

As far as the first question is concerned, there is authority to the effect that a discharge, following the initiation of proceedings, which is motivated by a desire to avoid judicial scrutiny, may be an act of contempt.[26] The test is whether there is a valid excuse for the failure to produce.[27] The author-

Internment Camp (1924) 58 ILTR 62; *Re Nicola Raine, The Times*, 5 May 1982. See below, p. 121 above.

[23] The television defence lawyer Perry Mason was confronted with this habeas corpus strategy in *The case of the grinning gorilla*, E.S. Gardner (London, 1958): 'You put a charge against her' Mason said, 'or I'll slam a writ of habeas corpus on you.' Tragg said: 'Go ahead, and slam the writ of habeas corpus on us, Mason, then we may charge her and we may turn her loose. Until you get a writ she's going to be right with us ... If you want, get out a writ of habeas corpus. You may have trouble finding a judge at night and it'll be tomorrow morning before you can get a writ and have it served. Give me a ring tomorrow morning and I may save you the trouble.' 'And in the meantime?' Mason asked. 'In the meantime Mrs. Kempton stays with us' (pp 114–15).

[24] (481 SS 1977), *Irish Times*, 5 Nov. 1977.

[25] *Irish Times*, 3 June 1984.

[26] In *Barnardo v. Ford* [1892] AC 326 Lord Watson stated (p. 335): 'A man who parts with the custody of a child after he is served with the process of the Court, or who evades service in order that he may get rid of such custody, commits a plain contempt for which he is answerable to the court.'

[27] Per Lindley LJ in *R. v. Barnardo* (1889) 23 QBD 305.

ities appear to suggest that a concern to avoid the process of habeas corpus (as where the body is not produced in order to perpetuate its concealment)[28] will not be a good excuse; on the other hand, a concern to address the complaint (by, for instance, bringing to an end a detention of doubtful legality without waiting for the habeas corpus hearing) may be a valid excuse. On this test, reasons unrelated to a concern to avoid habeas corpus (such as the expiry of the initial basis of the detention) may be enough to establish the reasonableness of the excuse, while a concern to frustrate a habeas corpus enquiry may not be a valid excuse to defiance of an order for production.

As to the second question, there is some authority at common law that the detaining authorities, even if not obliged to produce the prisoner, were not relieved of the obligation to make a return. The fact that the prisoner has previously been released did not relieve the former custodian from informing the court that this event had occurred. In *R. v. Gavin*[29] Lord Denman CJ was of opinion that the respondents, who had previously released the detainee, were technically in contempt in failing to make a return stating that they had discharged the detainee.

The High Court has, on occasion, maintained an Article 40.4.2 enquiry despite the intervening release by the Gardaí of the detainee. Two theories have been suggested as justifying such a post-release enquiry. In *The State (Breathnach) v. Hennessy*[30] the High Court appears to have adopted the view that a previously detained prisoner is in a form of constructive custody, so enabling the Court, notwithstanding prior release, to continue its Article 40.4.2 enquiry. Hamilton J is reported as having directed 'the release' of the detainee, even though he had earlier been released by the Gardaí:[31]

> ... in the mid-afternoon of 7 April 1976 an application was made to [Hamilton J] as judge of the High Court that Osgur Breathnach was being unlawfully detained in the Bridewell station. Having heard the application Justice Hamilton directed the Gardaí in charge of the

---

[28] *Barnardo v. Ford* [1892] AC 326.
[29] (1850) 15 Jur 329; *Re Thompson* (1888) 5 TLR 540.
[30] (127 SS 1976), *Irish Times*, 8 Apr. 1976.
[31] *Sunday Tribune*, 16 May 1992. (This account was based on a letter, sent through his solicitors, to the newspaper from Hamilton J correcting an earlier account of the proceedings).

Bridewell to bring Osgur Breathnach before the court at 5.00 pm that day. That happened and then a short adjournment took place to enable the Gardaí to be represented by the Chief State Solicitor and to enable medical evidence to be presented on behalf of Breathnach. Later that evening the case was heard by Justice Hamilton who, having regard to the nature of the alleged condition of Breathnach directed that he be removed to the Richmond Hospital for examination. That application was then adjourned until 11.00 am the following morning. When the case was brought before him again the following morning Mr Justice Hamilton directed that Breathnach be released although the Gardaí had stated that he had been released already.

It is difficult to see how Article 40.4.2 may permit such an extended interpretation. This constructive doctrine is evidently irreconcilable with the text of Article 40.4.2 which defines the remedy as one of 'order[ing] the release of such person from such detention.' 'Release' from 'such detention' in the final phrase of Article 40.4.2 has usually been understood as applying only to actual, and not just constructive, imprisonment, and as not being operable where the complainant has previously been discharged.[32]

A second justification for such post-release review is based on the contention that the duty to enquire under Article 40.4.2 is dependant solely on the Court's acceptance of the original complaint, and is, therefore, not affected by the fact that the complainant has subsequently been released. In *The State (Healy) v. Kenny*[33] an application was made following the failure of the applicant's solicitor (who had, allegedly, phoned every Garda station in counties Limerick, Clare and Kerry) to locate his client. On the return, it emerged that the detainee had, in fact, been released prior to the initiation of the enquiry. Counsel for the respondents asked therefore that the High Court terminate the proceedings. The newspaper report records Finlay P as refusing to discharge the enquiry on the ground that the Court's duty of enquiry was not affected by the pris-

---

[32] Thus the remedy, in the case of persons who have been released on bail pending the determination of an Article 40.4.2 complaint and whose detention is then found unlawful, is usually to discharge the persons from the conditions of bail and not an order of unconditional release; see above, p. 122.

[33] (10 SS 1975); *Irish Times*, 11 Jan. 1975.

oner's prior release: 'Mr Justice Finlay said that the enquiry which was being made before him was an enquiry into the legality of the detention, pursuant to the constitutional obligation which was imposed on him to carry out such an enquiry. He said he would be disposed to inquire further into the detention of Mr Healy.' It is difficult to see how the text of Article 40.4.2 could permit the High Court to exercise such post-detention review: Article 40.4.2 is restricted to just one remedy, release (or, in the case of a complainant whom it has previously released on bail, discharge from the conditions of bail). It does not empower the High Court to grant general declaratory relief, or any such remedy as it thinks fit.

Re-arrest following dismissal of an Article 40.4.2 complaint

The right to re-commence interrogation in the case of a person whose habeas corpus application turns out to have been unfounded[34] has been expressly addressed by section 8(A) of the Criminal Justice Act, 1984:

> Where a person detained pursuant to subsection (2) is taken to court in connection with an application relating to the lawfulness of his detention, the time during which he is absent from the station for that purpose shall be excluded in reckoning a period of detention permitted by this section.

The suspension of custody is contingent upon the detainee being 'taken to court.' But this does not necessarily always follow. The jurisdiction to order production is, as the Supreme Court has confirmed, merely an enabling power,[35] and it is not always directed. Further, assuming that production is ordered, section 8(A) will only exclude periods during which the detainee 'is absent' for the purpose of being 'taken to court.' It does not include periods when the detention is suspended on other grounds. It may not operate to exclude a period after the primary order, but before production,

---

[34] Where a complaint is upheld the High Court may recommend the re-arrest of the complainant at common law for the purpose of charge only: *The State (Walsh) v. Garda Commissioner*, Irish Times, 29 Jan. 1975; *The State (Bowes) v. Fitzpatrick* [1978] ILRM 195; *The State (Gilheany) v. Officer in Charge of the Bridewell*, Irish Times, 12 Jan. 1984; *Hand v. Governor of Mountjoy Prison*, Irish Times Law Reports, 29 May 1989.

[35] *The State (Woods) v. Kelly* [1969] IR 269; *The State (Rogers) v. Galvin* [1983] IR 249; *RT v. Director of Central Mental Hospital* [1995] 2 IR 65.

during which interrogation has been suspended, or a period after being taken to court when the complainant is granted temporary release, or when the detainee is remanded with a direction that interrogation be suspended. Further, section 8(A) only applies in the case of investigative arrest under section 4 of the Criminal Justice Act, 1984. It does not apply in the case of detention under the Offences Against the State Acts, 1939–1998. Nor does it apply in the case of detention under the Criminal Justice (Drug Trafficking) Act, 1996.

The grounds of Article 40.4.2 review of investigative detention

In *Brogan v. United Kingdom*[36] the European Court of Human Rights held that the scope of review available on habeas corpus at common law complied with the standard required under Article 5(4) of the European Convention on Human Rights. This, it was said, was because the common law remedy provided review not only of compliance with the formal statutory conditions 'but also of the reasonableness of the suspicion grounding the arrest and the legitimacy of the purpose pursued by the arrest and ensuing detention.' That epitome of the scope of review on the common law remedy, with its capacity to review both the reasonableness of the underlying suspicion and the legitimacy of the purpose of the arrest, corresponds with the scope of review under Article 40.4.2.

The evidential basis of arrest

Where the basis of the complaint is that the arrest is not supported by the evidential standard required by the constitutive legislation the High Court would appear to be competent to exercise *de novo* review, and not to be limited to a review merely of the reasonableness of the arrest. Under Article 40.4.2 the High Court is entitled to intervene where the evidential basis of a decision is unreasonable.[37] A reasonable suspicion is equivalent to the apprehension of a reasonable possibility of criminal responsibility; accordingly, arrest for which there is not even a reasonable possibility of responsibility is close to an arrest affected by a total want of objective evidence. Even on the most conservative formulation of the scope of

---

[36] (1988) 11 EHRR 117, 137. The European Court of Human Rights was reviewing the issue of whether habeas corpus review of the operation of s. 12 of the Prevention of Terrorism Act, 1984 complied with Article 5(4).

[37] Above, p. 40.

evidential review under Article 40.4.2, review has always been available on grounds of no evidence.

Secondly, the European Convention on Human Rights requires where the process of detention is administrative rather than judicial, and where there is no dedicated system of appeal, that there be, in default, a comprehensive judicial review exercisable by the High Court.[38] Police investigative arrest is, by reason of its non-judicial and non-appealable character, included in that category of detention. In *Brogan v. United Kingdom*[39] the European Court of Human Rights held that Article 5(4) required that applicants should have available to them a remedy allowing the competent court to examine 'the reasonableness of the suspicion grounding the arrest and the legitimacy of the purpose pursued by the arrest and ensuing detention.' However, it is, as we have seen, questionable whether the incorporation of the European Convention can alter the standard of review under Article 40.4.2.[40] That does not mean that the Article 5(4) standard of review has not been incorporated into domestic law. The objections which may affect the application of European Convention standards to Article 40.4.2 do not apply so strongly to alternative remedies for investigating the legality of police detention, such as the application for judicial review. The requirement under section 2(1) of the European Convention on Human Rights Act, 2003 that a court interpret a 'rule of law' in accordance with the Convention may require that the High Court interpret the standard of review on the remedy of judicial review in accordance with the enhanced standard required by Article 5(4).

Review of the legitimacy of the purpose of arrest

Challenges on the ground of improper purpose have provided one of the most common bases for Article 40.4.2 review of investigative detention. *Re McLaughlin*,[41] a decision of the Irish King's Bench Division in 1919, provides one of the earliest examples anywhere of the use of habeas corpus to correct an improperly motivated arrest. McLaughlin, a 14-year-old boy had been witness to the murder of a Resident Magistrate in a disturbed part of Mayo. He was detained by the Royal Irish Constabulary for a period of seven weeks for the purely illegitimate purpose of preventing his intimidation by IRA supporters. Following a habeas corpus application taken by

---

[38] See above, p. 51.   [39] (1988) 11 EHRR 117, 136–7.   [40] See above, pp 51–2.
[41] [1921] 2 IR 51, 92.

the boy's father, the High Court held that the objective supporting the detention was illegitimate, that the detention was unlawful and directed the boy's discharge.

The more common case involves a plurality of motives: a dominant illegitimate motive and a subsidiary benign purpose. At common law, the legality of an administrative act motivated by a plurality of purposes, is determined according to the dominant intention.[42] Where the dominant intention is unlawful the act will not be saved by a legitimate, but purely subsidiary, intention. That was also the rule on habeas corpus prior to the decision of the Supreme Court in *The People (DPP) v. Walsh*[43] and an associated line of cases in the 1980s. *Re O'Duffy*[44] illustrates the pre-*Walsh* approach. O'Duffy was the leader of the Army Comrades Association, which was a prescribed organization and membership of which had been incriminated by the Constitution (Amendment No. 17) Act, 1931. In December 1933 O'Duffy was arrested as he tried to address a political meeting in defiance of requests by the Garda Síochána. However, Johnston J, following a habeas corpus application taken on behalf of O'Duffy, held that the real reason for the arrest was one not justified by the Act: in effect, to prevent his addressing a political meeting. The High Court, accordingly, directed O'Duffy's release. This was despite the fact that the Gardaí might plausibly be said to have had a legitimate ancillary motive, having sound grounds for believing that O'Duffy was a member of an unlawful association, and so may have had (as was demonstrated by his subsequent prosecution) a genuine, if subsidiary interest in having him prosecuted. But, it was, apparently, the dominant intention which was decisive, and since this was illegitimate the application succeeded.

However, in the 1980s the accent changed. The legitimacy, or illegitimacy, of the dominant intention ceased to be decisive. Instead, reversing the earlier understanding, it was held that a legitimate but subsidiary intention would sustain an arrest for which the dominant intention was irregular. In *The People (DPP) v. Walsh*[45] the defendant had been arrested on suspicion of malicious damage to a window even though the real purpose was to investigate a murder of which he was strongly suspected. However, in a challenge to the admissibility of the evidence derived from the period of custody the Supreme Court applied, and found satisfied, a

---

[42] *Cassidy v. Minister for Industry and Commerce* [1978] IR 297.
[43] [1986] IR 722; [1988] ILRM 137.   [44] [1934] IR 550.   [45] [1986] IR 722, 731.

test which validated an arrest with a dominantly irregular motive: 'The real question in this case is whether on the evidence there resides in the minds of the Garda Síochána a genuine interest in the malicious damage, and a desire to pursue it.' The Court of Criminal Appeal specifically dealt with habeas corpus, holding that the 'genuine interest' test applied in habeas corpus proceedings as well as in determining the admissibility of evidence: O'Hanlon J held that had a habeas corpus application been taken while the detainee was being held in Tralee Garda station on suspicion of doing damage to the window the High Court would have been bound to refuse the application.[46] The *Walsh* principle, which still appears to be treated as the governing test, may, however, not be consistent with European human rights jurisprudence. In *Brogan v. United Kingdom*[47] the European Court of Human Rights held that Article 5(4) required that the scope of review extend to review of the legitimacy of the purpose pursued by the arrest and ensuing detention. The case law of the European Court of Human Rights has also proscribed domestic doctrines which, where rights protected by the Convention are engaged, impair the effectiveness of the judicial intervention required by the Convention.[48] The subsidiary, legitimate purpose doctrine clearly reduces the scope of effective review of improperly motivated arrest required by Article 5(4); arguably, therefore, the doctrine offends Article 5(4).

The *Walsh* formula requires that the authorities have at least a 'genuine interest' in the subsidiary ground of arrest. An arrest will, therefore, be unlawful where there is no such 'genuine interest': where the dominant intention is disingenuous and where, despite the claim that there is a valid subsidiary intention, there is no sincere interest in pursuing that subsidiary ground. The leading modern example is *The State (Trimbole) v. Gordon*[49] where the High Court found that there was no ground supporting the alleged suspicion that the arrestee had been in possession of firearms, but that the real reason was to ensure the availability of the Australian national, whose arrest had been requested by the Australian Government on a series of grave charges, pending the completion of an extradition arrangement between the Governments of Ireland and Australia. *The State (Bowes) v.*

---

[46] [1988] ILRM 137, 142.   [47] (1988) 11 EHRR 117, 137.
[48] *X v. United Kingdom* (1982) 4 EHRR 188; *Chahal v. United Kingdom* (1996) 23 EHRR 413; *Smith & Grady v. United Kingdom* (2000) 29 EHRR 493.
[49] *Irish Independent*, 27 Oct. 1984; this application is the origin of the cause célèbre, *The State (Trimbole) v. Governor of Mountjoy Prison* [1985] IR 550.

Fitzpatrick[50] is another instance of such bad faith detention. The complainant had been arrested on suspicion, it was rather disingenuously claimed, of malicious damage to a knife. The knife in question had been the weapon used in a fatal stabbing. The damage to the knife was minor, if not non-existent, and the real reason for the arrest was plainly to have the complainant interrogated under section 30 of the Offences Against the State Act, 1939 (for which there was no power of arrest for murder) about the homicide.

Article 40.4.2 review of conditions of investigative arrest
In 1976, in *Re Article 26 and the Emergency Powers Bill, 1976 Reference*[51] the Supreme Court gave its approval to a doctrine under which conditions of Garda custody which infringe the constitutional rights of a detainee could invalidate the legality of detention, and might justify habeas corpus. The conventional orthodoxy had been that conditions of detention were irrelevant to the legality of detention, the legality of which was determined solely according to whether the preliminary conditions had been complied with. The previous year the High Court had applied the traditional principle in holding that it had no jurisdiction to review a complaint that the detention of children in overcrowded and unhealthy conditions in the Bridewell Garda Station rendered their detention unlawful.[52] The *Emergency Powers* case amounted to an extension in the understanding at common law of the capacity of habeas corpus. The doctrinal advance made in the *Emergency Powers Bill, 1976 Reference* has still been only cautiously received in other common law jurisdictions.[53]

---

[50] [1978] ILRM 195.   [51] [1977] IR 159.
[52] *The State (Ward & others) v. Hanley* (31 SS 1975), *Irish Times*, 24 Jan. 1975.
[53] The proposition that abusive conditions of custody might be a ground of habeas corpus was originally accepted by the High Court in England and Northern Ireland: *R. v. Metropolis Police Commissioner, ex p. Nahar*, The Times, 28 May 1983; *Re Gillen's Application* [1988] NI 40. Then, in 1992, the House of Lords in *R. v. Deputy Governor of Parkhurst Prison, ex p. Hague* [1992] 1 AC 58 rejected the proposition that conditions of detention could give rise to an action either for false imprisonment or (per Lord Bridge) for habeas corpus. However, the principle in *Hague* may subsequently have been refined. In *Cullen v. Chief Constable RUC* [2004] 2 All ER 237 Lords Millett and Hutton distinguished cases of exceptional abuse, such as that alleged in *Re Gillen* [1988] NI 40 (where the applicant had allegedly been assaulted in police custody) from the general rule in *ex p. Hague*, and appeared to accept that abuses of this character might constitute grounds of habeas corpus.

The issue of whether conditions of detention will, in fact, invalidate the legality of detention depends on the relative seriousness of the breach. In *Re the Emergency Powers Bill, 1976* O'Higgins CJ stated:[54]

> It is desirable to state that the section is not to be read as an abnegation of the arrested person's rights (constitutional or otherwise) in respect of rights such as the right of communication; the right to have legal and medical assistance and the right of access to the courts. If the section were used in breach of such rights the High Court might grant an order for release under the provisions for habeas corpus contained in the Constitution.

The use of 'might' in the final sentence indicates that the remedy is relative and operates in proportion to the gravity of the breach. The gravity issue would, in turn, appear to depend upon the extent to which the breach was deliberate, or a breach of process, and upon the seriousness of the impact upon the human rights of the suspect.[55] Secondly, even a potentially invalidating defect may be rectified and neutralized by the time of the enquiry. In *The State (McCann) v. O'Herlihy*[56] the applicant was detained in a Garda station in County Kerry in an unheated cell, with, it was alleged, an open drain functioning as a urinal. Following the initiation of Article 40.4.2 proceedings the complainant was removed to a police station in Dublin. Counsel for the complainant conceded during the subsequent proceedings before Hamilton J that the removal to a Garda station where physical conditions were constitutionally acceptable had cured the previous unconstitutionality. In *Re Gerard Hynes*[57] an application was taken on the basis that the detainee had not been informed of the offence of which he was suspected when he had been arrested under section 30 of the Offences Against the State Act, 1939. On the return later that evening the Gardaí gave evidence of specific offences of which they suspected the complainant. The detention was held to have been retroactively validated, and the enquiry was discharged.[58]

---

[54] [1977] IR 159, p. 173.
[55] In *Re Gillen's Application* [1988] NI 40, 55 it was held that in order to merit release an assault must be 'serious.' O'Higgins CJ, in stating in the *Emergency Powers Bill 1976 Reference*, that release might be ordered if exceptional powers 'were used to breach such rights' appears to be referring to acts of deliberate abuse.
[56] *Irish Times*, 30 Oct. 1976.
[57] High Court, 7 Feb. 1984.
[58] In *The State (Leonard) v. Officer in Charge, Clontarf Garda Station, Irish Times,*

ARTICLE 40.4.2 AND REVIEW OF EXTRADITION PROCEEDINGS

Review of detention consequent on the process of extradition from the State had provided one of the most common occasions for deployment of Article 40.4.2. However, with the enactment of the Extradition (European Union Conventions) Act, 2001 and of the European Extradition Warrant Act, 2003 there may now be some uncertainty over the extent of the place of Article 40.4.2 in the extradition process. The entire extradition process has now been committed to the High Court. Section 20 of the Act of 2001[59] transfers to the High Court the jurisdiction previously exercised by the District Court as the court of committal under Part II of the Extradition Act 1965 (which now regulates extradition requests from outside the European Union). The judicial component of the process under the European Extradition Warrant Act, 2003 (which regulates requests from within the European Union) is also committed to the High Court which becomes the 'executing judicial authority in the State.' As part of this re-organization, a right of appeal to the Supreme Court, though on points of law only, has been constituted.[60] There was at common law a well-established prohibition against the exercise of habeas corpus (itself a superior court process) to review the legality of orders of the superior courts. This raises the question of whether this common law prohibition has been perpetuated under the Constitution, so that Article 40.4.2 is subject to an implicit jurisdictional restriction forbidding its use where the objective is to attack the legality of an order of extradition sanctioned by a judge of the High Court.[61]

---

3 Apr. 1985 an Article 40.4.2 enquiry was ordered following a complaint that the suspect's legal representative had been denied access to him. However, the enquiry was discharged when it was established that the Gardaí had subsequently allowed a consultation.

[59] S. 20(1) of the Extradition (European Union Conventions) Act, 2001 provides: 'The principal Act is hereby amended by (a) the substitution of "High Court" for "District Court" in each place that it occurs.'

[60] Extradition Act 1965, s. 29(5) (as amended by s. 20 (f) of the Extradition (European Union Conventions) Act, 2001); European Arrest Warrant Act, 2003, s. 16 (12).

[61] This formula would not prevent its being used to review legal objections deriving from sources other than the High Court order, such as a defect deriving from the manner of execution of the extradition order.

Article 40.4.2 and review of a High Court extradition order

The general (though not unanimous)[62] practice has been to review orders under the modern extradition code by means of an appeal to the Supreme Court. The principal objection to habeas corpus review of a High Court extradition order is the traditional understanding that habeas corpus is not, except in exceptional circumstances, available to review the decision of a judge of co-ordinate jurisdiction.[63] The Constitution imposes an unavoidable duty on 'any and every judge of the High Court' to conduct an enquiry into the legality of detention. Unless there is a qualification excluding from this duty orders of imprisonment of the High Court it would follow that a High Court judge who has made an order of detention would be required to conduct an enquiry into the legality of his own order. Further, the use of Article 40.4.2 as a means of reviewing a determination of the High Court was unprecedented under the previous extradition code. The new extradition arrangements differ from the previous regime in the degree of issues transferred to the High Court. Under Part III of the 1965 Act certain important legal conditions to extradition were committed to the High Court in a system of joint determination between the High Court and the District Court.[64] Here the practice was always to prosecute review of a High Court extradition ruling by means of an appeal to the Supreme Court rather than by means of an application under Article 40.4.2. The absence by either the High Court or the Supreme Court throughout the period 1965–2003 of any reference to the existence of a right of collateral review under Article 40.4.2, in addition to appeal to the Supreme Court, would be surprising if such a right was, in fact, understood to exist.

---

[62] In *O'Rourke v. Governor of Cloverhill Prison*, High Court, 26 Feb. 2004 the complainant challenged by means of Article 40.4.2. an order of remand which had been made in extradition proceedings by the High Court.

[63] *Re Roe* (1828) 1 Law Recorder 310; *Re Aylward* (1860) 12 ICLR 448; *In re Aikin* (1881) 8 LR Ir 50.

[64] Extradition Act, 1965, s. 50. At the time that the 1965 Act was being enacted the English Backing of Warrants (Republic of Ireland) Act, 1965, which Part III of the Irish Act was intended to reciprocate, had already been passed, and this had provided for claims for exemption from the legislation to be determined by a magistrates' court. As a deliberate improvement upon the English position it was decided that that such issues should be determined by the High Court and not entrusted to the District Court. The High Court was thereby constituted an institution of original competence in an arrangement of joint determination between the District and High Courts.

The problem with this argument is that the extradition code itself envisages Article 40.4.2 as continuing to function as a means of review. Section 20(4)(b) of the 2003 Act requires that the High Court, on making an extradition order, inform the person of 'his or her right to make a complaint under Article 40.4.2 of the Constitution' while section 20(6) provides that where 'a person makes a complaint under Article 40.4.2 of the Constitution he or she shall not be surrendered to the issuing state while proceedings relating to the complaint are pending.' Under section 29(3)(a) of the Extradition Act, 1965 the High Court is obliged to inform the person of 'the provisions of section 4.2 of Article 40 of the Constitution (which relates to the making of a complaint to the High Court by or on behalf of any person alleging that that person is unlawfully detained),' while under section 31, in a formula which is wider than its equivalent under the 2003 Act,[65] no surrender may be made 'until the conclusion of any habeas corpus proceedings brought by him or on his behalf.'

The fact that the legislation provides that persons committed under the 1965 and 2003 Acts are entitled to be informed of their right to make an application under Article 40.4.2, and that the process is suspended while the application is processed,[66] certainly indicates that the legislature intended a role for Article 40.4.2. This is significant because the common law rule against habeas corpus review of the legality of an order of a superior court was not absolute. Habeas corpus jurisdiction could be exercised over the order of a superior court where Parliament indicated an intention that such review should be available. In *Re Keller*[67] it was held that the Queen's Bench Division was competent to review a decision of the Court of Bankruptcy despite the status of the Bankruptcy Court as a superior court: 'where the legislation manifests an intention that such conditions shall be examinable [on habeas corpus], it is immaterial whether the Court is or is not a "Superior Court."' In the express references to the remedy in the extradition code the legislature (which, of course, under Article 36(iii)

---

[65] Article 40.4.2 suspension under the 2003 Act only applies in the case of a complaint taken by the person who is the subject of the order, whereas suspension under the 1965 Act also operates in the case of an application taken by a third party; suspension under the 2003 Act lasts only while proceedings are 'pending', while under the 1965 Act suspension lasts until 'the conclusion' of proceedings.

[66] Extradition Act, 1965, ss. 29(3) & 31; European Arrest Warrant Act, 2003, ss.16 (4)(b) & 16(6).

[67] (1888) 22 LR Ir 158, 202.

has control over the distribution of business amongst the courts) appears to be signaling an intention that the remedy under Article 40.4.2 operates as a concurrent means of redress.[68]

Article 40.4.2 as remedy for detention in breach of section 34 of the Extradition Act, 1965

Section 34 of the Extradition Act, 1965 institutes a special jurisdiction to direct the discharge of a person held in excess of one month pursuant to an extradition order made under Part II of the 1965 Act:

> if any person awaiting his surrender under this Part is not surrendered and conveyed out of the State within one month after the committal, or within one month after the conclusion of habeas corpus proceedings brought by him or on his behalf, whichever is the later, the High Court may, on application made by or on behalf of that person and upon proof that reasonable notice of the intention to make the application has been given to the Minister, order the person to be discharged from custody.

A rather technical point arises as to whether an applicant seeking discharge under section 34 must proceed by way of a *sui generis* application for statutory relief under section 34, or whether an application may also be made under Article 40.4.2. English practice suggests that an application under the statutory procedure is the only proper remedy.[69] In *Mallows v. Governor of Mountjoy Prison*[70] the English practice was apparently adopted by the High Court where 'the application for habeas corpus was deemed ... to be an application for his discharge pursuant to [the statutory provision].' The principal argument against the appropriateness of habeas corpus is that the provision is discretionary so that detention past one

---

[68] The fact that the legislation requires that the information as to the right to submit a complaint under Article 40.4.2 must be given at the time that the order is made suggests that the legislative intent was that review under Article 40.4.2 would apply to grounds concerned with the High Court order itself and not just to matters extraneous, or subsequent to, the High Court order.

[69] *R. v. Governor of Brixton Prison, ex p. Enahoro* [1963] 2 QB 455; *Re Chetta*, Queen's Bench Div, 30 Apr. 1997.

[70] [2002] 2 IR 385. This case concerned an application under s. 53(1) of the Extradition Act, 1965 (now repealed).

month does not make the detention unlawful (thereby justifying habeas corpus), but merely activates a contingent entitlement to release dependent on an exercise of pure discretion. On an immediate, literal reading of section 34(1) the word 'may' plainly indicates nothing more than a discretion. Section 34(1) can be contrasted with section 34(2). Under section 34(2) the High Court may postpone the date of extradition where 'the state of health of the person claimed or other circumstances beyond the control of the State or the requesting country have prevented the person claimed from being conveyed out of the State'; the Court may then 'fix a period within which he may be surrendered' and if not so surrendered he *'shall be released.'* But the impression changes when section 34(1) is placed alongside its antecedents under the Extradition Act, 1870, the Fugitive Offenders Act, 1881, and under its (now repealed) analogue in the case of Anglo-Irish extradition, section 53 of the Extradition Act, 1965. Each of these provided for a defence where 'sufficient cause [was] shown to the contrary' or where 'reasonable cause [was] shown for the delay.'[71] It can be argued that the omission of grounds of excuse (something that, in light of the provisions *in pari materia*, is unlikely to have been mere oversight) from the jurisdiction under section 34 signals a deliberate legislative intention that delay in excess of the statutory period was to be regarded as inexcusable, and consequently accessible to intervention under Article 40.4.2.[72]

---

[71] S. 12 Extradition Act, 1870; s. 7 Fugitive Offenders Act, 1881; s. 53(1) Extradition Act, 1965.

[72] A small conflict appears to arise between Article 40.4.2 and the statutory procedure under s. 34: the jurisdiction under s. 34 is predicated upon proof that reasonable notice of the intention to make the application has first been given to the Minister. However, access to Article 40.4.2 may not be encumbered by statutory conditions (*The State (Aherne) v. Cotter* [1982] IR 188). Accordingly, the presumption of constitutionality must be applied and the condition be read as applying only if the application for discharge is made by way of a *sui generis* application under s. 34, but not where the detainee seeks to process the application under Article 40.4.2.

ARTICLE 40.4.2 AND THE PRE-TRIAL PROCESS

Article 40.4.2 and the remand process

An order made under section 24 of the Criminal Procedure Act, 1967 of remand in custody following charge is conditional on two findings: that there is sufficient evidence against the accused to justify prosecution, and, in the event that there is that evidential basis, that an order of detention, rather than conditional release, is necessary. Article 40.4.2 is, notwithstanding some contrary authority, probably a legitimate instrument for challenging the first of these findings, the issue of sufficient evidence; however, an application for bail rather than habeas corpus is the more proportionate, and proper, remedy to challenge a finding that detention rather than temporary release be ordered.

The issue of the appropriateness of habeas corpus in a case where an accused alleges that he has been remanded in custody without any evidence appears to have been addressed in only one recent case, a decision of the High Court of Northern Ireland, *Re McAleenan's Application*.[73] The Court held that habeas corpus was not appropriate even in cases where there was no evidence: 'even if we had concluded that there was no evidence against the applicant which justified his remand in custody, we would not have had jurisdiction to issue a writ of habeas corpus on that ground.' It is unquestionable now that review on Article 40.4.2 is available where the evidential basis of a decisive finding is unreasonable.[74] Moreover, *McAleenan's* case was based upon a sample of authorities (*R. v. Morn Hill Camp Commanding Officer*[75] in 1917, and *R. v. Board of Control, ex parte Rutty*[76] in 1956) which denied absolutely the existence of a capacity to review, in any circumstances, the weight of evidence. The absolute proposition endorsed in those cases, that the weight of evidence is in all circumstances unreviewable on habeas corpus, no longer represents the modern common law position (nor, of course, that under Article 40.4.2).

The second finding, that detention rather than temporary release is necessary, usually arises in the context of an application for bail, and is usually challenged by means of an appeal against the refusal of bail. Habeas

---

[73] [1985] NI 496, 504.
[74] Above, pp 40–1.
[75] [1917] 1 KB 176.
[76] [1956] 2 QB 109.

corpus,[77] and judicial review,[78] have occasionally, been used as remedies for persons refused bail both in Ireland and elsewhere.[79] It is certainly easy to see the theoretical attraction of habeas corpus as a remedy for irregular refusal of bail. In *The People (AG) v. O'Callaghan*[80] Walsh J characterized the entitlement to bail as a presumptive right which could only be displaced in a case of necessity. It follows that a person unlawfully refused bail is unlawfully deprived of an entitlement to liberty, and has been unlawfully detained. In strict theory habeas corpus appears appropriate in a case where, for instance, bail is refused in breach of fair procedures, or by the setting of a bail bond at an excessively high figure. The difficulty, however, with the application of habeas corpus (or judicial review for that matter) is that the remedy, unconditional release, is a disproportionate one. The use of habeas corpus would defeat the security obtained by the conditions which are attached to a grant of bail. It would provide a windfall for persons unlawfully declined bail, and would provide an incentive for persons allegedly unlawfully deprived of bail to pursue a remedy by means of habeas corpus or judicial review rather than by appeal. The practice in England[81] and the

---

[77] In 2000 a constitutional challenge by a 13-year-old boy to refusal of bail, by reason of his inability to comply with the statutory requirement under the Bail Act, 1997 to provide one-third of the recognizance, was initiated under Article 40.4.2: *Irish Times*, 23 May 2000. In *Re Rice*, High Court, 5 Mar. 2004 (described in *Rice v. Mangan*, High Court, 30 July 2004) the complainant had been committed following his refusal to comply with a condition of bail requiring him not to enter County Clare. The legality of the condition was challenged by means of an Article 40.4.2 application. In *Re Leahy*, *Irish Times*, 12 Jan. 2005, a decision by the District Court to refuse bail was later that day successfully challenged by means of a habeas corpus application in the High Court. In *McDonagh v. Governor of Cloverhill Prison*, Supreme Court, 28 Jan. 2005, Article 40.4.2 was used to challenge the validity of a detention consequential upon refusal of bail.

[78] In *Re Bacadanu*, *Irish Times*, 7 Mar. 2003 an application was sought under Article 40.4.2 complaining of refusal of bail contrary to fair procedures. The Article 40.4.2 complaint was converted by the High Court into application for judicial review.

[79] *Ex p. Thomas* [1956] *Criminal Law Review* 119.

[80] [1966] IR 501.

[81] *R. v. Kray*, *The Times*, 17 Feb. 1965; *R. v. Richmond JJ, ex p. Moles*, Queen's Bench Div., 22 Oct. 1980. In *Moles* the remedy of release on habeas corpus for a person irregularly refused bail was described as unthinkable. Donaldson LJ said 'it cannot be seriously suggested that upon his being brought before the court pursuant to such writ the court would be unable to consider whether hereafter he should be remanded on bail or in custody, but we would, as [counsel] does faintly suggest, be obliged to release him.'

United States[82] has been to resist the attempts to develop habeas corpus into a remedy for unlawful refusal of bail. In English law habeas corpus to challenge refusal of bail has been declined in favour either of remittal to the original court, or a direction to pursue an appeal against refusal of bail.[83] Irish practice is occasionally less certain. *McDonagh v. Governor of Cloverhill Prison*[84] is one of a number of cases in which the High Court and Supreme Court has dealt with a complaint that bail had been illegally refused by means of an application under Article 40.4.2. The security of the pre-trial criminal process is likely to be compromised if the less flexible remedy of unconditional release on habeas corpus was to supersede the appeal (and conditional release on bail) as the proper remedy for refusal of bail.

Article 40.4.2 and detention following an order sending forward for trial

The legal conditions to the order sending an accused forward for trial are, following the amendments introduced by the Criminal Justice Act, 1999, now quite sparse. Under sections 4A and 4B of the Criminal Procedure Act, 1967 (as amended by the Criminal Justice Act, 1999) the conditions to an order sending forward for trial are merely that the prosecution has consented, and that the accused has been served copies of the seven categories of document specified in section 4B of the Criminal Procedure Act, 1967 (as amended). The accused is entitled, following his being sent forward for trial, to be tried at the first available court. It is a corollary of the accused's right to be tried at the first available court that the order sending the accused forward for trial should direct that the accused be remanded in custody to the next available court having jurisdiction to try him. This principle has been the source of a number of habeas corpus challenges. In *Re Singer*[85] the applicant was remanded in custody consequent upon an order sending him forward 'for trial at the next Circuit Criminal Court.' The next session of the Circuit Criminal Court having passed without any further explicit order having been made, Singer was discharged under Article 40.4.2.[86] On the other hand, a warrant directing

---

[82] *Stack v. Boyle* 342 US 1 (1951).
[83] *R. v. Richmond JJ, ex p. Moles*, Queen's Bench Div., 22 Oct. 1980.
[84] Supreme Court, 28 Jan. 2005.
[85] (1963) 97 ILTR 130.
[86] *Re McIntyre*, *Irish Times*, 27 Jan. 2000 (warrant sending accused forward for trial

that the accused be detained 'until legally discharged' does not require a further warrant to sustain detention past the first session of the court of trial. However, a further warrant may be required where the charges recited in a warrant directing detention 'until legally discharged' have been excised, and a set of charges different to those recited in the original warrant have been substituted.[87]

ARTICLE 40.4.2 AS A MEANS OF POST-CONVICTION REVIEW: CONVICTION ON INDICTMENT

The evolution of the restriction upon review

The doctrine that criminal convictions are inaccessible to habeas corpus review is long established at common law. But the underlying basis of the doctrine has been expressed in various ways. In *Re Sullivan*[88] Palles CB rationalized the prohibition against habeas review of a criminal convictions following trial on indictment as a form of estoppel:[89]

> There is this distinction between an investigation into the guilt or innocence of a party before jurors and before justices. The finding of the former is followed by judgment on record, which, in cases where there is jurisdiction to inquire amounts to estoppel by record; but there is no estoppel in cases before justices.

The proposition that a criminal conviction was an estoppel by record was a technical expression of the general principle that a conviction on indictment was unreviewable. The rationale underlying this prohibition on habeas corpus was a concern to protect the principle of the finality of a criminal conviction. To have permitted habeas corpus to operate would have been to subvert the strict finality principle. It was said that the 'security which the public has against the impunity of offenders is the principle that the trial court must be considered competent to convict.'[90]

---

to the 'present sittings of the Central Criminal Court' held to have lapsed when those proceedings had ended without the case being called over to the next sittings; release on Article 40.4.2 ordered).
[87] *In re Francis* (1963) 97 ILTR 151.   [88] (1888) 22 LR Ir 98.   [89] Ibid., p. 113.
[90] Per Denman CJ in *Carus Wilson's Case* (1845) 7 QB 984, 1009; 115 ER 759, 769.

Intervention by habeas corpus would carry the risk, it was said, that persons would be set at large for grave offences. Criminal convictions would be vulnerable to being undermined by disputes of the most refined and minute character.[91] Injustice could be remedied by the application of the prerogative of mercy.[92] The general rule was sustained by a series of ancillary doctrines: (i) that a conviction by a superior court was not required to show jurisdiction on its face;[93] (ii) that inaccurate factual statements on the face of an order of conviction were not accessible to challenge;[94] (iii) that proof of legal errors, or infringements of jurisdiction which were not contained on the face of a record would not be permitted to displace the almost irreversible presumption of legal propriety attributed to convictions by criminal courts.[95]

With the establishment of the Court of Criminal Appeal in 1924 the earlier rule was superseded by an alternative principle which, instead, reflected a concern to protect the integrity of the Court of Criminal Appeal. As the finality principle was relaxed so the restriction on habeas corpus was reformulated: the old absolute prohibition against post-conviction review evolved into a prohibition on post-conviction review otherwise than through the Court of Criminal Appeal. The concern now was that to allow habeas corpus operate as a post-conviction remedy would undermine the principle that a conviction was final save where overturned by the Court of Criminal Appeal. That rule, which continues to represent the law, is applied in two contexts: (i) as a prohibition on using Article 40.4.2 in place of an appeal to the Court of Criminal Appeal, and (ii) as a prohibition against the use of Article 40.4.2 in a case where an appeal to the Court of Criminal Appeal has already been exhausted.

Article 40.4.2 as a post-conviction remedy where appeal to the Court of Criminal Appeal has not been pursued

The institutional precedence of the Court of Criminal Appeal over habeas corpus is long established. The earliest rehearsal of the principle occurred

---

[91] See, e.g. the arguments of Jervis CJ in *Re Newton* (1855) 16 CB 97, 101; 139 ER 692, 693.
[92] *Ex p. Lees* (1860) El, Bl & El 828; 120 ER 718.
[93] *Ex p. Fernandez* (1861) 10 CBNS 3; 142 ER 349.
[94] *Re Newton* (1855) 16 CB 97; 139 ER 692.
[95] *Carus Wilson's Case* (1845) 7 QB 984; 115 ER 759.

in *The State (Canon) v. Kavanagh*,[96] where Maguire CJ dismissed an application for habeas corpus taken by a convicted person, describing the proceedings as 'strange', and advising the applicant to pursue the orthodox route of appeal to the Court of Criminal Appeal. In *The State (Edge) v. Governor of Mountjoy Prison*[97] an application for habeas corpus was initiated by a prisoner convicted of the offence of kidnapping, an offence which he alleged (and subsequently established) was not known to the law. The High Court, applying the principle of the priority of the Court of Criminal Appeal, adjourned the application until an appeal had been determined before the Court of Criminal Appeal. The principle was, once again, rehearsed in *Kelleher v. Governor of Portlaoise Prison*.[98] The complainant had been convicted of drug offences on the basis, he alleged, of evidence which had been unconstitutionally obtained. He initiated an appeal before the Court of Criminal Appeal, but while the appeal was pending, he submitted a complaint under Article 40.4.2. Although conceding (as the Court has previously done) that there might be 'exceptional circumstances'[99] which would justify the exercise of concurrent post-conviction review, the Supreme Court dismissed the application:[100]

> If there is any validity in the submissions made by [counsel for the applicant] the proper venue for the determination of these issues is the Court of Criminal Appeal. It is submitted that there are exceptional circumstances in the case which would justify this Court directing the High Court to conduct a full enquiry into the lawfulness

---

[96] [1937] IR 428, 435.
[97] Noted (1942) 76 *Irish Law Times & Solicitors' Journal* 199.
[98] Supreme Court, 30 Oct. 1997.
[99] *The State (Cannon) v. Kavanagh* [1937] IR 428, 436; *The State (McDonagh) v. Frawley* [1978] IR 131, 136. Such 'exceptional circumstances' would, it is suggested, require that the complainant, as a minimum, satisfy two conditions: (i) that a late application to the Court of Criminal Appeal is not admissible, and (ii) that the ground of complaint is of such gravity that if it were established on a criminal appeal the complainant would be discharged. To admit intervention where either of these conditions is not present would undermine the jurisdictional superiority of the Court of Criminal Appeal. On the other hand, an applicant to whom access to the Court of Criminal Appeal is foreclosed, and who has a case of such strength that if it was heard by the Court of Criminal Appeal he would be entitled to discharge, seems to have a reasonable claim to relief.
[100] Supreme Court, 30 Oct. 1997.

of the detention ...These are questions that occur regularly in the course of proceedings in the criminal courts and before the Court of Criminal Appeal, and in my opinion there is nothing exceptional about the circumstances in this case.

However, adherence to the rule prioritizing the Court of Criminal Appeal over review by Article 40.4.2 has not always been consistent. In *The State (Royle) v. Kelly*[101] the complainant was allowed to proceed directly by means of habeas corpus in order to raise some fairly routine post-conviction complaints, in spite of the fact that no appeal to the Court of Criminal Appeal had been instituted. In *O'C v. Governor of Curragh Prison*[102] the applicant was allowed to argue by means of a complaint under Article 40.4.2 that the offence of indecent assault, for which he had been prosecuted and sentenced to three years' imprisonment, had been implicitly repealed by section 28 of the Non-Fatal Offences Against the Person Act, 1997 (an argument which would clearly have been within the jurisdiction of the Court of Criminal Appeal). In *McCowan v. Governor of Mountjoy Prison*[103] no objection was raised to the complainant's argument on an Article 40.4.2 application that the addition of new charges to the indictment had prejudiced his opportunity to prepare a defence. The Supreme Court accepted jurisdiction without any reference to the orthodox principle that the argument had to be prosecuted before the Court of Criminal Appeal.

Were this tendency to allow habeas corpus (or, equally, the remedy of judicial review) operate as a concurrent means of criminal appeal to become established, the danger is that habeas corpus might develop into a rival court of appeal, marginalizing and undermining the Court of Criminal Appeal.[104] The specialist system of post-conviction review which

---

[101] [1974] IR 259.   [102] [2000] 2 ILRM 76.   [103] Supreme Court, 8 Nov. 2001.
[104] The logical corollary of the principle that habeas corpus should not be permitted to undermine the jurisdictional priority of the Court of Criminal Appeal is that habeas corpus may legitimately operate in default of the Court of Criminal Appeal where the Court of Criminal Appeal does not have jurisdiction. So, the High Court may have jurisdiction in cases where the point of law involved is one over which the Court of Criminal Appeal does not have jurisdiction. An obvious example is a challenge to the constitutionality of the legislation under which the accused has been incriminated, a matter over which the jurisdiction of the Court of Criminal Appeal does not extend. It was probably on this ground that the High Court was entitled to administer

the Court of Criminal Appeal was created to provide would be in danger of being pushed aside. The requirement of a prior certificate of leave to appeal would be avoided.[105] The strict time limits in Order 86, r. 5 of the Rules of the Superior Courts, 1986 (requiring the initiation of an application for leave to appeal to the Court of Criminal Appeal within seven days of refusal of leave by the trial court) would be overridden. A particular danger is that habeas corpus, with its remedy of unconditional release, would be adopted as a means of avoiding the jurisdiction to direct a re-trial which is available to the Court of Criminal Appeal.[106]

The prohibition on Article 40.4.2 where appeal to the Court of Criminal Appeal has been exhausted

It is implicit in the appellate scheme created by the Courts of Justice Act, 1924 that the legislative intention was that there be merely a single appeal to the Court of Criminal Appeal: instead of constituting a free-standing, renewable right of appeal available throughout the entire post conviction period an application for leave to appeal must be based on an application submitted to the trial judge.[107] It is unlikely that the legislature, if it intended there to be a continuous, free-standing right of appeal, would have restricted the facility of appeal to an application made to the trial judge (who might then be dead, or have retired). If following a criminal appeal a convicted person could simply proceed again by Article 40.4.2 this legislative intention, that there not be a perpetual right of post-conviction

    post-conviction review in *The State (O'Connor) v. Ó Caomhanaigh* [1963] IR 112. The issue in this case, whether s. 3 of the Tumultuous Risings Act, 1831 was religiously sectarian and thereby inconsistent with the guarantee in Article 44.2.3 of religious non-discrimination, was a question involving the constitutional vires of a law, which in the legal understanding of the time, could only be raised in the High Court, and over which the Court of Criminal Appeal would not be competent. A second instance might be a challenge to a summary conviction for criminal contempt. Since the Court of Criminal Appeal has jurisdiction to review a conviction following trial on indictment only, Article 40.4.2 may be a legitimate form of post-conviction relief where conviction follows trial other than on indictment, such as a conviction for criminal contempt tried summarily.
[105] Ss. 31 & 33 of the Courts of Justice Act, 1924.
[106] S. 5(1)(b) Courts of Justice Act, 1928.
[107] Under ss. 31 & 33 of the Courts of Justice Act, 1924 the right to appeal is predicated on the appellant having been granted, or refused (in which case the appellant may seek leave to appeal from the Court of Criminal Appeal) 'a certificate from the judge who tried him.'

appeal, would be avoided. Further, under section 29 of the Courts of Justice Act, 1924, the determination of the Court of Criminal Appeal is expressly declared to be final.[108] A conviction may only be impeached on new grounds in the circumstances described in section 2 of the Criminal Procedure Act, 1993. The principle of finality under section 29 would be subverted if a complaint could, notwithstanding a prior determination by the Court of Criminal Appeal, be submitted under Article 40.4.2.[109]

However, since the late 1960s the High Court has, on occasion, permitted convicted persons, who have unsuccessfully pursued appeals before the Court of Criminal Appeal, to re-litigate their conviction by means of an application under Article 40.4.2. A significant number of post-conviction habeas corpus cases appear to fall into this category: *Application of Lucey*,[110] *The State (Langan) v. Donohue*,[111] *In re Tynan*,[112] *The State (McNally) v. O'Donovan*[113] and *The State (Williams) v. Kelly (No.2)*[114] in the 1960s; *The State (Byrne) v. Frawley*[115] in the 1970s; *Hardy v. Ireland*[116] in the 1990s. All of these complaints consisted of points which were raised, seemingly as an afterthought, on a post-conviction Article 40.4.2 application, in spite of a previous unsuccessful appeal to the Court of Criminal Appeal. In 2001 in *Breathnach v. Manager of Wheatfield Place of Detention*[117] some highly technical objections[118] to the complainant's

[108] *The State (AG) v. Killian* (1951) 1 Frewen 115.
[109] This argument was rehearsed in *Egan v. Governor of Mountjoy Prison*, Supreme Court, 6 July 1990: 'the use of Article 40 Bunreacht na hÉireann for the purpose of circumventing section 29 of the Courts of Justice Act, 1924 is not acceptable to this Court'. The point was made again in *Hardy v. Ireland*, High Court, 25 June 1993.
[110] [1972] IR 347.
[111] [1974] IR 251.
[112] [1969] IR 273.
[113] [1974] IR 272.
[114] [1970] IR 271. However, in the High Court (24 Feb. 1969) Henchy J had refused the application on the ground that the applicants had not raised the defect on their appeal in the Court of Criminal Appeal (1969 SS No.18).
[115] [1978] IR 326.
[116] [1994] 2 IR 550; see, also, *Kavanagh v. Governor of Mountjoy Prison*, High Court, 29 June 2001 and *Holland v. Governor of Portlaoise Prison*, Supreme Court, 8 Mar. 2001, in both of which an application was processed under Article 40.4.2 despite the complainant's previous appeal to the Court of Criminal Appeal.
[117] Supreme Court, 22 Feb. 2001.
[118] The complainant had argued that the certificate required by s. 47(2) of the Offences Against the State Act, 1939 had not been properly proved, and that the

detention were, despite an earlier unsuccessful appeal to the Court of Criminal Appeal, considered by the Supreme Court on an Article 40.4.2 application. The objection to such jurisdictional informality as that in *Breathnach* is that, by treating the complaint as admissible, the principle that a convicted person is only entitled to one post-conviction appeal was subverted. Further, it is difficult to see why the complainant should have been allowed pursue by means of Article 40.4.2 (with its remedy of unconditional release) a complaint which, if it had been established in the Court of Criminal Appeal, may have resulted in no more than an application of the proviso.[119]

The residual jurisdiction on Article 40.4.2 where appeal to the Court of Criminal Appeal has been exhausted

The availability of an Article 40.4.2 enquiry following the earlier disposal of an appeal to the Court of Criminal Appeal undermines the principle, evidently intended by the Courts of Justice Act, 1924 of the finality of a criminal conviction following the conclusion of an appeal before the Court of Criminal Appeal. On the other hand, the High Court does, as it was said in *Clarke v. McMahon*,[120] have 'inherent powers for the protection of constitutional rights'. In balancing these competing concerns it has been accepted by the Supreme Court that there may be 'exceptional circumstances' in which Article 40.4.2 review might, despite an earlier appeal, be appropriate.[121] In working out a framework for identifying such 'exceptional circumstances' it appears that at least two conditions should be fulfilled. The first is that the complainant should be in a position to excuse the failure to raise the ground at the earlier appeal proceedings thereby removing the objection that the principle, that a convicted person should submit the grounds of appeal promptly, has been abused. (This condition to admissibility has been adopted in some High Court decisions: in *McGlinchey v. Ireland and the Governor of Portlaoise Prison*[122] the High

order of conviction was bad on its face since it had not specified the place where the sentence was to be carried out.
[119] S. 5(1)(a) Courts of Justice Act, 1928.
[120] [1990] 1 IR 228, 236.
[121] *The State (Cannon) v. Kavanagh* [1937] IR 428, 436; *The State (McDonagh) v. Frawley* [1978] IR 131, 136; *Kelleher v. Governor of Portlaoise Prison*, Supreme Court, 30 Oct. 1997.
[122] [1990] 2 IR 215.

Court permitted the complainant, who had pursued an earlier appeal to the Court of Criminal Appeal, to raise new grounds on the basis that he had previously been unaware of those grounds.) The second condition concerns the gravity of the complaint. The complaint should, as a minimum, be of such gravity that it would, if raised in the Court of Criminal Appeal, result in the complainant's discharge (and not just in an order of retrial, or in the application of the proviso). Article 40.4.2 post-conviction jurisdiction is restricted to 'exceptional' defects, and merely technical deficiencies hardly qualify as 'exceptional.' It was probably to accommodate this concern that in *The State (Royle) v. Kelly*[123] (a case where the applicant had previously pursued an appeal to the Court of Criminal Appeal) Henchy J formulated the standard of legal error in such exacting terms:[124]

> Where, as in the present case, the prisoner has been sentenced and convicted by a court established by law under the Constitution and the jurisdiction of that court to try the offence and impose sentence has not been challenged, it would be necessary to show that the procedure had been so flawed by basic defects as to make the conviction a nullity before it could be held that the detention was not in accordance with the law.

Defective sentence following conviction on indictment

Since the jurisdiction of the Court of Criminal Appeal extends to matters of sentencing it follows that the principle of the jurisdictional superiority of the Court of Criminal Appeal applies to matters of sentencing as well as to the matters affecting the initial conviction.[125] The leading rule, that appeal to the Court of Criminal Appeal is the primary means of review, appears to have been overlooked in a number of more recent Supreme

---

[123] [1974] IR 259.
[124] Ibid., p. 269.
[125] On the other hand, the obligation to pursue an appeal to the Court of Criminal Appeal could not be insisted upon where the ground of appeal relates to some matter outside the competence of the Court of Criminal Appeal: where there has, for example, been some abuse in the manner in which the sentence has been put into execution by the executive, or where the prison authorities have miscalculated the length of the sentence, and are holding the prisoner in excess of the time permitted.

Court decisions. In *McConnell v. Governor of Castlerea Prison*,[126] for instance, the complainant had been sentenced by the Circuit Court to a sentence in excess of the period which could, legally, have been imposed for a first offence. The complainant had not, at the time of the application, begun to serve the unlawful portion of the sentence. However, it was conceded that the principle, that a valid conviction is not severable from an unlawful sentence, applied. Accordingly, the legal basis of the entire imprisonment dissolved, and the prisoner was entitled to be discharged. The applicant profited considerably by prosecuting an application under Article 40.4.2, rather than by adopting the conventional route and appealing the legality of the sentence to the Court of Criminal Appeal. Had he appealed to the Court of Criminal Appeal, the Court could, under section 3(2) of the Criminal Procedure Act, 1993, have substituted a regular sentence. In *O'Brien v. Governor of Limerick Prison*[127] the complainant had been sentenced by the Central Criminal Court to ten years' imprisonment, with four of those years to be served without remission, and with the remaining six years being conditionally suspended. The Court held that two components (the requirement that the sentence be served without remission, and the conditionally suspended remanet of the sentence) were *ultra vires*.[128] The Supreme Court went on to hold that the irregular components of the sentence (the condition that the first four years be served without any remission, and that the four years be followed by a further six years suspended) could be severed from the valid part of the sentence. By excising the 'without remission' clause the sentence became a sentence of four years subject to remission. Then by applying remission to that four-year sentence, the applicant's sentence contracted to three years. Since the applicant had been detained for more than three years his release was directed. There appear to be two problems with the

---

[126] Supreme Court, 26 Oct. 2001.
[127] [1997] 2 ILRM 349. In *Carroll v. Governor of Mountjoy Prison*, High Court, 12 Jan. 2005, the complainant was discharged on a habeas corpus application merely on the ground that the precise date of commencement of the Circuit Court sentence which he was undergoing was uncertain.
[128] It was held (i) that a sentence of four years without remission was in defiance of the Prisons (Ireland) Act, 1907, which provided for the remission of all sentences; and (ii) that a sentencing scheme divided into one definite component, and another contingent component, was inconsistent with the legislative intention underlying the Prisons (Ireland) Act, 1907: a definite sentence served in one single episode.

decision in *O'Brien*: first, what justified the Court in severing the sentence? Severance is justified where the effect does not compromise the essential purpose of the impugned order, or upset its nature. The effect of severance was to convert the sentence into one significantly more lenient than that intended by the sentencing judge. Second, what grounds were there for overriding the jurisdictional superiority of the Court of Criminal Appeal? An appeal to the Court of Criminal Appeal might have produced a more balanced outcome. The power of the Court of Criminal Appeal under section 3 of the Criminal Procedure Act, 1993 to vary the sentence imposed by the court of trial might have achieved a result more consistent with the sentencer's intention than that much reduced sentence produced after severance on habeas corpus.

ARTICLE 40.4.2 REVIEW OF SUMMARY CONVICTIONS

Article 40.4.2 review of summary convictions is potentially reduced by two exclusionary principles. The first of these principles is the requirement referred to in one decision of the Supreme Court, *Rock v. Governor of St Patrick's Institution*,[129] that a complainant is obliged to exhaust an appeal to the Circuit Court instead of pursuing an application for judicial review or a complaint under Article 40.4.2. The second is the rule in *McSorley v. Governor of Mountjoy Prison*,[130] that certiorari or judicial review, and not the procedure under Article 40.4.2, is the appropriate remedy for correcting defects in summary proceedings.

The Circuit Court appeal requirement

The balance of authority suggests that where a summary conviction is challenged there is no obligation to exhaust an appeal to the Circuit Court, in the same way that there is an obligation to exhaust an appeal to the Court of Criminal Appeal where a conviction on indictment is challenged. The theory is that the process of summary conviction is made up of two separate hearings: a hearing before the District Court acting within jurisdiction, and a further entitlement to an appeal by way of rehearing before the Circuit Court. To compel a defendant whose conviction is *ultra*

---

[129] Supreme Court, 22 Mar. 1993.   [130] [1997] 2 IR 258.

vires to pursue a complaint by way of appeal has the consequence that, if convicted on the rehearing, the defendant has still only had the benefit of a single proper hearing. If, on the other hand, the matter proceeds by way of judicial review the worst outcome that the defendant can expect is to have the prosecution remitted to the District Court. But, even if remitted, the accused is still entitled to a proper hearing by the District Court and, if convicted, to avail of the right to a rehearing before the Circuit Court.[131] Were a person convicted by the District Court acting in excess of jurisdiction to be denied judicial review, and restricted to a re-hearing before the Circuit Court, the defendant would be disadvantaged in two respects: he or she would be deprived either of the chance that the prosecution will not be remitted, or, in the event that the matter is remitted to the District Court, of the entitlement to *two* trials (before the District Court and, on appeal, before the Circuit Court) carried out within jurisdiction. In light of this principle, it is doubtful whether *Rock v. Governor of St Patrick's Institution*[132] was correctly decided. Here the Supreme Court held that an Article 40.4.2 complaint was inappropriate in a case where a District Court conviction was alleged to have been tainted by a serious breach of fair procedures. This was, the Supreme Court held, '*par excellence* a case that should have been dealt with by way of an appeal.' However, in two subsequent decisions the Supreme Court has rejected the proposition that there is any rule that judicial review should be subordinate to the remedy of appeal to the Circuit Court. In *Arnold v. Windle*[133] the Supreme Court ruled:

> if it were established that the learned judge had acted unconstitutionally in imposing penalties on 24 September 1998 then it could be argued with considerable force that the availability of an appeal to the Circuit Court, already and contingently invoked by the applicant, would not provide an adequate remedy for him. He was entitled to have the penalty to be suffered by him imposed in the court of first instance in accordance with the requirements of natural justice, and to exercise the right of appeal, if he thought fit, from the penalty so determined.

---

[131] *Arnold v. Windle*, Supreme Court, 4 Mar. 1999; *R. v. Hereford Magistrates' Court, ex p. Rowlands* [1998] QB 110.
[132] Supreme Court, 22 Mar. 1993.
[133] Supreme Court, 4 Mar. 1999.

The Supreme Court confirmed the principle in *Nevin v. Crowley*:[134] 'where a trial, whether summary or on indictment, has been conducted in such a manner as to be in breach of fundamental principles of constitutional justice, the mere existence of a right of appeal cannot be an obstacle to the granting of an order of certiorari.' As a matter of principle the same rule should also apply in the case of an application under Article 40.4.2.

The principle in McSorley v. Governor of Mountjoy Prison[135]

The decision in *McSorley v. Governor of Mountjoy Prison* (which held that a challenge to detention by way of summary conviction must be pursued by judicial review rather than habeas corpus)[136] would appear to have pushed Article 40.4.2 to the margins of post-conviction review. If followed, it means that the application for judicial review will nearly always have to be preferred in place of habeas corpus. The Supreme Court in *McSorely* did, however, recognize one exception to the general principle that judicial review was to be preferred to Article 40.4.2, cases where the defect is apparent *ex facie*. The Court distinguished its earlier decision in *Sheehan v. Reilly*[137] and conceded that the principle would not operate where the error was apparent on the record.

The prisoner in *Sheehan's* case had been sentenced in November 1990 to sixteen months' imprisonment. In January 1991 he was sentenced to a further ten months' imprisonment to commence on the expiry of the first sentence, a clear infringement of the twenty-four months' sentencing limit prescribed by section 12 of the Criminal Justice Act, 1984. When the matter came before it on habeas corpus, the High Court converted the Article 40.4.2 application into an application for judicial review, and adjourned the proceedings. However, on appeal the Supreme Court strongly censured the order to convert the habeas corpus proceedings into judicial review proceedings. It was 'quite inappropriate to convert the application under Article 40.4.2 into judicial review proceedings which might conceivably cause delay.'[138] However, *Sheehan's* case, which had appeared to suggest that the High Court should dispense with judicial review and immediately undertake a habeas corpus enquiry, was, four years later, distinguished by *McSorley v. Governor of Mountjoy Prison* which

---

[134] [2001] 1 IR 113, 118–19.   [135] [1997] 2 IR 258.   [136] See above, pp 86–8.
[137] [1993] 2 IR 81.   [138] Ibid, p. 92.

appeared to suggest the direct opposite: that in complaints concerned with District Court convictions the High Court should dispense with the habeas corpus proceedings and investigate the matter by judicial review.

In *McSorley* the Supreme Court distinguished *Sheehan* on the ground that the defect in that case was apparent upon the face of the record:[139] 'The *Sheehan* decision is distinguishable in that it was clear by reference to the record that the applicant in that case was in unlawful custody.' The distinction drawn in *McSorley* appears to be that habeas corpus is appropriate where the defect is apparent on the record. On the other hand, the *McSorley* doctrine holds that Article 40.4.2 is not appropriate where the defect is not self-evident; in such a case judicial review must be sought. But the attempt to reconcile *Sheehan's* case on the basis that the grounds of complaint fell within the first category, and that the error was purely self-evident on the face of the record is, arguably, not so successful. Exposure of the illegality of the imprisonment in *Sheehan's* case also depended the disclosure of matters of fact not evident on the record: when had the lawful part of the sentence begun to be served?; was the applicant entitled to remission? Furthermore, the distinction between patent defects (which may be reviewed under Article 40.4.2) and extraneous defects (which may only be reviewed by judicial review) is artificial in principle. The concern in *McSorely* is that the process under Article 40.4.2 does not enable proper participation by any party implicated in the detention other than the detainer. But in *Re Zwann*[140] the Supreme Court held that, where the ground of an Article 40.4.2 complaint related to a defect on the record, all of the parties implicated must be afforded fair procedures; there was no mention of judicial review, and it was assumed that the procedure under Article 40.4.2 was perfectly sufficient to enable the exercise of those rights. In *McSorley* the Supreme Court conceded that, at least where defects on the record were concerned, natural justice could be accomplished through the Article 40.4.2 procedure, and did not require judicial review. But if the natural justice entitlements of the agency responsible for the detention can, as *Zwann* held, be accomplished through Article 40.4.2 for the purpose of a complaint of error on the record, why may those rights not be capable of being accomplished through Article 40.4.2 where non-documentary defects are at issue?

Recent evidence suggests that it is *Sheehan*, rather than *McSorley*, which

---

[139] [1997] 2 IR 258, 262.   [140] [1981] IR 395.

is being applied by the Supreme Court. In a number of cases the Court has permitted the use of Article 40.4.2 in circumstances which, if *McSorley* was applied, could only have been challenged by means of an application for judicial review. For instance, in *Dalton v. Governor of Glengarrif Parade*[141] no objection was raised to the use of Article 40.4.2 to challenge the delayed execution of a District Court warrant of committal. Again, the ground raised on Article 40.4.2 by the complainant in *McCowan v. Governor of Mountjoy Prison*[142] (that his trial in the Circuit Court had been affected by the late addition of charges to the indictment) was one which according to the *McSorley* principle ought to have been prosecuted by means of judicial review. Yet the Supreme Court held the application admissible on Article 40.4.2.

The grounds of Article 40.4.2 review of summary convictions

Historically, summary convictions had been subject to an invasive habeas corpus/certiorari regime under which convictions might be annulled on the basis of highly technical defects. Indeed, in the early 1940s consideration was given by the Government to the enactment of an amendment of Article 40.4.2 which would ensure that the remedy not be used to discharge persons from custody 'on purely technical grounds or because of some trifling flaw in procedure.'[143] The following passage, from Gibson J's judgment in *R. (Martin) v. Mahony*,[144] used to provide the leading breviate of the grounds of review on certiorari, or habeas corpus, of summary convictions. Certiorari, it was said, would only lie:[145]

> (a) where there is want or excess of jurisdiction when the enquiry begins, or during its progress; (b) when in the exercise of jurisdiction there is an error on the face of the adjudication; (c) where there has been an abuse of jurisdiction ... or disregard of the essentials of justice; (d) where the decision maker is shown to be disqualified by the likelihood of bias or by interest; (e) where there is fraud.

[141] Supreme Court, 29 Feb. 2000. Another instance is *Casey v. Governor of Cork Prison*, High Court, 13 Sept. 2000.
[142] Supreme Court, 8 Nov. 2001.
[143] NAI, Taoiseach files, S. 10299.
[144] [1910] 2 IR 695.
[145] Ibid., at p. 731.

Over the last hundred years or so, these categories of review have been both supplemented, and restricted. In addition to the five categories referred to in Gibson J's account, at least two new grounds have been recognized: error of law and certain categories of evidential error. On the other hand, categories (a) and (b) (procedural error, and error on the face of the record) have been reduced and review on grounds of procedural defect now only operates where the degree of procedural error is serious. The statement of Henchy J in *The State (Aherne) v. Cotter*[146] is one of a number of such cases in which the Supreme Court has emphasized how high the threshold of intervention is now set:[147]

> Before a convicted person who is serving his sentence may be released under our constitutional provisions relating to habeas corpus, it must be shown that the detention resulted from more than an illegality, or a mere lapse of jurisdictional propriety, but that it derived from a departure from the fundamental rules of natural justice according as these rules require to be recognized under the Constitution in the fullness of their evolution at a given time, and in relation to the particular circumstances of the case. Deviations from regularity short of that are outside the range of habeas corpus.

This marks a shift in the standard of review. Twenty-five years earlier the Supreme Court was applying a much more technical approach. The habeas corpus case *The State (Browne) v. Feran*[148] is an exemplar of this approach. Browne had been summarily tried for, and convicted of, an indictable offence, burglary. Under section 2 of the Criminal Justice Act, 1951 an indictable offence may only be tried summarily where three conditions are satisfied: (1) where the facts alleged show a minor offence fit to be tried summarily; (2) where the defendant has been informed of his right to be tried by a jury; (3) where the defendant does not object to being tried summarily. The District Judge's minute book set out the first requirement. It also set out the third requirement. It did not, however, recite the fact of the defendant having been informed of his right to be tried by a jury. The Supreme Court held that the conviction was bad for failure to show jurisdiction, and ordered the complainant's release. This was despite the fact that the District Court had heard the uncontroverted evidence of a Garda

---

[146] [1982] IR 188.   [147] Ibid., p. 203.   [148] [1967] IR 147.

Superintendent present at the trial that the accused had in fact been informed by the District Justice of his right to trial by jury.[149] It is, in light of the 'fundamental rules of natural justice' standard prescribed in *The State (Aherne) v. Cotter*, most unlikely that a technicality like that in *The State (Browne) v. Feran* would be treated in the same way now.

REVIEW OF THE CONDITIONS OF IMPRISONMENT BY ARTICLE 40.4.2

The legal history of the jurisdiction

The doctrine that illegal conditions of detention did not impair the legality of imprisonment was probably established by the early seventeenth century[150] and this view continued to be applied in Ireland down to the mid-1970s. (Indeed, the doctrine has continued to represent the law in most common law jurisdictions.)[151] An instance of the application of the approach in Irish law can be found in *The State (Ward) v. Hanley*[152] where the High Court rejected a complaint, submitted on behalf of itinerant children detained in unsuitable conditions, on the basis that it raised questions not justiciable on habeas corpus. Finlay P is reported to have said that only the legality of proceedings, and not the conditions of detention could be inquired into. He illustrated the point by saying that if the complainants had been detained in a first class hotel, but there was some defect attaching to the order of detention, the Court might be obliged to direct their release.

---

[149] The decision was the subject of a very critical anonymous note, 'Certiorari: its use and abuse' (1969) 103 *Irish Law Times & Solicitors' Journal* 431. The commentator concluded: 'the law in England [is] that normally a person who has been convicted of an offence to which he has pleaded guilty will not be later granted a certiorari to quash that conviction. The decision of the Supreme Court in *The State (Browne) v. Feran* may be regarded as having reached a high water mark in technicality.'

[150] See the opinion of the judges, delivered 19 June 1636, to the effect that habeas corpus was an inappropriate remedy for the relief of prisoners detained during time of plague: G.R. Elton (ed.), *Politics and the Bench: the judges and the origins of the English Civil War* (London, 1971), pp 182–3; the same principle was applied in *Anon.* (1654) Style 432; 82 ER 838.

[151] *R. v. Deputy Governor of Parkhurst Prison, ex p. Hague* [1992] 1 AC 58; *Cullen v. Chief Constable RUC* [2004] 2 All ER 237; *Prisoners A-XX v. State of New South Wales* (1995) 38 NSWLR 622.

[152] *Irish Times*, 24 Jan. 1975.

However, within a year, the common law doctrine rehearsed by Finlay P had been reversed. In *The State (C) v. Frawley*,[153] an informal application was received from a highly disturbed prisoner with a sociopathic personality disorder, who complained that for most of the time he was being detained in solitary confinement, was sedated, and was held in a cell which was unfurnished. The High Court, applying traditional common law doctrine, refused to consider the application. However, on appeal, the Supreme Court held that the legality of a prisoner's detention might be affected if it could be established that conditions of detention were inhumane or degrading, and the complaint was remitted to the High Court.

Following *The State (C) v. Frawley* the view took hold that the jurisdiction to order an enquiry under Article 40.4.2 was activated whenever the prisoner complained of an act of prison administration of a character which could be classified as a breach of a personal constitutional right. The difficulty with this standard was that any complaint of prison maladministration, no matter how trivial, could be formulated in constitutional terms. In the *State (Gallagher) v. Governor of Portlaoise Prison*[154] the applicant complained that his correspondence was being opened. The High Court accepted that the defect was a constitutional one (an interference with the prisoner's right to communicate) and directed an initial enquiry. In another case a prisoner alleged that copies of the Sinn Féin newspaper, the *Irish People*, were being withheld from him.[155] The High Court held that since a constitutional right (the right to communicate) was at issue, it was required to conduct an Article 40.4.2 enquiry. In none of these cases was the prisoner released; the only consequence of the prisoner being able to raise an arguable claim of breach of constitutional rights was that the High Court was obliged to go through the motions of conducting an Article 40.4.2 enquiry. The effect was that the most routine prison complaints were being processed through the quite inappropriate remedy of habeas corpus. This was particularly inappropriate because the only remedy available on Article 40.4.2, an order of release, was clearly disproportionate, while the more precisely targeted remedies, mandamus or injunction, were being disregarded.

---

[153] [1976] IR 365.   [154] *Irish Times*, 7 Mar. 1978.
[155] *The State (Keane) v. Governor of Curragh Military Detention Barracks*, *Irish Times*, 14 Mar. 1978. In perhaps the most absurd of these cases the ground of complaint was that cereal had been removed from the breakfast menu: *The State (Rutherford) v. Governor of Arbour Hill Prison*, *Irish Times*, 1 Feb. 1980.

The current standard of review

A disassociation between Article 40.4.2 and the remedying of prison conditions was eventually effected in *The State (McDonagh) v. Frawley*.[156] McDonagh, a well known prisoner litigant, taking advantage of the very permissive standard being applied by the High Court, was granted an enquiry on the basis that a back ache complaint from which he suffered, was not being adequately treated. The Supreme Court took the opportunity to correct what it saw as the misuse of habeas corpus. The Court held that complaints relating to conditions of post-conviction imprisonment would hardly ever attract the remedy of release under Article 40.4.2. While it did not exclude the remote, theoretical possibility that Article 40.4.2 might exceptionally be an appropriate remedy, it held that in the ordinary course such complaints would normally be remediable by alternative means. O' Higgins CJ said:[157]

> The confinement of orders of release under Article 40, s.4, to cases where the detention is not 'in accordance with the law' in the sense I have indicated means that applications under Article 40, s.4, are not suitable for the judicial investigation of complaints as to conviction, sentence or conditions of detention which fall short of that requirement. These fall to be investigated, where necessary, under other forms of proceedings. But in cases where it has not been shown to the satisfaction of the court that the detention is 'in accordance with the law' in the sense indicated, the release of the detained person must be ordered.

In no case, whether prior or subsequent to *The State (C) v. Frawley*, has a prisoner actually been released on the ground of oppressive post-conviction conditions of detention. It appears, however, that the weighting in favour of the Article 40.4.2 remedy will increase according to the exceptional gravity of the abuse, and, in particular, according to the intention with which such ill-treatment has been applied. In *Brennan v. Governor of Portlaoise Prison*[158] Budd J speculated that the deliberate violation of a

---

[156] [1978] IR 131; the principle was re-stated by the Supreme Court in *Walsh v. Governor of Limerick Prison* [1995] 2 ILRM 158.
[157] Ibid., at p. 137.
[158] [1999] 1 ILRM 190.

prisoner's rights by systematic torture might justify habeas corpus, while in *The State (Richardson) v. Governor of Mountjoy Prison*[159] the High Court held that an order of habeas corpus might be appropriate if the court were 'convinced that the authorities were taking advantage of the fact that a person was being detained consciously and deliberately to violate his constitutional rights, or to subject him to inhuman or degrading treatment the court might order his release ... likewise if the court was convinced that the conditions were such as to seriously endanger his life or health, and that the authorities intended to do nothing to rectify these conditions.' The extent of the public interest in the maintenance of imprisonment may also be important. In the post-conviction setting, the personal remedy under Article 40.4.2 is, as the Supreme Court explained in *The State (C) v. Frawley*, subordinate to the public interest in the maintenance of imprisonment. But that interest is relative. The public interest will not be as compelling at the pre-conviction stage and conditions of detention affecting pre-trial remand may be subjected to a different standard of review. Even at the post-conviction stage there may be circumstances (the fact, for instance, that the imprisonment follows conviction of a minor offence, that the person undergoing imprisonment is pre-adult, or that the sentence is about to expire) which might reduce the weighting attached to maintenance of that interest and, correspondingly, expand the scope of operation of Article 40.4.2.

IRREGULAR POST-CONVICTION TRANSFER

No successful challenge to the administration of post-conviction transfer can be identified since the late 1960s. In all of the cases in which an application succeeded the conventional order was to direct that the prisoner be released from the current place of detention, re-apprehended and taken to the appropriate place of confinement.[160] In *The State (Dillon) v. Kelly*[161] an order transferring a convicted prisoner from Mountjoy Prison to

---

[159] [1980] ILRM 82, 90–1.
[160] *The State (Dickenson) v. Kelly* [1964] IR 73; *The State (Holden) v. Governor of Portlaoise Prison* [1964] IR 73, 80.
[161] [1970] IR 174. The power assumed by the court to manufacture its own order has been analysed above at pp 167–9.

Portlaoise Prison under the provisions of the Criminal Justice Administration Act, 1914 was held invalid on the grounds of a technical mis-recital in the ministerial transfer order. The High Court held that the requirement of unconditional release under Article 40.4.2 allowed it no option but to order Dillon's release. However, the Supreme Court held that the proper order was a binary order of release combined with re-apprehension:[162]

> It has repeatedly been stated in this Court that, where a prisoner is unlawfully undergoing a sentence of imprisonment but his detention has been temporarily rendered illegal by his being detained in a prison not authorized by law it is the duty of the court which orders his release from such unlawful detention to ensure that the prisoner is immediately re-arrested and lodged in a lawful place of detention to serve out the unexpired part of his sentence. Therefore, the Court will issue its warrant directed to the Commissioner of An Garda Síochána for the apprehension of the prisoner Joseph Dillon and for his conveyance to, and lodgment in, Mountjoy.

However, as has been argued earlier, the *Dillon* order appears inconsistent with the general principle (a corollary of the doctrine that Article 40.4.2 requires unconditional release) that an order of release may not be combined with an order of re-arrest.[163] Secondly, it is questionable whether any order of release, even if momentary and purely technical, is consistent with the general law on Article 40.4.2 review of post-conviction error. The Supreme Court has consistently taken the view that the integrity of a conviction on indictment should be preserved by narrowing the range of intervention on Article 40.4.2 against irregularities in sentencing or in the administration of imprisonment, and requiring that such irregularities be remedied by means less disruptive than habeas corpus.[164] In light of this sort of approach, it is doubtful whether Article 40.4.2 is ever the proper remedy for defects of equivalent, if not even lesser, technicality such as errors in the administration of prison transfer.

---

[162] Ibid., pp 178–9.
[163] *The State (Williams) v. Kelly* [1970] IR 271.
[164] *The State (McNally) v. O'Donovan* [1974] IR 272; *The State (McDonagh) v. Frawley* [1978] IR 131.

By analogy with the principle on irregular sentences, the appropriate order might be to refuse a remedy under Article 40.4.2, and instead to remit the order for correction.[165]

---

[165] *The State (McNally) v. O'Donovan* [1974] IR 272, 282–3. The Supreme Court has more recently confirmed this principle holding that an irregularity in the transfer process would not justify the release of a convicted prisoner: *Breathnach v. Garda Commissioner and Manager of Wheatfield Place of Detention*, Supreme Court, 22 Feb. 2001. In *Re Ward*, Irish Times, 22 Feb. 1975, the High Court rejected as 'absurd' the contention that the detention of a hunger striker in Jervis Street Hospital under a transfer order under s. 17(6) of the Criminal Justice Administration Act, 1914 was invalid because the order had been made just after, and not prior to, the prisoner's actual transfer.

CHAPTER FIVE

Habeas corpus review of administrative detention, and detention ancillary to civil litigation

ARTICLE 40.4.2 AND REVIEW OF AN ADMISSION ORDER
UNDER THE MENTAL HEALTH ACT 2001

The admission process under the Mental Health Act, 2001

The power to make an admission order under the Mental Health Act, 2001 is restricted to a person suffering from a 'mental disorder', defined in section 3 as a condition of either mental illness, severe dementia, or significant intellectual disability. However, a person suffering from a 'mental disorder' only becomes accessible to involuntary detention where there is a risk of serious harm occurring to the patient or others, or the risk of serious deterioration.[1] The power of review under Article 40.4.2 extends

---

[1] The criteria by reference to which a person with a mental disorder then becomes accessible to involuntary detention are defined in ss. 3(1)(a) and (b):
   (a) because of the illness, disability or dementia, there is a serious likelihood of the person concerned causing immediate and serious harm to himself or herself or to other persons, or
   (b) (i) because of the severity of the illness, disability or dementia, the judgment of the person concerned is so impaired that failure to admit the person to an approved centre would be likely to lead to a serious deterioration in his or her condition, or would prevent the administration of appropriate treatment that could be given only by such admission, and
       (ii) the reception, detention and treatment of the person concerned in an approved centre would be likely to benefit or alleviate the condition of that person to a material extent.

The s. 3(1)(a) criterion only applies in a case in which there is a high probability of immediate, serious harm. The phrase 'serious likelihood' might not capture cases of lesser probability, including a 'significant risk' of harm. The definition requires that there be a risk of the patient causing serious harm; it does not extend to another causing harm to the patient, and is unlikely to cover cases of apprehended exploitation by others.

to review of the existence these substantive conditions. In *Croke v. Smith*[2] the Supreme Court held that the scope of Article 40.4.2 review of mental health detention extended to review of the issue of whether 'the person detained is a person of unsound mind, and in need of care and attention.'[3]

The procedure leading to the making of an admission order to an approved centre begins with an application to a registered medical practitioner for a recommendation that the person be admitted. The initial examination must be carried out within twenty-four hours of the 'receipt' of the application.[4] There is no power to enter property for the purpose of carrying out the preliminary examination. Nor is there (by contrast with the position regulating examination for the purpose of an admission order) any power to take charge of a person for the purpose of carrying out a section 10 examination. By contrast with the position under the Mental Treatment Act, 1945, where the term had been undefined, 'examination' for the purpose of the Mental Health Act, 2001 is defined exactingly, requiring a personal examination with reference to each of the following four conditions: the process and content of thought, the mood and the behaviour of the person concerned.[5] In *Re Brady*[6] an Article 40.4.2 complainant, who had been detained following an examination (under the Mental Treatment Act, 1945) in which the medical practitioner had made no real effort to see whether the person was suffering from a medical illness, and who relied too heavily on collateral history provided by her family, was released by the High Court, and a similar outcome could be expected under the stricter requirement in the 2001 Act. By contrast with the case law under the 1945 Act,[7] there is no provision for relaxing the standard of assessment in a case where a full examination may (because, for instance, the person is under sedation) be impractical.

---

[2] [1998] 1 IR 101, 125.
[3] In administering that form of enquiry the President of the High Court has available to it the power under s. 241 of the Mental Treatment Act, 1945 to order the Inspector of Mental Hospitals to examine, and to report to the Court on the condition of, any detained person. The s. 241 power was used in the habeas corpus case *Orton v. St John of God Hospital*, 15 Nov. 2004.
[4] S. 10(2) Mental Health Act, 2001.
[5] S. 2(1) Mental Health Act, 2001.
[6] *Irish Times*, 16 & 17 Feb. 1990.
[7] In *O'Reilly v. Moroney*, Supreme Court, 16 Nov. 1993, the Supreme Court, noting the absence in the 1945 Act of a definition of 'examine' held that a clinical interview was unnecessary in the case of a patient in a highly disturbed state.

The recommendation of admission made by the registered medical practitioner is then transmitted to the approved centre. The sole officer authorized to receive a recommendation is the director of the approved centre,[8] and the function of receiving a recommendation may not (by contrast with the delegation procedure instituted by the Mental Treatment Act, 1953)[9] be delegated to any other officer. The authority to make an admission order is conditioned by two time limits. Firstly, the recommendation lapses within seven days (and not seven 'clear days'[10] as under the preceding regime);[11] within that period the recommendation must be received by the clinical director, and the person conveyed to the approved centre. Secondly, the examination at the approved centre must be carried out 'as soon as may be'[12] and must be completed within 24 hours.

The admission order authorizes reception, detention and treatment for a period of twenty-one days.[13] The period may be further extended under a 'renewal order' for a period not exceeding three months.[14] The only condition to such a renewal order is that the consultant psychiatrist responsible for the care and treatment of the patient[15] certifies that he has examined the patient not more than one week before the making of the order, and certifies, in a form specified by the Mental Health Commission, that the patient suffers from a mental disorder. Section 15(3) authorizes two further renewal orders: 'detention may be further extended by order made by the consultant psychiatrist concerned for a period not exceeding 6 months, beginning on the expiration of the renewal order made by the psychiatrist under subsection (2), and thereafter may be further extended by order made by the psychiatrist for periods each of which does not exceed 12 months.' Section 15 appears to require an extended continuity of identity of the person making the renewal order: 'the psychiatrist' (the

---

[8] S. 14(1) Mental Health Act, 2001.
[9] S. 3 of the Mental Treatment Act, 1953.
[10] S. 167(2) Mental Treatment Act, 1945.
[11] Conveyance to the district mental hospital was required to be effected within seven clear days after the making of the recommendation.
[12] S. 14(1) Mental Health Act, 2001.
[13] S. 15(1) Mental Health Act, 2001.
[14] S. 15(2) Mental Health Act, 2001.
[15] The function is non-delegable; contrast the procedure for the detention of voluntary patients under which an admission order may be made by a consultant psychiatrist acting on behalf of the psychiatrist who is responsible for the care and treatment of the patient (s. 24(6)).

persona designata in section 15(3) who is authorized to make the 12 months' extension order) appears to correspond to the 'consultant psychiatrist concerned' (the *persona designata* referred to earlier in section 15(3) who is authorized to make an extension order of up to six months' detention), who, in turn, appears to correspond to 'the consultant psychiatrist responsible for the care and treatment of the patient' referred to in section 15(2). A break in continuity may, on this interpretation, impair the power of renewal.

Under section 18 it is a condition of the validity of an admission order that the order be reviewed by a Mental Health Tribunal. The regularity of the confirmation order of the Tribunal is made part of the wider chain of legality.[16] The review required of a Mental Health Tribunal under section 18 is, presumably, a valid review, so that an irregularity in the review process will impair the entire detention order. In choosing, therefore, to integrate Tribunal review into the process of detention the legislature has greatly increased the opportunity for interference by Article 40.4.2 and judicial review. The review process is initiated following the making of an admission order, or a renewal order; pending confirmation by a Mental Health Tribunal such an order has merely provisional status. The Tribunal is obliged to determine whether the procedural provisions in sections 9, 10, 12, 14, 15 and 16 have been complied with.[17] However, the jurisdiction appears incomplete: the Tribunal has no jurisdiction to determine a claim that the procedural conditions which are contained in sections 4 or 11 or 17 have been disregarded.

Techniques for avoiding discharge of the dangerously mentally disordered

At common law the operation of habeas corpus in the context of commitment for mental disorder was heavily conditioned by the concern that the remedy should not be used to facilitate the release of persons who, by reason of their illness, may constitute a threat to public security. Two techniques were developed especially for this purpose. The first was to postpone the disposal of the habeas corpus in order to achieve the retrospective validation of the order.[18] In the early nineteenth-century Irish

---

[16] Ss. 16,17 & 18 Mental Health Act, 2001.
[17] S. 18(1)(a).
[18] Retrospective validation of an irregular order on Article 40.4.2 is discussed above at pp 72–4.

decision, *Ex parte Carpenter*[19] the detainee had been detained as a lunatic in an institution in Finglas, County Dublin, without the essential preliminary of a finding by a commission of lunacy having been made. The Irish Court of King's Bench, in place of directing the applicant's release, directed that the matter be adjourned in order that a commission of lunacy, whose determination might legitimize the detention of the applicant, could take place. The Court's order was: 'enlarge the time for showing cause until the first day of next term, a commission of lunacy having issued out of the Court of Chancery and now being in progress.' A similar approach can be found being applied almost 170 years later in the English case, *Re Briscoe*[20] where the High Court, having found that the applicant's detention had been irregularly administered, refused, nonetheless, to direct the applicant's discharge. Adjourning the habeas corpus application, Tucker J said:

> Normally I would say, on an application such as this, that the applicant should be released. But I am reluctant to take that course because it is perfectly clear to me that there have been difficulties in the past there is an unhappy history of an unstable mental condition. I am reluctant to force the respondents to release this lady without having further opportunity to consider the matter.

It was well established at common law that, where a detainee posed an immediate danger to himself or others, the court possessed an overriding jurisdiction to deny release even if the detention was indisputably unlawful. In *Re Riall*[21] Lefroy CJ refused to direct the release of a person detained as a dangerous lunatic saying that 'supposing that at the time the conditional order was obtained he was not a dangerous lunatic, yet, if he is now we will not grant the habeas corpus to bring him up to be discharged, because the magistrate will immediately recommit him.' The leading expression of the view is the judgment of Lord Denman in *Re Shuttleworth*:[22] 'but I go a little further. If the Court thought that a party unlawfully received or detained was a lunatic we should still be betraying the common duties as members of society if we directed discharge. But we

---

[19] (1824) Sm & Bat 81.
[20] Queen's Bench Div., 22 July 1998.
[21] (1860) 11 ICLR 279, 287.
[22] (1846) 9 QB 651, 662; 115 ER 1423, 1428.

have no power to set aside the order, only to discharge. And should we as judges be justified in setting such a party at large?"[23] It is at least possible that the same exceptional jurisdiction might exist under the Constitution. The proviso to Article 40.4.2 restricts the power to refuse release to circumstances where the Court is satisfied that the detention is in accordance with the law, and, by implication, prevents the Court refusing release on any other ground. But, if, as argued earlier,[24] the High Court possesses a wider jurisdiction to withhold release in the interests of an overriding constitutional concern, a power equivalent to the common law power might be capable of being invoked under Article 40.4.2.

ARTICLE 40.4.2 AND IMMIGRATION-RELATED DETENTION

Section 5 of the Illegal Immigrants (Trafficking) Act, 2000 and the operational range of Article 40.4.2

An order of detention may be made at two stages of the ordinary immigration control process: firstly, imprisonment may follow an order of removal (most commonly following refusal of leave to land); secondly, under section 5 of the Immigration Act, 1999 there is a power of detention where it is necessary to prevent evasion of a deportation order made under the Immigration Act, 1999. However, the primary remedy where these powers are unlawfully executed is now judicial review, and not Article 40.4.2. The detainee's entitlement to intervention under Article 40.4.2 to review the legality of any of these categories of detention has been greatly restricted by section 5 of the Illegal Immigrants (Trafficking) Act, 2000. The effect of section 5 is that challenges to the legality of the underlying administrative order on which the detention is predicated must be conducted through judicial review, and intervention on Article 40.4.2 is, in these cases, withdrawn, or merely incidental.[25]

Notwithstanding this, there are some residual cases which are not excluded by the prohibition in section 5, and where Article 40.4.2 may still be deployed. Section 5 of the Immigration Act, 2003[26] provides for the

---

[23] The statement was approved by the Irish Court of Appeal in *Re O'Reilly* (1894) 29 ILTR 33, 35.
[24] See above, pp 100–2.
[25] See above, pp 88–92.
[26] S. 5(1) has been amended by s. 16(8) of the Immigration Act, 2004.

detention and removal of an immigrant on one of four grounds.[27] The principal of these grounds of removal is activated where an immigrant has been refused leave to land under section 4(3) of the Immigration Act, 2004. Section 5(1)(dd) of the Illegal Immigrants (Trafficking) Act, 2000, as amended,[28] prohibits review by any means other than judicial review of a decision to refuse permission to land. It thereby prohibits an Article 40.4.2 challenge to the legality of a refusal of permission to land from which a consequential removal order and detention has followed. But, there are three other grounds of removal and section 5 of the Act of 2000 does not affect the power to review under Article 40.4.2 the underlying basis of a detention which is predicated upon any of these grounds. Even where challenges against an underlying order must be processed through judicial review, objections to the subsequent administration of the removal order may be raised by way of an Article 40.4.2 complaint (for here the challenge is not directed to the refusal of leave to land but to the manner in which that removal has been operated).

There is a similar displacement of Article 40.4.2 in favour of judicial review in the case of deportation-related detention. Section 5(1) of Immigration Act, 1999 provides for the arrest and detention of a person against whom a deportation order is in force on one of four grounds: where a member of the Garda Síochána suspects that the person either (a) has failed to comply with any provision in the deportation order, or (b) intends to leave the State and enter another state, or (c) has destroyed his or her identity documents or is in possession of forged identification documents, or (d) intends to avoid removal from the State. Section 5(1)(c) of the Illegal Immigrants (Trafficking) Act, 2000 disallows challenges to a deportation order, or notification of deportation, otherwise than by way of an application for judicial review under Order 84 of the Rules of the Superior Courts, 1986.[29] But, detention may only be authorized where one of the

---

[27] Removal may be directed (a) in the case of a non-national who has failed to comply with s. 4(2) of the Immigration Act, 2004 (failure to present himself to an immigration officer); (b) in the case of a non-national who has been refused leave to land under s. 4(3) of the Act of 2004; (c) in the case of a non-national who is in the State in contravention of s. 5(1) of the 2004 Act (being in the State in contravention of the terms of a permission to land); (d) in the case of a non-national who has landed in the State in contravention of s. 6(1) of the 2004 Act (having landed at a place other than at an approved port).

[28] S. 16(6) of the Immigration Act, 2004.

[29] On the other hand, there have been cases where the habeas corpus ouster clause

four statutory contingencies arise, and while section 5 prohibits review of the legality of the underlying deportation order it does not prohibit a challenge by means of Article 40.4.2 targeted at the issue of compliance with the further conditions necessary to justify deportation-related detention. Nor does it affect a challenge directed to the manner in which that detention is administered. Finally, the exclusion of Article 40.4.2 by section 5 of the Illegal Immigrants (Trafficking) Act, 2000 only applies to detention under the ordinary immigration code; it does not apply to the two forms of detention constituted under the Refugee Act, 1996.[30]

HABEAS CORPUS AND IMPRISONMENT
FOR CONTEMPT OF COURT

Priority between Article 40.4.2 and appeal as means of review of imprisonment for contempt

Imprisonment for contempt of the High Court, Circuit Court, or District Court, may follow one of three types of proceeding: the process of attachment or committal, for civil contempt;[31] summary proceedings for criminal

---

in s. 5 appears to have been disregarded. In *Gabrel v. Governor of Mountjoy Prison*, Supreme Court, 8 Feb. 2001, and *Re Laiham*, *Irish Times*, 9 Feb. 2003, the complainants challenged by means of Article 40.4.2 the validity of their arrest on the basis that there had been non-compliance with the condition that a deportation order be preceded by notice of intention to make the order. But since the ground of challenge was to the manner of notification under s. 3(3) of the Immigration Act, 1999, and since, by s. 5 of the Illegal Immigrants (Trafficking) Act, 2000, a challenge on this ground is withdrawn from challenge under Article 40.4.2, the court was only competent to hear the application by way of judicial review.

[30] S. 9(8) of the 1996 Act provides for the detention of an applicant for a declaration of refugee status where any one of six contingencies exist. The authority to make such an order is entrusted to a judge of the District Court. Redress of such detention is not restricted to judicial review by section 5 of the Illegal Immigrants (Trafficking) Act, 2000. S. 17(2) of the Refugee Act, 1996 creates a unique form of deportation order, providing for the deportation of a person granted a declaration of refugee status, but who, in the interests of national security or public policy, the Minister considers it necessary to deport. S. 17(2) has also been omitted from the list of provisions catalogued in s. 5 of the Illegal Immigrants (Trafficking) Act, 2000.

[31] The jurisdiction of the District Court to imprison for civil contempt dates only to 1999, when power to make orders of attachment or committal were inserted

contempt; or, proceedings tried on indictment for criminal contempt. An application under Article 40.4.2 sometimes competes with the remedy of appeal among the remedies for persons imprisoned for contempt, and issues of priority amongst those remedies arise. The question whether habeas corpus is a primary, or merely a reserve, remedy for persons imprisoned for contempt varies according to the nature of those contempt proceedings and the court through which they have been processed.

There are probably three categories of contempt proceeding for the redress of which Article 40.4.2 functions as a proper method of review notwithstanding the co-existence of a right of appeal. Firstly, where imprisonment follows proceedings in the Circuit Court for civil contempt, it has long been accepted that habeas corpus functions as one of the detainee's primary remedies. In the 1870s, in *Trousdell v. Kearse*,[32] the Irish Court of Queen's Bench dismissed an argument that a contemnor imprisoned by a County Court was bound to proceed by way of appeal to the

---

into the District Court Rules, 1997: the District Court (Attachment and Committal) Rules, 1998, S.I. No. 124 of 1999 and the District Court (Attachment and Committal) Rules, 2000, S.I. No. 196 of 2000. However, the District Court has no express statutory power to make an order of committal for contempt. The *vires* of these rules may be questionable. (i) Under s. 91 of the Courts of Justice Act, 1924 the District Court rule-making body has jurisdiction to prescribe rules in relation to practice and procedure. But while the District Court Rules Committee has jurisdiction to prescribe rules in relation to the substantive powers conferred by statute or inherent in the court, the rule-making body has no jurisdiction to institute any new jurisdiction: *The State (O'Flaherty) v. O'Floinn* [1954] IR 295. It is arguable that the creation by the Rules of the District Court of a power to commit for civil contempt is such a new jurisdiction. The Law Reform Commission in its *Consultation Paper on Contempt of Court* (Dublin, 1991) favoured (pp 187–8) the view that the District Court had jurisdiction to commit for civil contempt, arguing that the District Court by virtue of its being constituted a court of record (by s. 13 of the Courts Act, 1971) necessarily had a power of committal for contempt. However, at common law the status of a court as a court of record only invested the court with power to commit for contempt committed in face of the court (and not for civil contempt): *Griesley's Case* (1588) 8 Co Rep 38, 77 ER 530; *Lady Throgmorton's Case* (1610) 12 Co Rep 69, 77 ER 1347. (ii) The power of the District Court Rules Committee is (by s. 91 of the Courts of Justice Act, 1924) restricted to 'the adaption or modification of any statute' that may be necessary for the purpose. S. 9 of the Petty Sessions Act, 1851 limits the District Court's jurisdiction in case of wilful insult or 'any other contempt' to committal for seven days. The unlimited committal potentially permitted by O. 46B might exceed a mere 'modification or adaption' of s. 9.

[32] (1873) IR 8 CL 25, 29.

High Court, and was disentitled to proceed by way of an application for habeas corpus: 'it has been argued ingeniously by counsel for the plaintiff that habeas corpus does not lie as the party might have appealed; but we think the right of appeal does not affect the right of the party where the act done to his prejudice is in excess of jurisdiction and void.' Significant prejudice would be caused to a prisoner if a High Court appeal were to be rigidly insisted upon in preference to an application under Article 40.4.2. To require an appeal to the High Court, at the expense of Article 40.4.2, would have the effect of obliging the prisoner to pursue the procedure prescribed by the Courts of Justice Act, 1936, and would deny the detainee a number of significant procedural rights guaranteed by Article 40.4.2. The Courts of Justice, Act, 1936 distinguishes the appeal rights of persons tried at the Circuit Court outside Dublin, and persons tried before the Dublin Circuit Court. In the case of a person committed by a Circuit Court sitting outside Dublin there is no immediate right of *ex parte* access to the High Court (as there is on Article 40.4.2). The appellant must either await the arrival of the High Court on Circuit,[33] or make a special application to have the matter heard immediately in Dublin. But such an application may, in a process far more long-winded than that under Article 40.4.2, be made *ex parte* only with the consent of the other party, or, if that is not forthcoming, by means of an *inter partes* hearing.[34] In addition, a detainee who appeals under the Courts of Justice Act, 1936 loses the opportunity (which he would have under Article 40.4.2) to appeal to the Supreme Court: section 39 of the Courts of Justice Act, 1936 makes the decision of the High Court on appeal final and unappealable.

Imprisonment for criminal contempt prosecuted summarily would appear to provide a second category of case where habeas corpus functions as a primary remedy. There is no right of appeal to the Court of Criminal Appeal available to a person convicted summarily for criminal contempt in the Circuit Court. An appeal to the Court of Criminal Appeal is only available following a trial on indictment. It follows that a complaint under Article 40.4.2, or an application for judicial review, is probably the most

---

[33] S. 38(1)(b): where a judgment or order is made or given by a judge of the Circuit Court sitting outside the Dublin Circuit the appeal must be to the High Court sitting in the appeal town for the county or county borough in which the action was heard or determined.

[34] S. 38(5)(b) Courts of Justice Act, 1936, as amended by s. 43 of the Courts and Court Officers Act, 1995.

effective remedy available to a person alleging an irregular conviction following a summary conviction for criminal contempt in the Circuit Court. Finally, habeas corpus functions as a primary remedy when the District Court illegally exercises its power to commit for civil or criminal contempt; this is in line with the general principle that a person imprisoned by the District Court is entitled to test the legality of the detention by habeas corpus or judicial review in the High Court without having to appeal to the Circuit Court.[35]

On the other hand, there are at least two species of committal for contempt for the redress of which Article 40.4.2 is inappropriate: imprisonment for criminal contempt following trial on indictment is subject to the general rule that appeal to the Court of Criminal Appeal takes precedence over Article 40.4.2. Further, at common law imprisonment for contempt ordered by a superior court was subject to the rule against habeas corpus review of committal by superior courts. In *In re Aikin*[36] Fitzgerald J dismissed a habeas corpus challenge made to the Queen's Bench Division against an order of attachment made by the Lord Chancellor: 'The present case comes before us as a division of the High Court of Justice, and there is a comity between the several divisions of the High Court of Justice exercising co-ordinate jurisdiction which ought to lead [the court] in the present case from questioning the procedure or practice of another Division.' It is, as we have seen earlier, arguable that an analogous prohibition against the use of Article 40.4.2 to review orders of detention made by the High Court has been perpetuated under the Constitution.[37] But even if this is so, two exceptions to the general prohibition against habeas corpus review of High Court-directed committal may be identified. Firstly, the principle appears not to apply where the ground of challenge relates, not to the actual decision of the High Court, but to the subsequent execution of that order.[38] A complaint which is concerned with the subsequent administration of the order does not trespass on the correctness of the decision of the committing High Court judge, and is therefore outside the

---

[35] See above, pp 215–17.
[36] (1881) 8 LR Ir 50, 53; See, also, *Re Roe* (1828) 1 Law Recorder 310, 312.
[37] See above, p. 199.
[38] In *The State (Gildea) v. Hipwell* [1942] IR 485 the applicant (who had been committed by order of the High Court in Bankruptcy) was permitted to challenge by means of a habeas corpus application a committal order which had been executed sixteen months after the original order of committal.

rationale of the rule. Secondly, the ordinary rule may be dispensed with in cases of extreme abuse of power. In *Re Aylward*[39] the Irish Court of Common Pleas, while declining to accept a habeas corpus challenge to an order which had been made by the Court of Queen's Bench committing Sister Margaret Aylward, noted that this did not preclude the Court from exercising jurisdiction in cases of exceptional abuse: 'if the Court of Queen's Bench had set upon themselves so far as to order the lady to have been imprisoned in the coal hole of the Lord Chief Justice, and then in rotation to those of the other judges of the Court habeas corpus might lie.'

The technical bias on judicial review of committal for civil contempt

Traditionally, the courts apply a strict standard of review to compliance with the procedural conditions to committal.[40] In *In re O'Neill*[41] Hanna J epitomized the standard of review of committal for contempt in as highly exacting:[42]

> The Court should always bear in mind that the liberty of the subject is inviolable and no person should be deprived of his liberty save in strict accordance with law. The jurisdiction to commit should be exercised with scrupulous care and searching scrutiny to see that the requisites of the legal power have been complied with.

Unease at the use of the committal power against distressed, or over-principled, persons may have underlain the traditional sympathy to purely technical challenges. However, the development of doctrines designed to ensure that imprisonment only operates *in extremis* now provide more

---

[39] (1860) 12 ICLR 448, 453.

[40] 'Attachment: strict procedure' [1932] *Law Journal (Irish Free State)* 212. A further corollary of the strict approach is the rule that the party applying for committal or attachment must affirmatively prove compliance with each of the required steps to committal. Where the party applying fails to set out compliance with all of the steps a direction may be obtained that the motion be dismissed. In *Dempsey v. Dempsey* [1933] *Law Journal (Irish Free State)* 213 the affidavit of service of an order directing payment of alimony did not state that the copy served contained a penal endorsement. O'Byrne J rejected the suggestion that the defect might be remedied by a subsequent affidavit, saying that 'the Court had to decide the matter on the evidence before it'.

[41] [1932] IR 548.

[42] Ibid., at p. 577.

direct means of limiting the operation of the jurisdiction.[43] A change of approach to the non-prejudicial irregularity had been endorsed in English law. In *Nicholls v. Nicholls*[44] the Court of Appeal pointed out that an over-technical standard prejudiced not just the immediate parties involved, but also the integrity of the committing court:[45]

> Today it is no longer appropriate to regard an order of committal as being no more than a form of execution available to another party against an alleged contemnor. The court itself has a very substantial interest in seeing that its orders are upheld. If committal orders are to be set aside on purely technical grounds which have nothing to do with the justice of the case, then this has the effect of undermining the system of justice and the credibility of the court orders.

Although the traditional approach may have stressed strict compliance, even here minor deviations from the legal framework would not always warrant discharge. In *Gore-Booth v. Gore-Booth*[46] the contemnor tried to argue that one of the affidavits was irregular for incorrectly stating the abode of the deponent. Lavery J held that even if there had been an irregularity it was of a technical character that could be overlooked. Irregularities may also be disregarded if they are over-remote, as in *The State (McKeever) v. Governor of Mountjoy Prison*,[47] where the defect, which was merely in the civil bill preceding the order for defiance of which the defendant had, in turn, been committed, was dismissed as over-technical. A defect may also be excused where it might have been, but was not, raised in the application to commit. In *Re Earle*[48] FitzGibbon J disposed of an argument that there had been an irregularity in the service of the notice of motion of attachment on the ground that the defendants had failed to

---

[43] The use of imprisonment has been reduced by the recognition of the requirement that committal should only be ordered where it is likely to be effective (*Danchevsky v. Danchevsky* [1974] 3 WLR 709; *Ross Co. Ltd v. Swan* [1981] ILRM 416), and by the recognition of new alternatives to imprisonment such as the fine or suspended committal order (*Heatons Transport v. Transport & General Workers Union* [1973] AC 15).
[44] [1997] 1 WLR 314.
[45] Ibid., at p. 326.
[46] (1962) 96 ILTR 32.
[47] Supreme Court, 19 Dec. 1966.
[48] [1938] IR 485.

raise the argument on the motion to commit. Blemishes in documentation, or in the character of the order, have been cured by remitting the order for correction.[49]

IMPRISONMENT FOR DEBT

Orders of imprisonment on grounds of the non-payment of debt are authorized under section 6 of the Debtors Act, 1872[50] and section 6 of the Enforcement of Court Orders Act, 1940. The power of imprisonment under the Enforcement of Court Orders Act, 1940 may only be exercised by the District Court; in the case of the Debtors Act, 1872, jurisdiction is given to the High Court, and also to the District or Circuit Court. In practice, of the two statutes, it is the power under the 1940 Act which is the more commonly exercised.

---

[49] *Keegan v. de Burca* [1973] IR 223.
[50] S. 6 of the Debtors (Ireland) Act, 1872 provides:

> Subject to the provisions hereinafter mentioned and to the prescribed rules, any court may commit to prison for a term not exceeding six weeks, or until payment of the sum due, any person who makes default in payment of any debt or instalment of any debt due from him in pursuance of any order or judgment of that or any other competent court, made or recovered after the passing of this Act in respect of a debt contracted after the passing of this Act.
>
> Provided–(1) That the jurisdiction by this section given of committing a person to prison shall, in the case of any court, other than the superior courts of law and equity, be exercised only subject to the following restrictions; that is to say,
>
> (a) Be exercised only by a judge, and by an order made in open court, and showing on its face the ground on which it is issued
> (b) Be exercised only as respects a judgment of a superior court of law or equity when such judgment does not exceed fifty pounds exclusive of costs
> (c) Be exercised only as respects a decree of a civil bill court by a chairman of quarter sessions or recorder.
>
> (2) That such jurisdiction shall only be exercised where it is proved to the satisfaction of the court that the person making default either has or has had since the date of the order or judgment the means to pay the sum in respect of which he has made default, and has refused or neglected, or refuses or neglects, to pay the same.
>
> Proof of the means of the person making default may be given in such manner as the court thinks just; and for the purposes of such proof the debtor and any witnesses may be summoned and examined on oath, according to the prescribed rules ...

The conditions to committal under the section 6 of the Debtors Act, 1872 and sections 6 & 8 of the Enforcement of Court Orders Act, 1940

In 1926 the jurisdiction to order imprisonment for non-payment of debt under the Debtors Act, 1872 was supplemented by a more extended power of imprisonment under the Enforcement of Court Orders Act, 1926. The procedure under the 1926 Act was then superseded by section 6 of the Enforcement of Court Orders Act of 1940; that latter provision provides:

> (a) where a debtor is liable, by virtue of an instalment order to pay a debt and costs either in one payment or by instalments and such debtor fails to make such payment or fails to pay any one or more of such instalments accruing due while such order is in force at the time or times appointed in that behalf by such order, the creditor may, at any time while such order is in force or within twelve months after it has ceased to be in force, apply to a Justice of the District Court for the arrest and imprisonment of such debtor;
>
> (b) on the hearing of an application under the preceding paragraph of this section, the Justice may, if he so thinks proper but subject to the next paragraph of this section, order the arrest and imprisonment of the debtor for any period not exceeding three months and thereupon the debtor shall be arrested and imprisoned accordingly;
>
> (c) the Justice shall not order the arrest and imprisonment of the debtor under the next preceding paragraph of this section if the debtor (if he appears) shows, to the satisfaction of such Justice, that his failure to pay was due neither to his wilful refusal nor to his culpable neglect.

Section 8(1) of the Enforcement of Court Orders Act, 1940 regulates the procedure for committal of a family maintenance payment defaulter:

> Where a sum or sums payable by virtue of an order[51] [made under the Family Law (Maintenance of Spouses and Children) Act, 1976] is or are not duly paid, a Justice of the District Court may, on the applica-

---

[51] The definition of 'order' was amended by s. 29 of the Family Law (Maintenance of Spouses and Children) Act, 1976, and by s. 3 (5) of the Courts (No. 2) Act, 1986 to include an order of costs made in conjunction with the primary order.

tion of the person to whom such sum or sums is or are payable under such order (in this section referred to an the applicant), by warrant cause the person by whom such sum or sums is or are payable under such order (in this section referred to as the defaulter) to be brought before him and thereupon such Justice, after hearing the applicant and the defaulter and such evidence (if any) as they may respectively adduce, may, if he so thinks proper, either direct such sums or sums together with the costs of such application to be levied by distress and sale of the goods of the defaulter or, unless the defaulter shows to the satisfaction of such Justice, that the failure to pay was due neither to his wilful refusal nor to his culpable neglect, sentence the defaulter to imprisonment for any term not exceeding three months.

The jurisdiction to make an order of committal under section 6 of the Enforcement of Court Orders Act, 1940 Act is predicated on the failure to comply with a section 17 instalment order: an order that the debtor pay 'the debt and costs of the proceedings in the District Court either in one payment, or by such instalments and as such times as the justice shall in all the circumstances consider reasonable.' The power to make an instalment order is, in turn, conditional on there having been default in observing a lawful judgment. However, the Supreme Court has held that release under Article 40.4.2 will not be granted in the case of highly technical challenges to the validity of that predicate judgment.[52]

The substantive findings precedent to arrest and imprisonment are: that the instalment order have been served upon the debtor;[53] that there have been a failure to pay the sum; and that (in the case of the 1872 Act) the defendant has either 'refused or neglected', or, (in the case of proceedings under the Enforcement of Court Orders Acts, 1926–1940) that the defendant has been guilty of either 'wilful refusal or culpable neglect' in failing to observe an instalment order.[54] The formula in the 1940 Act is stricter. Under the 1872 Act it is sufficient that the debtor have merely neglected or refused to comply; accordingly, a debtor may be committed under the

---

[52] *The State (McKeever) v. Governor of Mountjoy Prison*, Supreme Court, 19 Dec. 1966.
[53] O. 53, r. 8(5), District Court Rules, 1997.
[54] The provision in O. 53, r. 8(5), District Court Rules, 1997 providing for imprisonment merely on proof that 'the debtor has failed to comply with such order' appears *ultra vires*.

1872 Act even where the refusal has been induced by a mistake of fact, or a mistaken impression of law, or because the debtor has felt conscientiously compelled to prefer the competing claims of others for whom he is responsible. The requirement under the 1940 Act that the failure be contumacious excludes such non-culpable default. On the other hand, some authority suggests that there is no requirement under the 'wilful refusal or culpable neglect' standard required by the Enforcement of Court Orders Acts, 1926 and 1940 that the defendant actually have the means to pay. In *Brennan v. Gilligan*[55] it was held that a deliberate failure to generate the means to pay a debt could count as a deliberate refusal, and that the Acts would apply in a case where the debtor is 'dishonestly avoiding work for the purpose of frustrating the enforcement of the decree.'[56] This is, perhaps, questionable. Committal is predicated upon the defendant's failure to honour an instalment order. However, the scale of instalment order is determined according to the debtor's means, defined as the defendant's 'assets and liabilities, his income earned and unearned,' suggesting that it was the legislative intention that actual assets be the measure of a debtor's responsibilities. The Acts do not refer to the defendant's potential income, or potential assets and it does not appear to have been the legislative intention to create liability to imprisonment merely for failure to maximise a potential income.

The burden of proof varies according to which of the statutory regimes applies: under the 1872 Act the jurisdiction to commit is only capable of being exercised where 'it is proved to the satisfaction of the Court' that the person has been guilty of refusal or neglect. By contrast, under the Enforcement of Court Orders Acts, 1926 and 1940 the burden is expressly placed on the defendant. The power to commit under both sections 6 and 8 is presumed to be established unless 'the debtor shows to the satisfaction of such Justice that his failure to pay was due neither to his wilful refusal nor to his culpable neglect.'[57] There may be constitutional problems with this reversal of the onus proof clause. The process of committal under

---

[55] (1944) 78 ILTR 191.
[56] See also the judgment of the English High Court in *R. v. Poole Magistrates, ex p. Benham*, Queen's Bench Div., 8 Oct. 1991, holding that a failure to accept work could constitute 'culpable neglect' where there was 'clear evidence that gainful employment for which he was fit, was on offer to the debtor and that he had refused that offer.'
[57] S. 18(c).

sections 6 and 8 of the Enforcement of Court Orders Acts, 1926–1940 may be characterized as specialized forms of civil contempt. Since it is accepted that committal for civil contempt requires proof beyond reasonable doubt[58] it follows, in principle, that the party seeking committal for non-payment of debt carries the burden of proof and the degree of that proof must be beyond all reasonable doubt. The right not to be committed save on proof to an exacting standard, since it is a component of the individual's right to fair procedures, can be classified as a constitutional right, and there is at least a prima facie case that the encroachment upon that right by sections 6 and 8 is unconstitutional. An alternative source of challenge to the burden of proof arrangement is the European Convention on Human Rights. In *Benham v. United Kingdom*[59] the European Court of Human Rights classified committal proceedings for non-payment of debt premised on the debtor's wilful refusal or culpable neglect as criminal for the purpose of the application of Article 6 of the Convention. One effect of this classification is that the proceedings under sections 6(c) and 8(1) of the Enforcement of Court Orders Acts, 1926–1940 may attract the presumption of innocence prescribed by Article 6(2) of the European Convention. There is at least a prima facie incompatibility between the statutory imposition of the burden of proof upon the debtor and the European Convention requirement that the burden of proof be carried by the prosecuting party. Finally, there is a technical difficulty with the proof of neglect or refusal for the purpose of the Debtors Act, 1872. Section 6(2) of the Debtors Act, 1872 provides that for the purpose of proof of means both the debtor and any witnesses may be summoned and examined on oath 'according to the prescribed rules.' While rules for the examining and summoning of witnesses have been prescribed for the purpose of the High Court, none have been made for the Circuit Court, or for the District Court.

The power of arrest and committal may be lost in two circumstances. Firstly, arrest must be executed in close proximity to the making of the order. The High Court in *Berryman v. Governor of Wheatfield Prison*[60] referred to the 'considerable discretion' entrusted to the District Court either to commit or not to commit, or to vary the instalment order. Where

---

[58] *Graham v. National Irish Bank* [1994] 1 IR 215.
[59] (1996) 22 EHRR 293.
[60] [1993] 3 IR 573.

there is a long interval between the order and its execution there is a risk that the circumstances no longer correspond to those which originally justified the exercise of discretion in favour of committal. Second, the creditor, in accepting a part payment after the order of committal, and before the execution of that order, may be held to have waived execution.[61] In *Commercial Banking Co. v. William Foley*[62] negotiations took place, subsequent to the grant of a committal order, and a payment was made on account of the amount due under the committal order. The creditor's acceptance of part payment of the amount due was held to amount to a waiver of the right of execution and the debtor was discharged on habeas corpus. The High Court appears to have been particularly influenced by the provision in section 18(e)[63] which requires that a debtor be entitled to be released immediately upon payment by him, or on his behalf, of the amount of all instalments of the debt which are outstanding at the date of the order. The statutory right to discharge might, the Court suggested, be interfered with since no account could be taken of the earlier part payment. The waiver principle was applied more restrictively in *The State (Ring) v. Governor of Mountjoy Prison*.[64] The debtor in the *Ring* case had defaulted in several instalment orders, one of which was the subject of a committal order. Following the committal order, the debtor made a payment to the creditor which was accepted. The High Court refused, however, to direct the applicant's release: applying the principle under which a creditor, unless otherwise directed, is entitled to appropriate part payment to any particular part of a debt, the Court accepted the creditor's evidence that the payment had been appropriated to another instalment order. The position would, it was said, have been different if the debtor had taken the precaution of appropriating the payment to the instalment order which was the subject of the committal order, or to any other instalment order

---

[61] Contrast the approach in *Re Fereday* (1895) 2 Ch 437, holding that acceptance of part payment could not affect the validity of an order of imprisonment under the English Debtors Act, 1869 (virtually identical to the Irish Act of 1872).

[62] (1933) 67 ILTR 54.

[63] Para. 10 of s. 6(2) of the Debtors Act, 1872 provides a statutory right to discharge upon production of a certificate verifying satisfaction of the debt signed 'in the prescribed manner'. No such form has been prescribed. It would seem to be contrary to the legislative intention that the provision could survive without the entitlement to discharge; the right to discharge may, however, have been frustrated by the failure to put in place the prescribed machinery.

[64] (1971) 105 ILTR 113.

falling due at the time of the committal order. On the other hand, appropriation may be implicit as well as express.[65] It is surely a reasonable inference that where a debtor with an order of arrest and imprisonment hanging over him or her makes (like the debtor in *Ring* did) a part payment, that it is intended in respect of the instalment order which is the subject of the order of imprisonment?

---

[65] *Chitty on contracts*, ed. H.G. Beale (London, 1999) para. 22–059.

Table of cases

AA v. Medical Council [2003] 4 IR 302 ....131, 134
Adams v. DPP [2001] 2 ILRM 401 139
Aer Rianta v. Commissioner for Aviation Regulation, High Court, 16 Jan. 2003 46
AG (O'Gara) v. Callanan (1958) 92 ILTR 74 65
AG (SPUC) v. Open Door Counselling Ltd (No. 2) [1994] 2 IR 333.............................177
AG for Hong Kong v. Kwok a Sing (1873) LR 5 PC 179..166
AG v. Blennerhasset (1932) 67 ILTR 136...122
AG v. Borek, High Court, 11 Sept. 2003..66
AG v. Kirwan (1950) 89 ILTR 120...149
Aikin, In re (1881) 8 LR Ir 50 ....114, 199, 237
Allen, Re (1860) 30 LJ QB 38 73
Amand, Re [1941] 2 KB 239...118, 122
Amuur v. France (1996) 22 EHRR 533..114
An Taisce v. Dublin Corporation, High Court, 31 Jan. 1973...182
Anon. (1654) Style 432; 82 ER 838...221
Anon. (1673) 1 Mod 103; 86 ER 765...72
Anon. (1681) 1 Vent 357; 86 ER 230...140
Anon. (nd) Rowe's Reports 415..18n
Anon. (nd) Rowe's Reports 640..21
Arnold v. Windle, Supreme Court, 4 Mar. 1999..216
Article 26 and the Emergency Powers Bill, 1976 Reference, Re [1977] IR 159 196–7
Article 26 and the Illegal Immigrants (Trafficking) Bill, 1999, Re [2000]
  2 IR 360...88–90, 92, 109–10
Associated Picture Houses v. Wednesbury BC [1948] 1 KB 223 47–8
Aylward, Re (1860) 12 ICLR 448 ....199, 238
Baby A, Re [2000] 1 IR 430..116
Bacadanu, Re, Irish Times, 7 Mar. 2003..204
Bailey, Re (1854) 3 El & Bl 607; 118 ER 1269..42, 95
Baker, In re (1857) 2 H & N 219; 157 ER 92...42, 95
Barnardo v. Ford [1892] AC 326 ....138, 159–60, 188–9
Barrow's Case (1811) 14 East 346; 104 ER 635..136
Barry v. Waldron, High Court, 23 May 1996...155, 183–5
Barth v. Clise 12 Wall 400; 79 US 393 (1870)..150
Beckman & Dahlstrom, Re, Irish Times, 25 July 1977 184
Benham v. United Kingdom (1996) 22 EHRR 293...244
Berryman v. Governor of Wheatfield Prison [1993] 3 IR 573.....................................244–5
Blehein v. Murphy [2000] 2 IR 231..174, 177
Blues, Re (1855) 5 El & Bl 291; 119 ER 490...95
Bolger v. Garda Commissioner, Supreme Court, 2 Nov. 1998 ....145–6, 181
Bolger v. Garda Commissioner, High Court, 15 Dec. 1998 ....98, 105, 119–20, 181
Bowers v. Gloucester Corporation [1963] 1 QB 881..58
Brady, Re, Irish Times, 16 & 17 Feb. 1990..228

247

Breathnach v. Manager, Wheatfield Place of Detention, Supreme Court,
  20 Oct. 2000 ....134, 136
Breathnach v. Manager, Wheatfield Place of Detention, Supreme Court,
  22 Feb. 2001 ....133, 136, 211–12, 226
Brennan v. Gilligan (1944) 78 ILTR 191 243
Brennan v. Governor of Mountjoy Prison, Irish Times, 8 Mar. 1975 135
Brennan v. Governor of Portlaoise Prison [1999] 1 ILRM 190 223–4
Briscoe, Re, Queen's Bench Div. (EW), 22 July 1998 231
Brogan v United Kingdom (1988) 11 EHRR 117 ....192–3, 195
Brown, Re (1852) 18 LT OS 224 144
Bryan v. Irish Land Commission [1942] IR 185 171
Bushfield, Re (1886) 32 Ch D 123 139
Cahill v. Governor of Curragh Military Detention Barracks
  [1980] ILRM 191 ....97, 100–1, 127, 155
Carpenter, Ex p. (1824) Sm & Bat 81 ....74, 231
Carroll v. Governor of Mountjoy Prison, High Court, 12 Jan. 2005 ....64–5, 214
Carron v. McMahon [1990] 1 IR 239 175
Casey, Re (1873, Court of Queen's Bench, Ireland) 22
Casey v. Governor of Cork Prison, High Court, 13 Sept. 2000 219
Cassidy v. Minister for Industry and Commerce [1978] IR 297 194
Central Development Trust v. AG (1975) 109 ILTR 69 181
Chahal v. United Kingdom (1996) 23 EHRR 413 195
Chetta, Re, Queen's Bench Div. (EW), 30 Apr. 1997 201
Child, Ex p. (1854) 15 CB 238; 139 ER 413 125
Clarke v. Hogan [1995] 1 IR 310 65
Clarke v. McMahon [1990] 1 IR 228 ....53–4, 212
Clarke v. Member in Charge, Terenure Garda Station [2001] 4 IR 171 ......179, 184
Clarke, Ex p. (1890) 26 LR Ir 1 95
Clarke, Re Philip [1950] IR 235 67–8
Clifford & O'Sullivan, Re [1921] 2 AC 570 26
Commercial Banking Co. v. William Foley (1933) 67 ILTR 54 245
Condon v. Minister for Labour [1981] IR 62 179
Copeland's Application, Re [1990] NI 301 ....135, 185
Corcoran, Re (1950) 86 ILTR 6 116
Creedon v. Criminal Injuries Compensation Tribunal [1988] IR 51 40
Crilly v. Farrington [2001] 3 IR 251 179
Croke v Smith (No. 2) [1998] 1 IR 101 ....39, 53–4, 145, 182, 228
Cullen v. Chief Constable RUC [2004] 2 All ER 237 ....196, 221
Daganayasi v. Minister for Immigration [1980] 2 NZLR 130 44–5
Dalton v. Governor of Glengarrif Training Unit, Supreme Court, 29 Feb. 2000..........219
Danchevsky v. Danchevsky [1974] 3 WLR 709 239
Darnel's Case (1627) 3 St Tr 1 3
De Burca v. AG [1976] IR 38 102
De Wilde, Ooms, Versyp v. Belgium (1971) 1 EHRR 30 51
Dempsey v. Dempsey [1933] *Law Journal (Irish Free State)* 213 238
Dickson v. Capes (1860) 11 ICLR 345 139
Dodd's Case (1857) 2 De G & J 510; 44 ER 1087 181
Dolphin, Re Martin, High Court, 27 Jan. 1972 125–6
DPP (Ivers) v. Murphy [1999] 1 IR 98 187
DPP v. Corcoran [1995] 2 IR 259 59

TABLE OF CASES

DPP v. Early [1998] 3 IR 158 85
DPP v. Somers [1999] 1 IR 115 70
Duncan v. Governor of Portlaoise Prison [1997] 1 IR 558 76
Duncan v. Governor of Portlaoise Prison [1998] 1 IR 433 .... 145, 155, 157
Dunne v. Minister for the Environment, High Court, 8 Mar. 2005 182
E v. Norway (1990) 17 EHRR 30 .... 50, 154
Earle, Re [1938] IR 485 .... 160, 239–40
Egan v. Governor of Mountjoy Prison, Supreme Court, 6 July 1990 211
Egan v. Macready [1921] 1 IR 265 .... 22, 25–29, 35, 159, 161–2
Eggington, Re (1853) 2 E & B 717; 118 ER 936 .... 95, 143–4
Eleko v. Officer Administering the Government of Nigeria [1931] AC 662 41
Ellis v. O'Dea (No. 2) [1991] 1 IR 251 155
F v. Ireland, Supreme Court, 27 Feb. 1995 182
F (M) v. Superintendent Ballymun Garda Station [1991] 1 IR 189 .... 116, 157, 178
Farrell v. AG [1998] 1 IR 203 .... 39, 57
Fereday, Re (1895) 2 Ch 437 245
Fernandez, Ex p. (1861) 10 CB NS 3; 142 ER 349 .... 65, 207
Finucane v. McMahon [1990] 1 IR 165 .... 76, 155
Fisher v. Irish Land Commission [1948] IR 3 171–2
Flood, In re Simon, Saunders Newsletter, 20 May 1818 34
Francis, In re (1963) 97 ILTR 151 .... 61, 66, 206
Franic v. Wilson [1993] 1 NZLR 318 118
Fusco v. O'Dea (No. 2) [1998] 3 IR 470 175–6
G(D) & G(M) v. An Bord Uachtála, High Court, 23 May 1996 116
G (J) v. Governor of Mountjoy Prison [1991] 1 IR 37 155
G (OE) v. Minister for Justice, Equality and Law Reform, High Court, 27 May 2004 49
Gabrel v. Governor of Mountjoy Prison, Supreme Court, 8 Feb. 2001 234
Gallagher, Re, Irish Times, 26 July 1983 .... 101–2, 102, 132–3
Gallagher v. Director, Central Mental Hospital/ Re Maguire [1996]
  3 IR 1 .... 75–6, 88, 138, 158
Gallagher v. Director, Central Mental Hospital [1996] 3 IR 10 .... 155, 157
Gallile, Ex p. (1798) 7 TR 673; 101 ER 1192 136
Georgopoulus v. Beaumont Hospital Board [1998] 3 IR 132 81
Gillen's Application, Re [1988] NI 40 .... 83, 151, 196
Gooden v. Waterford Regional Hospital, Supreme Court, 21 Feb. 2001 60
Gore-Booth v. Gore-Booth (1962) 96 ILTR 32 239
Graham v. National Irish Bank [1994] 1 IR 215 244
Greene v. Governor of Mountjoy Prison [1995] 3 IR 541 62
Gregg, Re /R. (Gregg) v. Kelly (1841) 3 I LR 316 .... 114, 146
Griesley's Case (1588) 8 Co Rep 38; 77 ER 530 234
Guerin, Re (1888) 60 LT 538 42
Gutrani v. Minister for Justice [1993] 2 IR 427 39
Hanafin v. Minister for the Environment [1996] 2 IR 321 182
Hand v. Governor of Mountjoy Prison, Irish Times Law Reports, 29 May 1989 ... 186–7, 191
Hardy v. Ireland, High Court, 25 June 1993 211
Hardy v. Ireland [1994] 2 IR 550 133
Harte v. The Labour Court [1996] 2 IR 171 57
Hawkins v. Fackman (1795) Ridgeway 537 160
Hay v. O'Grady [1992] 1 IR 210 175–6
Heaphy, Re (1888) 22 LR Ir 500 99

Heatons Transport v. Transport & General Workers Union [1973] AC 15 239
Hegarty v. DPP, High Court, 29 Nov. 1996..146–7
Hegarty v. Governor of Limerick Prison [1998] 1 IR 412 ....76, 155
Henderson v. Henderson (1843) 3 Hare 100; 67 ER 313 131
Hensley v. Municipal Court San Jose Milpitas Judicial District 411 US 345 (1973) 118
Herbert's Case (1811) 16 East 165; 104 ER 1051..136
Hobhouse's Case (1820) 3 B & Ald 420; 106 ER 716 134
Holland v. Governor of Portlaoise Prison, Supreme Court, 8 Mar. 2001 211
Hopkins, Ex p. (1732) 3 PWMS 152; 24 ER 1009...115
Hottentot Venus (1810) 13 East 195; 104 ER 344...126
Houston and Byrne v. Lake, Dublin Evening Post, 25 Nov. 1797 21
Howel's Case (1587) 1 Leon 70; 74 ER 66...3
Hynes, Re Gerard/The State (Hynes) v. Officer in Charge, Crumlin Garda Station, High Court, 7 Feb. 1984..197
Irish Times Ltd v. Ireland [1998] 1 IR 359 153
J, In re (1954) 88 ILTR 120 67
Jablonski v. Poland (2003) 36 EHRR 27 154
Jahromi v. Secretary of State for the Home Department [1996] Imm AR 20 66
Jennings v. Government of the United States of America [1983] 1 AC 624...................120
Johnson, Case of the Honourable Mr Justice (1805) 29 St Tr 81......................................34
Jones v. Cunningham 371 US 228 (1963) 118
Junior v. Clifford, High Court, 17 Dec. 1993 133–4
Kajli & Nisli v. Minister for Justice, High Court, 21 Aug. 1992..64
Kavanagh v. Governor of Mountjoy Prison, High Court, 29 June 2001 211
Keating v. Governor of Mountjoy Prison [1991] 1 IR 61 ....176, 186–7
Keegan v. de Burca [1973] IR 223 ....160, 240
Keenan, Re [1972] 1 QB 533 140
Kelleher v. Governor of Portlaoise Prison, Supreme Court, 30 Oct. 1997 ....208–9, 212
Keller, In re (1888) 22 LR Ir 158...65–66, 94–5, 114, 134–5, 200
Kelly & Clare, Re, Irish Times, 3 Aug. 2002..187
Kelly v. Deighan [1984] ILRM 424 160
Kelly v. O' Sullivan, High Court, 11 July 1990..64–5
Killeen v. DPP [1997] 3 IR 218...57
Kindersley, In re [1944] IR 111 116–17
Kolompar v. Belgium (1993) 16 EHRR 197..154
L v. United Kingdom (2005) 40 EHRR 761...49
Laiham, Re, Irish Times, 9 Feb. 2003..234
Launder v. Governor of Brixton Prison [1998] 3 WLR 221 120
Lavery v. Member in Charge, Carrickmacross Garda Station [1999] 2 IR 390................178
Leahy, Re, Irish Times, 12 Jan. 2005...204
Lees, Ex p. (1860) EL Bl & El 828; 120 ER 718 207
Levy v. Moylan (1850) 10 CB 189; 138 ER 78 65
Liversidge v. Anderson [1942] AC 206..43
Lloyd, Re (1845) 9 JP 115..143
Lucey, Application of [1972] IR 347n..211
MacCurtain, Re [1941] IR 83..72
Maguire, Re/Gallagher v. Director of Central Mental Hospital [1996] 3 IR 1 ....75–6, 88, 138, 158
Mahmod, In re [1995] Imm AR 311 66
Mallows v. Governor of Mountjoy Prison [2002] 2 IR 385..201

TABLE OF CASES

Maloney v. Member in Charge, Terenure Garda Station, Supreme Court,
  18 May 2004 179
Mangan v. DPP, High Court, 30 July 2004 151
Mathews, Re (1860) 12 ICLR 233 .... 138, 159
McAleece, Re (1873) IR 7 CL 146 65
McAleenan's Application, Re [1985] NI 496 203
McConnell v. Governor of Castlerea Prison, Supreme Court, 26 Oct. 2001 .... 75, 214
McCowan v. Governor of Mountjoy Prison, 8 Nov. 2001 .... 209, 219
McDonagh, Re Thomas, High Court, 24 Nov. 1969 .... 101, 102, 132–3
McDonagh v. Governor of Cloverhill Prison, Supreme Court, 28 Jan. 2005 204–5
McDonagh v. Governor of Mountjoy Prison, Irish Times, 29 May 1973 41
McEvoy v. Meath CC, High Court, 23 Jan. 2003 182
McGlinchey v. Ireland, Irish Times, 28 July 1987 134
McGlinchey v. Ireland and the Governor of Portlaoise Prison
  [1988] IR 671 .... 125, 155, 157, 174–6
McGlinchey v. Ireland [1990] 2 IR 215 .... 157, 212–13
McGowan v. Governor of Mountjoy Prison, Supreme Court, 8 Nov. 2001 209
McIlraith v. Grady [1968] 1 QB 468 65
McIlwraith v. Fawsitt [1990] 1 IR 343 157
McIntyre, Re, Irish Times, 27 Jan. 2000 205–6
McLaughlin v. Scott/ Re McLaughlin [1921] 2 IR 51 .... 183, 193–4
McLoughlin, Application of [1970] IR 197 70
McMahon v. Leahy [1984] IR 525 .... 66, 73, 122, 177
McSorley v. Governor of Mountjoy Prison [1997] 2 IR 258 .... 75, 86–8, 145, 215, 217–19
Mohan v. Secretary of State for the Home Department, Court of Appeal,
  20 Dec. 1988 148
Mohsen v. Minister for Justice, High Court, 12 Mar. 2002 48
Morgan v. Garda Commissioner, Irish Times, 3 June 1984 121
Mullins v. Harnett [1998] 4 IR 426 58
Musial v. Poland (2001) 31 EHRR 29 154
Mwenya, Ex p. [1959] 3 WLR 767; [1960] 1 QB 241 .... 113, 140–1
Nevin v. Crowley [2001] 1 IR 113 217
Newton, Re (1855) 16 CB 97; 139 ER 692 207
Nicholls v. Nicholls [1997] 1 WLR 314 239
Nicholls v. Governor of Mountjoy Prison, Irish Times, 24 July 1998 98
O v. Minister for Justice [2003] 1 IR 1 .... 48–9, 53
O'Brien v. Governor of Limerick Prison [1997] 2 ILRM 349 214–5
O'C v. Governor of Curragh Prison [2000] 2 ILRM 76 209
O'Connor v. Carroll [1999] 2 IR 160 157
O'Connor v. Governor of Curragh Prison, Supreme Court, 3 Dec. 1999 .... 174, 177
O'Connor v. Nenagh UDC, Supreme Court, 16 May 2002 182
O'Duffy, Re [1934] IR 550 .... 59, 125, 183, 194
O'Dwyer v. Boyd [2003] 1 ILRM 112 152
O'Keeffe v. An Bord Pleanála [1993] I IR 39 40
Ó'Laighléis, Re [1960] IR 93 .... 77, 145
O'Neale, Murray and Graham, The Times, 10 Jan. 1799 18
O'Neill, In re [1932] IR 548 .... 66, 238
O'Reilly, In re James (1895) 29 ILTR 33 .... 124, 232
O'Reilly v. Moroney, Supreme Court, 16 Nov. 1993 228
O'Rourke v. Governor of Cloverhill Prison, High Court, 26 Feb. 2004 199

O'Shea v. Garda Commissioner, Irish Times, 15 July 1980, (1981) 2 Frewen 57..............112
O'Shea v. Governor of Mountjoy Prison, High Court, 28 June 1991 136
O'Sheil v. Minister for Education, High Court, 10 May 1999 182
Ojo v. Governor of Mountjoy Prison, High Court, 8 May 2003
Orton v. St John of God Hospital, High Court, 15 Nov. 2004
Page v. Williams (1851) 1 ICLR 527 34
Payne v. Governor of Portlaoise Prison, Supreme Court, 7 Apr. 2003....................131, 176
Peerless, Re (1841) 1 QB 143; 113 ER 1084 61–2
People (AG) v. Gilliland [1985] IR 643 147–8
People (AG) v. O'Brien [1965] IR 142..65–6
People (AG) v. O'Callaghan [1966] IR 501..204
People (AG) v. Sigal (1946) 12 Ir Jur 21..148
People (DPP) v. McGinley [1998] 2 IR 408..86
People (DPP) v. Pringle (1981) 2 Frewen 57..125–6
People (DPP) v. Shaw [1982] IR 1..103–4
People (DPP) v. Sweetman [1997] 3 IR 448..149
People (DPP) v. Walsh [1986] IR 722; [1988] ILRM 137..194–5
People v. Ferris, Judgments of the Court of Criminal Appeal, 1984–1989, 114 58
People v. Kelly (No. 2) [1983] IR 1..65–6
People v. O'Shea [1982] IR 384..177–8
Pereira v. Portugal (2003) 36 EHRR 49 154
Philpot, Re [1960] 1 All ER 165..70
Prisoners A–XX v. State of New South Wales (1995) 38 NSWLR 622 221
Proctor, Re [1903] 2 IR 117..181
Quigley, Re [1983] NI 245..76, 153
Quinlivan v. Governor of Portlaoise Prison (No. 1) [1998] 1 IR 456................................157
R. (Alconbury Ltd) v. Environment Secretary [2001] 2 WLR 1389..................................45
R. (Boylan) v. Londondery JJ [1912] 2 IR 347..62, 64, 65
R. (Caherty) v. Belfast JJ [1978] NI 94..122
R. (Childers) v. Adjutant General of the Provisional Forces [1923] 1 IR 5................125, 138
R. (D'Arcy) v. Carlow JJ [1916] 2 IR 313..42
R. (de Vesci) v. Queen's County JJ. [1908] 2 IR 285..42–3
R. (Gallagher) v. Martin (1874) IR 8 CL 556..95
R. (Garde) v. Strickland [1921] 2 IR 317..25–6
R. (H) v. N & E London Mental Health Tribunal [2002] QB 1 80
R. (Martin) v. Mahony [1910] 2 IR 695 ....24, 39–40, 55, 219–20
R. (McCann) v. Belfast JJ [1978] NI 153..67
R. (Mulholland) v. Monaghan JJ [1914] 2 IR 156..65
R. (O'Neill) v. Tyrone JJ [1917] 2 IR 96..70
R. (O'Brien) v. Military Governor of North Dublin Union Internment Camp
  [1924] 1 IR 32..83–5, 124
R. (O'Reilly) v. AG [1928] IR 83..124
R. (O'Sullivan) v. Military Governor of Hare Park Internment Park (1924)
  58 ILTR 62 ....121, 124, 187–8
R. (Ronayne) v. Strickland [1921] 2 IR 333..25–6
R. (Ryan) v. Starkie (1920) 54 ILTR 15 ....24, 39–40
R. (Wilson) v. Guardians of the Poor of Mallow Union (1860) 12 ICLR 35..................57–8
R. v. Allen [1921] 2 IR 241..25–6
R. v. Barnardo (1889) 23 QBD 305..188
R. v. Birmingham City Court, ex p. Birmingham City Council [1988] 1 WLR 337..........179

TABLE OF CASES 253

R. v. Board of Control, ex p. Rutty [1956] 2 QB 109 .... 42, 118–19, 203
R. v. Bolton (1841) 1 QB 65; 113 ER 1054 23
R. v. Bournewood Mental Health N.H.S. Trust, ex p. L [1999] 1 AC 458 112
R. v. Butler (1860) LT NS 730 145
R. v. Canons Park Mental Health Review Tribunal, ex p. A [1995] QB 60 60
R. v. Canterbury Prison, ex p. Craig [1991] 2 QB 195 68–9
R. v. Carrick (nd) Rowe's Reports 67 19
R. v. Clerk (1697) 1 Salk 349; 91 ER 305 145
R. v. Cody (1852) 5 Ir Jur 175 125
R. v. Cowle (1759) 2 Burr 834; 97 ER 587 139–40
R. v. Crewe, ex p. Sekgome [1910] 2 KB 576 139
R. v. Criminal Injuries Board, ex p. A [1999] 2 AC 330 45–6
R. v. Dartmoor Board of Visitors, ex p. Smith [1987] 1 QB 106 179
R. v. Delaval (1763) 1 Black. 411; 96 ER 234 115
R. v. Deputy Governor of Parkhurst Prison, ex p. Hague [1992] 1 AC 58 .... 196, 221
R. v. Despard (1798) 9 TR 736; 101 ER 1226 21
R. v. Dillon (1888) Judgments of the Superior Courts in Ireland 181 66
R. v. Eden (1813) 2 M & S 226; 105 ER 366 115
R. v. Eggington (1853) 2 El & Bl 717; 118 ER 936 144
R. v. Feeny (1843) 5 ILR 437 .... 66, 88
R. v. Gavin (1850) 15 Jur 329 .... 121, 187, 189,
R. v. Governor of Ashford Prison, ex p. Postlethwaite [1988] AC 924 60
R. v. Governor of Brixton Prison, ex p. Ahsan [1969] 2 QB 222 .... 43, 79–81
R. v. Governor of Brixton Prison, ex p. Enahoro [1963] 2 QB 455 201
R. v. Governor of Brixton Prison, ex p. Osman (No. 3) [1992] 1 WLR 36 .... 100, 102
R. v. Governor of Brixton Prison, ex p. Percival [1907] 1 QB 696 74
R. v. Governor of Brixton Prison, ex p. Pitt-Rivers [1942] 1 All ER 207 66
R. v. Governor of Brixton Prison, ex p. Schtraks [1964] AC 556 42
R. v. Governor of Brixton Prison, ex p. Servini [1914] 1 KB 77 71
R. v. Governor of Brixton Prison, ex p. Shuter [1960] 2 QB 89 74
R. v. Governor of Brixton Prison, ex p. Stallman [1912] 3 KB 424 165
R. v. Governor of Pentonville, ex p. Azam [1973] 2 WLR 949 99
R. v. Governor of Pentonville Prison, ex p. Tarling [1979] 1 WLR 1417 ...... 100, 102, 134
R. v. Gustavson (2005) 193 CCC (3d) 545 137
R. v. Hallstrom, ex p. W [1986] QB 1090 61
R. v. Heath (1744) 18 St Tr 1 .... 124, 159
R. v Hereford Magistrates Court, ex p. Rowlands [1998] QB 110 216
R. v. Hughes [1879] 4 QBD 614 187
R. v. Hull University Visitor, ex p. Page [1993] AC 682 57
R. v. Johnson (1724) 1 Str 579; 93 ER 711 115
R. v. Kray, The Times, 17 Feb. 1965 204
R. v. Leicester Crown Court, ex p. DPP [1987] I WLR 1371 179
R. v. Merrick (nd) Rowe's Reports 550 164
R. v. Metropolitan Police Commissioner, ex p. Melia [1957] 1 WLR 1065 158
R. v. Metropolitan Police Commissioner, ex p. Nahar, The Times, 28 May 1983 ... 196
R. v. Morn Hill Camp Commanding Officer, ex p. Ferguson [1917] 1 KB 176 203
R. v. Mountnorris (1795) Ir Term Rep 460 .... 66, 151
R. v. Murphy [1921] 2 IR 190 24
R. v. Northumberland JJ, The Times, 13 Mar. 1888 24
R. v. O'Brennan (1854) 3 ICLR 589 95

R. v. O'Flagherty (1841) 1 Leg Rep 72 .... 151, 173
R. v. Oldham JJ, ex p. Cawley [1997] QB 1 .... 61–2, 93
R. v. Olson (1987) 38 CCC (3d) 534 157
R. v. Pinckney [1904] 2 KB 84 142
R. v. Poole Magistrates, ex p. Benham, Queen's Bench Div (EW), 8 Oct. 1991 243
R. v. Reader (1723) 1 Str 532; 93 ER 681 150
R. v. Reynolds (1795) 6 TR 497; 101 ER 667 143
R. v. Riall (1860) 11 ICLR 279 .... 92, 99, 108, 124, 231
R. v. Richmond JJ, ex p. Moles, Queen's Bench Div. (EW), 22 Oct. 1980 204–5
R. v. Secretary of State for Home Affairs, ex p. O'Brien [1923] 2 KB 361;
  [1923] 2 AC 603 .... 118, 138, 142
R. v. Secretary of State for Home Affairs, ex p. Greene [1942] 1 KB 87 79
R. v. Secretary of State for the Home Department, ex p. Begum [1990] COD 107 136
R. v. Secretary for State for the Home Department, ex p. Bugdaycay [1987]
  AC 514 .... 43, 46, 47–8
R. v. Secretary of State for the Home Department, ex p. Jeyeanthan [2000]
  1 WLR 354 70
R. v. Secretary for State for the Home Department, ex p. Khawaja [1984]
  AC 74 .... 42, 44, 46, 79, 80–1
R. v. Secretary for State for the Home Department, ex p. Muboyayi [1992]
  1 QB 244 .... 92–4, 96, 98
R. v. Secretary of State for the Home Department, ex p. Phansopkar [1975]
  3 All ER 497 114
R. v. Secretary of State for the Home Department, ex p. Rahman, Queen's
  Bench Division (EW), 16 Aug. 1993 148
R. v. Secretary for State for the Home Department, ex p. Rahman [1996]
  4 All ER 945 85–6
R. v. Secretary for State for the Home Department, ex p. Turgut [2001]
  1 All ER 719 47
R. v. Secretary for State for the Home Department, ex p. Zamir [1980] AC 930 43
R. v. Spilsbury [1898] 2 QB 615 120
R. v. Ward (1762) 1 Black 386; 96 ER 218 115
R. v. Watton (1979) 68 Cr App Rep 293 149
Radio One Limerick Limited v. IRTC [1997] 2 IR 291 57
Raine, Re Nicola, The Times, 5 May 1982 188
Ramsey, Re (1867) 1 *ILT& SJ* 622 95
Rasul et al. v. Bush 124 S Ct 2686 (2004) 141
Rea (No. 2), In re (1879) 4 LR Ir 345 95
Reynolds v. AG, High Court, 14 Feb. 1973 181
Rice v. Mangan, High Court, 30 July 2004 204
Rice, In re (1873) IR 7 CL 74 70
Ring v. Minister for the Environment, High Court, 27 Feb. 2004 182
Rock v. Governor of St Patrick's Institution, Supreme Court, 22 Mar. 1993 215–16
Roe v. Wade 410 US 113 (1973) 179
Roe, Re (1828) 1 Law Recorder 310 .... 199, 237
Ross Co. Ltd v. Swan [1981] ILRM 416 239
Rowe, Re, Irish Times, 12 Oct. 1983 137
Rumble and Bonello, Re (1868) 3 IRCL 271 .... 158, 168
Russell v. Fanning [1988] IR 505 .... 56–7, 83–4, 176
Ryan v. Compensation Tribunal [1997] 1 ILRM 194 57

TABLE OF CASES

Ryanair v. Flynn [2000] 3 IR 240..........46
Sanchez-Reisse v. Switzerland (1986) 9 EHRR 71..........154
Scott, Re (1841) 2 Leg Rep 77..........107
Searche's Case (1587) 1 Leon 70; 74 ER 65..........3
Secretary of State for Education v. Tameside MBC [1977] AC 1014..........45
Shaughnessy v. US, 345 US 206 (1953)..........114
Sheehan v. Reilly [1993] 2 IR 81..........98, 135–6, 176, 217–18
Sherman & Apps, Re (1980) 72 Cr App R 266..........122
Shuttleworth, Re (1846) 9 QB 651; 115 ER 1423..........100, 231–2
Singer, In re (1960) 97 ILTR 130..........108, 137, 145, 181, 205
Singer (No. 2), In re (1960) 98 ILTR 112..........163–6
Sinnot v. Minister for Education [2001] 2 IR 545..........179
Smith & Grady v. United Kingdom (2000) 29 EHRR 493..........195
Smith v. Molloy (1905) 39 ILTR 221..........160
Smithers v. Governor of Mountjoy Prison [1998] 2 IR 392..........70–1
Stack v. Boyle 342 US 1 (1952)..........205
State (AG) v. Durcan [1964] IR 279..........44
State (AG) v. Killian (1951) 1 Frewen 115..........211
State (Aherne) v. Cotter [1982] IR 188..........52, 75, 92, 98, 105, 108–9, 151, 202, 220–1
State (Bond) v. Governor of Mountjoy Prison (1964) 102 ILTR 93..........70, 72, 102
State (Bowes) v. Fitzpatrick [1978] ILRM 195..........191, 195–6
State (Breathnach) v. Hennessy & others, Irish Times, 8 Apr. 1976..........122, 151, 184, 189–90
State (Brien) v. Kelly [1970] IR 69..........65–6
State (Browne) v. Feran [1967] IR 147..........63, 170, 173, 177, 220–1
State (Burke) v. Lennon [1940] IR 136..........31–2, 63, 95, 124–5, 155, 169–70, 177
State (Byrne) v. Frawley [1978] IR 326..........102, 211
State (C) v. Frawley [1976] IR 365..........222–4
State (C) v. Minister for Justice [1967] IR 106..........76, 180
State (Caddle) v. McCarthy [1957] IR 361..........63–4, 122
State (Cahill) v. Commissioner of An Garda Síochána, Irish Times, 15 Apr. 1975..........181, 183
State (Cannon) v. Kavanagh [1937] IR 428..........135, 208, 212
State (Carney) v. Governor of Portlaoise Prison [1957] IR 25..........182
State (Comerford) v. Governor of Mountjoy Prison [1981] ILRM 86..........97
State (Conneely) v. Governor of Limerick Prison, Irish Times, 3 Feb. 1937..........65
State (Costello) v. Governor of Mountjoy Prison, Irish Times, 8 Aug. 1987..........62
State (Coveney) v. Special Criminal Court [1982] ILRM 284..........68
State (Cremin) v. Cork Circuit Court Judge, Supreme Court, 8 Feb. 1965..........152
State (D) v. Groarke [1990] 1 IR 305..........69, 74, 155, 157
State (de Paor) v. O'Connor, Irish Times, 5 Nov. 1977..........121, 188
State (Dickenson) v. Kelly [1964] IR 73..........224
State (Dillon) v. Kelly [1970] IR 174..........168, 224–5
State (Dowling) v. Kingston [1937] IR 483..........73–4, 76–7, 139, 148
State (Dowling) v. Kingston (No. 2) [1937] IR 699..........35–7, 76, 128, 164, 166
State (Doyle) v. Carr [1970] IR 87..........67
State (DPP) v. Walsh [1981] IR 412..........160–1
State (Dunne) v. Martin [1982] IR 229..........148–9
State (Edge) v. Governor of Mountjoy Prison (1942) 76 ILT & SJ 199..........208
State (Fagan) v. Governor of Mountjoy Prison, Irish Times, 14 Sept. 1977..........151
State (Furlong) v. Kelly [1971] IR 132..........55–6, 71–2
State (Gallagher) v. Governor of Portlaoise Prison, Irish Times, 7 Mar. 1978..........222

State (Gildea) v. Hipwell [1942] IR 485 237
State (Gilheany) v. Officer in Charge of the Bridewell, Irish Times,
    12 Jan. 1984 .... 167, 184, 191
State (Gilliland) v. Governor of Mountjoy Prison [1987] IR 201 .... 171–2, 174
State (Greene) v. Governor of Portlaoise Prison, High Court, 20 May,
    28 Nov. 1977 .... 124, 181
State (Griffin) v. Bell [1962] IR 355 .... 77–8, 150
State (Hanley) v. Governor of Mountjoy Prison (1973) 108 ILTR 102 .... 32, 40, 122
State (Harrington) v. Garda Commissioner, High Court,
    14 Dec. 1976 .... 76, 82–3, 125, 135, 138, 151, 183–5
State (Healy) v. Donohue, Irish Times, 8 Mar. 1975 149
State (Healy) v. Kenny, Irish Times, 11 Jan. 1975 .... 122, 138, 183–4, 190–1
State (Hoey) v. Garvey [1978] IR 1 .... 138, 157, 184
State (Holden) v. Governor of Portlaoise Prison [1964] IR 73 224
State (Holmes) v. Furlong [1967] IR 210 .... 64, 177
State (Hully) v. Hynes (1961) 100 ILTR 145 .... 96, 122, 139, 150, 158
State (Hynes) v. Officer in Charge Crumlin Garda Station/Hynes,
    Re, High Court, 7 Feb. 1984 197
State (Keane) v. Governor of Curragh Military Detention Barracks,
    Irish Times, 14 Mar. 1978 222
State (Kenny) v. Ó hUadhaigh [1979] IR 1 67
State (Kinsella) v. Governor of Portlaoise Prison, (387 SS 1984), High Court,
    23 July 1984 124
State (Kugan) v. O'Rourke [1985] IR 658 127
State (Langan) v. Donohue [1974] IR 251 .... 149, 177, 211
State (Leonard) v. Officer in Charge, Clontarf Garda Station, Irish Times,
    3 Apr. 1985 197–8
State (Magee) v. O'Rourke [1971] IR 205 .... 76, 85, 150
State (McCann) v. O'Herlihy, Irish Times, 30 Oct. 1976 197
State (McCarthy) v. Lennon [1936] IR 485 181
State (McDonagh) v. Frawley [1978] IR 131 .... 208, 212, 223, 225
State (McFadden) v. Governor of Mountjoy Prison [1981] ILRM 113 127
State (McFadden) v. Governor of Mountjoy Prison (No. 2) [1981] ILRM 120 .... 164, 166
State (McGinley) v. Durcan, High Court, 5 May 1975 70
State (McKeever) v. Governor of Mountjoy Prison, Supreme Court,
    19 Dec. 1966 .... 239, 242
State (McKenna) v. Durcan (1952) 87 ILTR 62 149
State (McNally) v. O'Donovan [1974] IR 272 .... 211, 225–6
State (O) v. O'Brien [1973] IR 50 .... 75, 177
State (O'Connor) v. Ó Caomhanaigh [1963] IR 112 210
State (O'Dare) v. Sheehy [1984] ILRM 99 70
State (O'Duffy) v. Bennett [1935] IR 70 59
State (O'Flaherty) v. Ó Floinn [1954] IR 295 234
State (O'Shea) v. Chief Superintendent, Galway & Garda
    Commissioner, Irish Times 15 July 1980 .... 121, 181, 184
State (Quinlan) v. Kavanagh [1935] IR 249 60–1
State (Quinn) v. Ryan [1965] IR 70 .... 126, 138, 142, 159–60, 177
State (Richardson) v. Governor of Mountjoy Prison [1980] ILRM 82 .... 131, 224
State (Ring) v. Governor of Mountjoy Prison (1971) 105 ILTR 113 .... 157, 245–6
State (Rogers) v. Galvin, Irish Times, 20 Oct. 1980 112

TABLE OF CASES

State (Rogers) v. Galvin [1983] IR 249 .... 101, 112, 143–5, 156–7, 191
State (Rossi) v. Bell [1957] IR 281 182
State (Royle) v. Kelly [1974] IR 259 .... 177, 209, 213
State (Rutherford) v. Governor of Arbour Hill Prison, Irish Times, 1 Feb. 1980 222
State (Shannon) v. Clifford, Irish Times, 25 Oct. 1983 66
State (Sheerin) v. Kennedy [1966] IR 379 .... 149, 150, 170–1, 173, 180
State (Summers Jennings) v. Furlong [1966] IR 183 180
State (Trimbole/Hanbury) v. Gordon, Irish Independent, 27 Oct. 1984 195
State (Trimbole) v. Governor of Mountjoy Prison
  [1985] IR 550 .... 76, 78, 84, 101, 134, 143–5, 162, 167, 184, 187, 195
State (Walsh) v. Commissioner of the Garda Síochána (32 SS 1975),
  Irish Times, 29 Jan. 1975 .... 138, 184, 186–7, 191
State (Ward) v. Governor of Mountjoy Prison/Re Ward, Irish Times,
  22 Feb. 1975 .... 136, 226
State (Ward & others) v. Hanley, Irish Times, 24 Jan. 1975 .... 196, 221–2
State (Whelan) v. Governor of Mountjoy Prison [1983] ILRM 52 .... 147, 149, 151, 153–4
State (Williams) v. Kelleher [1983] IR 112 67
State (Williams) v. Kelly [1970] IR 259 .... 174–5, 259
State (Williams) v. Kelly (No. 2) [1970] IR 271 .... 135, 168–9, 211
State (Wilson) v. Windle, Irish Times, 19 Aug. 1987 97
State (Woods) v. Governor of Portlaoise Prison (1974) 108 ILTR 54 130
State (Woods) v. Kelly [1969] IR 269 .... 101, 124, 143, 176, 191
Sullivan, Re (1888) 22 LR Ir 98 .... 22–4, 35, 95–6, 206
T (R) v. Director of Central Mental Hospital [1995] 2 IR 65 .... 101, 143, 155, 172–3, 191
Thomas, Ex p. [1956] Criminal Law Review 119 204
Thompson, In re (1888) 5 TLR 540 .... 159, 189
Throgmorton's Case (1610) 12 Co Rep 69; 77 ER 1347 234
Tone's Case (1798) 27 St Tr 613 .... 18–19, 124
Toohey v. Governor of Central Mental Hospital (1967 No. 158 SS),
  High Court, 24 Oct. 1967 136
Toth v. Austria (1991) 14 EHRR 551 51
Trarore v. Refugee Appeals Tribunal, High Court, 14 May 2004 44
Trousdell v. Kearse (1873) IR 8 CL 25 234
Tynan, In re [1969] IR 273 .... 66, 137, 211
Van der Leer v Netherlands (1990) 12 EHRR 567 154
Victorian Council for Civil Liberties v. Minister for Immigration [2002]
  1 LRC 189 .... 111, 113, 125
Vilvarajah v. Secretary of State for the Home Department [1990] Imm AR 457 148
W(J) v. W(M) [1978] ILRM 119 141
Wales v. Whitney 114 US 564 (1885) 111, 113
Walsh v. Governor of Limerick Prison [1995] 2 ILRM 158 223
Walsh v. R. (1888) 22 LR Ir 314 67
Re Ward/ State (Ward) v. Governor of Mountjoy Prison; Irish Times, 22 Feb. 1975 226
Warman's Case (1778) 2 Black. 1204; 96 ER 709 115
Watson's (Leonard) Case (1839) 9 A & E 731; 112 ER 1389 72
Weynell v. Camocke (1707, Court of Queen's Bench, Ireland) 9
Wills v. Bowley [1982] 2 All ER 654 58
Wilson's (Carus) Case (1845) 7 QB 984; 115 ER 759 .... 143, 206–7
Wilson, Re Charles (No. 1), Supreme Court, 11 July 1968 134
Winterwerp v. Netherlands (1979) 2 EHRR 387 51

Wood's Case (1770) 2 Wm Bl 745; 96 ER 436 1
Woods, Application of [1970] IR 154 .... 101, 124, 125, 131–2, 179
Wynne v. Boughey (1666) O Bridge 570; 124 ER 750 1
X v. United Kingdom (1982) 4 EHRR 188 .... 49–50, 195
Z v. DPP [1994] 2 IR 476 153
Z v. Minister for Justice [2002] 2 ILRM 215 48
Zwann, Re [1981] IR 395 .... 105, 156, 178–9, 218

Table of statutes

ACTS OF THE PARLIAMENT OF IRELAND

1495	Poynings' Law (10 Hen. 7)	6
1782	Habeas Corpus Act (21 & 22 Geo. II, c. 11) 8, 16, 19, 20, 22, 30, 105–8, 134, 156, 164–7	
1796	Insurrection Act (36 Geo III, c. 20)	18
1797	Habeas Corpus Suspension Act (37 Geo III, c. 1)	17–8, 20–1
1798	Habeas Corpus Suspension Continuation Act (38 Geo. III, c. 14)	20
1799	Rebellion Act (39 Geo. III, c. 11)	19
1800	Habeas Corpus Suspension Act (40 Geo. III, c. 18)	20, 21–2

STATUTES OF THE OIREACHTAS

1924	Courts of Justice Act	210–12, 235
1924	Criminal Justice (Administration) Act	68
1926–1940	Enforcement of Court Orders Acts	240–6
1927	Juries Act	102
1928	Courts of Justice Act	210, 212
1931	Constitution (Amendment No. 17) Act	59–60, 194
1936	Courts of Justice Act	236
1939–1998	Offences Against the State Acts 63, 77, 84, 103, 133, 167, 169, 178, 192, 196–7, 211	
1941	Second Amendment of the Constitution Act	31, 130, 155, 170
1945	Mental Treatment Act	54, 60, 68, 228–9
1951	Criminal Justice Act	220
1953	Mental Treatment Act	229
1961	Courts (Establishment and Constitution) Act	128–30
1961	Courts (Supplemental Provisions) Act	152–3
1964	Guardianship of Infants Act	116
1965	Extradition Act	64, 72–3, 171–2, 198, 199, 201–2
1967	Criminal Procedure Act	203, 205
1975	Law Reform Commission Act	128
1976	Family Law (Maintenance of Spouses and Children) Act	241
1978	Road Traffic (Amendment) Act	59
1984	Criminal Justice Act	191–2
1986	Courts (No.2) Act	241
1991	Child Care Act	117
1993	Criminal Procedure Act	211, 214–15
1995	Courts and Court Officers Act	236
1996	Refugee Act	234
1996	Criminal Justice (Drug Trafficking) Act	192

1997	Criminal Law Act	106
1997	Bail Act	150–1, 204
1997	Non-Fatal Offences Against the Person Act	209
1999	Criminal Justice Act	205
1999	Immigration Act	232–3
2000	Illegal Immigrants (Trafficking) Act	88–91, 110, 232–4
2001	Mental Health Act	227–30
2001	Extradition (European Union Conventions) Act	198
2003	European Convention on Human Rights Act	51–2, 154, 193
2003	Immigration Act	232
2003	European Extradition Warrant Act	198, 200–1
2004	Immigration Act	232–3

ACTS OF PARLIAMENT OF ENGLAND, AND OF THE UNITED KINGDOM

1543	Trial of Treason Act (35 Hen. VIII, c. 2)	13
1640	Habeas Corpus Act (16 Car. 1, c. 10)	3
1677	Sunday Observance Act (29 Car. 2, c. 7)	95
1679	Habeas Corpus Act (31 Car. 2, c.2)	5, 6, 8, 12, 13, 15, 17
1800	Habeas Corpus Suspension Act (41 Geo. III, c. 15)	20
1801	Habeas Corpus Suspension Act (41 Geo. 3, c. 26)	20
1803	Habeas Corpus Suspension (43 Geo. III, c. 116)	20
1803	Habeas Corpus Suspension Act (44 Geo. III, c. 8)	20
1805	Habeas Corpus Suspension (45 Geo. III, c. 4)	20
1816	Habeas Corpus Act (56 Geo. III, c. 100)	17, 134
1822	Habeas corpus Suspension (3 Geo. IV, c. 2)	20
1831	Tumultuous Risings Act (1 & 2 Wm. 4, 44)	210
1834	Prevention of Smuggling Act (3 & 4 Will. 4, c. 54)	61
1842	Dublin Police Act (5 & 6 Vict., c. 24)	62
1848	Habeas Corpus Suspension Act (11 &12 Vict., c. 35)	20
1849	Habeas Corpus Suspension Act (11 & 12 Vict., c. 2)	20
1851	Petty Sessions Act (14 & 15 Vict., c. 53)	77, 177, 235
1866	Habeas Corpus Suspension Act (29 & 30 Vict., c. 1)	20
1867	Habeas Corpus Suspension Act (30 & 31 Vict., c. 1)	20
1868	Habeas Corpus Suspension Act (30 & 31 Vict., c. 25)	20
1870	Extradition Act (34 & 35 Vict., c. 52)	71, 202
1871	Protection of Life and Property (Ireland) Act (33 & 34 Vict., c. 9)	20, 22
1872	Debtors (Ireland) Act (35 & 36 Vict., c. 57)	240–6
1877	Judicature (Ireland) Act (40 & 41 Vict., c. 57)	34, 181
1881	Land Act, 1881 (44 &45 Vict., c. 49)	158
1881	Fugitive Offenders Act (44 & 45 Vict., c. 69)	120, 202
1883	Trial of Lunatics Act (46 & 47 Vict., c. 38)	158
1887	Criminal Law and Procedure Act (50 & 51 Vict., c. 20)	23–4
1908	Prevention of Crime Act (8 Edw. 7, c. 59)	171
1908	Children Act (8 Edw. 7, c. 67)	62
1914	Criminal Justice Administration Act (4 & 5 Geo. 5, c. 58)	225–6
1920	Restoration of Order in Ireland Act (10 & 11 Geo. 5, c. 31)	25, 142

1948	Criminal Justice Act (11 & 12 Geo. 6, c. 58)	70
1959	Mental Health Act (7 & 8 Eliz. 2, c. 72)	49
1962	Commonwealth Immigrants Act (10 & 11 Eliz. 2, c. 21)	80
1965	Backing of Warrants (Republic of Ireland) Act (c. 45)	199
1983	Mental Health Act (c. 20)	61
1984	Prevention of Terrorism Act (c. 8)	
1985	Prosecution of Offences Act (c. 23)	68

ACTS OF THE PARLIAMENT OF NEW ZEALAND

2001	Habeas Corpus Act	116

Index

abuse of process
  staggering grounds of complaint, 101,
    131–4
  delay, 102
  waiver, 102
  disingenuousness, 102
acquiescence, effect on complaint, 72, 102
Admiralty, Court of Leinster, 1
affidavits
  untruthful affidavits as contempt, 159
  grounding affidavits and initial
    complaint, 184–5
aliens: *see* nationals/non nationals
'any person', construction of, 127
appeals against release,
  jurisdiction, 32, 37, 169–70, 177–9
  moot, 178–9
appeal, Supreme Court,
  right of, 91
  remittal to the High Court, 174–5
  scope of review on Supreme Court
    appeals, 175–6
  procedure, 176–7
  moot appeals, 178–9
applicant in person, 136–7
Article 40.4.3
  as interpretative guide to Article 40.4.2,
    147
  origins, 32–4, 169–70
  'such law is invalid', construction of,
    170–2
  where detention is about to expire,
    172–3
  rules of court, 173
  See also bail, Second Amendment of the
    Constitution Act, 1940
Attorney General's scheme, 179
audience, right of
  at initial application for enquiry, 136–7
  at hearing, 143–4
autrefois convict: *see* summary convictions

bail
  under the Habeas Corpus Act, 1782,
    106
  power to grant under Article 40.4.2,
    146–7
  principles regulating grant of bail,
    147–50
  suspension of sentence where bail
    granted, 149–50
  conditions attached to the grant of bail
    pending Article 40.4.2 enquiry, 150–1
  pending determination under Article
    40.4.3, 173–4
  refusal of, habeas corpus as a remedy
    for, 203–5
  remedy where applicant granted bail
    succeeds on Article 40.4.2 challenge,
    122–3, 190
  re-arrest where breach, 150–1, 173
Bankruptcy, Court of, 200
Broadstreet, Samuel, 15–16
burden and standard of proof: *see* evidence
  on Article 40.4.2 enquiry
Butler, James, first duke of Ormond, 3

certificate of grounds of detention
  contents of the certificate under Article
    40.4.2, 145–6
  detainer's right to make a certificate, 156
  whether obligation to make a return
    where prisoner already discharged,
    189
  See also return
certiorari, inter-relationship with Article
  40.4.2
  where the ground of complaint
    implicates party other than the
    immediate detainer, 86–8, 217–19
  statute requiring complaints to be
    processed through judicial review,
    88–92

comparative differences in the scope of review on the remedies at common law, 94–6
scope of review on Article 40.4.2 and certiorari, 96–7
Chancery, Court of Ireland, 1–2
Chief Justice, competence to hear complaints under Article 40.4.2, 128–130
child custody, 141: *see also* detention
Circuit Court, competence of President of to hear Article 40.4.2 complaint, 128–30
Claims, Court of, 1
Committee on the Amendment of the Constitution, 1940, 31–4
Common Pleas, Court of, 1
conditional/absolute order procedure, 108, 123
Confederates, 3
construction of Article 40.4.2
literalist and flexible approaches, 100–1
conversion of an application under Article 40.4.2 into an application for judicial review, 97–8
conviction on indictment
common law prohibition of review by habeas corpus, 206–7
Article 40.4.2 review of conviction where appeal to the Court of Criminal Appeal has not been exhausted, 212
Article 40.4.2 review of conviction where appeal to the Court of Criminal Appeal exhausted, 207–10
residual Article 40.4.2 post-conviction review, 209–10, 212–13
conviction, summary
requirement to pursue appeal to the Circuit Court, 215–17
requirement to pursue by means of judicial review in preference to habeas corpus, 217–19
grounds of review, 219–20
remittal following successful complaint, 216
contempt of Article 40.4.2
forms of contempt of Article 40.4.2, 159–60, 188–9

classification as criminal or civil contempt, 160–1
contempt of court
order, documentary error, 65
habeas corpus as a means of review of committal for contempt of court, 234–8
technical approach in review of committal, 238–9
corporations as applicants for habeas corpus, 125
corpus cum causa, 1
costs
discretion as to costs in Article 40.4.2 proceedings, 182–3
parties subject to liability to pay, 182
court fees, 180
Court of Criminal Appeal, relationship with Article 40.4.2, 207–15
Curran, John Philpot, 18
custody: *see* detention

death penalty, 33
debt, imprisonment for non-payment of
procedure under the Debtors Act, 1872 and the Enforcement of Court Orders Act, 1940, 240–6
grounds of habeas corpus review of imprisonment for non-payment of debt, 242–6
delay, effect on complaint, 72
detainer
procedural rights, 156–7
change in identity of, 158–9
orders against persons other than immediate detainer, 137–8
detention,
the concept of detention, 110–19
restriction upon autonomy as a form of detention, 118–19
detention within a large geographical expanse, 112–13
child guardianship disputes, 116–17
the concept of liberty under Article 40.4.2, 116, 119
applicant at liberty when initial application submitted, 120–1
applicant on bail when initial complaint submitted, 120
de Valera, Eamon, 33–4, 37

discretion to refuse release
  common law, 98–100
  discretion under Article 40.4.2, 100–2
  abuse of process and discretion to refuse release, 101–2
divisional High Court, 33–4, 155
documentary error
  misdescription, 63
  requirement to show jurisdiction on the face of the record, 61–5, 207, 219–20
  exceptions to the requirement to show jurisdiction, 65
  curing documentary error, 65–6
  impregnability of superior court orders, 65
  modification of common law rule by statute, 65
Duggan, Eamon, 30
Dunning, John, 14

Eden, William, 8
emergency complaints to High Court judges at home, 153, 183, 185
Emmett, Robert, 21
enquiry, decision to direct an initial enquiry
  standard of proof, 89–90, 134–5
  sources of ground of complaint, 135–6
  hearing ex parte / on notice, 91, 136
error of law
  historical evolution of capacity to review error of law, 55
  common law standard, 57
  modern Irish position, 55–7
European Convention of Human Rights
  incorporation of, and scope of review on Article 40.4.2, 51–2
  Article 5(4), 49–51
  speedy determination, 154
  review of police investigative detention, 192–3, 195
evidence on Article 40.4.2 enquiry
  hearsay on Article 40.4.2, 85–6
  burden and standard of proof, 76–85
  balance of probabilities flexibly applied standard, 80–2
  rules of evidence, interrelationship with Article 40.4.2, 76
  evidential sources on the Article 40.4.2 enquiry, 75–6

estoppel: *see* conviction on indictment
ex parte, initial application, 136
extradition
  prohibition of by the Habeas Corpus Act of 1679, 12–13
  procedural conditions, excusing non-compliance, 71–2
  bail, pending challenge to extradition, 147–8
  jurisdiction to review extradition orders under Article 40.4.2, 199–201
  review of delayed execution of extradition orders under Article 40.4.2, 201–2
  documentary error, 64
extra-territorial operation of habeas corpus, 139–42

fair procedures, on an Article 40.4.2 enquiry
  procedural rights of custodian at common law, 88
  right of custodian to justify detention, 87–8, 107, 156–7, 218
  complainant's right to notice, 157
  right of victim to representation, 158
Figgis, Darrell, 27, 29
findings of fact, review of evidential findings on habeas corpus
  fresh evidence, admissibility of, 39–40
  review of weight of evidence at common law, 39–44, 203
  unreasonable evidential findings, 40–1
  condition precedent doctrine, 41–4, 80
  misinformation or misunderstanding of evidence, 44–6
  'anxious scrutiny' standard, 46–9
  failure to take account of relevant considerations doctrine and review of evidence, 47–8
  European Convention of Human Rights and review of evidence, 49–52, 193
  Constitution and review of evidence, 52–5
'forthwith enquire', construction of, 153–4

Garda custody
  discharge after enquiry initiated, 185–191

effect of charge after enquiry initiated, 186–7
re-arrest and interrogation following dismissal of Article 40.4.2 complaint, 191–2
review of the evidential basis of arrest, 192–3
European Convention on Human Rights and standard of review, 193
review of the legitimacy of the purpose of arrest, 193–6
bad faith arrest, 195–6
review of conditions of Garda custody, 196–7
Grey, William de, 10, 14
guardianship disputes, 116–18

Habeas Corpus Act, 1640, 3
Habeas Corpus Act, 1679
section 7, 5, 8, 10
Habeas Corpus Act, 1782
right to bail, 106
right to bail/discharge where not indicted, 106
procedure, 106–7
prohibition on re-arrest, 164–7
survival under Article 40.4.2, 106–8
regulation by rules of court, 108–9
See also re-arrest
Habeas Corpus Act, 1816, 17
hearsay: *see* evidence on Article 40.4.2 enquiry
'High Court or any judge thereof', construction of, 128–130
High Court, President of
power to constitute Court hearing complaint, 155

immigration
bail pending Article 40.4.2 application, 148
habeas corpus review of immigration-related detention, 232–4
illegal immigrants and detention for the purpose of habeas corpus, 114
See also relationship between certiorari and Article 40.4.2
imprisonment, conditions of, review on habeas corpus
review at common law, 221–2

development of the jurisdiction under Article 40.4.2, 221–2
current standard of review, 223–4
in camera hearings on Article 40.4.2, 152–3
information, right to about basis of detention, 136
Inspector of Mental Hospitals, 228
intermediary orders on Article 40.4.2
suspension of interrogation, 151–2, 184
access to prisoner, 151
medical treatment, 151, 184
intervening release
effect on habeas corpus proceedings, 121–2
Irish Free State Constitution, 27–31

Johnson, General Henry, 19

Kennedy, Hugh, 28–9

legal aid: *see* Attorney General's scheme
legislation, inability to regulate Article 40.4.2 by, 52, 91–2, 108–10
Liberty of the Subject Bills, 6–17
locus standi: *see* third party complainant

Macready, Sir Nevil, 26
martial law, 18–19, 25–7: *see also* 'state of war or armed rebellion'
mental health
procedural conditions, approach to compliance with, 68
substantive conditions, review of compliance with on Article 40.4.2, 227–8
procedure regulating admission order, 228–30
release of dangerously mentally ill, 231–2
misdemeanour/felony distinction, 11–12, 106
Moynihan, Michael, 32

'named day', construction of, 144–5
nationals/non-nationals
and personal liberty, 127
and the right to habeas corpus, 29, 127
necessity as a justification for detention, 103–4
notice parties, 157–8

oath of Supremacy, 6
O'Brien, George, 28–9
O'Higgins, Kevin, 29–31

'person in whose custody such person is detained,' construction of, 138
'personal liberty', construction of, 119
Pitt, William, 99
'Plan of campaign,' 23–4
Poynings' law, 6
Privy Council of Ireland 2, 3
Privy Council of England, 3
procedural conditions, non-compliance with as a ground of habeas corpus review
  mandatory/directory construction, 66–70
  principle of substantial compliance, 70–2
  non-prejudicial defects, 70–2
  retrospective validation, 65–6, 72–4, 197
procedural models of habeas corpus
  common law two-stage procedure, 123
  rule nisi process, 123
  one-stage model, 124
production of the prisoner
  stay of order of production, 162
  during the application for an enquiry, 137
  during the enquiry, 101, 142–44
  expense of, 181

Queries, the, 1640, 4, 5

re-arrest
  section 5 of the Habeas Corpus Act, 1782, 164–7
  jurisdiction of High Court to order re-arrest, 163–9, 225–6
reasons
  for refusal/grant of initial enquiry, 137
release
  stay on release, 161–2
  meaning of 'release', 163
  peremptory order of release, 156
  extended order of release, 187
  See also re-arrest
remand in custody, pre-trial
  habeas corpus review of sufficiency of evidence, 203
  See also bail

remittal
  on adjourning proceedings or refusal of release, 74
  consequent upon release, 74–5
  discretion to order, 74
  jurisdiction to remit ancillary to Article 40.4.2, 75
  judicial review and remittal, 216
repeated applications, 131–4
res judicata, 134
return
  detention by Privy Council, 3
  ability to controvert, 17
  amendment of return, 66
  scope of review on habeas corpus and, 94–6
  extraneous defects, 93–96
  contents of return at common law, 145–6
  obligation to make return where prisoner discharged, 189
  See also 'certificate of grounds of detention'
riot and affray, 11–12
Robinson, Christopher, 8, 10–13
Roman Catholics, exclusion of from the constitution, 6, 11
Ross, Sir John, 26–7
rules of court, 105, 108–10

Second Amendment of the Constitution Act, 1941, 33–8, 130–1, 170
selection; right to select judge, 154–5
sending forward for trial, order
  habeas corpus review of, 205–6
sentence,
  bail on post-conviction challenge, 148–50
  Article 40.4.2 review of, 213–15
  improper execution of, 213
  severance, 214–15
setting aside initial order, 143
Sidney, Henry, 6
'state of war or armed rebellion'
  Article 6, Irish Free State Constitution, 30–1, 83–4
  Article 40.4.5, Constitution of Ireland, 31
statutory construction
  ambiguity, resolution in favour of liberty, 58

principle against straining language, 59
where principle of strict construction may be displaced, 59–60
principle against disproportionate interference with liberty, 60–1
successive applications for habeas corpus
at common law, 34–7
Irish Free State Constitution, 28–9, 35–6
following refusal of initial enquiry, 37–8, 130–1
following refusal of release, 34–8
complaint concurrently before other judge of High Court, 134
See also Second Amendment of the Constitution Act, 1941
suspension of habeas corpus, legislation, 17–22
third party complainant, 101, 124–7, 183

Thurlow, Edward, 15
time of disposal
'named day,' production upon, 144–5
speed of disposal, 153–4, 184
under European Convention on Human Rights, 154
Tone, Theobald Wolfe, 18
Townshend, George, 13
transfer, habeas corpus review of inter-prison transfer, 224–6

United Irish rising, 17–19

victim, right of representation, 158

Wedderburn, Alexander, 15
writ of error, 140

Yorke, Charles, 10